Alvar Aalto

Between Humanism and Materialism

Alvar Aalto

Between Humanism and Materialism

**Edited by
Peter Reed**

With essays by

Kenneth Frampton
Pekka Korvenmaa
Juhani Pallasmaa
Peter Reed
Marc Treib

The Museum of Modern Art, New York
Distributed by Harry N. Abrams, Inc., New York

Published on the occasion of the exhibition *Alvar Aalto: Between Humanism and Materialism,* organized by Peter Reed, Associate Curator, Department of Architecture and Design, The Museum of Modern Art, New York, with the cooperation of the Alvar Aalto Foundation and the Museum of Finnish Architecture, Helsinki, February 19–May 19, 1998.

The exhibition is made possible by a major grant from Mrs. Celeste Bartos and by generous support from Artek.

Additional funding has been graciously provided by Elise Jaffe and Jeffrey Brown.

The publication accompanying the exhibition is made possible by the generosity of Jo Carole and Ronald S. Lauder, in memory of Lily Auchincloss, and of The International Council of The Museum of Modern Art.

The exhibition will travel to Italy and Japan under the auspices of The International Council of The Museum of Modern Art.

Produced by the Department of Publications
The Museum of Modern Art, New York
Edited by Harriet Schoenholz Bee
Designed by Michael Beirut, Pentagram,
and by Antony Drobinski, Emsworth Design, Inc.
Production by Christopher Zichello
Composition by Emsworth Design, Inc.
Printed and bound by Tien Wah Press, Singapore

Texts by Marja-Riitta Norri and Vilhelm Helander were translated from the Finnish by Hildi Hawkins.

Library of Congress Catalogue Card Number: 97-76094
ISBN 0-87070-107-x (MoMA, T&H, clothbound)
ISBN 0-87070-108-8 (MoMA, paperbound)
ISBN 0-8109-6183-0 (Abrams, clothbound)

Published by The Museum of Modern Art
11 West 53 Street, New York, New York 10019
www.moma.org

Clothbound edition distributed in the United States and Canada
by Harry N. Abrams, Inc., New York. www. abramsbooks.com

Clothbound edition distributed outside the United States and Canada
by Thames and Hudson, Ltd., London

Printed in Singapore

Front cover: Alvar Aalto. Church of the Three Crosses, Vuoksenniska, Imatra, Finland. 1955–58. Interior detail

Back cover: Alvar Aalto. Experimental House and Sauna for Elissa and Alvar Aalto, Muuratsalo, Finland. 1952–53. Courtyard wall detail

Frontispiece: Alvar Aalto. Villa Mairea, House for Maire and Harry Gullichsen, Noormarkku, Finland. 1938–39. Fireplace detail

Contents

The Trustees of The Museum of Modern Art dedicate this book, *Alvar Aalto: Between Humanism and Materialism,* to the memory of their beloved colleague and friend, Lily Auchincloss. She took her role as a Trustee seriously and, during her twenty-six years on the Board, devotedly and imaginatively touched virtually every area of the Museum. Her uncanny wisdom, style, humor, and vitality of spirit challenged the Trustees and staff alike to reach beyond expected goals to new and unknown heights. Whether it was an exhibition that was without a sponsor, the acquisition of a rare example of an artist's work, an International Council visit abroad, or an Annual Fund appeal, her focus and her spontaneity were inspiring and contagious. Finally, this Aalto book is a fitting remembrance for Lily Auchincloss because it symbolically attests to one of her most abiding interests, the Department of Architecture and Design, where she enjoyed a special place, had been an active participant since 1970, and was Chairman of its Trustee Committee from 1981 until her death in June 1996.

Foreword

THIS PUBLICATION accompanies the exhibition *Alvar Aalto: Between Humanism and Materialism*, a comprehensive retrospective of the achievement of the great Finnish architect. It is particularly fitting that The Museum of Modern Art's long-hoped-for plan to mount such an exhibition not only celebrates the architect's centenary in 1998 but also occurs sixty years after the first museum exhibition and publication on Aalto were organized by The Museum of Modern Art in 1938. The exhibition and the scholarly essays in this publication provide fresh insights into the national and international contexts in which Aalto developed the extraordinary architectural output of his prolific fifty-four year career. They demonstrate Aalto's critical role in modern architecture and design through an exploration of his extraordinary sense of form, materials, production, his keen understanding of the human condition, and ultimately his continuing relevance to the issues that confront the world at the turn of the century.

This historic endeavor would not have been possible without the steadfast cooperation of the Alvar Aalto Foundation and the Museum of Finnish Architecture, Helsinki. A particular debt of gratitude is owed the directors of these institutions, Kristian Gullichsen and Marja-Riitta Norri, respectively. The Aalto Foundation has granted the Museum unprecedented access to its archives, which has been critical to the realization of the project. The staffs of both organizations have collaborated diligently, graciously, and effectively with the Museum. We are also very grateful to numerous other lenders, public and private, whose generosity has made this exhibition possible.

Crucial support for the exhibition was graciously provided by Mrs. Celeste Bartos, a Life Trustee of this Museum, whose interest in Aalto and generous encouragement guaranteed the project's realization. We are also deeply grateful for a major grant from Artek, the manufacturer of Aalto's now classic line of furniture since 1935. Artek's commitment to high-quality production of these landmarks of twentieth-century design is manifested in their continuing success and wide appeal. Robert Weil, Chairman, and Ulf Ericsson, President, of Proventus Invest, and Mauri Heikintalo, President of Artek, deserve our thanks. Generous support was also received from Elise Jaffe and Jeffrey Brown, and from the American-Scandinavian Foundation. This volume is made possible by generous support from Jo Carole and Ronald S. Lauder and from The International Council of The Museum of Modern Art under the leadership of Sir Brian Urquhart and Jo Carole Lauder. The book is dedicated to the memory of the Museum's beloved Lily Auchincloss, a Trustee who served as Chairman of the Trustee Committee of the Department of Architecture and Design. It is a fitting and moving testament to Lily's remarkable dedication to architecture and design and to this Museum.

Peter Reed, Associate Curator in the Department of Architecture and Design, director of the exhibition, and a contributor to this volume has achieved a sensitive and thoughtful presentation of the work of one of the great figures of twentieth-century architecture. Ably assisted by Bevin Howard, Research Assistant, of this Museum and Elina Standertskjöld of the Museum of Finnish Architecture, he has worked energetically over the past three years, with the essential support of Terence Riley, Chief Curator in the Department of Architecture and Design, under whose direction an insightful balance between contemporary and historical figures of the modern period has been maintained at the Museum.

Glenn D. Lowry
Director
The Museum of Modern Art

Preface

WHEN THE NEW BUILDING for The Museum of Modern Art was inaugurated, concurrently with the New York World's Fair in May 1939, the work of Alvar Aalto was presented at the Museum by its architecture department, alongside that of Frank Lloyd Wright, Le Corbusier, and others. My parents, Maire and Harry Gullichsen, had traveled to New York by ship to attend these events. Aalto was already in New York supervising the work on the Finnish Pavilion at the fair. Meanwhile, work on the Villa Mairea was in progress at home in Finland. Once they arrived at the Museum, my parents saw, to their great surprise, their own new home, finished and free from scaffolding at last, and complete with its Aalto interiors. The photographs of the fully realized house had arrived at the very last minute by airplane.

Alvar Aalto enjoyed a deep appreciation within The Museum of Modern Art circle, and his furniture was terrifically popular. The Museum had already honored Aalto with an extensive exhibition in 1938: *Alvar Aalto: Architecture and Furniture*. The highly praised Finnish Pavilion at the New York World's Fair further consolidated Aalto's reputation in America. Upon seeing Aalto's installation at the fair, Frank Lloyd Wright is said to have exclaimed, "He is a genius!"

At this time, Aalto stood on the summit of his career, which had progressed, in twelve years, from the obscurity of a provincial small-town practice to the limelight of the international arena. But the success in New York was also to be Aalto's final flourish at the end of an epoch that soon disappeared in the smoke and ashes of war.

When the weapons were finally silenced, the world had changed, and so had Alvar Aalto. He never returned to his architectural gold mine of the prewar period. The contemporary spirit in his work was replaced by glances at the past and reflections of the classical heritage. To ask why he abandoned that distinctly personal architectural idiom he had created during those years is as irrelevant as it would be to ask why Pablo Picasso did not remain faithful to his wonderful Cubist *nature-morte* motifs. As Picasso turned to classical themes in his art—goddesses, centaurs, and bulls—Aalto sought inspiration in classical architecture. Nonetheless, Aalto remained the eternal rebel, who refused to join the mainstream of the modern movement, which he had helped to create.

Aalto's work shows an intellectual and an emotional dimension not often seen in high modern architecture. The empathetic dimension is expressed on many levels in his work: an emphasis on the physical and psychological comfort of the occupants, the ambition to balance the abstract with familiar motifs, and a tactile sensitivity for materials and textures. The obvious sensuality in his approach to the details reflects his Dionysian appetite for life.

With time, Aalto's mythical relationship with Mediterranean cultures gained increasing prominence in his work. His restless ambition to constantly outdo himself acquired rhetorical overtones, and the relaxed bohemian took on a certain authoritarian arrogance. A popular anecdote about Aalto in his later years (although anecdotes are notoriously unreliable) was that Frank Lloyd Wright had taught him that nobody listens to an architect unless he is sufficiently arrogant.

In my own opinion, the intimate Town Hall in Säynätsalo stands out among Aalto's works. The strict tectonic stature of the building is balanced against the bizarre impression of a fragment of fourteenth-century Tuscany, which seems somehow to have lost its way in the deep Finnish forest. In the summer of 1952, while work on the town hall was in progress, I had the opportunity to hold the position of errand-boy at Aalto's office. My main task was to sharpen the pencils each morning. "How is the boy doing?" my mother would ask Aalto. "He's very good at sharpening pencils," Aalto would reply. He chose not to mention that my duties also included making sure there was a bottle of Chianti at hand at all times.

On behalf of the Alvar Aalto Foundation, I would like to say that it has been a great pleasure to cooperate with The Museum of Modern Art on this exhibition. At the Foundation, we realized from the outset the importance of this great project, not least with a view to the Museum's long tradition in spreading Aalto's message. We have had the honor of contributing fragile original documents, which can only rarely be shown to a larger public.

Aalto had many faces, and much of his work still awaits closer analysis. The ambitious work of documenting Aalto's entire life's work, which The Museum of Modern Art now presents, is an important contribution that will hold great significance for a deeper understanding of one of the foremost figures in twentieth-century architecture.

Aalto wrote: "Architecture cannot save the world, but it may serve as a good example." These memorable words, as well as Aalto's entire body of architectural work, may be worth contemplating as we are about to enter the next century.

Kristian Gullichsen
Chairman
Alvar Aalto Foundation, Helsinki

Appreciation

FORTY YEARS AGO, in 1958, *Arkkitehti*, the Finnish architectural review, published a special issue in celebration of Alvar Aalto's sixtieth birthday. Asked to contribute a statement, Aalto wrote briefly about his ideas of architecture in the form of an imaginary interview with his friend, the great historian Sigfried Giedion. The imaginary dialogue, titled "Instead of an Article," is one of Aalto's most important essays. In it, he crystallizes the basis of his architecture: "True architecture exists only where man stands in the center." The comment seems self-evident, but its adoption in practice is often overwhelmingly difficult. Why did it succeed with Aalto?

Perhaps the following example can offer a partial answer. Aalto once recounted that he was ill during the early design stage of the Paimio Tuberculosis Sanatorium. As a patient, he found himself examining the hospital environment from the vantage point of the sick person, rather than the care givers, a situation in which, as he said, the individual is "at his weakest." He noted the ceiling lights that dazzled the eyes, the freezing ventilation, the unpleasant color of the ceiling, and the disturbing sounds. This experience provided the basis of the unique designs in the patients' rooms at Paimio: carefully modulated light and air, cheerful colors, and soft materials (which were, sadly, replaced by standard products in a renovation a couple of decades ago). A similar approach characterizes Aalto's later buildings, too: care is taken not only with the general impression (the dynamics of volume and structure, and the balance of proportions), but the entire building in all its details is the result of a sympathetic design and choice of materials for both small and large elements. In the case of the Paimio Tuberculosis Sanatorium, we can cite a detail that still attracts attention: the vibrant yellow linoleum floor, which reflects an ethereal glow on the ceiling to soothe a patient lying flat on a stretcher.

Essential to Aalto's design process is a "liberation of sensibility." This is expressed through a spirit of experimentation, play, and fantastical visions illustrated with "childish drawings" to which Aalto refers in his poetic essay, "The Trout and the Mountain Stream." Aalto's aim was to achieve a kind of laboratory to test innovations suitable for mass-housing production in Finland and internationally. According to Aalto, "the simultaneous solution of opposites" was the first necessary condition for a building or any human achievement to attain the level of culture. In Aalto's public buildings, a central feature is, indeed, the simultaneity of the monumental and the intimate, their combination through variations in scale, light, and space.

At the same time, Aalto emphasized a social perspective, particularly in housing design, and linked the built environment to the human scale. In various different connections, he demanded a broad interpretation of rationalism so that it would include psychological factors. Aalto once placed a wild lion on a drawing by a student whose diploma project was based on mere calculations; the lion represented a free imagination and, at the same time, common sense in the jungle of norms and regulations. Aalto's principle of the organic growth of the environment and his ideas about flexible standardization did not even begin to influence real Finnish housing construction in its most productive years, the 1970s. Aalto's later frustration with the predominant, narrow-minded financial and technical rationalism was reflected in his facetious remark that his module was a millimeter or less.

Although Aalto was, above all, a builder, he also took part in organizational activities, particularly during the 1950s. As chairman of the Finnish Association of Architects, he was influential in setting up certain central institutions that were subsequently important to the development of professional practice. In 1954 he drafted guidelines for the Museum of Finnish Architecture, founded two years later, as a new type of institution. The museum was to serve as a central museological establishment for architecture and provide educational programs in Finland. "The task of architecture is, in a constructive sense, to participate in building the country, and thus it has a duty in an educational sense to develop our country's culture," wrote Aalto. But he also recognized the museum's role in exhibiting Finland's architecture to an international audience. Its first prominent achievements were exhibitions of Finnish architecture held in London and Moscow. Thus, he said: "In recent times the old idea of the museum has been

replaced by a new mode of operation, whose most prominent example may be cited as The Museum of Modern Art in New York." It was precisely the outward orientation, the extension of activity beyond the local establishment, which represented the new way of thinking that Aalto wanted to lay down as the foundation of the new architectural museum.

No school of followers, as such, has ever developed around Aalto on a formal level, for this would only have led to lifeless imitation. From early on, Aalto's individuality and sovereign position gave rise to a vacuum around him: the younger generation did not wish to follow along the same lines, but presented an antithesis. This dialogue of creative work produced results, and different ways of thinking stimulated one another: a competitive situation developed into which architects threw themselves as equals, Aalto included. Appreciation of Aalto was, however, never as pervasive in Finland as internationally. That this continues to be the case is demonstrated by the long and continuing attempts to change the "landmarked" facade of Finlandia Hall to gray or pink granite.

When I began my own architectural studies, Aalto was over seventy years old, a natural master, but distant. He was considered exclusively a designer of monumental buildings, which was foreign to the spirit of the time, with its emphasis on social values, rationalism, and the exact sciences. But just as the student world is often sensitive to the vibrations of distant changes, the view of my own profession soon developed in a direction that stressed creative individual effort, and our interest in Aalto and other masters increased. Sadly, Aalto had already died by the time this respect became a universal phenomenon.

Aalto's written works, while limited in number, are unusually weighty. They say everything essential about architecture, concretely and with a strong link to reality; there is no need to read between the lines. In the characteristic manner of the pioneers of modernism, however, he hardly ever explained the factors behind his own architecture. He wrote that architecture is "an art based on material," but the question of how its most beautiful examples are born of the interaction of the immaterial elements of light and space can be answered only through the buildings themselves.

Marja-Riitta Norri
Director
Museum of Finnish Architecture, Helsinki

Introduction

FOR OVER SIXTY YEARS, the work of Alvar Aalto has been interwoven with The Museum of Modern Art's evolving commitment to the presentation and understanding of the architecture and design of the twentieth century. During the summer of 1930, Philip Johnson and Henry-Russell Hitchcock traveled the breadth of Europe to see firsthand the new buildings that were to become, two years later, the subject of the Museum's first exhibition of architecture, *Modern Architecture—International Exhibition.* Known popularly as the International Style show, the exhibition presented the work of the leading figures of a young generation of architects—Le Corbusier, Ludwig Mies van der Rohe, and J. J. P. Oud among them. While a number of these figures had already gained a limited amount of recognition in Europe as well as in the United States, the exhibition also featured a survey of projects from around the world designed by a great number of lesser-known figures. The inclusion of a project by Aalto, the Turun Sanomat Building in Turku, Finland, of 1928–30, comprising newspaper offices and printing presses, was a testament to Johnson and Hitchcock's keen understanding not only of modern architecture's seminal roots but of its future direction as well.

The International Style exhibition codified a certain tendency among the leading figures of the European avant-garde: the planar, abstract manner known as the machine aesthetic. However, it was neither Le Corbusier nor Mies van der Rohe who was featured in The Museum of Modern Art's first in-depth exhibition of an International Style architect but Aalto, whose architecture, furniture, and design objects were presented at the Museum in 1938. Among the buildings shown in the exhibition, *Alvar Aalto: Architecture and Furniture,* were the Turun Sanomat Building, the Paimio Tuberculosis

Sanatorium in Paimio, Finland, of 1929–33, and the Viipuri City Library in Viipuri, Finland (now Vyborg, Russia), of 1927–35—all evidence of the architect's commitment to the tenets of the International Style. In addition, however, the curving sensuous lines of Aalto's glassware and furniture in the exhibition distinguished his design vocabulary from that of his contemporaries. Shortly thereafter, the free-form organic profiles of his design objects were prominent features of Aalto's Finnish Pavilion at the 1939 New York World's Fair (which opened just thirteen months after the exhibition at The Museum of Modern Art), and prefigured the direction his work would take after World War II, when he emerged as one of the leaders of the second generation of modern architects. This work included celebrated projects in Europe, such as Säynätsalo Town Hall in Säynätsalo, Finland, of 1948–52 and the Church of the Three Crosses in Vuoksenniska, Imatra, Finland, of 1955–58. But two important buildings were constructed in the United States as well: Baker House, the Senior Dormitory for Massachusetts Institute of Technology in Cambridge of 1946–49 and Mount Angel Abbey Library in St. Benedict, Oregon, of 1964–70.

In 1951, Arthur Drexler was hired as a curator in the Museum's Department of Architecture and Design by Philip Johnson, the department's founding chairman. While he shared Johnson's enthusiasm for the work of Mies van der Rohe, after his appointment as director of the department in 1956, Drexler also championed alternative visions of postwar modern architecture, including Johnson's own turn from Miesian purity toward a more eclectic modernism. Two architects who figured prominently in Drexler's curatorial constellation, in addition to Mies van der Rohe, were Frank Lloyd Wright and Alvar Aalto. Unfortunately, he never was able to realize his aspiration to stage major retrospective exhibitions of either of these two seminal figures of twentieth-century design (*Ludwig Mies van der Rohe: Centennial Exhibition* was shown in 1986). Because Wright considered himself to be the author, not merely the subject, of exhibitions of his work, mounting an ambitious presentation of his architecture at the Museum was not feasible during his lifetime. This attitude was assumed by his successors after his death in 1959, severely limiting the prospects for a critically and curatorially independent appraisal of Wright's life's work during Drexler's tenure. In 1962, Drexler was able to stage a modest homage to the architect: *Frank Lloyd Wright: Drawings.*

Drexler's hoped-for retrospective exhibition of Aalto's work foundered for different reasons. Originally planned to open in March 1974, the exhibition was ambitiously conceived with the collaboration of Stuart Wrede, the Finnish-American architect and scholar, trained at Yale University (who became the director of the Department of Architecture and Design after Drexler's death in 1987). Unfortunately, the scale of Drexler's plans was matched, inversely, by an increasingly negative economic situation in Finland, the principal potential source of funding for the project. Drexler's plans were further undercut by a generational—and negative—reappraisal of Aalto's work at home. By the late 1960s, the seventy-year-old architect was the undisputed leader of his profession, but, to many younger Finnish architects, he had also come to represent the political and cultural establishment. Official sources of support, already stretched thin, backed away from a potentially controversial commitment. Drexler retained his interest in the project throughout the years but, again, was unable to see it materialize into a major exhibition. After repeated attempts to revive the project, the department staged a greatly reduced exhibition in 1984, *Alvar Aalto: Furniture and Glass*, organized by J. Stewart Johnson, then curator of design.

This exhibition, organized by Associate Curator Peter Reed, on the occasion of Aalto's centennial, is, thus, the realization of a project that started nearly thirty years ago. Even so, *Alvar Aalto: Between Humanism and Materialism* is not simply a matter of implementing a long-formulated plan. It has been part of a general reappraisal of the institution's presentation of the art of the twentieth century by The Museum of Modern Art's curators in order to identify those masters whose oeuvres may not have been comprehensively featured at the Museum and whose contributions were so significant that they could not be further overlooked before the turn of the century. For the Department of Architecture and Design, those figures were Louis I. Kahn, Frank Lloyd Wright (presented at the Museum in 1992 and 1994, respectively), and Alvar Aalto. The current exhibition, thus, not only fulfills a long-held ambition but is the result of a recent critical reappraisal that has benefited enormously from research undertaken by a new generation of architectural historians who have come to the fore since Aalto's death in 1976.

This catalogue represents a distinguished synthesis of that research and affords the reader insights into not only Aalto's great accomplishments but also the architectural culture of Finland and the trajectory of modernism before and after World War II. In his dual role as curator of the exhibition and editor of the catalogue (with the assistance of Bevin Howard), Peter Reed has contributed enormously, in both style and substance, to The Museum of Modern Art's chronicle of the artistic achievements of this century.

Finally, I would like to note that this volume is dedicated to Lily Auchincloss, a long-time Trustee of The Museum of Modern Art and, at the time of her death in 1996, the honorary chairman of the Trustee Committee for the Department of Architecture and Design. She was a true friend to the department, and was an outstanding example of the intelligent, committed, and endlessly supportive women who have had such a profound influence on this institution over the decades. Her grace, generosity, and inimitable presence are vividly remembered and will be as long as those attributes are regarded as highly as they should be. A rose is a rose is a rose, except when it's a Lily.

Terence Riley
Chief Curator
Department of Architecture and Design
The Museum of Modern Art

Acknowledgments

ALVAR AALTO: BETWEEN HUMANISM AND MATERIALISM would not have been possible without the cooperation of the Alvar Aalto Foundation and the Museum of Finnish Architecture in Helsinki. Since our initial meeting several years ago, when we spoke about this project as a major retrospective to occur during the 1998 Aalto centenary, Kristian Gullichsen, Chairman of the Alvar Aalto Foundation, and Marja-Riitta Norri, Director of the Museum of Finnish Architecture, have been enthusiastic supporters of the exhibition and catalogue. The Museum of Modern Art was given the extraordinary privilege of complete access to the Alvar Aalto Archives, part of the Foundation, from which the core of the exhibition is assembled. Their brilliant decision to appoint the architectural historian, Elina Standertskjöld, Curator of Archives at the Museum of Finnish Architecture, to assist me in virtually all aspects of the project guaranteed its organizational success in Finland. Her intimate knowledge of the drawings in the Alvar Aalto Archives (for which she established a system in the early 1980s), energy, enthusiasm, and perpetual good humor made months of work in Finland enjoyable and productive. I have also benefited from the expertise of curatorial consultant Kenneth Frampton, Ware Professor of Architecture, The Graduate School of Architecture Planning and Preservation, Columbia University, whose vast knowledge of modern architecture and contributions toward shaping the intellectual content of the catalogue and exhibition were important to their success.

Large exhibitions of this kind must rely heavily on enlightened individuals and institutions for their generous support. First and foremost, I wish to extend my deepest gratitude to Museum Trustee Mrs. Celeste Bartos for her unqualified support at a critical time. Her knowledge and appreciation of Aalto, shared by her husband, Armand Bartos, an architect and long-time member of the Museum's Trustee Committee on Architecture and Design, is reflected in her magnanimous gift to the project. Artek, the manufacturer of Aalto's furniture for over sixty years, provided a generous grant for the exhibition; Robert Weil, Chairman, and Ulf Ericsson, President, of the parent company, Proventus Invest, and Mauri Heikintalo, President of Artek, deserve our special thanks. Generous and enthusiastic support is also provided by Elise Jaffe and Jeffrey Brown, whose passion for modern architecture is inspirational. Additional funding is provided by the American-Scandinavian Foundation. This publication is made possible by generous support from Jo Carole and Ronald S. Lauder, in memory of Lily Auchincloss, and by The International Council of The Museum of Modern Art, under whose auspices the exhibition will travel internationally.

I would also like to acknowledge the Finnish Consulate in New York for its efforts in promoting the exhibition through the cultural campaign, "Finland: Europe Finnessed." In particular, I would like to thank Maija Lähteenmäki, Consul General; Pasi Natri, former Deputy Consul General; Riitta Korpivaara, Deputy Consul General; and Petra Tuomi, Press Officer.

The vast majority of the original drawings and models have been lent to the exhibition by the Alvar Aalto Foundation. The convivial staff of the Foundation was most helpful and hospitable during our several lengthy sojourns in Helsinki. Archivists Mia Hipeli and Arne Heporauta demonstrated enormous patience with our constant demands, as did Ulla Enckell with our requests for archival photographs; architects Tapani Mustonen, Mikko Merckling, and Sverker Gardberg aided our technical understanding of Aalto's buildings and provided critical information for the construction of new models. Marjo Pursiainen, secretary at the Foundation, was a model of gracious efficiency, and Raili Jokiniemi acquainted us with traditional Finnish cuisine. Virtually all of the loans from Finland were conserved, photographed, and prepared in Helsinki for the exhibition in New York. This enormous task, coordinated by Elina Standertskjöld, was carried out by a team of expert professionals: Paula Alavuo and Päivi Ukkonen, conservators; Matti Huuhka, photographer, and his staff at Museokuva; and Pekka Schemeikka, framer.

In addition to the Alvar Aalto Foundation, a number of private and institutional lenders have enriched the exhibition with loans from their collections. Aalto's son and daughter, Hamilkar Aalto and Johanna Alanen, and granddaughter, Johanna Aalto, made available to us sketches and sketchbooks for study as well as for inclusion in the exhibition. At the Alvar Aalto Museum in Jyväskylä, Markku Lahti, Director, Kaarina Mikonranta, Chief Curator, and Hanni Sippo, architect, assisted in coordinating loans from the Jyväsklyä Workers' Society, the Muurame Parish, and the Säynätsalo Town Hall Archive. I also wish to thank Krister Ahlström, President and CEO of the A. Ahlström Corporation, Hilkka Korhonen, secretary, and Inkeri Nyholm, former curator there; at the Iittala Glass Museum, Päivi Jantunen, Information Manager, Hackman

Designor Oy Ab, Marjut Kumela, Director of the Arabia Foundation, and Tiina Aaltonen, Registrar; Timo Keinänen, Head of Archives, Museum of Finnish Architecture; Pekka Tuomisto, Chairman of the Board and Director General of the National Pensions Institute, and Pekka Uitto, Administrative Assistant; Kauno Lentomäki, Säynätsalo Town Hall; Kaarina Lahti, Manager, Public Relations of the Helsinki University of Technology; Alfred Schmitz, Geschäftsführer of the Gemeinnützige Theater Baugesellschaft Essen mbH, and Franz-Peter Kothes, public relations officer, Essen Opera House; Clifford Tjørn, architect, Lyngby City Hall; Nina Hobolth, Director, Nordjyllands Kunstmuseum, Aase Bak, Curator, and Kirsten Andersen; Dr. Siegfried of the Institut für Museen und Stadtgeschichte, Wolfsburg, and Wolfgang Wittig, historic preservationist; Jöran Lindvall, Director, Swedish Museum of Architecture, Cecilia Wåhrner, and Susanna A. Janfalk; Bernard Tschumi, Dean, The Graduate School of Architecture Planning and Preservation, Columbia University, and David Hinkle; and Anna Hall-Teponoja, Curator, The Mairea Foundation.

Over the past three years, I have enjoyed numerous conversations with scholars, architects, and Museum colleagues about Aalto. In addition to the individuals already mentioned, I would especially like to thank the authors of the essays in this volume, whose significant contributions have greatly enriched the publication and my own understanding of Aalto's accomplishments: Kenneth Frampton, Vilhelm Helander, Pekka Korvenmaa, Juhani Pallasmaa, and Marc Treib. Göran Schildt, Aalto's biographer, was an enthusiastic supporter of this project, and his outstanding publications on Aalto are the crucial foundations upon which all present and future studies must rely. Stuart Wrede, architect and former director of this Museum's Department of Architecture and Design, was most helpful and encouraging. I would also like to acknowledge Aalto's former collaborators, Jean-Jacques Baruël and Kaarlo Leppänen; Ben af Schultén, design director, and Brian Lutz, export manager, at Artek; architect David Fixler at Perry, Dean, Rogers and Partners; Hannele Grönlund; Hildi Hawkins; Kirsi Leiman; Peter B. MacKeith; Riitta Nikula; Kristina Nivari; Sirkka Soukka of the Kotka Cultural Office; Eeva Maija Viljo; and Professor Frampton's former students, Matthew Baird and Chris McVoy. Other individuals assisted in many and various capacities, among whom I would like to acknowledge Aalto's grandson, Heikki Alanen, Deputy Chairman of the Alvar Aalto Foundation; Kjersti Board, Swedish Information Service, New York; Kimberly Alexander Shilland, Curator, Architectural Collections, The MIT Museum; Paula Hamilton, Library Director, Mount Angel Abbey Library, Emily Horowitz, Librarian and Gallery Coordinator, and Martha Schrader; Wilfried Russ, Gesellschaft für Wohnen und Bauen (GEWOBA), Bremen; Ilkka Kippola, Archivist, Finnish Film Archive; Anssi Blomstedt; Hannele Heporauta; Jari Jetsonen; Matti-Juhani Karila; Pekka and Pamela Mandart; Ritva Siukkola, Manager Housing Services, Center for International Mobility, Helsinki, whose organization provided accommodations for extended stays in Helsinki.

Both the exhibition and publication have relied on existing and new photography, and many people assisted us in assembling images for this endeavor. Rauno Träskelin demonstrated great stamina and skill in making new photographs of buildings and design objects in Finland; other new photographs of Aalto's buildings were commissioned from Steve Rosenthal and Peter Eckert of Strode Eckert Photographics. Katariina Pakoma of the Alvar Aalto Museum, was most resourceful. In addition to those mentioned in the Photograph Credits, I would like to thank Erica Stoller of Esto, the late G. E. Kidder Smith, Simo Rista, Matti Laajanen, Suomen Ilmakuva Oy, Jean-Jacques Baruël, Heinrich Heidersberger, Maija Holma, and Leonardo Mosso.

The exhibition includes a number of elements created specifically for it. Among these are new videos of several buildings, made by Yleisradio Oy [The Finnish Broadcasting Company Ltd.]/TV1, Helsinki. The videos were produced and directed by Eeva Vuorenpää, and edited by Markku Pulkkinen; arrangements for their inclusion in the exhibition were facilitated by Marjaleena Lampela, Head of Documentaries, and Päivi Moore, Head of Sales Department. The construction of a brick wall based on Aalto's House of Culture was made possible by the Glen-Gery Corporation, where Raymond J. Staub, Vice President and National Sales Manager, and Charles F. Cockrell, Vice President and General Manager, oversaw the making of new bricks for this project. At Ensto Ceramics, Börje Hildén, Managing Director, and Disan Sjöstrand, Sales Secretary, oversaw the manufacture of Aalto's glazed tiles. Seppo Sievä of Sievätyyli Oy produced new bronze door handles. New didactic drawings of Aalto's buildings were made by Manuel Gutierrez de Rueda and Richard Sturgeon; Peter B. MacKeith supervised the research and production of several complicated drawings. Pekka Korvenmaa and Jari Honkonen/Decode, Inc., produced the map in the Chronology. Two new models, constructed by Richard Sturgeon and Derek Conde, have greatly enriched the exhibition.

At The Museum of Modern Art, I am enormously grateful for the expertise and professionalism of the vast team of colleagues required to realize a project of this magnitude. Glenn D. Lowry, Director, and Terence Riley, Chief Curator in the Department of Architecture and Design, consistently provided enthusiastic support from the project's inception. Beverly M. Wolff, Secretary and General Counsel, and Stephen W. Clark, Assistant General Counsel, offered sound advice. Michael Margitich, Deputy Director for Development, and Monika Dillon, Director of Major Gifts, were most supportive and a pleasure to work with. I am also grateful for the superb efforts of Rebecca Stokes, Manager, Campaign Services, and Carol Coffin, Executive Director, The International Council.

Jennifer Russell, Deputy Director for Exhibitions and Collections Support, and Linda Thomas, Coordinator of Exhibitions, deserve special thanks, as does Eleni Cocordas, Associate Coordinator of Exhibitions, whose sage advice and careful attention to detail were invaluable in managing the exhibition. They and Jay Levenson, Director of the International Program, masterfully organized the exhibition's international tour. The arrangements pertaining to the careful shipment of the artworks were handled professionally by the Museum's Registration department, under the direction of Diane Farynyk, Registrar, and superbly orchestrated by Senior Registrar Assistant Carey Adler, with John Alexander and Cheryl Horwitt. Peter Omlor, Manager, Art Handling and Preparation, and his crew skillfully assisted with the installation. For the particularly complex installation, comprising a wide variety of mediums, we were blessed with the professional expertise and creative skills of Jerome Neuner, Director of Exhibition Design and Production, who designed and prepared the exhibition installation, assisted by his staff, including Andrew Davies and Mari Shinagawa. John Calvelli, Senior Graphic Designer, handled the graphics for the exhibition with supreme skill. Others who assisted in the preparation of artwork for the exhibition include Karl Buchberg, Senior Conservator, and Lynda Zycherman and Patricia Houlihan, Associate Conservators; John Martin, Foreman Matter/Framer, and Pedro Perez, Conservation Framer; and Mikki Carpenter, Director of Photographic Services and Permissions, and Kate Keller, Chief Fine Arts Photographer. Joshua Siegel, Curatorial Assistant, Film and Video, and Charles Kalinowski, Head Projectionist, provided valuable technical advice on the video components of the exhibition.

The Department of Education and the Museum's Library and Archives, under the direction of Patterson Sims, Deputy Director for Education and Research Support, provided essential program and research support. Cynthia Nachmani, Museum Educator, wrote the colorful brochure accompanying the exhibition. Josiana Bianchi, Assistant Educator/Public Programs Coordinator, organized public programs in conjunction with the exhibition, including two symposia on architecture and design. These were jointly sponsored with our colleagues at the Bard Graduate Center for Studies in the Decorative Arts; I would like to thank Nina Stritzler-Levine, Director of Exhibitions, and Lisa Beth Podos, Director of Public Programs, both of Bard, for their support in making this possible. The Museum's Archives and Library staffs facilitated our research efforts, and I would like thank Rona Roob, Chief Archivist, and her staff as well as Daniel Starr, Chief Librarian, Technical Services and Planning, Janis Ekdahl, Chief Librarian, Administration, and Eumie Imm Stroukoff, Associate Librarian, Reference.

The Communications and Marketing departments, led by Elizabeth Addison, Deputy Director for Marketing and Communications, were most effective in their efforts to promote the exhibition. I would like to thank Lisbeth Mark, Press Representative, Mary Lou Strahlendorff, Senior Press Representative/Electronic Media Coordinator, Alexandra Partow, Assistant Director, Elisa Behnk, Marketing Manager, and assistants, Kena Frank and Kim Mitchell. It was a pleasure to work with Aldona Satterthwaite, Director of Writing Services, Anna Hammond, and Tavia Fortt on the new Members' magazine. In Sales and Marketing, I would like to thank

James Gundell, Ruth Shapiro, Kara Orr, Brook Marcy, and Richard Dobbs for their efforts in the area of merchandising Aalto-related items in The Museum Stores and the mail-order catalogue. The celebratory events surrounding the exhibition were expertly and sensitively arranged by Ethel Shein, Director of Special Programming and Events, who was assisted by Francesca Goodwin, Assistant Director, Event Planning and Catering Services, and Anne MacGillivray, Event Planning and Corporate Services.

One of the greatest pleasures in undertaking a catalogue such as this is the opportunity to work with a great editor. Harriet S. Bee, Managing Editor in the Department of Publications, deserves our profound gratitude for her enormous contribution. Her sensitive handling of image and text, her wide-ranging knowledge of architecture, and her expertise in book-making played a vital role in shaping the intellectual and visual content of this volume. She was ably assisted editorially in the preparation and proof-reading of the texts by Jasmine Moorhead. Christopher Zichello, Associate Production Manager, demonstrated unwavering patience in his ability to cope with unforeseen delays, and, at the same time, managed to produce a book of the highest standards of quality on time. I would also like to acknowledge the contributions of Marc Sapir, Production Manager, and Nancy T. Kranz, Manager, Promotion and Special Services, who oversaw production planning and arrangements for several editions of the book, respectively. The graphic designers of the catalogue, initially Michael Beirut, Pentagram, and Antony Drobinski, Emsworth Design, Inc., who brought it to completion with skill and speed, created a handsome publication. I would also like to thank Jody Hanson, former director of Graphics at the Museum for her assistance and supervision of design.

Finally, I would like to extend sincere thanks to my colleagues in the Department of Architecture and Design: Matilda McQuaid, Associate Curator, Paola Antonelli, Associate Curator, Christopher Mount, Assistant Curator, Pierre Adler, Study Center Supervisor, Luisa Lorch, Cataloguer, Caren Oestreich, Assistant to the Chief Curator, and Abby Pervil, Executive Secretary. For nearly two years, Bevin Howard, Research Assistant, assisted me in nearly all aspects of the exhibition and catalogue. Her unwavering good humor, capacity for hard work, and informed opinions made her a valued colleague both in Helsinki and in New York.

Additionally, I would also like to thank my friend James Dart, architect, who accompanied me on my visits to many of Aalto's buildings. His astute insights and observations have enriched my appreciation and perception, not only in terms of Aalto's architecture but also with regard to many other aspects of this project.

Peter Reed
Associate Curator
Department of Architecture and Design

Alvar Aalto: Toward a Synthetic Functionalism

Juhani Pallasmaa

In every case one must achieve a simultaneous solution of opposites. . . .
Nearly every design task involves tens, often hundreds, sometimes
thousands of different contradictory elements, which are forced into a
functional harmony only by man's will. This harmony cannot be
achieved by any other means than those of art.

—Alvar Aalto[1]

ALVAR AALTO'S ASPIRATION for a synthetic solution to the technical and psychological complexities of design sets him apart from the core group of the modern movement, which sought expressive power through reduction and polarization. Aalto, on the other hand, sought a mediation of antagonistic elements both in his architecture and in his writings. His architecture was an unorthodox, inclusive fusion of opposite intellectual categories and design strategies. Instead of aiming at conceptual and formal purity, it sought to reconcile opposites such as nature and culture, history and modernity, society and the individual, tradition and innovation, standardization and variety, the universal and the regional, the intellectual and the emotional, the rational and the intuitive.

During an extraordinarily prolific career that lasted more than half a century, Aalto's creative activity encompassed myriad aspects of the man-made environment—industrial design, individual domestic and public buildings, civic centers, and regional planning. His architecture at any scale developed through a number of stylistic phases, but he established his fundamental philosophical position early on in his career. His ideas developed gradually, and he frequently returned to earlier themes, often years or even decades after their first appearance. Aalto's concepts characteristically first appeared as vague images in his sketches; later they were elaborated and repeated in various projects, and eventually they became elements in his

Alvar Aalto. Viipuri City Library, Viipuri, Finland (now Vyborg, Russia). 1927–35. Auditorium detail office routine. In his writings and speeches Aalto expressed an evolutionary viewpoint, and his entire life's work is an interacting and intertwining series of ideas and sensibilities.

Aalto's ambition to achieve an architectural synthesis is grounded in the classical background of his education and early professional years. The broad-minded attitude of the neoclassicism of the 1920s served as a point of departure for a relatively easy transformation to modernism. "It seems that in terms of form Aalto remained a Classicist. This he did ideologically, too,"[2] argued Göran Schildt, Aalto's devoted biographer and intimate friend during his later life. Scholars have shown that Aalto often elaborated classical architectural themes in his work and used historical motifs and references.[3] But Aalto also remained a devout functionalist throughout his later stylistic changes.[4] Regardless of their artistic expressiveness, Aalto's buildings fulfill rigorous functional and technical criteria.

After a short engagement with orthodox rationalism[5] at the end of the 1920s and early 1930s, in the wake of recent Continental thinking, Aalto began to develop his synthetic philosophy. This synthesis extended the scope of rationality from technical considerations into the psychological realm. "Salvation can come only or primarily through an expanded rationality," he wrote in 1935.[6] Aalto's conflation of opposites had to transcend the limits of rational criteria, and he began to search for an inclusive artistic and emotive logic. He wrote: "The problems of architecture cannot usually be solved at all using technical methods.... Architecture is thus a super-technical form of creation in which this harmonizing of various forms of function plays a key role.... A building is not a technical problem at all—it is an archi-technical problem."[7] In a later essay he emphasized the synthesizing task of architecture even further: "Gradually our shoulders have been made to bear the increasingly heavy weight of a machine dictatorship. We must rely on philosophical methods, and in this case, if we master the material, the name of the philosophy is architecture and nothing else."[8]

The terms *romantic, irrational,* and *organic,* which are frequently applied to Aalto's mature work, suggest that he abandoned rationality altogether after his short rationalist period. But this is not the case; in fact, Aalto had redefined the concept of rationality. Paraphrasing his own notion above, Aalto's approach represented a form of "super-rationality," one that deliberately incorporated psychological, intuitive, and subconscious factors within the design equation. He also incorporated images of time, history, and vernacular tradition into his modernist vocabulary. In the same way that the late phase of Cubism is known as Synthetic Cubism, in order to distinguish the mature development from its earlier, Analytic, phase, Aalto's mature architectural thinking can be regarded as the synthetic phase of functionalism.

Even in his earliest writings in the mid-1920s Aalto had already outlined his philosophy of synthesis and the unification of opposites. In 1926 he praised the image of the Italian hill town in Andrea Mantegna's painting *Christ in the Garden* (1540; Tours Museum, France) as "a synthetic landscape."[9] In his own mature work Aalto created synthetic landscapes, condensed architectural microcosms that integrated architecture with its geographical and cultural setting. Aalto did not conceive buildings as detached architectural objects; his buildings are sensitive situational responses that seek a dialogue with their context. In another early essay he wrote about the paradoxical ambition of turning an outdoor space into an interior and vice versa, and called this strategy of reversed opposites "a piece of the philosophers' stone."[10] The reversed imagery of outdoors and indoors became a favorite motif in Aalto's numerous designs for courtyards and entry halls. The abstracted forms of his rationalist period were replaced by suggestive and associative shapes that evoke unconscious memories and images.

Central to Aalto's idea of an architectural synthesis was the subordination of technology to the cultural task of architecture. In the mid-1930s he began to develop the idea of flexible standardization, a way of industrializing construction that would allow flexibility and variety. He made a number of attempts to initiate architectural research as a system of international cooperation in order to establish scientific ground for architectural education and practice. Ironically, by the time full-scale industrial construction actually started in Finland in the 1960s, Aalto had already grown skeptical of industrialization as well as theoretical analysis. The new rationalist and constructivist movements that developed in Finland, along with the rapid industrialization of construction and the new societal and political concerns of the Nordic welfare state, emerged as ideologically antithetical to the viewpoint of the aging academician.

The two decades that have passed since Aalto's death have provided sufficient distance from his overpowering presence to reveal the profound significance of his philosophical thinking and design work. Indeed, Aalto's philosophy suggests a valid synthesis for an architecture that seeks culturally and ecologically sound values and means at the turn of the millennium.

The Classicist Aalto

Aalto began his architectural work in the eclectic classicist idiom that was later labeled Nordic classicism.[11] Having received his architect's diploma from the Helsinki University of Technology in 1921 at the age of twenty-three, Aalto entered practice in Jyväskylä, his hometown in central Finland. The name of his first office, The Alvar Aalto Office for Architecture and Monumental Art, was set in two-foot-high letters next to the entrance,[12] reflecting the unusual self-confidence and ambition of the young man. In addition to seeking architectural commissions through keen participation in competitions and active self-promotion, he drew cartoons for a comic paper; wrote articles; designed furniture, objects, book covers, and typography; served as a visual and applied-arts critic for a newspaper; and even functioned as a sales agent for a company producing gravestones.[13] Along with leading artists of the decade, Aalto set out enthusiastically to shape the cultural profile and material image of Finland. In the mid-1920s his ambition was to turn his remote and rural hometown into a "northern Florence."[14]

Aalto's early commissions included the renovation and restoration of nine country churches,[15] which undoubtedly acquainted him with various issues of architectural style (figure 1). The influence of his professors, Usko Nyström and Armas Lindgren, whom Aalto remembered with respect and gratitude in his later years, certainly reinforced an understanding and appreciation of architectural history.[16] The young architect drew shamelessly from a variety of sources for his designs. In a single interior design he could combine elements from the Renaissance, the baroque, neoclassicism, and Art Nouveau,[17] whereas his early furniture derives from a multitude of eighteenth- and nineteenth-century European and American eclectic sources.[18] Many of Aalto's wild stylistic innovations were as outrageous as any of the products of postmodernism half a century later (figure 2). He loved to startle people with his design inventions as much as he enjoyed confounding and embarrassing them through his unorthodox behavior.[19]

Some historians consider Nordic classicism a preparatory phase for modernism in the Nordic countries, and it is evident that the spirited and ascetic aesthetic, relying on sparse ornamentation, precision of contour and profile, and clear distinction between figure and ground, as well as the emerging social concerns of the period, paved the way for modernity. The period was characterized by an unorthodox interest in architectural history, an attitude that produced both ponderously serious and naively playful buildings in all of the Nordic countries. Nordic classicism combined a strong sense of tradition with a desire for individual stylistic invention. The Atrium House for Väinö Aalto that Aalto projected for his brother in 1925 (plate 26) exemplifies the fusion of classical imagery into the context

of modern life, as well as the combination of seriousness and a sense of humor. Nordic classicism was inspired by the anonymous and unassuming folk classicism of northern Italy rather than monumental high classicism of Rome. This interest in vernacular classicism carried with it a sense of humility, and it anticipated the functionalist engagement with societal issues, such as housing and buildings for recreation, industry, and transportation. The broad-minded attitude of the period provided a fertile ground for Aalto's inventiveness and evolutionist aspirations.

His appreciation of inspiration derived from history is clear in his early writings: "And when we see how in times past one succeeded in being international, free of prejudices and at the same time true to oneself, we can with full awareness receive currents from ancient Italy, from Spain, and from modern America. Our ancestors will continue to be our masters."[20] Surprisingly, however, Aalto's attitude toward the Finnish national romanticism of the turn of the century was negative. He condemned it as "that absurd 1905-period of the flowering of the birch-bark culture when all that was clumsy and coarse was considered so very Finnish."[21] His deprecation of national romanticism is unexpected, indeed, both because his teachers, Nyström and Lindgren, were esteemed practitioners of this style and because his own later work was to develop formal aspects (such as fluid organicism and plastically molded shapes), as well as his architectural strategies (such as an aspiration for *Gesamtkunstwerk*) in the spirit of national romanticism. Ironically, the critical view of Aalto that developed during the 1960s in Finland regarded him as a continuation of this movement.

1. Alvar Aalto. Viitasaari Church renovation. 1925 (original church, 1777, moved from Viitasaari to Haapasaari, 1877–78). Sections. Alvar Aalto Foundation, Helsinki

2. Alvar Aalto. Gas Station, Jyväskylä, Finland. 1924. Elevation. Alvar Aalto Foundation, Helsinki

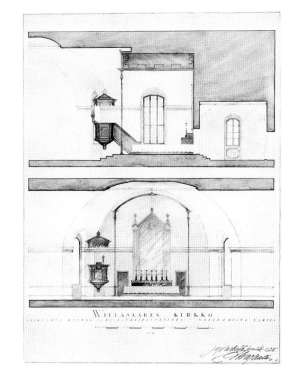

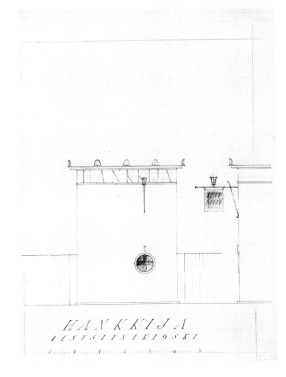

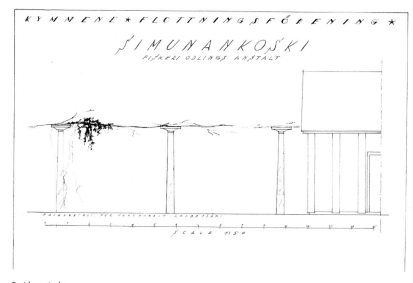

3. Alvar Aalto.
Simunankoski Fishery,
Simunankoski, Finland.
Project, 1924. Colonnade
elevation. Alvar Aalto
Foundation, Helsinki

During his first years as a professional, Aalto designed many projects and executed buildings for his hometown and its vicinity. These include residential designs, club houses, exhibitions, kiosks, religious buildings, and urban schemes. One of his most interesting early projects is the proposal for a fishery conceived as a classical garden, with pergolas supported by Doric columns (figure 3); the project reveals Aalto's desire to expand his activities beyond established architectural tasks. The Railway Employees' Housing, Jyväskylä, of 1924–26 is an example of ascetic and refined classicist design, which hints at his later modernist work. The Jyväskylä Workers' Club of 1924–25 (plates 15–22) is a more ceremonious building using Doric classicism with occasional Palladian details combined with characteristic Aaltoesque innovations; for instance, the theater lobby is treated as a miniature urban square evoking an experience of the outdoors (plate 21). The building has a fairly complex program, and it is the first demonstration of Aalto's aspiration for *Gesamtkunstwerk*, a synthesis of various art forms, which extends from architecture to furnishings, door handles, and light fittings. A complete grasp and control of the architectural ensemble became an Alvar Aalto signature. The Defense Corps Building of 1924–29, facing the central square of Jyväskylä, with its stately facade articulated by square windows, sparse horizontal moldings, and a simple frieze running the entire width of the building at the top of the facade, also contains aspects of Aalto's later work in Turku.

Aalto's classicist designs executed in wood, such as the Defense Corps Building in Seinäjoki of 1924–29 (plates 11–14) and his residential buildings in Jyväskylä, combine unorthodox and inventive classical detailing with an atmosphere that echoes the vernacular classicism of the eighteenth- and nineteenth-century Finnish towns built of wood as well as the naive classicism of peasant architecture. Aalto also expressed admiration in his writings for peasant architecture in its primordially rustic and more refined classicist modes.

The Functionalist Utopia

In 1927, Aalto won the competition for the Southwestern Finland Agricultural Cooperative Building in Turku (completed 1930), and the subsequent commission prompted his move from the small town of Jyväskylä to Turku, Finland's former capital on the western coast, which had a strong cultural and architectural heritage. Aalto's exceptional professional ambition and energy seemed excessive in the rural town of his youth, whereas the geographic location, scale, and cultural climate of Turku provided an appropriate challenge. At the time, the architectural environment in Turku was more liberal than in Helsinki, where authoritative traditionalists were outspokenly critical of emerging modernist sensibilities. Among Finnish intellectuals, the modernist ideology was strongly supported by the seminal literary magazine *Tulenkantajat* [The Torch Bearers], the first issue of which was published in November 1928.[22] On the cover of issue number 6, 1930, the magazine published a photograph of Aalto's newly completed Turun Sanomat Building (figure 4) along with a polemical question: "Is Turku the most modern city in Finland?" Inside the issue, a caption to a photograph of the roof terrace of the building stated explicitly: "The modernist architecture of Turku . . . has already become proverbial."[23] The simultaneous critical hesitation of the older generation in Helsinki is well illustrated in an article by Bertel Jung,

4. Cover of *Tulenkantajat*,
no. 6 (1930)

himself a radical at the turn of the century: "What is functionalism and what does it want? What gives this passing fancy the right to throw overboard most of the laws that earlier determined all architectural creation?"[24]

Aalto's move to Turku in 1927 must have also been motivated by the fact that it situated him closer to his new circle of friends in Sweden and made further travel to the Continent more convenient. Aalto was internationally oriented and excited about everything that represented a modern, international lifestyle. He was also excited about the nascent field of flying, and in 1924 Aalto and his new bride, Aino Marsio, traveled on their honeymoon to Europe by hydroplane.[25] He furnished his Turku home with modern chairs by Marcel Breuer, and he acquired a gramophone in order to practice fox-trot dancing at home.[26] Aalto purchased his first car in 1927 with the prize money from a competition, and a movie camera in 1929. He turned abruptly away from explicit historical motifs that he had used in his designs and admired in his writings. "The designer did not even dream of including the affected forms of ethnographic or vernacular architecture," he proclaimed proudly in the description in his competition entry for vacation houses organized by *Aitta* magazine in 1928 (plate 73).[27]

Aalto wanted to project a cosmopolitan image of himself, and he customarily arranged a press conference after returning from his frequent travels. "Early morning coffee in Paris, lunch in Amsterdam, afternoon coffee in Hamburg, and dinner in Malmö," he remarked during an interview in 1928. Continuing, in a tone of combined arrogance and irony, he added: "Flying is the only acceptable form of travel for modern civilized man, since trains and ferries are full of all sorts of folk, whereas in aeroplanes one only meets select people in whose company one need never feel embarrassed."[28] It was commonly believed that Aalto even wrote his interviews himself, and the literary style of some of his published interviews does support that assumption.[29] That Aalto succeeded in projecting the combined image of a cosmopolitan intellectual and an artist with natural endowments is evident in a 1932 characterization of him by Gotthard Johansson, the well-known Swedish architectural critic: "Aalto…is a character that one can equally often run into in Paris, Berlin, Stockholm, or Turku, a heretic and resourceful thinker, who treats architecture as a big Mecano-box. At the same time, he is a refined artist with the same instinctive and assured sense of proportion characteristic of Le Corbusier."[30]

In his youth Aalto often aroused opposition through his outspoken, arrogant, and sometimes even outrageous behavior. His association with the radical group of Swedish architects, *acceptera*, known for its leftist aspirations, and the similarly inclined *Projektio* film club in Helsinki gave him a radical leftist label. During his rationalist phase, Aalto undoubtedly had leftist affinities, but early on he became disillusioned by political doctrines altogether.[31]

Aalto often adapted the ideas and inventions of others and turned them into elements of his personal idiom.[32] However, the essential point is that Aalto was capable of improving the ideas that he drew from the work of his architectural colleagues and literary sources. His evolutionist philos-

5. Erik Gunnar Asplund. Skandia Cinema, Stockholm. 1922–23. Interior

ophy enabled him to consider artistic ideas as shared intellectual capital, a heritage that could be improved upon incrementally. Tradition and individual innovation were not exclusive aspects of artistic development according to Aalto's thinking.

Aalto's most important mentor was the Swedish architect Erik Gunnar Asplund, who was thirteen years his senior. In 1920 Aalto even sought an apprenticeship with his highly respected and influential Swedish colleague. In his eulogy of Asplund, two decades later, Aalto recalled his first encounter with the Swedish architect in 1923, in the Skandia Cinema in Stockholm (figure 5) that Asplund was just completing: "I had the impression that this was an architecture where ordinary systems hadn't served as the parameters. Here the point of departure was man, with all the innumerable nuances of his emotional life and nature."[33] Asplund's strong influence can be seen throughout Aalto's classicist period in Jyväskylä, and during his transition to the modern ideology, only a few years later, Aalto was equally influenced by him. During the 1930s, Aalto visited Stockholm frequently and customarily dropped by Asplund's office.[34] Another influential Swedish friend and colleague of Aalto's was Sven Markelius.

In Turku, Aalto became a close friend and briefly a partner of Erik Bryggman, who was seven years his senior and who provided a balance to Aalto's zealousness. Regardless of Aalto's vigor and talent, Bryggman seems to have had a more mature and integrated understanding of architecture than his younger colleague at the time of their association.[35] The impact of Bryggman's restrained Hospits Betel building of 1927–29 (figure 6), which

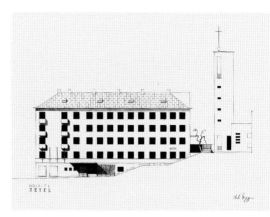

6. Erik Bryggman. Hospits Betel, Turku, Finland. 1927–29. Elevation. Museum of Finnish Architecture, Helsinki

reflected functionalist influences from his visit to the Weissenhofsiedlung in Stuttgart of 1927, on the final character of Aalto's Southwestern Finland Agricultural Cooperative Building in Turku was substantial. The competition scheme and building permission drawings for this extensive building within a regular urban-block structure in Turku were originally conceived in a fairly rich classicist idiom. But, while the construction work progressed, Aalto eliminated almost all of the classical elements. Certain parts of the building, such as the lobby and interior of the Turku Finnish City Theater (figures 7–8), the interior and furnishings of the restaurant, and the treatment of the courtyard facades, were boldly simplified and anticipated Aalto's functionalist work.

The building that first brought Aalto into the international limelight was the Turun Sanomat Building of 1928–30 (plates 42–51).[36] This newspaper plant and office building constitutes the one work of Aalto's that is stylistically close to Continental precedents; the scheme actually utilizes all of the five points toward a new architecture propagated by Le Corbusier in 1926. The building was designed down to the last door handle, sign element, and light fixture. Furthermore, this comprehensive conception illustrates well Aalto's astounding skill and swiftness in adapting to an entirely new stylistic vocabulary.

Color had been an important element for the Nordic classicists, and subtlety of color was often transferred to their functionalist work[37]; the main stair hall of the Turun Sanomat Building has an exquisite color combination of grayish blue and brown. The building contains several ideas that reach their mature application in Aalto's later works, such as the plastically molded columns, system of skylights, specially designed fittings, and the integration of graphic elements with the architecture. But the pure functionalist expression of the Turun Sanomat Building had been developing quietly in Aalto's classicist work. For example, the transition from the 1924–26 Railway Employees' Housing project to the Tapani Standard Apartment Block in Turku of 1927–29 (figure 9), and further to the Turun Sanomat Building, is a matter of stylistic aesthetic preference rather than fundamental differences of architectural thinking.[38] In all cases, the most skillful architects of Nordic classicism transformed themselves into practitioners of functionalism before

and around 1930, with astonishing swiftness and without apparent conflict or frustration. In retrospect, it is evident that the classicist engagement is to be credited for the refined sense of composition, articulation, scale, and detail characteristic of Nordic functionalism.

The Turku 700th Anniversary Exhibition and Trade Fair, which Aalto and Bryggman designed together in 1929, is considered the most significant single breakthrough of functionalism upon Finnish public awareness (plates 77–84). Functionalism quickly became the dominant style in Finnish architecture at the turn of the decade. In addition to the Turku fair, the influential lecture, "Rationalization Trends in Modern Housing Design," given in 1928 by Aalto's friend Markelius, one of the

7. Alvar Aalto. Turku Finnish City Theater, Southwestern Finland Agricultural Cooperative Building, Turku, Finland. 1927–28. Competition drawing: interior perspective (1927). Whereabouts unknown

8. Alvar Aalto. Turku Finnish City Theater, Southwestern Finland Agricultural Cooperative Building, Turku, Finland. 1927–28. Interior

leading Nordic promoters of the new style, at the annual conference of the Finnish Association of Architects in Turku effectively propagated the new ideology.[39]

The Stockholm Exhibition of 1930, organized and designed by Aalto's progressive Stockholm friends, Erik Gunnar Asplund, Gregor Paulsson, Sven Markelius, and Uno Åhren,[40] declared a new architecture that extended its decisive impact to all the Nordic countries (figure 10). Aalto had closely followed the development of the Stockholm Exhibition, and the Turku fair architects were able to realize some of the novel ideas before their Swedish colleagues. The Turku exhibition was conceived as a sequence of enlarged newspaper pages; the expressive pylon constructions and modernist graphics and lettering show influences from De Stijl, the Bauhaus, and possibly Russian Constructivism (although there is surprisingly little evidence that Finnish functionalist architects were familiar with the work of the Russian avant-garde).[41] At this stage Aalto had already begun to develop a more personal plastic expression within his newfound functionalist idiom. The new approach appeared in certain detail solutions, such as the freely shaped orchestra stand of the Itämeri Restaurant in the Southwestern Finland Agricultural Cooperative Building and the freely molded shape and surface textures of the choir platform at the Turku fair (plates 83–84), all of which anticipated aspects of his later mature work in the 1950s and 1960s.

After having completed the Turun Sanomat Building and the Turku fair, Aalto was introduced into the Congrès Internationaux d'Architecture Moderne (CIAM) circles by Sven Markelius before the second CIAM conference in Frankfurt in 1929; these two newly completed projects served to introduce Aalto's work on an international stage. Aalto also participated in subsequent CIAM conferences—in Brussels a year later and in Athens in 1933. He usually arrived late at the conferences and, reportedly, did not take the ideological discussions very seriously, but he provided charming company outside the official program. Aalto developed close friendships with Walter Gropius, Fernand Léger, László Moholy-Nagy, and Sigfried Giedion. Moholy-Nagy, who was well acquainted with the latest artistic ideas in Europe, became an especially strong intellectual stimulus for Aalto.[42] Aalto's work and thinking is usually seen as an explicit contrast to Bauhaus rationality and aesthetics, and it is surprising to learn how much inspiration Aalto actually drew from the Bauhaus circles through Gropius and Moholy-Nagy. Typically, Aalto later deprecated the achievements of the Bauhaus. Giedion and his wife Carola Giedion-Welcker introduced Aalto to another circle of artist friends that included Max Ernst, Constantin Brancusi, Hans Arp, and Alexander Calder.[43] Of Aalto's international artist friends, Léger seems to have been closest to his own exuberant personality and sanguine view of art; the transformation of Aalto's rationalist architecture to his later sensuous designs parallels Léger's transition from abstracted images of machines to his plastically lush late paintings. As the secretary general of CIAM, the most respected architectural historian of his time,

9. Alvar Aalto. Tapani Standard Apartment Block, Turku, Finland. 1927–29. Exterior

10. Erik Gunnar Asplund. Stockholm Exhibition. 1930. Advertising mast

and shareholder in the Zurich furniture shop, *Wohnbedarf*, Giedion was in a position to promote Alvar Aalto in numerous ways.[44]

Functionalism began to find support also in Helsinki. *Arkkitehti*, the Finnish architectural journal, became an important supporter of functionalism through its newly appointed editors, Hilding Ekelund and Martti Välikangas,[45] who were both esteemed architects. Ekelund in particular promoted the new style by publishing defeated functionalist competition entries in the magazine; by 1930 functionalism had become the prevailing style in Finnish architectural competitions. By the beginning of the decade even the board of the Finnish Association of Architects was dominated by supporters of the new style. Through the impact of Erkki Huttunen (figure 11), who directed the building department of the Central Society of Cooperative Stores, functionalism became the corporate style of the organization, and buildings designed in the new style were erected even in remote parts of the country.

There was certainly professional and public resistance to the modern style in Finland, but the absence of an established urban bourgeois tradition made the acceptance of modernism easier in Finland than on the Continent. Regardless of its radicality, the modern aesthetic of restraint could also be associated with the traditional peasant aesthetic of necessity and scarcity; in this sense in Finland the modern style had simultaneous futuristic and traditionalist readings. An ethical appreciation of austere simplicity and of the everyday environment is a line that can be followed in Finnish architectural writing from the end of last century up to the present day.[46]

Mass housing was of course a central concern in the development of modern architecture. The exhibition, *Rationalization of the Minimum Dwelling*, held in Helsinki in 1930 (figure 12),[47] and the Nordic Building Conference of 1932 focused on this problem. Aalto spoke and wrote diligently about the problems of mass-produced housing and the standard dwelling. Aalto wrote in the catalogue of the 1930 housing show: "The exhibition intends to initiate a way of thinking that regards the solution of the problem of dwelling... as one of the most important socio-economic issues.... The solution to the problem has to be based on human 'similarities,' as they appear as results of scientific analysis... a psychologically correct line has to be drawn between 'similarities' and 'differences.'"[48] Thus, he pointed out the conflict between standardization and the need for individuality and variety—the central theme of his later writings. Due to societal and political circumstances, however, the first functionalist housing schemes were not realized before the end of the 1930s,[49] and extensive construction of housing areas and new suburbs actually took place only after the wars.[50]

A major drawback for the dissemination of progressive architectural thinking occurred in 1931 when J. S. Sirén was chosen to be a professor of architecture at the University of Technology over Aalto, the second candidate. Sirén[51] was the widely respected architect of the newly completed neoclassicist Parliament Building, whereas Aalto had been working in Jyväskylä and Turku, and had not built in Helsinki.[52] Onni Tarjanne, a noted architect and professor, judged Alvar Aalto's qualifications for the post in the following manner: "Undoubtedly he is very talented and possesses noteworthy artistic qualifications, which will probably in the future, if given the opportunity, even leave beautiful traces in our architecture. He has, however, mainly worked in the wake of the currently emerging fashionable architecture, functionalism, a style the development potential, duration, and permanent value of which cannot be foreseen."[53] In the course of the next few years Aalto was to give convincing proof of his elder colleague's assertion through the completion of his two functionalist masterpieces, the Paimio Tuberculosis Sanatorium of 1929–33 (plates 52–72) and the Viipuri City Library of 1927–35 (plates 89–109).

11. Erkki Huttunen. Store for the Aitta Cooperative, Sauvo, Finland. 1931–33

Considering Aalto's meager experience in hospital design,[54] the complexity and scope of the Paimio Tuberculosis Sanatorium project, the number of technical and architectural inventions devised by Aalto there, and the stylistic transition that he had just barely begun, the artistic maturity of the project is astounding. The task was demanding, indeed, for an architect who had just reached the age of thirty. In fact, Aalto's scheme was such a radical step away from professional conventions that respectable members of the Finnish Association of Architects discussed whether the young daredevil ought to be stopped from creating a public scandal that might have harmful consequences for the entire profession. Aalto was given firm support, however, by Sigurd Frosterus, the esteemed architect and philosophical writer, and the architect and critic Gustaf Strengell, who had recognized Aalto's genius early on.[55] Upon completion of the building, Strengell judged it to be the most important building designed in Finland during the three decades since national romanticism. He expressed his unreserved admiration for "the deep, tenacious will to achieve clarity and purity without any regard to incidental considerations."[56]

The Paimio Tuberculosis Sanatorium also drew wide interest abroad, and it was instantly recognized as a work of universal significance. The building fulfilled the promise of exceptional talent hinted at in Aalto's earlier work. In the design of the sanatorium Aalto synthesized all his knowledge of rationalist architecture. The basic disposition of the complex, as well as a number of detail solutions, clearly reveal the impact of Johannes Duiker's Zonnestraal Tuberculosis Sanatorium in Hilversum, the Netherlands, of 1926–28, which Aalto had visited in spring 1928 in conjunction with his trip to Paris.[57] There are also reflections of the work of Le Corbusier as well as André Lurçat, another French architect friend of Aalto's. But regardless of any amount of influence, Aalto's synthesis is

12. Alvar Aalto. Furnishings
for the exhibition
*Rationalization of the
Minimum Dwelling,*
Helsinki Art Hall. 1930

convincingly personal and integrated. The unique quality of the sanatorium design lies in the combination of rigorous functional and technical criteria with astute psychological considerations. Even today, more than sixty years after its completion, the sanatorium exudes a rare atmosphere of optimism, healing, and inspiration.

The general layout and many of the details of the sanatorium reflect contemporary medical theories in the treatment of tuberculosis. Aalto explained his design intentions in the following manner: "The main purpose of the building is to function as a medical instrument.... One of the basic prerequisites for healing is to provide complete peace.... The room design is determined by the depleted strength of the patient, reclining in his bed. The colour of the ceiling is chosen for quietness, the light sources are outside the patient's field of vision, the heating is oriented towards the patient's feet and the water runs soundlessly from the taps to make sure that no patient disturbs his neighbour."[58] In another context, Aalto reported that he happened to have been hospitalized himself at the time the sanatorium design was conceived and that his personal experience made him emphasize the hospital environment from the patient's perspective, the experiences of "a person in the weakest possible condition."[59] For this project Aalto developed a host of technical solutions (such as heating and ventilation systems, daylight arrangements, light fixtures, color schemes, inventions to eliminate noise disturbances, special door handles, etc.) that were based on a careful observation of functional, physiological, and psychological factors in hospitals. The canary yellow floor of the main stair and hallway evokes the experience of sunshine and warmth even during the dark winter months (plate 58). The building was designed by Aalto to the last detail, including washbasins, spittoons, hospital beds, wardrobes, lamps, and outdoor reclining chairs (plates 66–72).

The Paimio Tuberculosis Sanatorium is a complete work of art conceived in a singular inspired atmosphere, and it deserves to be called

"heroic" as much as any other architectural masterwork of the twentieth century. In 1930 Aalto wrote: "It requires radicalism to avoid creating a superficial comfort and instead to search out the problems whose solution could create the conditions for better architectural work and achieve truly usable criteria for people's well-being in their everyday lives."[60] The Paimio sanatorium is convincing proof of Aalto's own creative radicalism.

After his active engagement in furniture design from his student days[61] and lengthy experiments with Otto Korhonen, the owner of Huonekalu- ja Rakennustyötehdas Oy [Furniture and Construction Factory, Ltd.] in Turku,[62] Aalto finally achieved a technically and aesthetically satisfactory concept of the molded-wood and plywood chair in the model that he designed for the sanatorium in 1931–32, known as the Paimio Chair (plates 63, 65). This bentwood chair completed Aalto's efforts to transform principles of tubular-steel furniture into wood, the material he preferred because of its tactile, visual, and psychological qualities. Aalto criticized the narrow and reductive understanding of rationalism in the design of tubular-steel furniture (he used one of Marcel Breuer's first models as an example):

> But a chair has an endless series of requirements that it should, when finished, fulfill, and not till it fulfills all of them in a reasonable way, without different requirements coming into conflict with each other, can it be regarded a thoroughly rational creation. One can of course understand the word rational in a variety of ways, but the main criterion is fulfilling all the definable rational requirements so that they form a totality without conflict. If we wish to list the requirements that these chairs do not succeed in filling we could mention the following: a piece of furniture that forms a part of a person's daily habitat should not cause excessive glare from light reflection; ... it should not be disadvantageous in terms of sound, sound absorption, etc. A piece that comes into the most intimate contact with man, as a chair does, shouldn't be constructed of materials that are excessively good conductors of heat. I merely name these three criteria that the tubular metal chairs hardly fulfill.[63]

The principles of the Paimio Chair were later applied in a number of variations to create entire furniture series. Many of Aalto's furniture designs, as well as glass objects designed in the mid-1930s (plates 140–144), are produced today, sixty years after they were conceived, and these designs are still among the most popular successes of modern design.

The Paimio Tuberculosis Sanatorium was inaugurated in 1933 after four years of design work and construction. In the same year, immediately after the completion of the sanatorium, Aalto moved his office from Turku to Helsinki with great expectations. Helsinki was decisively closer to the eastern border city of Viipuri, where the construction of his library was finally beginning, and, more importantly, the capital was more central than Turku in the emerging cultural and economic situation. Aalto had every reason to expect commissions in the capital after the completion of his Paimio masterpiece.

He had won the competition for the municipal library in Viipuri in 1927, but, owing to difficulties in funding and an eventual change of the site, the library was only completed in 1935, after a many-faceted design process that lasted eight years (plates 89–109).[64] Aalto's engagement in the design of the library completely spans his transition from classicism to rationalist functionalism and finally to his personal synthetic idiom; the executed building reveals aspects of all three successive stylistic periods. The original competition entry of 1927 represents a refined and stately classicism (plates 89–90) heavily influenced by Asplund's somewhat earlier Stockholm Public Library of 1921–28. The second version, produced a year after the competition, with its totally glass-enclosed main stair and a surprisingly Miesian pavilion on a roof terrace within an enclosing parapet wall, is clearly inspired by Continental functionalism (plate 91). The dramatic stylistic change from the classicist competition entry again illustrates Aalto's capacity to make stylistic adaptations; the second version reflects features of the Turun Sanomat Building and anticipates aspects of the Paimio Tuberculosis Sanatorium. The final scheme submitted at the end of 1933 (plates 94–109) implied a decisive step away from the philosophy and aesthetics of the prevailing course of the modern movement. In this project Aalto moved toward a personal style that continued to develop until his last projects more than four decades later.

The Viipuri City Library's overall juxtaposition of two parallel volumes is a fairly standard modernist composition with historical precedents among, for instance, certain architectural images of the Russian Constructivists, such as Kasimir Malevich.[65] But, more importantly, the executed project introduced idiosyncratic solutions and details, and an overall architectural character that took the building well beyond the functionalist canon. It introduced certain unique characteristics of Aalto's later work, such as the fluent organization of circulation and various functions, the skylit library space with a sunken floor section, the juxtaposition of geometric and plastically molded shapes, ergonomic and tactile detailing, the use of natural materials as a counterpoint to immaterial whiteness, and a careful concern for conditions of both natural and artificial light as well as acoustics. These are all design features that became ingredients of Aalto's mature approach and can be found in countless variations in his later work.

Among the most extraordinary features of his oeuvre is the skylight system, which first appeared in his work at Viipuri. Aalto's explanation of the precise technical and psychological rationale of his skylight solution is a perfect illustration of his aspiration for a synthesis that widened rational considerations to include more subtle physiological and psychological realms:

> The ceiling (of the reading rooms and the lending room) has 57 round, conical openings, 1.8 meters in diameter, which function as skylights. The principle is as follows: the depth of the cones ensures that no light rays can penetrate at an angle of 52° or less. Thus the lighting is indirect all year round. This achieves two goals: first, the books are protected from direct sunlight and second, the reader is not disturbed by shadows or sharp light, whatever his position in relation to the book. The inner surfaces of the cones reflect daylight in such a way that the rays from each spread like a diffuse cluster over a large floor surface. Every seat in the reading room, receiving light from several cones, is thus bathed in a composite light.[66]

The undulating wood ceiling of the lecture hall is another design novelty, which was later articulated in countless variations as an Aalto signature (plates 101, 105; page 20). He explained the logic of the undulating ceiling:

> The ceiling of the auditorium consists of joined wooden slats, . . . which disseminate sound, particularly speech at close quarters, in an acoustically advantageous way. Since debate is as important as lectures, audibility is not merely in one direction, as in concert halls. My acoustic construction is aimed at making every point in the auditorium equal as a transmitter and a receiver of words spoken at normal loudness over the floor. I consider acoustic problems to be primarily physiological and psychological, which is why they cannot be solved by purely mechanical means.[67]

Aalto's account of the aim of his acoustical design (plate 103) even reveals a societal ideal—an aspiration for equality and democracy.

Beyond Modernist Functionalism: The Humanizing of Architecture

Despite his new international reputation, Aalto was not well known in Helsinki, and he was not welcomed in the way he had reason to expect. In addition to having lost the professorship to Sirén, Aalto was unsuccessful in most of the competitions he entered during the first half of the 1930s.[68] This must have caused some frustration for an architect who had launched functionalism in his country and had created internationally acclaimed masterworks in this style. In 1935–36, shortly after having moved to the capital, Aalto built his own house and studio in Munkkiniemi, a suburb of Helsinki (plates 125–129). Aalto's new contacts with Finnish industrial leaders led to commissions, such as the Sunila Pulp Mill and Housing at Kotka of 1936–38 (plates 113–119), but they were all some distance from Helsinki. His first commission in the city was the interior of the Savoy Restaurant in 1937, designed in collaboration with his wife Aino, as with so many of the Aalto interiors until Aino's early death in 1949. Although Aalto later won the important competitions for the National Pensions Institute in 1948 and the University of Technology in 1949, both in Helsinki (plates 240–276), his first design to appear prominently in the capital was the humble but elegantly detailed entry pavilion to an underground shelter facility built in 1951 at the Erottaja intersection of two main streets of the city.

In these years, his engagement in furniture and glass design also began to bear fruit; in fact his furniture spread his fame even more than his architecture.[69] The establishment of the Artek company in 1935 as a collaborative effort of Alvar Aalto, Maire Gullichsen, and the design critic Nils Gustav Hahl secured stable conditions for the further development of Aalto's furniture and other design products, as well as for their efficient production and international marketing. Maire's husband, Harry Gullichsen, the managing director of the A. Ahlström Corporation, had a crucial role in Aalto's career as the client for numerous commissions, including the first regional plan in Finland.

At the same time, the mid-1930s brought a dramatic transition in Aalto from that of an enthusiastic supporter of functionalism to a skeptic critical of rationalist principles. This abrupt change is clearly reflected in his writings, perhaps even more than in his designs. Aalto's conscious intellectual transitions were more dramatic than changes in his design work, which were perhaps guided more by intuition and emotion. After having consecrated himself to functionalism in 1928, Aalto had supported its rationalist ideology fervently. In one interview he had stated: "[The new architecture] strives to assess the content of the work (on which its form depends) correctly and to make it the only point of departure in creating form."[70] In another interview he elaborated upon his functionalist position: "Instead of form-based interior design, which starts exclusively from forms and then attempts to serve the practical purpose to the extent permitted by this constraint, the Functionalist method starts out from the real demands of life and then creates forms to suit needs."[71] By 1930 Aalto had appropriated a programmatic rationalist attitude in the spirit of Hannes Meyer, to the point of questioning the relevance of synthesis altogether: "I do not believe that it is sensible to concentrate on synthesis in tackling an architectural assignment.... The Functionalist architect is an entirely different professional type from the old-style architect. In fact he is not an architect at all; he is a social administrator."[72] Aalto's extreme confidence in analytic rationalism was well illustrated by the title he used for two of his lectures at the turn of the decade, "Non-Synthetic Aspirations in Architecture,"[73] and by his initiative to publish a book in Germany with the very same title.[74] Yet his subsequent conversion from rationalism was so complete that ten years later he was to make an exactly opposite statement with equal assurance:

Architecture is a synthetic phenomenon covering practically all fields of human activity. An object in the architectural field may be functional from one point of view and unfunctional from another.... If there were a way to develop architecture step by step, beginning with the economic and technical aspect and later covering the other more complicated human functions, then the purely technical functionalism would be acceptable; but no such possibility exists.... It is not the rationalization itself that was wrong in the first and now past period of modern architecture. The wrongness lies in the fact that the rationalization has not gone deep enough. Instead of fighting rational mentality, the newest phase of modern architecture tries to project rational methods from the technical field out to human and psychological fields.... Technical functionalism is correct only if enlarged to cover even the psychophysical field. That is the only way to humanize architecture.[75]

This expanded understanding of rationality is at the core of Aalto's mature thinking. Around 1935 he turned decidedly away from the universalist and abstract utopia of modernism and began to develop a multilayered, regionalist architecture that sought harmony with the Finnish geographical and cultural context, and reflected the subtle morphologies of its Finnish landscape of forests and lakes. Combining details and images of indigenous tradition with the modernist idiom became the overriding characteristic of Aalto's post-functionalist work. Resonance from the ageless peasant tradition can also be felt in Aalto's furniture designs. One of the reasons for the popular success of his furniture and glass designs undoubtedly lies in the relaxed dualism of tradition and radicality, which makes them equally acceptable in ordinary domestic settings or in high-style cultural environments. In one of his earliest essays Aalto revealed his appreciation for architectural atmosphere over conceptual or detail considerations: "I am led to believe that most people, but especially artists, principally grasp the atmosphere in a work of art. This is especially manifest in the case of old architecture. We encounter there a mood so intense and downright intoxicating that in most cases we don't pay a great deal of attention to individual parts and details, if we notice them at all."[76]

This view of the way in which architecture takes hold of the attention and emotions of the observer ultimately developed into a design strategy for Aalto, which lasted throughout his life. His works are dominated and held together by the cohesion of an atmosphere rather than by a unifying conceptual framework. Aalto created separate scenes, as it were—for the approach view of the building, the entry hall, main stair, and the main spaces—which could be experienced as a sequence of impressions rather than as an abstract idealized composition or entity. He did not seem to be concerned with the conceptual and geometric purity or with the organization of the design as presented graphically in the architectural drawing; his real interest was in the experiential and material encounter of the actual building. Aalto's designs may sometimes appear disorganized and clumsy as drawings, but the actual encounter makes the complex spaces and shapes appear convincingly motivated and unconstrained. Because of Aalto's emphasis on spatial, plastic, and material reality, the subtleties of his architecture cannot always be fully mediated by photographs. Aalto was a sensory realist in his design approach, not a conceptual idealist. In all his stylistic phases Aalto's designs project a rare sensuality and tactile intimacy.

Aalto expanded his understanding of rationality even further to include elements of intuition and play. From the mid-1930s on, his designs included playful details, whimsicalities, and improvisations. In the early 1950s, having built his own summer house at Muuratsalo as an architectural experiment that extended from the juxtaposition of various brick and tile textures to the aesthetic effect of decorative plants and mosses (plates 226–234), Aalto wrote about the need to unite research-oriented work with the mentality of play in our "calculating and utilitarian age…. It is only when the structural parts of a building, the forms logically derived from them, and empirical knowledge are imbued with what we can seriously call the art of play that we are on the right road. Technology and economy must always be combined with a life-enriching charm."[77]

This idea of "the art of play" had been maturing in Aalto's mind since his early youth. In a lecture given in his hometown as early as 1925 he wrote: "There is hardly anyone who would seriously deny that instinctive joy is the right response to an aesthetic experience. It is related to all intuitive activity, the joy of creation and the joy of work. Unfortunately, modern man, particularly Western man, is so deeply influenced by methodical analysis that his natural insight and immediate receptiveness have been greatly weakened."[78] There is a strong element of play and enjoyment in Aalto's inventively classicist works, and the playfulness re-emerges in his work after the Viipuri City Library. Aalto described the use of intuitive play and free association as a deliberate method of his design process in his celebrated essay, "The Trout and the Mountain Stream,"[79] which explained the design methods he used on the Viipuri library.

In this second ideological transition, Aalto was again inspired by Erik Gunnar Asplund. According to architect and author Stuart Wrede: "The later cross-pollenation of ideas between Asplund and Aalto was to have an even greater importance."[80] Here Wrede was referring to the similar transitions of both architects from rationalist modernism to a multilayered synthesis after the mid-1930s. Many of Aalto's mature design strategies have parallels in Asplund's later works, and these shared ideas presumably fermented in their frequent discussions.[81] Aalto's eulogy of Asplund in 1940 ended in words that could apply equally well to his own architecture: "A newer architecture has made its appearance, one that continues to employ tools of the social sciences, but that also includes the study of psychological problems—'the unknown human' in his totality. The latter has proved that the art of architecture continues to have inexhaustible resources and means which flow directly from nature and the inexplicable reactions of human emotions."[82]

In retrospect, it is clear that Aalto had begun to distance his architecture from the generally accepted tenets of the modern movement even

in many aspects of his functionalist works. Elements of his idiosyncratic designs began to appear in various aspects at Paimio and Viipuri as well as in many of his unsuccessful competition entries and, more explicitly and comprehensively, in the design of his own house in Munkkiniemi of 1935–36 (plates 125–129). This house combines a Cubist volumetric composition with traditional rustic references and details, as well as a host of spontaneous improvisations. The coziness, comfort, and relaxed atmosphere of this home of a young radical architect is surprising indeed. It shows clearly Aalto's rejection of the ideological, conceptual, and formal constraints of orthodox modernism in favor of sensuous pleasure and domestic comfort, and that his intention was to create images that evoked a sense of deep-rooted and timeless tradition instead of radical innovation and purist visual expression.

Toward the end of the 1930s, Aalto's synthetic functionalism developed into its first complete and fully orchestrated ensemble in the design of the Finnish Pavilion at the Paris International Exhibition of 1936–37 (plates 130–139).[83] Aalto secured this prestigious commission with two proposals, which were awarded the first and second prizes. Both schemes are sensitively woven into the context of the wooded slope of the Parisian park next to the Trocadero. The executed proposal elaborated ideas of freely flowing space, irregular spontaneous rhythms, the sunken central space and skylight system introduced in the Viipuri library, and an array of virtuoso inventions of wood structures and textures with a naturalist and rustic air. The spaces, shapes, textures, and materials evoked images of landscape and idyllic settings of nature. The multitude of lashed-pole supports and wood textures seems to have been inspired by the exotic products of colonial countries that Aalto had seen at the World's Fair in Brussels in 1935.[84]

The second competition entry, with its central themes of a terraced floor, a skylit hangar roof, and an undulating terrace was even more radical (figure 13).[85] The spatial impression hovers excitingly between the imageries of an indoor space and a bucolic garden. The project even included three wood-framed biplanes suspended from the ceiling over the stepped floor and the undulating terrace to reinforce the sense of the outdoors. The duality of Aalto's interests and inspirations—his excitement with technology and mobility symbolized by the airplanes, and his simultaneous aspiration to fuse architecture with the surrounding park and to introduce images of rustic origins—could hardly be made more clear.

Regardless of the fact that Aalto was obliged to make compromises in the displays because of the conservatism of the Finnish organizers, the pavilion was a great success for Aalto. Even Le Corbusier, who was as stingy as Aalto himself in giving credit to a contemporary colleague, acknowledged Aalto's success: "In the Finnish pavilion the visitor is delighted by its deep-rooted authenticity. It has been a point of honour for the authorities to choose the right architect."[86]

Around this time Aalto had also come under the influence of tradi-

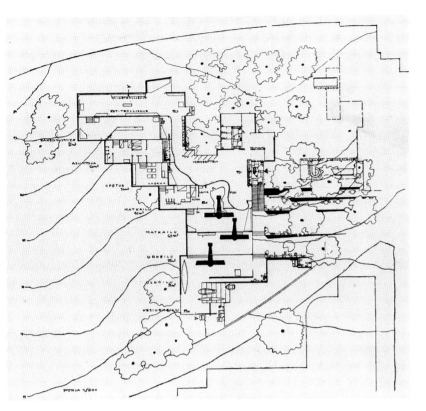

13. Alvar Aalto. Finnish Pavilion, Paris International Exhibition. 1936–37. Competition drawing: plan (1936). This scheme won second prize.

tional Japanese architecture and aesthetics, which affected not only the pavilion and his exhibition designs, but especially many of the details and the overall ambience of the Villa Mairea, the House for Maire and Harry Gullichsen, of 1938–39 (plates 155–169).[87] The Gullichsens had become his intimate friends and enabled Aalto to develop his new idiom without any restrictions. This was a project of special emotional significance for Aalto, an "opus con amore," as he himself acknowledged.[88] For both client and architect, the villa was an experiment in the potential offered by industrial technology and progressive architecture, design, and art for the realization of a shared vision of social utopia. They saw the special case of this private villa as a prototype for dwellings in the classless society of the future.[89]

The design evolved through a number of stages that represent fairly standard images of the modern movement. The earliest sketches also contain images of projecting balconies (plates 156–157) reminiscent of the volumetric composition of Frank Lloyd Wright's Fallingwater, the famous house for Edgar J. Kaufmann at Mill Run, Pennsylvania, of 1934–37.[90] If Aalto had seen pictures of Wright's masterpiece while working on the

Villa Mairea, his competitive spirit would certainly have been stimulated to challenge the older master. The final scheme achieves an extraordinary synthesis between nature and architecture. Aalto's architectural microcosm contains metaphors of the forest creating a rhythmic spatial flow with vaguely defined boundaries, a collage of materials, images, details, and numerous improvisations within an episodic painterly structure.

The imagery evoked by the house shifts from impressions of Continental modernity to Finnish peasant settings, with occasional Japanese refinements. For instance, the white-washed walls, flat roof, and ocean-liner handrails are juxtaposed with the rusticity of the wood sauna, the turf roof of the terrace, and the indigenous combination of fireplace and stair executed in natural stone. The imagery of an undivided living space with a rustic fireplace akin to the traditional Finnish peasant-cabin interior is combined with details and impressions of traditional Japanese architecture.[91] The Villa Mairea points simultaneously to the utopian modernist future and to the indigenous Finnish heritage. With these dualistic associations, the building attaches itself convincingly to the continuum of culture.

The intuitive and associative architecture of the Villa Mairea is closer to the way painters stage scenes than to the conventional structural principles of architecture. The way that Aalto assembles architectural images is more reminiscent of the Cubist technique of collage than the tectonic logic of architecture. In his presentation of the architectural principles of the house, Aalto referred directly to the affinity of his architectural approach with painting: "The unusual formal concept associated with the architecture [of the villa] also contains an intended link with modern painting.... Modern painting may be bringing forth a world of forms connected with architecture and generating personal experiences instead of the historical ornament which once served prestige purposes."[92]

The building's abundance of motifs, rhythms, textures, and materials is overwhelming. The interior teems with collagelike details: rattan-bound steel columns, the rough fiber facing of the studio staircase, a single concrete column in the library, the fireplace's fieldstone finish, and a variety of floor materials (plates 166–169). Aalto compiled motifs and textures as a painter adds dots of color, light, and shade on his paintings. The building is not unified by a single dominant architectural concept; instead, the conglomeration of ideas, impressions, and associations is held together by a sensuous atmosphere, in the same way that a great painting is integrated by the constancy of its light.

Aalto transformed the interior into a metaphorical forest punctuated by columns and wood poles; conversely, the courtyard, a metaphor for a peasant clearing in the pine forest, is transformed into a protected domestic space (plate 165; page 55). The Villa Mairea is a miniaturized world and a Cubist still life; it is the "synthetic landscape" and the "architectonic vision of landscape" that Aalto had written about in his 1926 essay on the Mantegna painting.[93]

While Aalto was developing the Villa Mairea design, he entered the competition for the Finnish Pavilion at the 1939 New York World's Fair, to be installed within a hangar structure provided by the organizers. He left nothing to chance this time. The office entered three proposals, and these won all three prizes.[94] The incredible fact that three different projects of such high quality were produced within three hectic days and nights[95] is conceivable only by remembering that the Paris International Exhibition had already acquainted Aalto with the necessary exhibition techniques, technologies, materials, and skills. Furthermore, he had already developed the idea of a freely undulating space in his design for the Forestry Pavilion at the agricultural exhibition at Lapua in 1938, as well as in his sketches of a central hall in one of the schemes of the Villa Mairea (plate 159). And, perhaps most interestingly, he had experimented with freely molded shape in miniature scale in his 1936 glass designs (plates 140–144).

The Finnish Pavilion at the New York World's Fair completed Aalto's journey from classicism through rationalist functionalism to convincing personal synthesis (plates 145–154). Today the pavilion remains a unique and unchallenged accomplishment in freely molded, amorphous architectural space. The undulating wall of the competition scheme seems to have been derived from an aerial image of the aurora borealis, but in the executed work it was transformed into an impression of forest space. Aalto had written in 1925 after his first trip to Italy: "We Northerners, especially the Finns, are very prone to 'forest dreaming', for which we have had ample opportunity up to now."[96] The New York pavilion is a virtuoso transformation of the episodic, amorphous, and poly-rhythmic forest space into an architectural concept. Aalto had in fact been developing the forest theme in several aspects of the Paris pavilion and the Villa Mairea, and bucolic elements had appeared in his work since the Viipuri library. Individual exhibits, displays, and objects were fully integrated into the architectural ensemble. Wood material in countless applications, shapes, and details played the leading role in this symphonic work. The space abounded with shapes, rhythms, textures, and details, yet the whole was integrated into an impressive singular experience resembling a walk through a forest landscape with its spectacular ever-changing play of light and shadow.

The exhibition was an immense success and enticed even Frank Lloyd Wright to call Aalto a genius.[97] The exhibition, *Alvar Aalto: Architecture and Furniture,* at The Museum of Modern Art, New York, in 1938, organized as a consequence of the success of Aalto's pavilion in Paris, had introduced him in America. But the success of the New York World's Fair pavilion brought Aalto invitations to numerous American universities and must have even made him consider the prospect of immigrating to the New World, following his countryman Eliel Saarinen, who had settled in the United States after his success in the *Chicago Tribune* Competition of 1923 and was carrying forward a successful second career at Cranbrook Academy of Art in Michigan.[98] In any case, Aalto directed much of his intellectual energy in the next few years to teaching and research initiatives in the United States.

The Idea of Flexible Standardization

Well before these new opportunities opened up in America, the ideas of facilitating industrial construction through standardization and of humanizing standardization through incorporating means to achieve flexibility and variety had occupied Aalto's thinking for some time. As early as his classicist work Aalto had used standard products and components, such as light fittings by Poul Henningsen, Marcel Breuer chairs manufactured by the Thonet company, and metal windows produced by Crittal-Braat in the Netherlands. Standardization had also become a central notion of Aalto's lectures and articles.

Aalto tackled the problem of standardization both philosophically and in his design tasks. Many of the drawings made for the Turun Sanomat Building, the *Rationalization of the Minimum Dwelling* exhibition, and the Paimio Tuberculosis Sanatorium, were obviously intended for repeated standard application, and possibly also for commercial manufacture (figure 14).[99] These drawings, stamped with a special label—"standard"—were made at the time in which Aalto developed an interest in standardization and mass production. "The use of standard elements is the manner of the industrial age; it is the only means to achieve scientifically sound results and raise quality… the architect creates the standards… he

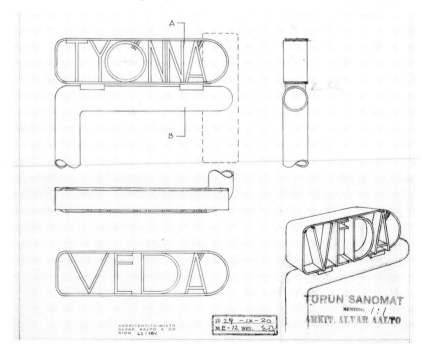

14. Alvar Aalto. Standard door handles for Turun Sanomat Building, Turku, Finland. 1928–30. Drawing, Erling Bjertnaes. Alvar Aalto Foundation, Helsinki. The handles are labeled: *työnnä* (push), *vedä* (pull).

may himself use these units in several buildings or someone else may use them. The architect creates an entity, a system of these units," Aalto stated in a 1929 interview.[100]

From 1935 onward he began to develop ideas of flexible, or elastic, standardization and to use biological metaphors for a principle of standardizing small units—"cells"—rather than complete buildings. Aalto's aspirations for flexible standardization paralleled his sharpening critique of modernist rationalism in the 1930s: "We have admitted, and probably agree, that objects which can with justification be called 'rational' often suffer from a considerable lack of human quality."[101] Aalto argued for a neutrality in the standardized product: "Now that standardization is a principle of production, we can see that formalism is enormously inhuman. A standardized object should not be a finished product, but on the contrary be made so that man and all the individual laws controlling him supplement its form. Only objects embodying some degree of neutrality can be used to alleviate standardization's constraint on the individual, and the positive sides of standardization thus used for the good of culture."[102] When mechanical standardization, such as that in the automobile industry, could aim at mass production of similar products, Aalto saw that architectural standardization should aim at differentiation and variety:

> *Whereas the course of development in relation to the automobile is for more and more effort to be made to concentrate on just a few types, the task of the architectural production process is exactly the opposite. By all right feeling and common sense, it should not be centralized standardization, but shall we say, 'decentralized' standardization. In architecture, the role of standardization is thus not to aim at a type, but on the contrary to create viable variety and richness which in an ideal situation is comparable to nature's infinite capacity of nuance.*[103]

By the mid-1950s, Aalto's conception of flexible standardization had reached the point of philosophical deliberation concerning the future of culture at large in the industrializing world:

> *But it is possible to use standardization and rationalization in the interests of man. The question is what we should standardize or rationalize. We could create standards which would raise the level not only of living but also of the spirit. It is very important for us to create elastic standardization which would not control us but which we would control. . . . We could try for what would offer man more. It is a matter of indifference how far electric cables and car wheels are standardized. But when we come into the human home, to things which are close to us, the problem is quite different—it is a question of the spirit, of the soul, a question of what is intellectual in standardization.*[104]

Regardless of the fact that Aalto devoted so much of his thinking to the idea of humanist standardization, he did not have an opportunity to

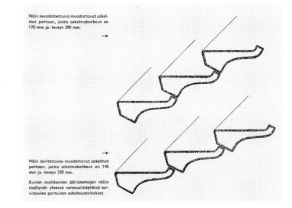

15. Alvar Aalto. Prefabricated standard stair. 1942

demonstrate these ideas in practice beyond isolated technical inventions, such as an ingenious standard stair of 1942 that would enable the construction of stairs with different tread-riser proportions by means of a single prefabricated unit (figure 15).[105] The wedge-shaped brick that he devised for the undulating wall of the House of Culture in Helsinki of 1952–58 (plate 288) is an invention to facilitate complete flexibility in creating an undulating wall surface. Aalto's furniture concepts are also systems of flexible modular standardization. His three furniture-leg configurations—X, Y, and Z, as they were called in Artek shop practice—enable one-, two-, and three-dimensional transitions of the supporting vertical leg to the supported horizontal plane, and offer an open-ended range of furniture applications. Aalto referred to the furniture leg as "the little sister of the architectonic column,"[106] but he never had a chance to develop an architectural parallel to his adaptable and variable furniture ideas.

Over several decades, Aalto and his assistants developed numerous technical and aesthetic solutions, which were repeatedly used as office standards. Such Aalto standards include different wall tiles, acoustical and textural surfaces, window and door details, ironwork, furnishings, light fittings, etc. Even the use of color in Aalto's postwar work was standardized to the application of indigo or violet blue and dark browns juxtaposed with white, gray, and black surfaces and the natural color of bronze, brick, and various species of wood. These gradually accumulated and developed office standards that enabled the realization of Aalto's *Gesamtkunstwerk*, regardless of his growing volume of work.

A concrete development in Aalto's idea of standardization was the AA-System of prefabricated houses, which he conceived for the A. Ahlström Corporation preceding World War II. The architectural character of the houses is surprisingly traditional and rustic considering the modern character of Aalto's other work. This speaks to Aalto's unique capacity to adapt his architecture to the requests of his clients and to the nature of each given task, but presumably it also reflects some degree of disillusionment with the modernist idiom. After the war years, the flat roofs, stuccoed facades, and metal windows of the radical modernist buildings of the prewar decade were in disrepair. It should also be noted that the aesthetic ideals of functionalism, such as flat roofs, imported from more favorable climates, had led to risky technical solutions. Hints of traditionalist architecture had emerged earlier in Aalto's residential designs for industrial plants, and Finnish functionalist architecture at large began to show regionalist and romantic tendencies toward the end of the 1930s; Bryggman in particular turned to a delicate romanticism before the war. The AA-System anticipated the type-house designs developed for the postwar reconstruction phase in the Reconstruction Bureau directed by Aalto. The reconstruction house types are exemplary in their economy, use of commonly available materials, and skills as well as in their functional efficiency.

In 1942, under Aalto's chairmanship, the Finnish Association of Architects founded the Standardization Institute,[107] which developed standard technical solutions and instructions for various building parts, compiled information on components and materials of construction, and prepared a system of modular coordination applied to the building industry; this work served as a basis for the full-scale prefabrication that began in Finland toward the end of the 1960s.

One of the myths of the elder Alvar Aalto presented him as an architect who did not write or theorize, but only spoke through his buildings. Aalto himself gave rise to this image through his explicitly stated position in the late 1950s. Until the war years, Aalto was an exceptionally prolific writer, lecturer, and propagandist, who even used daily newspapers and popular magazines as channels for promoting his ideas. His most ambitious idea in the literary field was his collaborative effort with Gregor Paulsson to publish an international weekly periodical in the field of cultural philosophy and politics. According to a memo, the aims of the publication (with the working title *The Human Side*) were:

> *To inform the general public in straightforward, nontechnical language about new, sociobiologically valid phenomena appearing today in culture, social life, industry and politics, in various parts of the world, and which together indicate that structures in these spheres are going through a complete metamorphosis. Furthermore, to direct attention to the necessity of forming a new system of values associated with the new structures to replace the value nihilism which is at the root of the present chaotic situation. The ultimate purpose is thus a synthesis of culture, social life, industry and politics. Along with this, to investigate "declined" cultural functions in order to distinguish them from others. This work shall be carried out quite independently of present political ideologies.*[108]

Instead of dropping the idea because of the outbreak of war in Europe in September 1939, Aalto and Paulsson stated: "In this time of war and conflict, the publication *The Human Side* is therefore considered even more important, if possible, than it would have been in a time of peace."[109] Regardless of their fairly vague plans, the editors had succeeded in acquiring a surprisingly authoritative and diversified collection of contributors for the planned journal.[110] When the Soviet Union attacked Finland at the end of November 1939, the editors altered their plans and circulated another notice: "The character of *The Human Side* has been revised and linked up as closely as possible with the war in Finland, but still within the ideological bounds of the original programme."[111] The further acceleration of the war, however, shattered the idealistic initiative.

The Aalto legend has also presented him as a pragmatic designer whose creative attitude was based on intuition rather than theoretical investigations or research. At the end of the 1930s Aalto, however, made successive attempts to initiate systematic research in architecture. During his second trip to the United States in conjunction with the opening of the New York World's Fair in 1939, Aalto presented the idea of establishing a network of international research institutes to a group of influential architects in San Francisco, gathered together by William W. Wurster.[112] Aalto proposed a system of international research institutes and was so emphatically engaged with the idea of architectural research organized on the basis of international collaboration that, immediately upon returning from New York for the erection of the Finnish pavilion, he published an article that suggested world's fairs be replaced with a system of permanent educational institutions in the participating countries, constituting a kind of a universal school network. By this arrangement, Aalto believed, universal exhibitions could be given back their "purpose as motors for humanity's development."[113]

In 1940 Aalto was invited to teach and do research at Massachusetts Institute of Technology (MIT) in Cambridge. In this role Aalto proposed another idea to advance architectural research. His paper, "Working Program for Architectural Research at M.I.T.,"[114] laid out the principles of an educational-research scheme to investigate issues of flexible standardization, human sensory reactions, and potentials of varied exterior surfaces in housing design. Two months after Aalto had submitted his proposal, he was called back to Finland to direct reconstruction activities, and the initiative had to be dropped.[115]

Aalto returned to his teaching position at MIT in 1945–48, but he concentrated on the design of Baker House Senior Dormitory there of 1946–49 (plates 181–195). The dormitory building, undulating along the Charles River, is a skillful application of the idiom that Aalto had established by the time of the war, but it also reveals regionalist and contextual interests and thus points to the new phase in Aalto's development, which was to materialize in such mature masterpieces of the 1950s as the Säynätsalo Town Hall of 1948–52, the Jyväskylä Pedagogical Institute of 1951–59, the Rautatalo Office Building of 1953–55, the National Pensions Institute of 1948–57, and the House of Culture of 1952–58, all of which utilize brick and copper as the main exterior materials (plates 196–214, 240–258, 280–288; see page 54).

By the time of publication of the 1949 edition of Sigfried Giedion's seminal history of modern architecture, Aalto was considered a leading figure in the development of contemporary architecture. His critical voice concerning the inhumanity of techno-economically dominated construction was beginning to be understood, as the lack of quality in International Style postwar building became evident. Nevertheless, Aalto had had to establish himself abroad before he became a publicly accepted and esteemed figure in his home country. Until late in life, he had to win important public commissions through architectural competitions. Kyösti Ålander, the founding director of the Museum of Finnish Architecture, acknowledged Alvar Aalto in print in 1954 as the greatest of the architects who have "transformed... narrow theory into a living architectural style [but did so] on account of foreign rather than Finnish acclaim."[116] But the lack of general recognition in his own country frustrated Aalto to the point that in 1954 he named his motorboat "Nemo Propheta in Patria" [No man is a prophet in his own country].

The Reemergence of Rationalism: The Aging Master

The rationalist and functionalist ideology became dominant among Finnish architects again in the early 1950s, even though Aalto had challenged this position in his designs and writings since the mid-1930s. The best accomplishments of Finnish architecture in the 1950s reflect a combination of rationalist and functionalist ideals with a refined sense of materials and a reassuring sense of tradition and place. It is of interest in the context of the development of Alvar Aalto's view of rationality to survey his relation to this reemergence of the rationalist and functionalist movement. This will also illuminate the professional position of the aging master in his own country.

In Aalto's early years, Asplund and Bryggman had provided a sober balance to his zealousness. During the functionalist era and in the years immediately after the war, another group of friends—P. E. Blomstedt, Yrjö Lindegren, and Aulis Blomstedt—provided an intellectual challenge to Aalto. The members of this group were all highly talented and respected architects: P. E. Blomstedt was a fervent functionalist, architect and theorist; Lindegren was the designer of such masterpieces as the Olympic Stadium; and Aulis Blomstedt was an important postwar theorist and educator, and the designer of ascetic but well-proportioned buildings. However, P. E. Blomstedt had died in 1935, Lindegren in 1952, and Bryggman in 1955; and the intimate friendship of Aalto and Aulis Blomstedt had broken down during the early 1950s. It has been suggested by contemporary observers that the loss of this circle of friends, which provided a collegial critique for Aalto, strengthened his tendency toward egotism, and facilitated his withdrawal from public participation in ideological discussions.[117] The tragic and untimely death of Aalto's first wife, Aino, in 1949 must have also deeply affected his mentality. Aino had been a professional partner and a balancing force ever since Aalto had established his office.[118]

After having guided the profession authoritatively for fifteen years in his role as the chairman of the Finnish Association of Architects, Aalto withdrew from public professional discussion in the early 1960s. In retro-

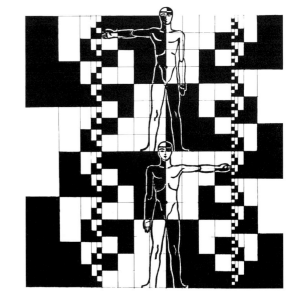

16. Aulis Blomstedt. Study of Pythagorean Intervals Applied to the Human Figure, n.d.

spect, it is easy to understand and accept his withdrawal from the obsessively political discussion that was emerging. He had disappointing experiences with democratic institutions as clients and later seemed inclined toward the enlightened patriarchal society of his youth in rural Finland and of his numerous industrial commissions.

Thus, a critical attitude toward Aalto had begun to develop toward the 1950s, even among his old friends. In 1948, Aulis Blomstedt, the younger of the architect brothers, wrote a scathing essay, titled "Snowballs," for the special issue of *Arkkitehti* celebrating Aalto's fiftieth birthday; but the editors did not dare to publish it. Blomstedt characterized Alvar with the following metaphor: "It is told that a certain world master in the game of chess always began his game with a theoretical mistake already in the second move. Aalto commits his mistake already in the first move, and in a number of other essential moves, but never in the last one. As I turn the other side of the coin to view, I see Aalto's eternally roguish and boyish face against the background of his own landscapes: the face of the Master."[119]

Aulis Blomstedt was temperamentally unlike Aalto, and he became passionately interested in proportional and modular theories. His graphic and numerical studies in musical and architectural harmony reveal a devoted Pythagorean ideology (figure 16).[120] In a later published article, Blomstedt openly criticized Aalto's favorite notion of elastic standardization: "There has been enough discussion of elastic standardization. In order that life could achieve elastic freedom, standardization, in accordance with the word, has to be non-elastic—in the right manner."[121] Aalto countered with the gibe that the module he had used in his design of the Rautatalo Office Building in Helsinki of 1953–55 was "one millimeter or a fraction of it."[122] This was his way of deprecating the important effort of Blomstedt in defining proportional and modular principles for large-scale industrial construction. In articulating this attitude Aalto also turned

17. Viljo Revell. Apartment Building, Tapiola, Finland. 1954

18. Cover of *Le Carré Bleu*, no. 1 (1956), with wood sculpture by Reima Pietilä

against his own rationalist aspirations as well as his own earlier attempts to create humanistic architectural research and standards.

After the mid-1950s, the end of the friendship between Aalto and Blomstedt and the growing distance between their philosophical positions gave rise in Finland to two schools of architectural thought with conflicting ideologies. The newly established Museum of Finnish Architecture became a counterpoint to Aalto and his followers.[123] Aalto had been one of the founders of the museum in 1956, the second museum in the world dedicated to architecture, but by the end of the decade architects and historians who participated in its activities, such as Viljo Revell (figure 17), represented more rationalistically and theoretically oriented views than those of the master. In a fictive Platonic dialogue with Sigfried Giedion, published in *Arkkitehti* in 1958, Aalto explicitly condemned theory and writing: "The Creator created paper for drawing architecture on. Everything else is, at least for my part, to misuse paper. *Torheit*, as Zarathustra would have said."[124] This statement not only audaciously contradicted the prolific writing of his own fairly recent past but also made professional silence a virtue for an entire generation of Finnish architects.

In 1956, the Finnish CIAM group, whose ideological leader was Aulis Blomstedt, established an international magazine called *Le Carré Bleu*, published in French as a forum for international theoretical discussion (figure 18).[125] Although Aalto's CIAM connections had been instrumental in the development of his thinking and international reputation, he did not attend CIAM meetings after the war. Yet it is ironic that his Finnish colleagues in CIAM were to form his critical intellectual opposition.

It is equally paradoxical that the younger generation, with a new social awareness and rationalist inclination, became critical of Aalto, who had passionately supported these same ideals three decades earlier. The generation of students that began its studies after the mid-1950s generally conformed to the rationalist line. Aalto's architecture was considered so

idiosyncratic that young architects sought more objective models.[126] In their roles as professors of architecture at the Helsinki University of Technology, Aulis Blomstedt and Aarno Ruusuvuori had a strong impact on the younger generation (figure 19). Aalto's exaggerated individualism even tended to make his architecture appear anachronistic in the intellectual air of the 1960s. Aalto's late monumentalizing tendency and use of white marble as facade material in the Enso-Gutzeit building of 1959–62 (page 85) and Finlandia Hall of 1962–71 (figure 20) in Helsinki were severely criticized by the younger generation, which hoped for a rationalist architecture that would express the ideals of democracy and equality. In the face of the growing political awareness of the late 1960s on the part of the student generation, Aalto became embattled and perhaps misunderstood. The younger generation was critical of the accentuated individualistic role of the established generation of architects and designers at large. Technologi-

19. Aarno Ruusuvuori. Marisauna, Bökars, Finland. 1968

cal rationality, societal solidarity, and aesthetic restraint were valued over expressive artistic aspirations. Kaj Franck, the designer of austere, sophisticated glass objects and an influential teacher at the Helsinki Institute of Arts and Design, propagated the anonymity of design products and won wide support among students. By the time of the Paris student uprisings in spring 1968, students at the schools of architecture and design in Helsinki had become critical of aesthetic aspirations altogether. Then, during the 1970s, the societally motivated student movement led to philosophical confusion, and Finnish architects lost their self-confidence and sense of social purpose.

Alvar Aalto died in 1976, and the pendulum began to swing back as Finnish architecture moved decisively toward his inclusive thinking and formal language. Aspects of Aaltoesque design, such as the counterpoint between rectangularity and free form, skewed coordinates, rich surface textures, and the use of skylight arrangements, became standard elements of Finnish architecture. Aalto's critical view of technology and flexible standardization also replaced the enthusiastic confidence in the benefits of rigid industrialization. Materiality and references to history, as well as detailing based on craftsmanship skills, became characteristics of Finnish architecture at large. Ironically, the absence of Aalto's overpowering figure on the professional scene allowed for the profession to comprehend his aspirations and to realize the depth and continued relevance of his thinking.

Aalto's own statement in one of his last published texts formulated the Aalto legacy that has had a decisive and lasting impact on architectural thought and practice in his country: "Every commission is different and so solutions to problems cannot be stereotyped. The examples I have given are individual and are only valid as a method in other applications. There is a great deal in architecture which never gets beyond the analysis level, though synthesis is what is actually needed. Nothing is more dangerous than to separate analysis and synthesis: they absolutely belong together."[127]

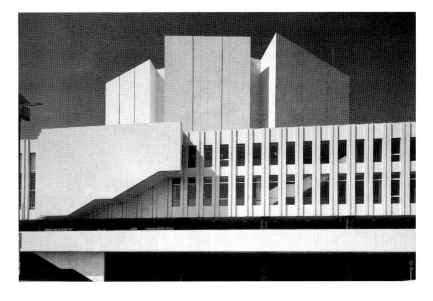

20. Alvar Aalto. Finlandia Hall, Helsinki. 1962–71. Exterior detail

Notes

1. Alvar Aalto, "Taide ja tekniikka" [Art and Technology], lecture, Academy of Finland, October 3, 1955, in Göran Schildt, ed., *Luonnoksia: Alvar Aalto* (Helsinki: Otava, 1972), pp. 87–88; trans. Juhani Pallasmaa. See also the collection of Aalto's writings in English: Göran Schildt, ed., *Sketches: Alvar Aalto*, trans. Stuart Wrede (Cambridge, Mass., and London: MIT Press, 1978), pp. 127–128.

2. Göran Schildt, "Alvar Aalto and the Classical Tradition," in Asko Salokorpi, ed., *Classical Tradition and the Modern Movement* (Helsinki: 2nd International Alvar Aalto Symposium, 1985), p. 137.

3. See, for example, Demetri Porphyrios, *Sources of Modern Eclecticism: Studies on Alvar Aalto* (London: Academy Editions,1982).

4. The term *functionalism*, denoting a new rationally oriented architecture, was used by leading architects in Finland from 1928 onward; the term became commonly used in Finland toward the end of the 1930s. Such terms as *rationalism, neorationalism, internationalism,* and *new objectivity* were used at the turn of the decade synonymously with functionalism. In his writings, Aalto also used the terms *new realism* and *functional architecture*. See Raija-Liisa Heinonen, *Funktionalismin läpimurto Suomessa* [Breakthrough of Functionalism in Finland] (Helsinki: Museum of Finnish Architecture, 1986), pp. 4–9. After the war, functionalism was commonly used in reference to Finnish modern architecture in general. This practice was justified by the fact that functionalist aesthetics, structural rationality, and societally oriented professional ethics guided the development of Finnish architecture and continues to do so today. The term *International Style* has also been used in Anglo-American literature to refer to functionalism. A noticeable return to functionalist ideals took place during the late 1950s and again in the 1980s.

5. A clearly articulated rationalist program was declared in Finland as early as 1904 by Gustaf Strengell and Sigurd Frosterus in opposition to the results of the Helsinki Railway Station competition. According to Strengell: "We have plenty of decorative and 'artistic' talent here in Finland at present. What we need is some guiding, clear and rational force. It's men we need, men who are prepared to break irrevocably with the past, to look boldly and resolutely to the future. Men who are not merely heart and soul but are made more of brains and good sense—heroes of thought, more than those *Deren ganze Seele in den Augen Steckt*." And Frosterus proclaimed: "We want rationalism that does not hesitate to call a task by its right name, that does not hesitate to believe in the beauty of reality, that rejects ready-made schemes and established norms for beauty…. We want an iron and brain style." Gustaf Strengell and Sigurd Frosterus, *Arkitektur: en stridsskrift våra motståndare tillägnad af Gustaf Strengell och Sigurd Frosterus* [Architecture: A Challenge to Our Opponents by Gustaf Strengell and Sigurd Frosterus] (Helsinki: Euterpes Förlag, 1904); repr. in English in *Abacus Yearbook 3* (Helsinki: Museum of Finnish Architecture, 1983), pp. 65, 77. The two architects were widely read humanists and early cosmopolitans.

Significantly, they were supporters of Aalto during the professional dispute concerning the Paimio Tuberculosis Sanatorium of 1929. Aalto mentioned Strengell and Frosterus respectfully in several contexts. For example: "The intellectualization of architecture, that exceptionally healthy feature which was represented in our country by Sigurd Frosterus and Gustav Strengell, can be traced to van de Velde." Alvar Aalto, "Henry van de Velde in Memoriam," *Arkkitehti*, nos. 11–12 (1957); repr. in English in Schildt, *Sketches*, p. 143.

6. Alvar Aalto, "Rationalismi ja ihminen" [Rationalism and Man], lecture, Swedish Society of Crafts and Design, May 9, 1935; in Schildt, *Luonnoksia.*; repr. in English in idem, *Sketches*, p. 50.

7. Alvar Aalto, "Euroopan jälleenrakentaminen tuo pinnalle aikamme rakennustaiteen keskeisimmän probleemin" [The Reconstruction of Europe Reveals the Central Architectural Problem of Our Time], *Arkkitehti*, no. 5 (1941); quoted in English in Aarno Ruusuvuori and Juhani Pallasmaa, eds., *Alvar Aalto: 1898–1976* (Helsinki: Museum of Finnish Architecture, 1978), pp. 113–114.

8. Alvar Aalto, "Taisteleva arkkitehtuuri" [Fighting Architecture], lecture, Royal Institute of British Architects, London, 1957; in Schildt, *Luonnoksia*; quoted in English in Ruusuvuori and Pallasmaa, *Alvar Aalto*, p. 142.

9. Alvar Aalto, unpublished manuscript, 1926; quoted in Göran Schildt*, Alvar Aalto: The Decisive Years*, trans. Timothy Binham (New York: Rizzoli, 1986), p. 11.

10. Alvar Aalto, "From Doorstep to Living Room" (1926); quoted in Göran Schildt, *Alvar Aalto: The Early Years*, trans. Timothy Binham (New York: Rizzoli, 1984), p. 216.

11. The classicism in the Nordic countries between 1910 and 1930 was at one time viewed as an interlude between the more significant architectural movements of Art Nouveau and functionalism; Aalto himself underrated his classicist works and did not want them to be included in presentations of his oeuvre. The movement was introduced to a wider international audience through the exhibition and catalogue *Nordic Classicism, 1910–1930*, organized in 1982 by the Museum of Finnish Architecture in collaboration with the other Nordic architecture museums. See Simo Paavilainen, ed., *Nordic Classicism, 1910–1930* (Helsinki: Museum of Finnish Architecture, 1982).

12. Schildt, *Early Years*, p. 126.

13. Schildt gave a vivid description of the ambitious young Aalto. See also Igor Herler, "Early Furniture and Interior Designs," in Juhani Pallasmaa, ed., *Alvar Aalto Furniture* (Helsinki: Museum of Finnish Architecture, Finnish Society of Crafts and Design, and Artek, 1984), p. 14.

14. Schildt, *Early Years*, pp. 168, 254.

15. Aalto's church renovations and restorations during the 1920s were: Toivakka Church (1923), Anttola Church (1924–26), Äänekoski Church (1924), Pertunmaa Church (1924), Viitasaari Church (1925), Kemijärvi Church (1926–29), Pylkönmäki Church (1926), Korpilahti Church (1926–27), and Ristiina Church (1927).

16. Another influential professor of architecture at the

time Aalto began his studies was Gustaf Nyström, who worked in a neo-Renaissance style but was an ingenious early user of cast-iron, steel, and concrete structures. His influence on Aalto was second-hand, as he died in 1918.

17. Schildt, *Early Years*, p. 167.

18. Herler, "Early Furniture," is an excellent and detailed analysis of the sources of Aalto's early furniture designs.

19. Aalto often repeated a slogan from his boyhood in Jyväskylä, "Lyödään hepnaadilla!" [Let's strike them with amazement], in a combination of Finnish and Swedish street slang. Schildt, *Early Years*, p. 47–48.

20. Alvar Aalto, "Menneitten aikojen motiivit" [Motifs from Times Past], *Arkkitehti*, no. 2 (1922); repr. in Schildt, *Sketches*, p. 2.

21. Alvar Aalto, "Eräs kaupunkimme kaunistustoimenpide ja sen mahdollisuudet" [A Step to Beautify Our Town and Its Feasibility], *Keskisuomalainen* (January 22, 1925), p. 3; quoted in Herler, "Early Furniture," p. 14.

22. The group was originally an informal literary conversation circle formed after Finland had won independence in 1917. *Tulenkantajat* was initially the title of a series of literary albums published from 1924 onward by Werner Söderström. *Tulenkantajat* magazine was published in Helsinki by Tulenkantajain Osakeyhtiö in two phases, in 1928–30 and 1932–39. During its first years, the magazine fervently promoted modernist ideals in literature, visual arts, architecture, theater, cinema, and music. The editors were spellbound by urbanity, machines, mobility, sports, nudity, travel, and jazz. The inaugural issue of November 1928 declared: "This journal implies that a new generation takes the lead in the artistic life of Finland." The first issue of 1929 declared a connection with Europe: "We are Europe," "We are the young Europe," and "Now the time for the young nations of Europe has come." The third issue of 1929 contains a respectful interview with Aalto about his Turku theater (pp. 36–38), and number six, 1930, reviews Aalto's radical stage design for Hagar Olsson's play, *S.O.S.* (pp. 86–88); trans. Juhani Pallasmaa.

23. *Tulenkantajat*, no. 6 (1930), p. 87; trans. Juhani Pallasmaa.

24. Bertel Jung, "Funktionalismi" [Functionalism], *Arkkitehti*, no. 4 (1930), p. 59; trans. Juhani Pallasmaa.

25. Flying and airplanes were a common source of inspiration for modernists. Le Corbusier's *Vers une architecture* included several images of airplanes, and he even published a book on the subject: Le Corbusier, *Aircraft* (London: Studio Publications, 1935). The seminal 1931 publication of the Swedish radical architects' group, *acceptera,* ends with an image of an aircraft; and an airplane also appears on the cover of *Tulenkantajat*, nos. 7–8 (1930).

26. Schildt, *Decisive Years*, pp. 13–14.

27. Kirmo Mikkola, "The Transition from Classicism to Functionalism in Scandinavia," in Salokorpi, *Classical Tradition and the Modern Movement*, p. 69.

28. Alvar Aalto, interview, in *Sisä-Suomi* (August 18, 1928); quoted in Schildt, *Decisive Years*, pp. 54–55.

29. Gustaf Strengell parodied Aalto's desire for fame with a quote from an imaginary American architectural journal, "The Architectural Tomfoolery," which purportedly said: "There is practically no architecture, nor are

there any architects in Finland of today, save Mr. Alvar Aalto, who resides in Åbo [Swedish for Turku]. This ancient but dethroned capital has, thanks to Mr. Aalto's genius, again become elevated to the rank and positions of Finland's cultural center." Gustaf Strengell, "Alvar Aalto: Finland's första funktionalist" [Alvar Aalto: Finland's First Functionalist], *Hufvudstadsbladet*, (July 10, 1932), p. 9; trans. Juhani Pallasmaa.

30. Kirmo Mikkola, *Aalto* (Jyväskylä: Gummerus, 1985), p. 10; trans. Juhani Pallasmaa.

31. Aalto's broad-mindedness extended to his political attitudes. In the 1920s he designed the leftist Workers' Club in Jyväskylä while working on the Seinäjoki Defense Corps Building for the extreme right nationalistic movement, and in his mature years he designed the House of Culture in Helsinki for the Finnish Communist Party while also being engaged in projects for Finnish industries. He also built a number of churches, although he was a humanist skeptic and hardly religiously inclined. Göran Schildt has emphasized Aalto's inclination for anarchistic thinking in its original utopian sense. The final chapter in Schildt, *Early Years,* is titled "Anarchism as an Architectural Principle," pp. 242–259.

32. Aalto's classicist and functionalist work synthesized discoveries of his Swedish and Continental friends. His bentwood furniture developed further technical innovations made earlier by others; and the free form, Aalto's trademark, was a commonly used modernist motif in the 1930s, applied frequently in sculpture, painting, object design, and graphic design. Many of his light fittings elaborated ideas introduced by Poul Henningsen, and his freely molded glass objects had precedents among the products of the Swedish Orrefors company. Hilding Ekelund wrote somewhat ironically in 1930: "With the same burning zeal that academic architects of the past sketched Roman baroque portals, Gothic finials, etc., in their sketchbooks in order to use them in their own buildings, Alvar Aalto seeks techno-rationalist novelties from various parts of Europe utilizing them resourcefully and casting them in his own mold. Regrettably, wittiness and a certain exaggerated mechanicalness tend to dominate his interiors." Hilding Ekelund, "Småbostadens rationalisering" [Rationalization of the Minimum Dwelling], *Hufvudstadsbladet* (November 18, 1930); trans. Juhani Pallasmaa.

33. Alvar Aalto, "E. G. Asplund in Memoriam," *Arkkitehti,* no. 1–12 (1940); repr. in Schildt, *Sketches*, p. 66. Aalto gave a wide-open answer to a question concerning the inspiration he had drawn from older colleagues: "It is a rather difficult question. I can only generally say that I am much indebted to my colleagues and predecessors. But they are many. It would turn into a long list all the way from archaic times to our days. It would not only consist of architects but the entire field of art and science. In addition to personalities, the list would contain achievements of scientists supporting various philosophies of architects, painters, sculptors, engineers and other disciplines." Göran Schildt, "Esipuheena keskustelu" [A Conversation as a Preface], in Leonardo Mosso, *Alvar Aalto, teokset: 1918–1967* [Alvar Aalto, Works: 1918–1967] (Helsinki: Otava, 1967), p. 6; trans. Juhani Pallasmaa.

34. Stuart Wrede, *The Architecture of Erik Gunnar Asplund* (Cambridge, Mass.: MIT Press, 1980), p. 337, n. 112.

35. Bryggman had made his first extensive trip to Italy by 1920. He had made another trip to Italy and Austria in 1927 and one to Germany in the summer of 1928. Aulis Blomstedt's eulogy of Bryggman gave a touching portrait of his personality: "A really great architectural talent is a very rare freak of nature. So far we seem to have only a dim conception of what the word architectural really means. Nevertheless, we know that Erik Bryggman had this gift. Everything he touched became alive. The most trivial building task, the simplest material changed under his hand into a kind of crystallised humanity, which cannot be described in words. The hidden flower of architecture had burst into full blossom. A master of architecture has passed away, after having left us the living wonder of his life's work." *Arkkitehti,* no. 12 (1955), p. 190; repr. in English in Riitta Nikula, "On Erik Bryggman and His Architecture," in idem, ed., *Erik Bryggman, 1891–1955: Architect* (Helsinki: Museum of Finnish Architecture, 1991), p. 70.

36. In its overall disposition and architectural expression, the newspaper building had close precedents in the competition entries for an office block in Vaasa (1927), conceived together by Bryggman and Aalto, and that for the Suomi Insurance company headquarters extension in Helsinki (1927), which Bryggman designed alone.

37. The interior of Asplund's Skandia Cinema was indigo blue and orange red. "While I was building this I thought of autumn evenings and yellow leaves," Asplund is reported to have said. Aalto, "Asplund in Memoriam," in Schildt, *Sketches*, p. 66. Aalto's Turku Finnish City Theater had a "Chinese" color scheme: the walls of the entry stair were red, the door to the theater was black with gold plates, and the theater interior entirely gray-blue.

38. Aalto's losing competition scheme for the Kinkomaa Tuberculosis Sanatorium (1927) and his stadium proposal in the Independence Monument competition for Helsinki (1928) contained programmatically modern aspects in their extreme simplicity. The stadium project especially was a proposition that could hardly be reduced further in terms of form.

39. Sven Markelius, "Rationalisointipyrkimykset nyky-aikaisessa huonerakennustaiteessa" [Rationalization Trends in Modern Housing Design], *Arkkitehti,* no. 5 (1928), pp. 71–72. Hilding Ekelund later remarked that the Markelius lecture marked the official breakthrough of functionalism in Finland. See Schildt, *Decisive Years,* pp. 47–48.

40. Erik Gunnar Asplund, Wolter Gahn, Sven Markelius, Gregor Paulsson, Eskil Sundahl, and Uno Åhren published the influential *acceptera* manifesto in 1931. The polemical tract analyzes emerging societal, cultural, technological, and aesthetic conditions and advises designers to accept the new reality and to base architecture and product design on these conditions.

41. P. E. Blomstedt was very interested in Russian Constructivism from the late 1920s on. See Elina Standertskjöld, *P. E. Blomstedt, 1900–1935: Arkkitehti* (Helsinki: Museum of Finnish Architecture, 1996), p. 70. Hilding Ekelund acquired books on the work of the Russian avant-garde during his trips to Moscow in

connection with the construction of the Finnish embassy he was designing in 1935. See Vilhelm Helander, "A Small Portrait," in Timo Tuomi et al, eds., *Hilding Ekelund (1893–1984) Architect* (Helsinki: Museum of Finnish Architecture, 1997), p. 47. Aalto must have been aware of the work of the Russian avant-garde through his friends André Lurçat and Hans Schmidt, who were both working in the Soviet Union. See Schildt, *Decisive Years,* pp. 87–88.

42. Göran Schildt, "Aalto, Bauhaus, and the Creative Experiment," in *Alvar Aalto vs. the Modern Movement* (Jyväskylä: 1st International Alvar Aalto Symposium, 1981), pp. 9–43.

43. In 1991 the Alvar Aalto Museum organized the exhibition *Fratres Spirituales Alvari,* which showed works by artists (Alexander Calder, Otto G. Carlsund, Le Corbusier, Fernand Léger, and László Moholy-Nagy) related to Aalto's artistic approach. See Teija Hihnala and Päivi-Marjut Raippalinna, eds., *Fratres Spirituales Alvari* (Jyväskylä: Alvar Aalto Museum, 1991).

44. In 1949 in the eighth printing of the second, enlarged, edition of his seminal history of the modern movement, *Space, Time and Architecture,* Sigfried Giedion added a chapter on Aalto: "Alvar Aalto: Elemental and Contemporary." He introduced Aalto with the following sentence: "Aalto is the strongest exponent of the combination of standardization with irrationality, so that standardization becomes no longer master but servant." Sigfried Giedion, *Space, Time and Architecture: The Growth of a New Tradition,* 9th printing, 2nd enl. ed. (Cambridge, Mass.: Harvard University Press, 1952), p. 453. Giedion also presented an admiring account of Aalto's personality: "One cannot speak about Aalto the architect without speaking about Aalto the man. People are at least as important to him as architecture. Aalto is interested in every human being, in each of their particular desires and experiences, no matter where they come from or to what social class they belong. He draws incentive and stimulation from contact with men of varied callings, much as James Joyce did. Indeed, Aalto cannot set foot outside his door without becoming involved in some human episode. He approaches people directly and without inhibitions, in the same way that he approaches the organic material wood." Ibid., p. 490.

45. See Tuomi, *Hilding Ekelund*; and Timo Keinänen and Kristiina Paatero, eds., *Martti Välikangas 1893–1973* (Helsinki: Museum of Finnish Architecture, 1993).

46. See, for example, Albert Edelfelt, "The Decline and Rebirth of Decorative Taste" (1898); repr. in *Abacus Yearbook 3,* pp. 23–32; and the writings of Ekelund in Tuomi, *Hilding Ekelund.*

47. The exhibition was organized by Alvar Aalto, and he was responsible for the overall planning of the exhibited standard dwelling. The furnishings and furniture for this model apartment were designed by Aino and Alvar Aalto, except for the interior of one of the bedrooms, which was designed by Werner West. The designers of various other parts of the exhibition were P. E. Blomstedt and Erik Bryggman.

48. Alvar Aalto, "Foreword," in *Pienasunto* [Minimum Dwelling] (Helsinki: Pienasuntojen rationalisointiosaston julkaisu taideteollisuusnäyttelyssä, 1930), p. 2; trans. Juhani Pallasmaa.

49. Aalto's residential area for the Sunila Pulp Mill of 1936–38 and the "Olympic Village" apartment blocks designed by Hilding Ekelund and Martti Välikangas for the 1940 Olympic Games planned for Helsinki were exemplary functionalist housing schemes sensitively adapted to the terrain and vegetation, aiming successfully at individuality and variety.

50. A unique concept of a new town, the "Forest Town," integrated inhabited areas with their natural context, which was characteristic of Finnish planning after the wars. This concept, based on functionalist precedents, was well demonstrated by the Tapiola Garden City outside Helsinki.

51. J. S. Sirén was a highly professional designer in the classicist idiom, but he remained a skeptic of modernity from 1931 until after he retired from his position at the University of Technology in 1957.

52. In his 1932 parody (see note 29) Gustaf Strengell mentioned that Aalto was not known in Helsinki: "An additional reason for the fact that Aalto is so extremely little known, one could even say that he is totally unknown, in Helsinki is naturally the condition that so far he has not been given an opportunity to execute any architectural work in the capital of the nation." Strengell, "Finland's First Functionalist," p. 9; trans. Juhani Pallasmaa.

53. Heinonen, *Funktionalismin läpimurto*, p. 40; trans. Juhani Pallasmaa.

54. Prior to the Paimio sanatorium, Aalto had designed and executed the miniature Municipal Hospital (1924–28) in Alajärvi, had also made plans for two homes for elderly people, and entered competitions for a health spa in Pärnu, Estonia (1927), and the central Finland Tuberculosis Sanatorium at Kinkomaa (1927). In 1929 Aalto was invited to participate in the competition for the Kälviä Tuberculosis Sanatorium; this competition was won by Jussi and Toivo Paatela. In 1931 Aalto entered the competition for the Zagreb Central Hospital in Yugoslavia, but his entry did not place.

55. Frosterus and Strengell were international and progressive supporters of rationalism, and were instrumental in the abrupt end of the national romanticist movement (see note 5). In 1903–4 Frosterus had worked in the office of the Art Nouveau architect Henry van de Velde, one of Aalto's respected friends, and Strengell worked in the office of C. Harrison Townsend in London.

56. Schildt, *Decisive Years*, p. 90.

57. Paul David Pearson, *Alvar Aalto and the International Style* (New York: Whitney Library of Design, 1978), p. 84.

58. Alvar Aalto, text in Alvar Aalto Archives, Helsinki; quoted in Göran Schildt, *Alvar Aalto: The Complete Catalogue of Architecture, Design and Art,* trans. Timothy Binham (New York: Rizzoli, 1994), pp. 68–69.

59. Alvar Aalto, "The Humanizing of Architecture," in Schildt, *Sketches,* p. 78. See also Alvar Aalto, "Humanismin ja materialismin välissä" [Between Humanism and Materialism], lecture, Central Union of Architects, Vienna, 1955; repr. in ibid., pp. 131–132.

60. Alvar Aalto, "Tukholman näyttely II" [The Stockholm Exhibition II], *Arkkitehti,* no. 8 (1930); repr. in ibid., p. 20.

61. Aalto's first known furniture design dates from 1919, and he had considerable experience in furniture design before he arrived at his classic bentwood designs of the 1930s. See Herler, "Early Furniture," p. 22.

62. The collaboration began in 1928 in conjunction with the manufacturing of furniture for the Itämeri Restaurant in the Southwestern Finland Agricultural Cooperative Building. See Schildt, *Decisive Years,* p. 33.

63. Aalto, "Rationalism and Man"; excerpt pub. in English in Pallasmaa, *Furniture,* pp. 115–116; see also Schildt, *Sketches,* p. 48.

64. In the beginning of 1928, simultaneously with the commission for the Turun Sanomat Building, Aalto won the commission for the Viipuri City Library. Half a year later, he produced a revised scheme, using the modern idiom he had been developing in the Turun Sanomat Building. Economic difficulties delayed the project, and rising critical, professional, and public opinion concerning the suitability of the site eventually made the city council decide on an adjacent site within the central park of the city. Toward the end of 1933, Aalto submitted yet another design, which was quickly approved and eventually completed in 1935.

65. Heinonen, *Funktionalismin läpimurto,* p. 256; ills. 184, 185.

66. Alvar Aalto, unpublished manuscript, Alvar Aalto Archives, Helsinki; quoted in Schildt, *Complete Catalogue,* p. 114.

67. Ibid.

68. Most of the prizes were won by Erik Bryggman, Hilding Ekelund, P. E. Blomstedt, Yrjö Lindegren, Erkki Huttunen, and lesser-known Finnish functionalists.

69. Aalto's furniture was introduced to an international audience principally by the English critic Philip Morton Shand, whom Aalto met at the Stockholm Exhibition of 1930. Shand published Aalto's designs in *Architectural Review* and *Architects' Journal,* and organized a show of Aalto furniture at the Fortnum & Mason department store in London in 1933, his first exhibition abroad. Shand was also a cofounder of the Finmar company, which imported and sold Aalto's furniture internationally.

70. Alvar Aalto, interview, in *Uusi Aura* (January 1, 1928); quoted in Schildt, *Decisive Years,* p. 207.

71. Alvar Aalto, interview, in *Uusi Aura* (October 21, 1928); quoted in ibid.

72. Alvar Aalto, interview, in *Nidaros* (Trondheim, Norway) (June 28, 1930); quoted in Schildt, *Decisive Years,* pp. 195–196.

73. Lecture, Swedish Association of Engineers and Architects, Stockholm, November 18, 1929; and lecture, Finnish Association of Architects, Helsinki, February 16, 1932. Only the titles are recorded in documents of the Alvar Aalto Archives. See Schildt, *Decisive Years,* p. 64.

74. Aalto corresponded in 1930 with Otto Völckers, editor of the magazine *Stein Holz Eisen.* The book was not published, and the manuscript has been lost (if it ever existed). See ibid.

75. Alvar Aalto, "Arkkitehtuurin lähentäminen ihmiseen" [The Humanizing of Architecture], *The Technological Review* (November, 1940); repr. in Schildt, *Sketches,* pp. 76–78.

76. Aalto, "Motifs from Times Past," in Schildt, *Sketches,* p. 1.

77. Alvar Aalto, "Koetalo, Muuratsalo" [Experimental House, Muuratsalo], *Arkkitehti,* nos. 9–10 (1953); repr. in Ruusuvuori and Pallasmaa, *Alvar Aalto,* pp. 39–40.

78. Alvar Aalto, undated manuscript for a lecture, mid-1920s; pub. in English in Schildt, *Early Years,* p. 193.

79. Alvar Aalto, "Taimen ja tunturipuro" [The Trout and the Mountain Stream], *Domus,* nos. 223–225 (1947), p. 3; repr. in Schildt, *Sketches,* pp. 96–98.

80. Wrede, *Asplund,* p. 84.

81. Among their shared ideas were combining technological refinement and sensuality, use of skew coordinates and deviation from rhythmic regularity, relation of building to landscape, counterpoint of abstraction and materiality, and interaction of tectonic and organic shapes. Asplund's 1936 speech "Art and Technology" to the Swedish Association of Architects (Aalto's inaugural lecture at the Finnish Academy in 1955 had the same title) expressed the same aspiration for an extended rationalism as did Aalto's writings of the same period: "One should not conceive of utility as an end in itself but merely as a means to increase choice and well-being for people in this life. Technology does not suffice to achieve this; what I would call art must be an ingredient." Asplund argued for a multisensory architecture of the kind that materialized fully in the work of Aalto after the mid-1930s: "The idea that only design, which is comprehended visually, can be art is a narrow conception. No, everything grasped by our other senses through our whole human consciousness and which has the capacity to communicate desire, pleasure, or emotions can also be art." Wrede, *Asplund,* p. 153.

82. Aalto, "Asplund in Memoriam"; repr. in Schildt, *Sketches,* pp. 66–67.

83. For a complete account of the Finnish pavilions at the Paris International Exhibition and the New York World's Fair, see Peter B. MacKeith and Kerstin Smeds, *The Finland Pavilions: Finland at the Universal Expositions, 1900–1992* (Tampere: Kustannus, 1993).

84. Schildt, *Decisive Years,* p. 134.

85. In the unexecuted second competition project Aalto was assisted by Aarne Ervi and Viljo Revell, who left the office soon after the competition to launch independent careers that turned them into significant architects in their own right. In 1942–44 Aalto collaborated once more with Ervi and Revell in the Reconstruction Bureau administered by the Finnish Association of Architects. After the mid-1950s Revell's rationalistically oriented office became an important counterpoint to Aalto's views.

86. Le Corbusier, in *Arkkitehti,* no. 9 (1937); repr. in Schildt, *Decisive Years,* p. 135.

87. Aalto was a founding member of the Finnish-Japanese Association and a personal friend of the Japanese ambassador to Finland in the mid-1930s. It is of interest in this connection to recall that early Nordic classicism had drawn inspiration from Chinese culture.

88. The expression is used in Karl Fleig, ed., *Alvar Aalto: Volume 1, 1922–1962* (Zurich: Éditions d'Architecture Artemis, 1963), p. 108.

89. The Villa Mairea is located on the Ahlström estate in the village of Noormarkku, north of the city of Pori in

western Finland; the A. Ahlström Corporation had its main offices there, and both Maire Gullichsen's grandfather and father had had their mansions built on the estate in styles characteristic of their times. "It is possible to use an individual architectural case as a kind of a laboratory, in which it is possible to realize aspects that are not possible in today's mass production, but from which these experimental cases gradually spread and become available for everyone as the machines of production develop," Aalto explained in his project description of the villa. Aino and Alvar Aalto, "Mairea," *Arkkitehti,* no. 9 (1939), p. 134; trans. Juhani Pallasmaa. (The project description is signed by both Aino and Alvar.) See also Schildt, *Decisive Years,* pp. 153–154.

90. Göran Schildt suggested that Aalto was inspired by Fallingwater. Schildt, *Decisive Years,* pp. 153–154. In response to an explicit question concerning Wright's influence on him, Aalto claimed: "I knew nothing about him before I came to the U.S.A. in 1939 and saw his buildings for the first time." Alvar Aalto, "Keskustelu" [Conversation], in Schildt, *Luonnoksia,* p. 112; repr. in idem, *Sketches,* p. 171. The reference to Wright is not included in the version of the text originally published as a preface to Mosso, *Alvar Aalto, teokset.*

91. Aalto's chief assistant on the Villa Mairea project, Paul Bernoulli, the Swiss-born architect, has informed me that Aalto used Tetsuro Yoshida's book *Das Japanische Wohnhaus* (Tübingen: Verlag Ernst Wasmuth, 1935) as a source for certain details in the villa. The Japanese teahouse, Zui Ki Tei, built in 1935 at the Ethnographic Museum in Stockholm, probably gave Aalto his strongest direct impressions of Japanese aesthetics. The influence of the Zui Ki Tei teahouse on Danish architecture is discussed in Fred Thompson, "En spaltet national-identitet" [A Split National Identity], *Arkitekten* (Copenhagen), no. 25 (1996), pp. 13–22.

92. Aino and Alvar Aalto, "Mairea," pp. 134–137; trans. Juhani Pallasmaa.

93. Aalto, "From Doorstep to Living Room," in Schildt, *Early Years,* pp. 214–218.

94. Aino Aalto had conceived the third-prize entry relatively independently.

95. Interview with Lisbeth Sachs, in Schildt, *Decisive Years,* pp. 161–164.

96. Alvar Aalto, "Keskisuomalaisen maiseman rakennustaide" [Architecture in the Landscape of Central Finland]; quoted in Schildt, *Early Years,* p. 207.

97. According to Göran Schildt, the source for this remark is Edgar Kaufmann, Jr., who accompanied Wright on a visit to the Finnish Pavilion at the New York World's Fair. Kaufmann related this story much later to Schildt in an interview, while Schildt was researching his Aalto biography; Göran Schildt, conversation with Peter Reed, February 1996.

98. Eliel Saarinen's entry won second prize but was the favorite of most architects and critics. It was ultimately more influential than the executed first-prize design by Hood and Howells. In his foreword to a book on Saarinen, Aalto wrote admiringly of the two careers of his colleague. Interestingly, Aalto also confessed that interior drawings by Saarinen, published in a popular magazine, had made an unforgettable impression on him at the age of nine. Alvar Aalto, "Foreword," in Albert Christ-Janer, *Eliel Saarinen: Finnish-American*

Architect and Educator (Chicago: University of Chicago Press, 1948).

99. The standard drawings contain doors, windows, light fittings, chairs, beds, sofas, tables, kitchen furnishings, coat racks, shelves, cupboards, fixed interior furnishings, and fixed outdoor furnishings. For an excellent discussion of Aalto's standard designs, see Elina Standertskjöld, "Alvar Aalto and Standardization," in *Acanthus 1992* (Helsinki: Museum of Finnish Architecture, 1992), pp. 74–84.

100. Elsa Enäjärvi, interview with Alvar Aalto, *Tulenkantajat,* no. 3 (1929), p. 37; trans. Juhani Pallasmaa.

101. Aalto, "Rationalism and Man"; quoted in Ruusuvuori and Pallasmaa, *Alvar Aalto,* p. 119.

102. Ibid., p. 141.

103. Aalto, "The Reconstruction of Europe Reveals the Central Architectural Problem of Our Time," in ibid.

104. Aalto, "Fighting Architecture," in ibid., p. 142.

105. The stair was prepared as a sample sheet of standards for building components at the Standardization Institute of the Finnish Association of Architects. The stair was published in the well-conceived publication, *Rakennustaide ja standardi: jälleenrakentamisen ydinkysymyksiä* [Architecture and Standard: Core Issues of Reconstruction] (Helsinki: Suomen Arkkitehtiliitto, 1942); repr. in facsimile, Jyväskylä, 1982. There is no direct proof of Aalto's authorship of the idea, but the Aaltoesque profile of the design makes it quite evident. The flexible stair is also illustrated in Aalto's thorough report on Finnish building standardization. See Alvar Aalto, "Finsk byggstandardisering," *Byggmästaren,* no. 1 (1943), pp. 1–7; and Ernst Neufert, *Bauentwurfslehre.* Aalto discussed the concept for the flexible stair in his 1957 lecture at the Royal Institute of British Architects. He reminded the audience that the worst thing in Dante's *Inferno* was the stair that had the wrong proportions; repr. in Schildt, *Sketches,* p. 147.

106. Alvar Aalto, introduction to catalogue of exhibition at NK department store, Stockholm, 1954; quoted in Pallasmaa, *Alvar Aalto Furniture,* p. 9.

107. The publication, *Rakennustaide ja standardi,* mentioned above analyzed the philosophy and aims of rationalization and standardization in building. The ethical humanist tone of the argument is impressive. The publication was considered so important that Mika Waltari, the leading Finnish writer of the time, was given the responsibility of formulating the literary style; Waltari is the only name given in the credits, but the text echos clearly Aalto's concurrent writings: "The solutions that we aspire to in rationalization of building have to be in harmony with human emotion.... The purpose of standardization is not to aim at a distinct building type but, on the contrary, the creation of variety and richness fit for life, which in the ideal case is comparable with the limitless capacity for nuances in Nature." (pp. 9, 11)

108. Schildt, *Decisive Years,* p. 182.

109. Ibid., p. 183.

110. The imposing list of contributors included, among others, Lewis Mumford, Walter Gropius, Alexis Carrel, James Johnson Sweeney, Frank Lloyd Wright, László Moholy-Nagy, Gunnar Myrdal, and George Bernard Shaw. Ibid., pp. 183–185.

111. Ibid., p. 184.

112. Memo of the meeting, June 1, 1939, in the William W. Wurster Archive, Berkeley, Calif.

113. Alvar Aalto, "Maailmannäyttelyt: New York World's Fair/The Golden Gate Exposition," *Arkkitehti,* no. 8 (1939); repr. in Schildt, *Sketches,* p. 65.

114. The program was divided into three parts: Division I. Examining of the Flexibility of Standardization; Division II. Examining of Special Sensitive Reactions of the Human Being to Architectural Elements in One Room; and Division III. The Surface Areas of the House. Aalto went into great detail in describing research to be done, for example, in investigating "the quality of artificial light in a room" according to its effect on a human being. Alvar Aalto, "Working Program for Architectural Research at M.I.T," unpublished typescript, September 3, 1940, MIT Archives, Cambridge, Mass.

115. Walter R. MacCornack, Dean, School of Architecture, reported to the president of MIT: "The work of [Aalto's] first group of students is exceptionally good," but regretted that "Aalto received an urgent command from the Finnish Government to return at once to carry out his agreement with respect to certain phases of the Reconstruction Program." Letter from Walter R. MacCornack to Karl T. Compton, October 23, 1940, MIT Archives, Cambridge, Mass.

116. Kyösti Ålander, *Rakennustaide renessanssista funktionalismiin* [Architecture from the Renaissance to Functionalism] (Porvoo-Helsinki: Werner Söderström, 1954); repr. in English in *Abacus Yearbook 3* (Helsinki: Museum of Finnish Architecture, 1983), pp. 217–218; trans. Desmond O'Rourke.

117. Kyösti Ålander and Viljo Revell suggested this to me in a number of conversations during the early 1960s.

118. Aino Aalto, née Marsio (1894–1949), was four years older than Alvar and had graduated from the University of Technology two years before he did. She was a talented designer and had an important role in the design of Aalto interiors and the management of the Artek company. Glass objects that Aino designed in 1932 are still being manufactured today. Aino Aalto died when Sigfried Giedion was writing his essay on Alvar Aalto for the 1949 edition of *Space, Time and Architecture,* and he gives a touching account of Aino's role in the work of the architect couple: "All Aalto's exhibitions and his work up to 1949 were signed 'Aino and Alvar Aalto.' It was not a gesture of chivalry that induced him to place the name of his wife before his own. This marriage was as singular as everything else related to him. Its steadfastness was based upon common sharing of all struggles and successes ever since their joint student days. But its real secret lay more likely in a profound reciprocation of human contrasts. Aalto is restless, effervescent, incalculable. Aino was thorough, persevering, and contained. Sometimes it is a good thing when a volcano is encircled by a quietly flowing stream.... [Aino's] name will always be connected with the work of Alvar Aalto. He always put her name before his own, but Aino herself always insisted, 'I am not creative, Alvar is the creative one.' This is not the moment to determine the extent of Aino's infuence on Aalto's production. But we know that she had her quiet say as an architect at all stages of his work and life." Giedion,

Space, Time and Architecture, pp. 491–492. For a detailed account of Aino Aalto's contribution see, Renja Suominen-Kokkonen, *The Fringe of a Profession: Women as Architects in Finland from the 1890s to the 1950s* (Helsinki: Suomen Muinaismuistoyhdistyksen Aikakausikirja 98, 1992).

119. Aulis Blomstedt, "Snowballs," unpublished manuscript, quoted in Mikkola, *Aalto*, pp. 14–15; trans. Juhani Pallasmaa.

120. See Juhani Pallasmaa, ed., *Aulis Blomstedt, Architect: Pensée et forme—études harmoniques* (Helsinki: Museum of Finnish Architecture, 1977); and idem, "Man, Measure and Proportion: Aulis Blomstedt and the Tradition of Pythagorean Harmonics," in *Acanthus 1992*, pp. 6–25.

121. Aulis Blomstedt, "Tutkielma teollisen rakentamisen rakennusyksiköksi" [A Study for a Structural Unit for Industrial Construction], *Arkkitehti*, no. 1 (1954), p. 6; trans. Juhani Pallasmaa.

122. Nils Erik Wickberg, "Finnish Architecture in the Early 1900's and Alvar Aalto," in *Alvar Aalto vs. The Modern Movement*, p. 60.

123. The rationalistically oriented architectural practices of Viljo Revell, Kaija and Heikki Sirén, and Aarno Ruusuvuori were commonly regarded as a rationalistic counterforce to Aalto. During the 1950s and early 1960s, Reima Pietilä also associated with the rationalist side because of his theoretical interests, early modular projects, and his association with the magazine *Le Carré Bleu*.

124. Alvar Aalto, "Artikkelin asemasta" [Instead of an Article], *Arkkitehti*, nos. 1–2 (1958); repr. in Schildt, *Sketches*, p. 160.

125. The founders of the journal were Aulis Blomstedt, Eero Eerikäinen, Keijo Petäjä, Reima Pietilä, André Schimmerling, and Kyösti Ålander. Since 1962 it has been published in Paris under the editorship of André Schimmerling.

126. The young generation of rationalist architects that emerged in the early 1960s was inspired by traditional Japanese architecture, Ludwig Mies van der Rohe, and the California rationalists, whose influential Case Study Houses were published in *Arts & Architecture* magazine during the 1950s.

127. Alvar Aalto, "Esipuheena keskustelu" [Conversation as a Preface], in Mosso, *Alvar Aalto, teokset*, p. 5; repr. in English in Ruusuvuori and Pallasmaa, *Alvar Aalto*, p. 167.

Aalto's Nature
Marc Treib

IN RESPONSE TO A QUESTION from a Danish journalist on what he thought a city should be like, Alvar Aalto replied: "You should not be able to go from home to work without passing through a forest."[1] The juxtaposition of forest and city may appear as an anomaly in many of the world's cultures; in Finland, however, the apparent contradiction is minor. The forest remains strong in the national consciousness, informing almost every aspect of life, including architecture. Alvar Aalto's attitude toward building in the landscape remained remarkably constant throughout his long years of professional practice. He drew inspiration from foreign sources as well as from his native landscape, and from their physical properties as well as their mythic dimensions. When the qualities of a site seemed to suggest a particular architectonic direction, Aalto usually emphasized the run of the land. When the qualities of a site were limited, Aalto constructed the landscape—outside the building, inside, or both. In almost all instances, however, architectural form complemented the attributes of the land, yielding a resonance that enhanced the prominence of each.

The perception of any place, whether natural or constructed, is inextricably linked to cultural experience. Alvar Aalto's own feeling for nature was, equally, the product of the Finnish countryside, his upbringing and education in the early twentieth century, and his conscious search for an architecture set "between humanism and materialism."[2] Since the idea of nature is itself a cultural construct, its definition varies with the people who articulate it and the times in which they do so. Dutch art historian Erik de Jong wrote: "There is, of course, no such thing as nature in the singular.... Our conception of it is dependent on the historical and social context."[3] Aalto's architecture, the creation of humane settings, urban or rural, was rooted in the Finnish landscape and experience, and in modern times.[4] Seen in this light, we need first to examine two of the cultural landscapes—the physical and the mythic—that informed Aalto's own ideas for constructing actual landscapes.

Road through a forest, central Finland

Despite a century of industrialization and urban expansion, extensive rural tracts and forested wilderness command the physical landscape of Finland to this day. Its vastness, relatively homogenous in its granite bedrock and forests of birch and pine, still conjures a sense of myth as strong today as half a century ago when the enraptured Curzio Malaparte, the Italian press attaché to the northern theater of war, described it: "As the snow thaws and changes color and the spring chrysalis bursts into flight out of the shining icy cocoon leaving the bare dead slough of winter, the forest regains mastery over the snow and the frost and becomes thick again—entangled, secretive—a green, mysterious and forbidden universe."[5] The writer, far from his Mediterranean peninsula, read Finland and its people almost as surreal objects under glass. Everything he described bore an aura beyond the physical; it was a land of similes and metaphors. The foreigner rarely adjusts easily to the extremes of light and dark that accompany the change of seasons in the far north, nor to the trees and water that prevail there. To the native, however, these are the materials with which to construct personal and collective experience.

To the young Aalto, the land possessed far more than a single, physical dimension. Born in the outer reaches of central Finland, Aalto was more immersed in the world of nature than the world of domestic space. His father, Johan Henrik Aalto, a surveyor posted in Kuortane, documented Finland's extensive land redistribution, which was necessary for more practical agricultural production using modern techniques. As a civil servant, and as one of the few educated persons in the rural village, the Finnish surveyor enjoyed a position of social prestige, which fostered in the boy a sense of responsibility as well as self-confidence. Forestry was also in the family on Aalto's mother's side; as his biographer Göran Schildt poignantly noted: "Like two fixed stars, the titles of surveyor and forester approach one another to form the constellation which for Alvar Aalto would always shine in the zenith of social values."[6] This boyhood experience greatly influenced Aalto's ethical values as well as his attitude toward the landscape. Despite his later interest in contemporary aesthetic ideas or in technology and standardization, architecture for Aalto would always be a social art, with the human being at its center.[7]

His father recorded the lay of the land, its bodies of water, and its forests, often spending weeks away from home on surveying expeditions. In time, the son was pulled into the orbit of terrain, lakes, and the mythic dimensions of the forest. Inside the surveyor's studio, a great white drawing table supported the work of his father's apprentices. To the young Alvar, the table was itself epic, as the architect recounted poetically late in life: "The white table is big. Possibly the biggest table in the world, or at least in the world and among the tables that I know."[8]

Beneath this white table, Aalto the infant began his exploration of space; in adolescence, he finally joined the group that gave measure to the land.[9] The white table served as Aalto's own metaphor for his work in general and his attitude toward the site in particular. He stressed the need to address both specifics and generalities, both nature and human need: "What is a white table? A neutral plane in combination with man, so neutral a plane that it can receive anything, depending on man's imagination and skill. A white table is as white as white can be, it has no recipe, nothing that obliges man to do this or that. In other words, it is a strange and unique relationship."[10]

While it is always possible to exaggerate the influence of childhood experiences and later memories of them, the young Aalto's exposure to man's marking of the land was, according to his own account, a decisive inspiration to his making of places. The regulating order of the survey, inherently a static construct laid upon a kinetic field, suggests Aalto's later use of architecture to ground construction in the landscape. Only in the high modernist work—the Paimio Tuberculosis Sanatorium of 1929–33 (plates 52–72), for example—is there a clear, if sympathetic, distinction of building from land. More commonly, Aalto's architecture achieves a relation to the landscape that is at once harmonic and dissonant. Each element retains its individual dimensions, and yet each contributes to the collective project of construction.[11] Furthermore, the interiors of several notable Aalto buildings themselves appear as interior landscapes, fields in which the column and the balcony replace the tree and the rocky ledge. While never literally replicating the outdoors inside a building, the constituents of Aalto's attitude toward nature transform the bionic or geologic idea, perception, and feeling into architecture.

Aalto's birth in 1898 coincided with the emergence of Finnish nationalism and a heightened sense of political identity, free from the cultural spheres of Russia or Sweden. Evangelical missions and colonial settlement had brought Finland under Swedish rule in the mid-twelfth century. With it had come Christian beliefs, a foreign political hegemony, and new architectural typologies for churches, manor houses, and fortifications. Historically, the population concentrated on the southwestern archipelago, the shores of the Baltic, and the Gulf of Bothnia, where the sea provided nourishment and facilitated travel. For centuries, the water-filled interior of lower Finland remained sparsely populated and removed from direct governmental control as well as external cultural influence.

In 1809, in the wake of the Napoleonic Wars, the governance of Finland had moved east to imperial Russia. Helsinki became the capital three years later, with the German architect, Carl Ludwig Engel, appointed director of public works in 1816. Engel soon built town halls, customs houses, barracks, and churches—and shaped a goodly portion of Helsinki in the empire style.[12] As the nineteenth century came to a close, Finland's autonomy continued to erode, with increased fiscal and military pressures placed upon the grand duchy. Against this political deterioration arose the opposing forces of nationalism that had swept across Europe and the British isles. In Finland, nationalism fed expressions in literature, the arts, and architecture, if not in politics. Aalto's years of architectural study included this period of turmoil and civil war.

1. Gesellius, Lindgren, and Saarinen. Finnish National Museum, Helsinki. 1902–12

Finnish literature, especially the *Kalevala* epic, expressed these political and cultural aspirations. As early as the 1820s, the physician and amateur anthropologist, Elias Lönnrot, had begun to collect the oral epics of Karelia, that imprecisely defined province on the border of Finland and Russia. Here, for centuries, the bards had chanted in pairs the heroic exploits of Väinämöinen and Lemminkäinen, and the unhappy fates of Kullervoo and Aino. Lönnrot collected, edited, and augmented the tales, ultimately forging them into a coherent work of fifty cantos.[13]

The *Kalevala*'s descriptions of Pohjola—the mystic province of the north—provided the Finns with their *Ur*-landscape, as did the Germanic Nibelungen or Icelandic Edda sagas. Encountering a newly created land bereft of vegetation and amenity, the hero Väinämöinen directs Sampsa Pellervoinen to plant seedlings for a more hospitable landscape:

> On the hills he sowed the pine-trees,
> On the knolls he sowed the fir-trees,
> And in sandy places heather,
> Leafy saplings in the valley.
> In the dales he sowed the birch-trees,
> In the loose earth sowed the alders,
> Where the ground was damp the cherries,
> Likewise in the marshes, sallows.
> Rowan-trees in holy places,
> Willows in the fenny regions,
> Juniper in stony districts,
> Oaks upon the banks of rivers.[14]

The epic poem provided inspiration and iconography for the paintings of Akseli Gallen-Kallela,[15] the tone poems of Jean Sibelius, and the architectural ornament of Eliel Saarinen and his partners Hermann Gesellius and

Armas Lindgren. Works such as the Finnish National Museum in Helsinki of 1902–12 by Gesellius, Lindgren, and Saarinen combined decorative programs based on the pine and the bear with fragments of historical architecture—a vaulted nave of a medieval church to display religious art, for example—to convey to the Finnish people the sources of their culture (figure 1). Although Continental ideas propelled the new style, direct references to familiar architectural forms rooted the new architecture in popular experience.

And the architecture was new; it was never the intention of these architects to literally duplicate historical forms. These buildings by Lars Sonck; Gesellius, Lindgren, and Saarinen; Selim Lindqvist; and others succeeded in balancing international contemporaneity and indigenous references.[16] The desire to engage foreign culture, to remain Finnish and yet appear European and modern, informed the cultural milieu in which Aalto trained and initiated his practice.

Tuscany in Central Finland

When Aalto completed his studies in 1921 and opened his office in Jyväskylä two years later (The Alvar Aalto Office for Architecture and Monumental Art), his work utilized a renewed classical vocabulary, which had replaced the national romanticism of the prior generation.[17] The grip of national romanticism on Finnish architects had loosened, undermined by an exhaustion of the vocabulary and a revised worldview that looked more actively beyond the borders of the country. In Finland, as in Sweden, the architectural expression of craft and texture was suppressed while attention to the mass of the building was emphasized.[18] Given the free interpretation of the architectural canon, the legislated proportions of classical architecture were commonly pushed to their limits. The reliance on the column, the pilaster, the pedimented window, and the round arch raised few doubts that the style was yet another classical derivation. But, in its simplification, distended forms, and mannered applications, there was little confusion that this architecture was anything but the product of the twentieth century.

While the *Kalevala* provided the mythic setting for Finnish architecture at the turn of the century, the cultural landscape of Tuscany provided its metaphorical counterpart in the 1920s and early 1930s. Finnish architects extolled the accomplishments of Italian builders and architects, as the lure of Italy swept through Finland, prompted by various writings and a cultural longing for participation on an international stage. Architect Hilding Ekelund, for example, rhapsodized about Vicenza in his 1923 article, "Italia la bella," published in *Arkkitehti:* "Palladio, Palladio, in dress uniform at every street corner, with columns, architraves, cornices—the whole arsenal. Between them simple, bare houses, just walls and holes, but with distinct harmonious proportions."[19] Finnish architects used a panoply of materials in which to execute buildings in the Italian mode, with little regard for the means by which their prototypes had been made. The Helsinki housing estate Käpylä, built by Martti Välikangas in the mid-1920s, crossed garden-city planning with classical motifs executed in wood; the monumental new parliament, on the other hand, was to be executed in 1930 in granite, to heroic classical designs by J. S. Sirén.[20] Given the difference in climate as well as materials, it is interesting to consider what attracted Finnish architects to Tuscan building: the overall picturesque effect created by its clustered prisms on the hillside or the inherent authority that only classicism carried throughout the Western world.

Although Finnish architects such as Ekelund were attracted to the volumes and dispositions of popular architecture, that appeal was not on composition alone. Models for agglomerative buildings were found much closer to home in the centuries-old vernacular tradition of Finland; they, too, contributed to Aalto's compositional predilections. In regions such as Ostro-Bothnia, courtyards or double-courtyards were the norm for rural planning. Farmsteads were not always configured so precisely, however. The oft-cited Niemelä croft, from Konginkangas, Häme, was itself an assemblage of stor-

age buildings, barns, pigsties, and residential structures.[21] While seemingly a haphazard grouping of diverse parts, the planning of the structures followed careful considerations of utility and climate (figure 2). The architect and critic, Gustaf Strengell, regarded the Munkkiniemi house of his friends, the Aaltos, as a contemporary version of the Niemelä farm.[22]

The functions of these modest domestic and agricultural compounds rarely required buildings of exceptional height. More commonly, they were horizontal, following the line of the terrain. Thus, the question of how to build monumentally on the hill, in the forest, or in the meadow was not answered with a look to Finland but with another—to Italy: "There are many examples of pure, harmonious, civilized landscapes in the world," Aalto instructed, "one finds real gems in Italy and southern Europe."[23] More recently, Richard Weston has claimed: "For Aalto, Italian hill towns offered a paradigm of such harmonious accommodation between man and nature. The town was subservient to the topography, which was in turn heightened by man's intervention—a cultural symbiosis."[24]

The nationalistic longing of the romanticists had become the international urge of the classicists. "We Northerners," wrote Aalto in 1925, "especially the Finns, are very prone to 'forest dreaming', for which we have had ample opportunity up to now. Sometimes, however, we feel that we do not have enough pure nature at our disposal, and then we try to plant the beauty of the wilds at our very doors. In fact we should apply the opposite principle, starting with the environment we live in, and adding our buildings to it, to the improvement of the original landscape."[25] According to Aalto, even a building in the rural landscape should be regarded as an act of civic improvement.

Aalto traveled to Italy for the first time, on his honeymoon with his wife and architectural partner, Aino Marsio, in the fall of 1924. By then, the architect was fully under the sway of things Mediterranean, which for him represented a vision for cultural emergence from the backwoods wilderness of central Finland. The Jyväskylä Workers' Club of 1924–25 (plates 15–22) looked both to the Palace of the Doges in Venice and Ragnar Östberg's Stockholm City Hall of 1913–23 (page 101). The club's design accommodated a complex program of mixed use set within a simple box, urbane and polished, if mannered and forced into a tight volume. It was an urban building that filled the site, and its details spoke more of Italy than of the forest.

2. Niemelä croft, Konginkangas, Häme (moved to Seurasaari Open-Air Museum, Helsinki)

There was no inherent contradiction in Aalto's mind about borrowing architectural ideas from prior cultures and alien places. In his first published article in *Arkkitehti*, "Motifs from Times Past," of 1922, Aalto proposed two arenas in which the architect might work. The first, folk architecture, uses local typologies, vernacular forms and technology, and is very much rooted to the place. It is indigenous, and an architect is not even necessary for its design. The second, far broader arena acknowledges "the conscious will to create form which is commonly associated with an architect's work."[26] For Aalto, foreign impulses must be transformed to render them applicable to local conditions. Any discrepancies between the parent architecture and its local variant do not constitute provincialism, Aalto argued; instead, he believed that "these motifs, even in their earliest versions, appear to be in total harmony with their surroundings."[27] Given this philosophical stance, to use the language of Filippo Brunelleschi or of the Italian hill town created no conceptual or operational discord. As a son of central Finland, and active cultural critic as well as architect, Aalto viewed Jyväskylä as a "stronghold of culture," a potential cultural capital for the province.[28] He held grand visions for his adopted hometown, but these visions remained for the most part unrealized.[29] Aalto's approach toward building in the landscape, however, transposed the Tuscan manner to the forests of Finland.

The lessons learned, and forcefully applied, were primarily those of building configuration and site planning. Of these projects, executed shortly after Aalto's return from Italy in the mid-1920s, the Muurame Church of 1926–29 provides the most vivid illustrations (plates 31–36). A preliminary perspective sketch situated the church on an exaggerated incline, as if the Italian *collina* could be imported through determined longing and a stroke of the pencil (figure 3). A sleek campanile, more than twice the height of the nave, complemented the heroic arch, which itself recalls Leone Battista Alberti's S. Andrea in Mantua (designed 1470). The counterbalance of vertical against horizontal, on the other hand, suggests the use of towers by Aalto's countryman, Eliel Saarinen, at the Finnish National Museum or the Railway Station in Helsinki. In these works, as in many of Aalto's own projects, the campanile becomes—as it had in Italy—an attenuated pivot for the architectonic composition. In Muurame, the transverse sacristy opened to the nave and rested upon a base of support spaces. These included a kitchen opening to an arcade and a walled garden, almost as in a vision taken from Renaissance painting. Acknowledging these Mediterranean precedents, Aalto composed the church as a group of tightly knit, articulated volumes on the grassed slope.

The exterior surfaces were stuccoed, concealing the masonry construction; astutely positioned string courses tied the elements of the building together, and were particularly effective in joining the protruding apse to the east wall of the nave.[30] A wood barrel vault spanned the interior, at once citing early Finnish churches such as the church for the Kemi Rural

3. Alvar Aalto. Muurame Church, Muurame, Finland. 1926–29. Preliminary perspective sketch. Alvar Aalto Foundation, Helsinki

Congregation (mid-sixteenth century) and the semicylindrical vaults of Romanesque Europe. The Muurame Church still sits comfortably on its Nordic hillside, perhaps evincing some yearning for the south but confident in its localized adaptation of foreign sources—as Aalto had proposed in his 1922 essay.

In other competitions of the 1920s, Aalto explored various schemes for clustering building parts, the smaller elements always supporting the greater conglomerate. He was selected in 1925 to replace Eliel Saarinen in the competition for a new church in Jämsä (plates 27–30).[31] The 1826 church had burned that year, and only the 1857 detached steeple in the classical empire style survived. Aalto's entry was strictly historicist, with a recessed porch and patterning recalling S. Miniato al Monte and other medieval Florentine churches. More radically, Aalto chose not to build directly on the site of the destroyed church, making it instead a piazza before the new structure. The bell tower would remain the focus of this tapering court enclosed by trees. Aalto's proposal was not selected for realization. Perhaps this congregation in the Finnish countryside was not quite ready for a product of decidedly Italian origin.[32]

In the 1927 competition for the new church in the Helsinki district of Töölö (plates 37–38), Aalto proposed a stepped entrance path that cut through the subsidiary rooms huddled at the base of the nave. The sanctuary itself rose heroically from the rocky outcropping on the edge of a park just beyond the city center. For his presentation drawings, Aalto eschewed soft pencil sketches and adopted the single-weight ink-rendering style of Engel's countryman, Karl Friedrich Schinkel, which had been resurrected more recently by Swedish architects such as Sigurd Lewerentz. Schildt noted the resemblance between Aalto's Töölö design and Le Corbusier's

5. Le Corbusier. Sketch of the Acropolis, Athens. From *Vers une architecture* (1923)

4. Alvar Aalto. Töölö Church, Helsinki. Project, 1927. Competition drawing: perspective. Alvar Aalto Foundation, Helsinki

presentation of the Acropolis of Athens in his 1923 *Vers une architecture*—complete with a statue resembling the Greek goddess Athena as a vital part of the plan (figures 4 and 5). Although set within the city, and integrating Aalto's developing ideas of monumentality, the scheme for the church reflected site-planning ideas from the architect's projects in the Finnish countryside.[33]

Two years before the Töölö competition, Aalto had suggested his future schemes: "Sometimes I would make the church stand out as a more dominating element among the houses by building a little colonnaded square in front of it or raising its spire. (The open square, surrounded by architecture, is one of the most powerful rhythmic accents available in hilly country)."[34] Five years later, Aalto shunned a strictly classical vocabulary, but the influence of Italy on his architectural composition and siting would remain in modified form in his architectural vocabulary throughout his career. The particulars of style and disposition became more relaxed as time progressed, but the gathering of subsidiary volumes to support a principal space always remained at the core of Aalto's civic and religious compositions. Nearly three decades later, in configuring the Church of the Plains and its flanking parish wings in Seinäjoki, in siting the town hall that faces the church across the street, and in creating the more liberally composed civic complex at Säynätsalo of 1948–52, the canons of Italian site planning recurred in the work of the Finnish master (plates 196–211, 367–375).

The Landscape Within

In 1926, to convince Finnish readers that the consistency between indoors and out was desirable, Aalto cited an Annunciation painted by Fra Angelico.[35] But he did not discuss its architectonic elements. For him, the painting illustrated two important aspects: "The unity between room, facade, and garden, and the shaping of these elements to reveal the human presence and reflect his moods."[36] Aalto admitted that it would be naive to believe that the contact between interior and exterior in Finland can rival the prolonged connections of southern climes. However, that qualification should not preclude a greater understanding of crossing the threshold nor the manner in which that transition affects the disposition of interior spaces:

> *The garden wall is* [the home's] *real exterior wall; within it, let there prevail a unity not only between the forms of the building and the garden, but also between them and the arrangement of the rooms. The garden (or courtyard) is as much a part of our homes as any one of its rooms. Let the step from the garden to the interior show less contrast than the one from the street or road to the garden. We might say: the Finnish home should have two faces. One, an aesthetically direct connection with the world outside; the other,* [its] *winter face, reveals itself in the modes of furnishing our most inner rooms.*[37]

Aalto took his own advice quite literally in a number of his subsequent residential designs, in particular, Villa Mairea, the House for Maire and Harry Gullichsen in Noormarkku of 1938–39 (plates 155–169). But that was over a decade later. For the moment, he took his own advice *too* literally, devising the Atrium House for Väinö Aalto, his brother, in Alajärvi in 1925 (plate 26). With its drying laundry visible through the roof's breach—which exposed the atrium to the northern elements—the design would have been far more at home in temperate Naples than in central Finland. The architect justified his proposal by asserting: "Simply by virtue of its ground plan, the atrium beautifully fulfills all the ideas developed [in my writing]."[38] The opening in the roof also afforded a visitor standing in the entry hall a glimpse of the full life within, with clothing hung out to dry as "a somewhat careless sign of daily life; everyday banality as a central architectural element, a piece of the Neapolitan street in a Finnish home!"[39] While this fragment of Aalto's polemic was hardly defensible, a corollary argument proposed an idea that would inform much of his later architecture, that the interior itself could be treated as a landscape: "For exactly the same reason as I previously desired to make your interior into a garden, I now wish to make your hall into an 'outside.' This is one way to reduce the contrast between them ... which aids the transition between 'outdoors and in.'"[40] In Aalto's later work, as we shall see, living rooms, theater lobbies, museums, and exhibition pavilions comprised ranges of interior space that roamed freely within a shaped periphery. Were they interiors, exteriors, or hybrids where such distinctions were no longer viable?

Aalto probably drew his inspiration for these spaces from the work of the Swedish architect Erik Gunnar Asplund, who first tested the idea of the indoor plaza in his Skandia Cinema in Stockholm of 1922–23, with an auditorium crowned by a ceiling suggesting an evening sky (page 25). The elaborate classicized doorways, lacquered scarlet and tinged with gilding, opened to seats placed under an ultramarine-blue ceiling. Lights irregularly hung in the vault suggested stars in a night sky, a conceit underscored by the recessed moon positioned high over the left-hand side of the screen. Although it was essentially a scenographic device, defensible within the fantastic setting of the cinema, Asplund developed the metaphor more abstractly in his later civic projects in a less pictorial manner.[41]

As Asplund's ideas for the Law Courts Annex in Gothenburg, Sweden, developed during the 1920s and 1930s, the interior piazza at its heart came to assume greater prominence. His original winning competition scheme of 1913 had suggested little of what would become, after almost a quarter of a century's study, an elegant structure supported by a precise concrete frame filled with a large glass wall and rich wood paneling (figure 6). Lounges, offices, and formal court rooms encircled a full three-story-high space: Asplund's civic forum brought indoors.[42] Perhaps Asplund sought for this space the openness and transparency embodied in

his modernist buildings for the 1930 Stockholm Exhibition (page 27). Although by the late 1930s Asplund, like Aalto, had retreated from the purity of high modernism, he still valued many of its original aspirations. The conceits used by both Asplund and Aalto in their early projects—Asplund in the Skandia Cinema and Aalto in the entry hall of the Jyväskylä Workers' Club—were clearly insufficient. To truly succeed architectonically, the bond between interior and exterior needed to be established on a much deeper, and more abstract, level.

Outdoor references within Aalto's buildings began to occur tentatively soon after his return from Sweden in 1923. By the late 1930s, the idea of the interior landscape was broadly applied, for example, in his 1937 competition entries for an art museum in Revel (now Tallinn), Estonia, and the Finnish Pavilion for the Paris International Exhibition (plates 130–139). Perhaps the most brilliant blending of interior and exterior was the design for the Finnish Pavilion at the 1939 New York World's Fair (plates 145–154). Given the restrictive building envelope, which was not of his own design, Aalto created an internal world detached from its rectangular box. Waving walls, freely curving in plan and stepped outward in section, created a dynamic space that suggested natural phenomena as widely diverse as the aurora borealis, the curving shoreline of a Finnish lake, eroded rock strata, and the glassware designed by Aino and Alvar Aalto.[43] The natural materials—plywood sheathing and randomly spaced wood battens—and large photomurals of the Finnish countryside and manufactured products reduced the distance between this pavilion in New York and the Finnish landscape it was intended to represent.[44] The pavilion remains Aalto's most brilliant use of architectural means for spatial effect.

In the postwar period, as Aalto's projects increased in scale, the idea of the enclosed "exterior" space took greater hold in his architecture. Given

6. Erik Gunnar Asplund. Law Courts Annex, Gothenburg, Sweden. 1937. Interior court

7. Lars Sonck. Stock Exchange, Helsinki. 1911. Interior court

8. Alvar Aalto. Rautatalo Office Building, Helsinki. 1953–55. Interior court

the harshness of Finnish winters, the idea of an enclosed courtyard was especially appealing. In the second decade of the century, Eliel Saarinen had proposed expansive glass-roofed spaces for urban developments in Helsinki's center, admitting light deep into the interiors of buildings; and in 1911 Lars Sonck had realized an early version of this in his light court for the Helsinki Stock Exchange (figure 7). But in Aalto's hands, the skylit courtyard was less a static void than an integral (and integrating) void around which the building swirled.

The central light court of the 1953–55 Rautatalo Office Building in Helsinki fulfilled the dream of a lobby that functioned, spatially and socially, as a piazza for the north. A gridded field of round skylights, first employed at the Viipuri City Library in 1927–35 (plate 94), relieved the sense of the ceiling's weight and closure and flooded the tiered space with daylight (figure 8). Animated by pedestrian traffic to and from the various offices and stores, enriched by a café that intruded on its marble paving, the Rautatalo's elevated courtyard succeeded in offering all the amenities of an open space except the breeze.

Two decades later Aalto configured the flowing entrance and lobby spaces of Finlandia Hall in Helsinki (1962–71) as a rendering in the polished marble of a rocky moraine (plates 402, 404). Grand stairs brought the visitors from the ground-floor vestiary and services to the lobby level, and direct entrance into the two principal auditoriums. Faceted balconies overlooked the central space, engaging columns, which, like trees in a forest, organized the visual as well as structural aspects of the space. Perhaps more than any of Aalto's other public spaces, the lobbies of Finlandia Hall completed the architect's enterprise of creating a metaphorical landscape using interior architectural space. Set on the shore of a

Baltic inlet within a park, the building linked the city's built fabric with the few vestiges of a natural landscape, which referred in turn to the larger landscape beyond the urban boundaries.

While these essentially urban buildings recalled the natural landscape through freely planned, structurally modulated, or light-filled interior spaces, the metaphor was most fully developed when nature was immediately at hand. Thus, the pastoral Villa Mairea must stand as the ideal illustration of Aalto's collapsing of natural and architectural systems.

Completed in 1939, this exquisite rural villa for Maire and Harry Gullichsen complemented a series of residences on the Ahlström family estate in Noormarkku, fifteen miles northeast of the coastal city of Pori (plate 160). Despite the luxurious budget, the Gullichsens directed Aalto to use the project as a test site for ideas that could be more broadly applied to buildings for those of lesser means. In describing the villa, Aalto explained: "It is possible to use the individual architectural case as a kind of experimental laboratory, where one can realize that which is not possible for the present in mass production; but out of these experimental cases gradually spread and in the developing machinery they change to become an objective available to everyone."[45] This particular aspect of the program remained stillborn, but the success of the design in its many aspects can hardly be challenged. The villa was cut from a singular piece of cloth, and, although it announced itself as architecture, without apologies to its forest setting, it retains an inextricable affinity with its landscape.

In fact, the entire living area of the villa can be read as a forest architecturally transformed. A lone concrete column, camouflaged by unpeeled saplings, which unwrap to form a visually permeable screen, supports the free-form canopy that defines the entrance (plate 163). Two additional sets of lashed composite "columns," saplings with their bark removed, complete the landscape of support beneath the sheltering canopy. Inside the front door, one encounters a copse of wood poles, more finished and ordered, removed from the rough textures and irregular order of the forest.

Living and service blocks enclose a courtyard and swimming pool (plates 161, 165). Light level and the sense of enclosure vary through the living zones. Perhaps Aalto was thinking of his 1926 characterization of the English hall when proposing the fluid spaces of the villa's living areas: "It symbolizes the open air under the home roof."[46] Although the structure of the living space comprises a regular grid, few of the steel columns are treated in just the same way (plates 166–168). In their variety, they suggest the intricate complexity of the surrounding pine forest and the villa's interior as a free-flowing landscape.[47] In two locations, black-lacquered columns are paired and bound together with rattan—the varying heights of the wrapping correspond to the height of the fireplace mantel, in one case, and the top of the library wall, in the other. Along the south bank of windows, one column has been tripled. Architectural critic Demetri Porphyrios alluded, somewhat melodramatically, to this play of columns as "an adulterous affair of incessant metaphoric substitution."[48] Wood strips sheath the structure and offer a convenient surface for the climbing vines that grow on slats above the radiators.

The principal stair leading to the bedrooms further reinforces the reading of the house as a refined humanized forest. Early sketches reveal an affinity with Japan: the poles containing the staircase resemble bamboo.[49] In time, a modulated composition of wood poles, like those found at the villa's entry, replaced this original Asian allusion, however. In the final spacing and clustering of the poles—and their cover by climbing indoor plants—the analogy with the forested setting was completed

(plate 169). It is important to stress, however, that through transmutation rather than reproduction Aalto's architecture achieved its own dimension and autonomy. This modern villa is a vehicle for human dwelling; it is not a rustic hut in the woods set at the mercy of the elements. Aalto made no attempt to mimic either vernacular farmhouses or the forest. Instead, he sought the transference of natural phenomena through architecture, distinguishing natural from constructed systems while at the same time establishing a strong psychological union between them (figure 9).

The Constructed Landscape

As physical compositions, Aalto's non-urban buildings tended to divide into two basic groups: concave or convex. The concave schemes reiterated the contours of fissures and valleys. The convex schemes complemented or reinforced rising landforms. And for those sites that lacked potent natural features Aalto constructed his own architectural landscapes.

Aalto's fascination with the classical amphitheaters of Greece and Italy is documented by his sketches as well as his architecture (figure 10). The amphitheater appears to have possessed nearly mythic proportions in his designs. A natural declivity providing enclosure and protection from the wind might suggest to an architect a rational manner in which to plan a site; but Aalto's use of the amphitheatrical form almost always expanded upon functional appropriateness. For example, the origin of the competition design for the Malmi Funeral Chapel in Helsinki of 1950 lay in the drift of the land (plate 219). The three chapels anchored the hillside and offered three walled courtyards to console the bereaved. While the scheme owed a certain debt to Asplund's crematorium chapels at the Woodland Cemetery in Stockholm of 1940 (figure 11), the use of architecture to intensify the landform is essentially Aalto's own.

In 1952, Aalto and Jean-Jacques Baruël entered a design competition for the Central Cemetery and Funeral Chapel in Lyngby-Taarbaek, Denmark (plates 220–225) with a scheme that furthered the idea of the Malmi project. The competition brief called for a single chapel to accommodate up to fifteen funerals each day. "Because Aalto recoiled from the idea of funeral ceremonies mass-produced in this fashion, he provided a group of several chapels instead of only the one chapel prescribed."[50] As in his Malmi proposal and in Asplund's Woodland Crematorium, Aalto

9. Alvar Aalto. Villa Mairea, House for Maire and Harry Gullichsen, Noormarkku, Finland. 1938–39. View of courtyard, pool, and sauna from living room, with Maire Gullichsen (left) and Aino Aalto (right)

10. Alvar Aalto. Travel sketch: theater, Delphi, Greece. 1953. Collection Alvar Aalto Family

devised a series of exterior courts to facilitate circulation loops that ensured privacy for each group of mourners. The chapels were sited at the crest of the ravine, almost as ships riding atop an earthen sea. The gravesites, terraced along the slope, created a great funereal amphitheater whose focus was ultimately the bowl itself (plates 221–222). Small streams of water accompanied the visitors down the slope, providing the water necessary for plants and maintenance, and terminating in two collecting ponds.[51] In both cemetery competitions Aalto employed the same basic strategy: he used the contours of the site as the foundation for the planning, and he reinforced the lay of the land through architectural means such as walls, courts, and buildings.

Amphitheaters appear in Aalto's architecture in some unlikely places, especially given the nature of the northern climate. For Aalto the amphitheater was a formal typological structure symbolic of citizen and/or campus interaction, and he used it in his winning competition entry of 1951 for the extension to the Jyväskylä Pedagogical Institute. It bore the motto "Urbs." To maximize vistas out over the countryside, the university was planned on a natural ridge at the edge of the town. In a written description, Aalto noted that one of the desired views looked toward the "volcanic cone" (a fantastic reading) of a hill called Ronninmäki. Eeva Maija Viljo has cited Aalto's description, noting: "With the Tuscan landscape as a model, Aalto envisages the hillsides of central Finland artfully strewn with architectural monuments, and he suggests a white campanile on Ronninmäki 'near the peak (not on

the peak)' in order to enhance the pictorial value of the ridge in the Jyväskylä landscape."[52]

The university's auditorium building, intended as a cultural forum, faced an existing municipal garden recast as a meeting ground for college and town. Included as a prominent feature of the scheme was an outdoor amphitheater that conceptually extended the seats of the main auditorium (figure 12). This Ceremonial Court, as the space was called, was a shallow, yet masterfully articulated slab of terrain. While the plan of the court maintained an underlying symmetry, its development was highly asymmetrical. Aalto fractured the rear wall of the auditorium into several vertical brick planes, undermining the weighty impact of the building's rear facade. Earthen terraces, stiffened with benches of granite and timber, defined the radiating levels of the amphitheater. Each seating segment used steps of varying widths; only the central void seemed calm. Within the simple figure of the arena, Aalto set the pieces of classical form in a nervous equilibrium, while localizing the archetype to better address the college's site and architecture.

At the North Jutland Art Museum in Aalborg, Denmark, completed in 1972, the amphitheater assumed a more rigorous architectural form (plate 342). Detached from the museum proper, the irregular bowl was paired with a terraced sculpture garden and set antithetically to the museum building across a green lawn. Juhani Pallasmaa noted that Aalto used the outdoor theater form in an "almost obsessive manner," suggesting that the inherent references to classical antiquity were compounded by the associations with ruins and the

11. Erik Gunnar Asplund. Woodland Cemetery, Stockholm, Sweden. 1940. Crematorium chapels, portico, and courtyard

passage of time.[53] The amphitheater thus underscored the position of the museum as a part of a continuing historical process.

The functional requirements of the building program also benefited from such adaptations of precedent, particularly those in which Aalto questioned the efficacy of symmetry. The auditorium of the House of Culture in Helsinki of 1952–58 applied the lessons of the amphitheater to an interior (plate 285). The facility's entry spaces and auditorium are set symmetrically; one enters the main room through vomitoria, as in a stadium. The varying depths of the stepped ranges of seating improved the hall's acoustics while granting the space an increased intimacy. Within the House of Culture Aalto made no analogies to the landscape, as he had in the Villa Mairea and would subsequently do for Finlandia Hall. This was clearly an urban structure on a limited site. But the stadium/amphitheater and auditorium typologies had more features in common than differences, and Aalto employed them to great effect.

In instances where the site itself offered no dramatic profile, Aalto created one. At the Seinäjoki Civic Center of 1958–87, Aalto mounded earth in structured contours to form transitions between the plaza and the council chamber on the building's first floor (plate 373). Essentially creating what more emphatic sites already provided, Aalto used this hillock to naturalize the linear plaza that joined the elements of the complex. The brilliantly conceived central block of the Helsinki University of Technology at Otaniemi, completed in 1966, fused the school's three principal lecture halls together within a single curving brick wedge, its angular profile following the "rising rhythm" of their floors (plates 267–269). The idea evolved from the history and contour of the site, as Aalto explained: "The main building of the Institute has been placed on a central hill which dominates the area: it was here that there stood the main building of the estate to which the fields at one time belonged. A part of the small park adjoining the estate could be utilised as accompanying surroundings to the main building of the Institute."[54] The triangular wing walls of brick enfold a granite amphitheater aimed toward the sun and intended as a focal point for the internal yard enclosed by the library, administrative, and lecture wings.[55] These two projects vividly illustrate, each in different ways, Aalto's use of architecture to compensate for the deficiencies of an undramatic site.

Aalto used convex as well as concave aspects to create a resonance between architecture and landform. Indeed, the possibility of prospect, and hence defense, has always been an important factor in the positioning of towns and buildings. Prospect has been equated with security and power, and Aalto himself wrote as early as 1926: "The town on the hill…is the purest, most individual and most natural form in urban design. Above all, it has a natural beauty in that it reaches full stature when seen from the level of the human eye, that is, from ground level."[56]

On hilltops or rocky outcroppings, Aalto frequently aggregated the elements of the building program to reinforce the morphology of the

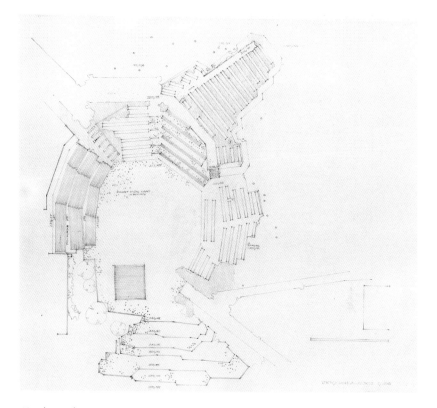

12. Alvar Aalto.
Pedagogical Institute,
Jyväskylä, Finland. 1959.
Ceremonial court plan.
Alvar Aalto Foundation,
Helsinki

existing site. We have already seen this idea inform his church designs of the 1920s. The internal organization of these structures often derived from the profile of the land, setting interior and exterior in symbiosis.

In 1956, construction commenced on a house for the art dealer Louis Carré at Bazoches-sur-Guyonne, outside Paris; the Maison Carré was completed three years later. The house site was a knoll rising from a rolling agricultural landscape and surrounded by groves of oaks. As a transition between landscape and dwelling, the convex contours of the site were geometricized and outlined with concrete retaining walls/steps radiating outward from the terraces (plates 310, 312–313). Here Aalto clustered the parts of the house almost as a small village, following the incline (a memory of Italy perhaps) and unified by a single-sloped roof joining the uphill entry with the living room below. Seen from without, the house appeared as an agglomeration of pieces, several of them complemented by an outdoor terrace. Inside, however, the staircase and wood furled ceiling

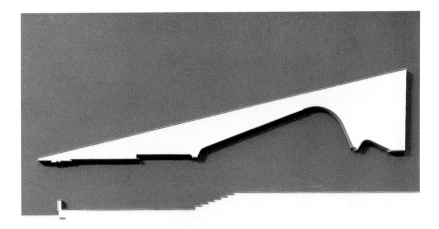

13. Alvar Aalto. Maison Carré,
House for Louis Carré,
Bazoches-sur-Guyonne, France.
1956–59. Section model. Alvar
Aalto Foundation, Helsinki

connected the various living levels together smoothly and invited the visitor to descend (plate 314). The house seen in section thus echoes the natural gradient of the land (figure 13), with the contour adjusted architectonically within. Like the forest embracing the Villa Mairea, the Bazoches landform was architecturally regraded, demonstrating the distance between what now exists and what once had been.

Aalto's travel sketches reveal an unusual interest in landscapes where terrain, rather than buildings, provides the primary structure. In his eyes, hillsides terraced for cultivation and classical Greek ruins ranked equally; stepped hilltops in the sketches appear ambiguously as ziggurats as well as cultivated fields (figure 14). Perhaps for Aalto agriculture and architecture shared a common base in culture expressed through cultivation or construction. The conceptual sketches for a proposed art museum in Iran manifest just those ideas (plates 386–388).

For a hilltop outside Shiraz (figure 15), Aalto proposed a structure developed as a stacking of horizontal layers, "an accumulation of rising terrace forms."[57] His architectural response to the site seems to have been immediate. For the few days following his visit to the site, Aalto avoided socializing, "instead devoting his limited hours working on a definitive concept of the building before departing the country."[58] Despite the predominant horizontal line of the early sketches, the faceted walls of the developed scheme demonstrated significant resemblances to other Aalto projects in Finland: the Forestry Pavilion for the Agricultural Exhibition in Lapua (1938), the Alvar Aalto Museum in Jyväskylä (1973), and even the libraries at Rovaniemi and Seinäjoki (plate 374). An entry between gently curved planes led to a centralized point of passage from which the galleries opened into a fan. The sloping roofs of the galleries radiated from this focal point, their far walls staggered to produce a serrated profile (plates 389–391). But the design was left incomplete. The project stalled when Aalto demanded control over construction as well as the initial design stage, and the fall of the Shah put an end to the undertaking.

In 1952–53, on the island of Muuratsalo, Aalto created his own summer house, a structure at once assertive and retiring. Known as the Experimental House and Sauna, the compound was decribed by Schildt in this way: "No self-obliterating humility, no tendency to mask the human guest's intrusion by choosing natural stone and wood as material, characterizes this ancient atrium house, which rests as proudly on its rocky shelf as a Byzantine monastery at Athos. The bridging over of the old gulf between man and nature, the pointing out of what they have in common, is probably the nucleus of Aalto's alternative."[59]

At Muuratsalo, the wedge shape of the building—set tactfully back from the shore along the forest edge—crowns the granite shelf looking out over Lake Päijänne to the south and west. In profile it is an architectonic extension of the convex rock outcropping. A string of diminutive wood structures culminates in the dwelling's central court with a fire pit in its heart (plate 226).[60] Even more literally than the Villa Mairea, the house was intended as an experimental site for building materials and techniques, to be tested in the architects' own domain far from public scrutiny. A site plan published in a 1955 book on Nordic architecture identifies the auxiliary buildings as follows: experiment with solar heating, free-form brick constructions, experiment with a nonlinear colonnade, experiment with a building without foundations, main building's central court.[61] Of these, perhaps the idea for a building without standard foundations, such as the sauna (plates 232–233), was the most radical, since it would have involved a structure that denied conventional wisdom and literally grew from the bedrock.

Once again, we encounter a mildly dissonant congruence of building and site, comforting in its seeming familiarity yet thwarting the visitor's expectation. This house, like the Villa Mairea, was zoned into living and sleeping wings. Curiously, the walls that surround the court rise to full height and outline the silhouette of the roof as if it were intended to continue over the court (plate 227). Grand dimensions give this house in the woods an air of monumentality and urbanity, a reading reinforced by the inversion of what one would consider the normal progression of architectural finishes: "Had he been an ordinary Finn, he would have built an outwardly primitive hut using logs from dry standing trees—a hideaway for a refugee from civilization," commented Schildt.[62] But Aalto was no ordinary Finn, and he instead inverted many of the common practices for building along the Finnish shore. He built not of wood but of brick painted white;

14. Alvar Aalto. Travel sketch: Calascibetta, Sicily. 1952. Collection Alvar Aalto Family

15. Alvar Aalto. Iran Museum of Modern Art, Shiraz, Iran. Project, 1969–70. Landscape sketch. Alvar Aalto Foundation, Helsinki

he built unnecessarily grand walls that hardly sheltered; he built courtyard walls of brick set in a crazy quilt of mixed bonds as experiments in masonry textures (plates 229, 231). Only the log sauna appears as a typical building, although its details do not precisely follow tradition.

Given its rural, almost wilderness site, one would expect the exterior of the summer house to be left unpainted, as were the national romantic villas of Gesellius, Lindgren, and Saarinen; Lars Sonck; and the artist Akseli Gallen-Kallela.[63] Greater degrees of finish would be found inside, where the dwelling became more polite. Instead, Aalto painted the outside surfaces of the court's brick walls white, possibly to assert the presence of the architecture in the forest. In contrast, the interior walls of the court were surfaced with red brick, set in a multitude of configurations and sizes, and glazed ceramic tile. This play, which Aalto believed to be an essential aspect of architectural design, constituted a significant part of the Muuratsalo "experiment" as realized, "where the proximity to nature can give fresh inspiration both in terms of form and construction."[64]

The plan configuration at Muuratsalo, using a building ell to shelter a courtyard, has a long history in Finland, in vernacular architecture and in Aalto's own work, where in the 1920s he had proposed several schemes that looked to Italy with utopian interpretations of the Mediterranean atrium house. Of these, only the 1928 scheme for a summer house was realized. Aalto entered two designs in a competition, sponsored by the shelter magazine, *Aitta*, for a small vacation house that could be built on a variety of sites. The "Merry-Go-Round" Summer Cottage was planned as a hemicycle gathered around a court (plate 73), maximizing its exposure to sunlight and its protection from the wind. Aalto noted that its compact circulation would help "spare the legs of the lady of the house for tango and jazz."[65] Despite its minute scale, the villa embodied many of the ideas proposed in Aalto's early articles, and its diagram would inform many of his designs in years to come, among them the AA Standard Summer Cottages (plates 172–175). This 1941 project for the A. Ahlström Corporation employed a system of prefabricated rooms/buildings, which could be combined in a variety of configurations. The variety of the sample designs drew upon Aalto's developing ideas on standardization, and he proposed nature as the ultimate model:

> *This immense variety of function and form, this total dissimilarity, has arisen within an extremely strict 'system of standardization'. Every blossom is made up of innumerable apparently uniform protocells, but these cells have a quality that permits the most extraordinary variety in the linkage of cells. This leads to a tremendous wealth of forms in the final product; yet all these forms are based on a specific system.*[66]

The prototypical vacation cottages included both orthogonal and angled plans, but most of them accepted the courtyard typology as a given.

That Aalto's architecture often confounds the visitor's expectations of siting, typology, configuration, and finish is one source of its strength. By introducing an initial geometric organization or a handling of materials Aalto created an expectation that these conditions would continue throughout the structure or site. But, just when expectation was highest, a surprise would jolt anticipation: a disjunction between the exterior form of the building and the actual contour of its interior spaces; the overlay of materials almost in the manner of a brushstroke or collage; or the frequent shift between orthogonal and curvilinear, or angular, planning. Found in projects large and small, and furthered by his deep understanding of twentieth-century abstraction, these unexpected conditions became the fundamentals of Aalto's architecture and method. "Abstract art at its best," Aalto believed, "is the result of a kind of crystallization process. Perhaps that is why it can be grasped only intuitively, though in and behind the work of art there are constructive thoughts and elements of human tragedy. In a way it is a medium that can transport us directly into the human current of feelings that has almost been lost by the written word."[67] Thus, one does not build by emulating nature, or by geometricizing it, but by abstracting natural systems. By varying form and materials, one more closely approaches the condition of nature. "For millennia, art has not been able to disengage itself from the nature-bound human environment," wrote Aalto, "and neither will it ever be able to do so. On the other hand, it must not be thought that freedom and independence ought to be denied to creative artists.... The

prime rule for the arts is therefore free creation of forms always with central reference to man."[68]

Aalto's treatment of siting might also be fairly termed abstract, since it draws from and ultimately reforms the conditions of the landscape. The conception of the Säynätsalo Town Hall of 1948–52 (plates 196–214) began with a reference to classical Rome, but its architectural planning began with an astute reading of the terrain.[69] By responding to the sloping hillside and utilizing the common practice of cut-and-fill, Aalto configured the building as a closed square that functions, in effect, as a retaining wall.[70] The uphill and side wings are partially buried. The lower wing, originally housing shops and a post office, with the library above, countered the movement of the earth downward, as a dam might withstand the pressure of water, creating a "pool" of earth behind it (figure 16). Within the enclosed precinct, a central plaza, or court, of grass, partially paved, provided a center for the community. The library and town offices occupied this level, and here began the procession toward the council chamber, which (with its own reference to Italy) rose as a crown, with dimensions far beyond those thought proper by the municipal authorities: "When the members of the municipal board of building tactfully inquired if a tiny, poor community like theirs really needed to build a council chamber 17 metres high, considering that brick was so expensive, [Aalto] replied: 'Gentlemen! The world's most beautiful and most famous town hall, that of Siena, has a council chamber 16 metres high. I propose that we build one that is 17 metres.'"[71]

The single-loaded corridor, liberally glazed on the court side, connected the office spaces surrounding the grassed plaza and inhaled the outdoor civic space into the building (plate 211).[72] Two stairs led to the elevated courtyard: a monumental stairway of granite leading to the building's entrance and a "stair" of earth, grass, and wood edging (plates 206, 208). Like those of the Maison Carré, the loosely zig-zagging steps excavate the natural slope of the land as visible contours. The diminutive scale of the building's components can be attributed to the architect's desire to sublimate the parts to the whole in order to emphasize the importance of the council chamber.[73] However, given the limited size of the structure, its inherently small-scale building material, and its articulation of parts, the

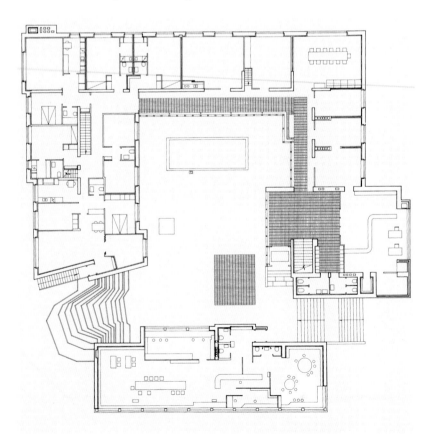

16. Alvar Aalto. Säynätsalo
Town Hall, Säynätsalo, Finland.
1948–52. Main-level plan.
Alvar Aalto Foundation, Helsinki

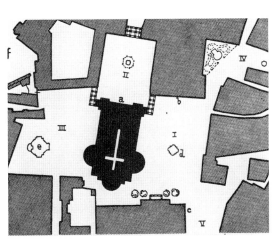

17. Camillo Sitte. Analytical sketch plan of central Salzburg, Austria. From *Der Städtebau nach seinen kunstlerischen Grundsätzen*, 1889

building's apparent monumentality is impressive.[74] By reconfiguring and stabilizing the forested hillside, and by conflating defined open space with the identity of the people, Aalto created a building at once civic and urbane, monumental and welcoming.

In many respects, the architect's ideas for this small complex were far from rational, especially for a town of only 3,000 citizens. Reaching the council chamber, in fact, requires a convoluted trek: mounting exterior granite stairs, entering an intimate lobby, turning back to climb a strictly enclosed and ever-narrowing brick stairway, and then finally entering the chamber. Aalto has left us no written explanation of his actions and ideas, but it seems that he configured this *promenade architecturale* to heighten the culminating impact of the civic room. To approach the council chamber is to ascend an architectural hillside, itself analogous to the newly modulated contour of the land within the town hall precinct. Once again we witness in Aalto's work a resonance of architectural form with natural landscape. At Säynätsalo, Aalto's modulation is neither purely convex nor purely concave but an occult hybrid that relies on one to reveal the other. As such, the town hall represents one of Aalto's most successful site designs.

For the most part, each of Aalto's approaches discussed above concerns the design of individual buildings. The larger commissions that came to him in the postwar years required a broader consideration of culture with complex programs involving sets of buildings. Even by the late 1930s Aalto had begun to avoid the classical formality expected for civic complexes, in some ways extending ideas proposed by the Austrian architect, Camillo Sitte, in his 1889 book, *Der Städtebau nach seinen kunstlerischen Grundsätzen*.[75] In response to the expansion of Vienna beyond the limits of its fortifications, which led to the destruction of defined architectural spaces, Sitte sought viable precedents through the study of historical plazas in northern Europe. The church and the city hall, he believed, required dignified spatial settings, and the plaza was the appropriate instrument for their realization (figure 17). He lamented the fact that the art of designing such spaces had been lost as cities had turned to surveyors and engineers for their design.

Within two years of its publication, Sitte's book began to exert an influence on urban design in Finland. The planning of Eira in southern Helsinki in 1907 (laid out by Bertel Jung, Armas Lindgren, and Lars Sonck) and the Töölö district (based on a plan by Sonck and Gustaf Nyström in 1906) drew heavily on the Austrian's principles of picturesque composition for the placement of monumental buildings and for creating civic open space. Gustaf Strengell's *Staden som konstverk* [The City as a Work of Art] of 1922 borrowed liberally from Sitte's ideas, although Strengell expanded his subject area to include the Finnish town itself.[76] But the most profound effect of Sitte's ideas was on the work of Eliel Saarinen. From 1925 virtually until his death in 1950, Saarinen's urban plans were particularly influenced by Sitte, who also held sway more generally in Finland.[77] Aalto seems to have shared this inheritance with Saarinen's protégé, Otto-Ivari Meurmann, who, interestingly, was the city architect for Viipuri at the time Aalto designed the municipal library there.[78]

Early in Aalto's career, the belief in the classical form and the vertical counterpoint coalesced in his suggestions for one of Jyväskylä's most prominent geographic features: "Ronninmäki Hill... would need only a white campanile (tower) near (not at) the top for the whole area to acquire an extremely refined character. Even a lookout tower would do, but not one of those needlelike towers which function as a point *for* observation but not as an object *of* it. A real tower would make the whole landscape Classical."[79] These dream images were left only as overly ambitious suggestions. But, in the mature work of the postwar period, Aalto applied these long-held visions for civic complexes on nearly level sites, where topography provided few suggestions for an architectural strategy.

The flat site for the Seinäjoki city hall, church, library, and theater (1958–87) had no exceptional natural features; it was essentially a topographic tabula rasa just beyond the town's more heavily developed districts. Here, architecture would define, although not truly enclose, civic space. An axis runs the length of the complex, from the court of the Cross of the Plains church to the east and terminates with the police station at its western limit (plate 371). Elements from the city hall and library, each set in plan at an angle, intrude upon the axis and render the composition dynamic. Like the buildings themselves, the civic complex is a collage of varying parts. An opening through the parish services wing admits the visitor to the court before the church, but the view is skewed and skirts the facade. Throughout the complex, the visitor's glance is diverted; the structures demand no perpendicular confrontation in the classical sense. The space is, in fact, more a dynamic path than a restrained plaza, more emphatically suggesting movement than stasis.

In Rovaniemi the space opens outward to the town, bolstered to the north by the municipal library, to the west by the city hall, and to the east by the city theater (figure 18). The orthogonal masses of the buildings set off the fan-shaped reading room of the library, the faceted walls of the council chamber, and the angled theater lobby as pearls within an oyster.

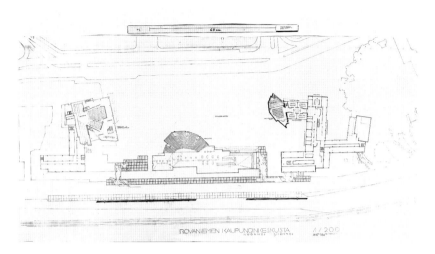

18. Alvar Aalto. Civic Center, Rovaniemi, Finland. 1965. Site plan. Alvar Aalto Foundation, Helsinki

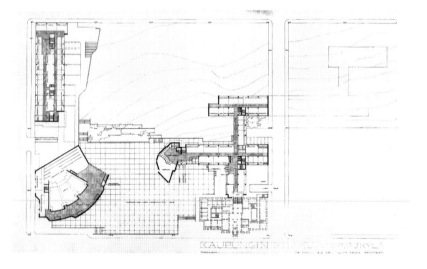

19. Alvar Aalto. Civic Center, Jyväskylä, Finland. 1965. Site plan. Alvar Aalto Foundation, Helsinki

The secondary volumes, which house the bulk of the buildings' functions, comprise a static boundary that increases the architectural cohesion of the complex. As Demetri Porphyrios astutely commented:

> *The monuments are not the Town Hall, the theatre, the library, or the church* in toto *but rather the assembly room, the auditorium, the book-stacks and the basilica-campanile themselves. The pronounced design of these monuments-fragments and their gift for impromptu composition distinguishes them from the nondescript fabric which sustains them and to which they are attached.*[80]

In the design of the civic complex for Jyväskylä, Aalto again articulated in plan the theater and the city hall, and emphasized the presence of the council chamber by forming it as a tower (figure 19). In its sculptured shape, the chamber tower was planned to assume the guise of Jyväskylä's civic beacon. As in Rovaniemi, by departing from a strictly orthogonal geometry, these shaped rooms attracted notice and announced the locus of the civic complex, much as the Italian campanile had announced the presence of the church. Despite their idiosyncratic geometry, Aalto's building clusters retained a memory of Italy, as Aalto himself confessed in 1954: "In my mind there is always a journey to Italy: it may be a past journey that still lives on in my memory; it may be a journey I am making or perhaps a journey I am planning. Be this as it may, such a journey is a conditio sine qua non for my architectural work."[81] While the edges of the orthogonal building parts again addressed the city's blocks and defined the plaza within, the irregular profiles of the theater and the council spaces address one another; their formal affinity suggests an almost magnetic tension, attracting and repelling simultaneously.

The most original of the city-hall complexes was the project for Kiruna, Sweden, which won first prize in a competition held in 1958 (plates 329–333). Here the council chamber assumed an even more prominent character, dominating the building group in a mode more common to Aalto's auditoriums or churches. In a rare instance of overt reference, Aalto recalled the forms of the slag heaps of this mining town in the distant north.[82] Addressing the area's climatic extremes, the municipal offices were cast as a giant snow fence set against the prevailing north winds. The public court was to be enclosed and heated, but the project was left unrealized, and a far less ambitious scheme was constructed in its place.

The Sublime Forest

In Aalto's view, architecture should displace neither the forest nor the farm; instead, it should complement them both. Arguing in 1936 for his housing plan for the Sunila industrial estate, Aalto wrote: "The various parts of the land should be used as God intended them—good forest should remain good forest and the same goes for good farmland."[83] Clearly, even after years of foreign travel, Aalto found Finland and nature at the core of his being and at the core of his architecture. Whether the forest was literal (the site of the building) or metaphorical (the interior space of the building) varied with the particular location and his architectural concept. But the sylvan idea remained central throughout all his work.

The myth of the forest continues to inform the contemporary Finnish consciousness, as it did the designs of Alvar Aalto. Architect and theoretician Juhani Pallasmaa has speculated upon the Finnish use of space, a "forest geometry," stressing that in early times, "The forest was...a sphere for the imagination, peopled by the creatures of fairytale, fable, myth, and superstition. The forest was a subconscious sector of the Finnish mind, in which feelings of both safety and peace, fear and danger lay."[84] While centuries have passed, and despite the introduction into Finland of industrial and post-industrial cultures, "the same symbolic and unconscious implications continue to live on in our minds. The memory of the protective embrace of woods and trees lies deep in the collective Finnish soul, even in this generation."[85] Aalto himself seems never to have entirely left the forest. He built in cities, and he built structures beyond Finland's borders. He received some of his greatest publicity for work produced in the United States (such as his Finnish Pavilion at the 1939 World's Fair in New York, or the postwar Baker House dormitory at Massachusetts Institute of Technology). While he brought a sense of landscape to urban plazas and the interiors of urban buildings, his works in the Finnish landscape generated the greatest resonance.[86] For Säynätsalo, Muuratsalo, and even (if to a slightly lesser degree) in the stridently modernist Tuberculosis Sanatorium at Paimio, Aalto's architecture and Aalto's nature are at their most coincident.

An examination of the sources of Aalto's ideas of landscape and the formal manner with which he executed his designs addresses the question of his relation to nature only partially. In order to suggest the full range of Aalto's accomplishment in conjoining architecture and landscape, we must look to the common denominator between his architecture and his familial heritage: the forest. This was not nature to be tended and cultivated, nature malleable with predictable results. As Schildt philosophized: "The forest calls for another kind of adaptation; it is not irrational, but a much more complicated biological unit, in which the parts work on one another and combine to form a more organic whole than a field."[87] In this sense, Aalto's architecture *is* the forest, the play of interrelated pieces that cohere as a symbiotic suspension, in the chemical sense of the word (figure 20). It is not the grand conception of classicism, in which the part must bow to the whole. Neither is it the picturesque composition of agglomeration, its sense of accretion over time created through contrivance. Aalto's architecture operates as nature does; it addresses the entity and the fragment simultaneously, the architectural fragment in relation to the prevalent order, and/or the relation of the building itself to its site.

The eighteenth-century philosopher, Edmund Burke, identified a source of the sublime in a sense of infinity.[88] Unlike the beautiful, whose formal reading was ultimately measurable and knowable, the sublime sug-

20. Alvar Aalto. Villa Mairea, House for Maire and Harry Gullichsen. Noormarkku, Finland. 1938–39. View from entrance.

gested a sense of the boundless, the unknowable. In the triad of the sublime, beautiful, and picturesque, the last stood as a mediating form of aesthetic appreciation. While lacking the scale of endeavor needed for a truly sublime experience—the grandeur of the Alps or even the vastness of St. Peter's in Rome—the picturesque could nonetheless initiate that provocation stemming from imperfection and the unknowable.

Perhaps we might cautiously position Aalto's work in landscape as picturesque and, at times, even sublime.[89] His are neither spaces nor forms that can be sensed by the static body; on the contrary, they require dynamic perception: one must move through the spaces, move around the forms, in order to truly discern them. Most important, in light and in the changing of the seasons, the architectural reading escapes codification. "Hence, the radical anti-intellectualism of Aalto," Demetri Porphyrios concluded, "his distrust of abstract ideas; his insistence on the lyrical transmutation of nature into sense-experience; in short, his symbolist preoccupation with nature as form."[90]

In an issue of *Arkkitehti* dedicated to Aalto's memory, Christian Norberg-Schulz told of the architect's late arrival to a reception at architectural historian Sigfried Giedion's house in Zurich. The occasion was the opening of Aalto's exhibition there in 1948. Giedion asked the master about his views on architecture, and Aalto "began to talk about the Finnish countryside and salmon fishing. For the first time we felt that architecture is *life* and that creation arises from contact with reality, a region inaccessible to analytical reflection.... Reality ... is largely *local*, tied to place, and it is the task of the architect to make people see the special character of the place and its properties."[91]

Addressing only the locale, however, might deny any greater aspiration; Aalto rarely stopped with the immediate conditions of program and place. To a group of Swedish city planners he said:

> *Architecture has an ulterior motive which always lurks, so to speak, around the corner: the thought of creating a paradise. It is the only purpose of our houses. If we did not always carry this thought around with us all our houses would become simpler and more trivial and life ... would it be at all worth living? Each house, each product of architecture that is worthwhile as a symbol is an endeavor to show that we want to build an earthly paradise for people.*[92]

In Aalto's architecture there is no direct replication of natural forms and little mimesis; instead, architecture transforms program and site into direct and/or metaphorical continuities between landscape and construction. "Architecture still has unused resources and means, which derive straight from nature," Aalto asserted, "and from the reactions springing from the human soul indescribable in words."[93] If the forest provides the bionic metaphor for Aalto's architecture created in both harmonic and dissonant resonance, the picturesque and the sublime offer philosophical readings. Thus, Aalto's body of work can be seen as the making of a sublime forest, constructed for the "little man," denying any grand formal scheme in deference to accommodating human activity and the nature of the site. Thus, while his buildings can be fully experienced, they can never be completely fathomed.

Notes

This essay is dedicated to Göran Schildt—biographer, cultural critic, and storyteller—from whom we have all learned so much, in such a humane manner. I also wish to thank Peter Reed, Mary McLeod, and Dorothée Imbert for reviewing an earlier draft of the text and for offering valuable suggestions.

1. Cited in Göran Schildt, *Alvar Aalto: The Mature Years,* trans. Timothy Binham (New York: Rizzoli, 1991), p. 272.

2. Alvar Aalto, "Between Humanism and Materialism," lecture given at the Central Union of Architects, Vienna, 1955; repr. in Göran Schildt, ed., *Sketches: Alvar Aalto,* trans. Stuart Wrede (Cambridge, Mass., and London: MIT Press, 1978), pp. 130–133.

3. Erik de Jong, "Nature in Demand: On the Importance of Ecology and Landscape Architecture," *Archis* (October 1996), p. 65.

4. At the dawn of the century, Finland was rapidly industrializing and urbanizing, a process lagging centuries behind similar revolutions in England and on the Continent. During the last quarter of the nineteenth century, the population of Helsinki grew threefold: in 1870, the population stood at about 30,000 people; by 1900 it had climbed to over 93,000. See Bo Lönnqvist and Marja-Liisa Rönkkö, *Helsingfors: Från kungsgård till huvudstad* [Helsinki: From Royal Estate to Capital] (Helsinki: Holger Schildts Förlag, 1988), pp. 105–118. For a more detailed study of population, disease, and city planning, see Sven-Erik Åström, *Samhällsplanering och regionsbildning i kejsartidens Helsingfors* [Social Planning and the Formation of Social Areas in Imperial Helsinki] (Helsinki: Mercators Tryckeri, 1957).

5. Curzio Malaparte, *Kaputt* (1944), trans. Cesare Foligno (Marlboro, Vt.: Marlboro Press, 1946); repr. 1991, p. 56. Curzio Malaparte was the pseudonym of Kurt Erich Suckert, who is better known in architectural circles as the client/designer of the Villa Malaparte on Capri, built with the help of the architect Adalberto Libera. As a Tuscan-red block set on a rocky ledge, the Villa Malaparte could hardly be more foreign to Aalto's manner of relating architecture and landscape, although each achieves stasis on its own terms. See Marida Talamona, *Casa Malaparte,* trans. Vittoria di Palma (New York: Princeton Architectural Press, 1992).

6. Göran Schildt, *Alvar Aalto: The Early Years,* trans. Timothy Binham (New York: Rizzoli, 1984), p. 25. Schildt also underscored the respect accorded the surveyor's vocation: "No profession could rival those of the land surveyor or forester, employed by the State, with a technical training, doing his work impartially, respected by all." Ibid.

7. Schildt attributed a characteristic of Aalto's formal vocabulary to a friction between public service and personal desire: "The most important point of resemblance for Aalto between the surveyor's and the architect's office, however, was his desire to work objectively, to rise above all private interests, as civil servants do in their work in the service of society. His attempt to combine this attitude with an architect's private business, the quest for artistic expression, and social criticism or at least involvement in reform, is one of the conflicts which give Aalto's creative work its inner tension." Ibid., p. 27.

8. Alvar Aalto, quoted in ibid., p. 12.

9. "There were two storeys in that big table. In the middle: precision instruments, everything up to three-metre steel rulers, compasses, scale gauges and other such things.... In the lower storey, I lived from the moment I had learned to crawl on all fours. It was like a large market place which I ruled all by myself, until I was ready to be moved up to the upper storey, the white table top itself." Ibid.

10. Ibid., p. 13.

11. For a discussion of the "inflected" landscape, an architectural condition between absolute contrast and absolute merger, see Marc Treib, "Inflected Landscapes," *Places,* vol. 1, no. 2 (1984), pp. 66–77.

12. The term *empire style,* used in the north to describe buildings of Italian neoclassical origin (popular the first half of the nineteenth century), should not be confused with the Empire style (which prevailed in France early in the century) or the third empire style (popular late in the century). On Engel and his work, see Nils Erik Wickberg, *Carl Ludwig Engel* (Helsinki: City of Helsinki, 1973); and the monumental Henrik Lilius, ed., *Carl Ludvig Engel* (Helsinki: Museum of Finnish Architecture, 1990).

13. Elias Lönnrot, ed., *Kalevala* (1835; 1849); Michael Branch explained that the *Kalevala* embodied "late-eighteenth-century ideas most closely associated with the German thinker, J. G. Herder (1744–1803). Herder had argued that a 'nation' could exist only if it possessed a distinctive cultural identity founded on the language and oral literature of the ordinary people." See Michael Branch, "Kalevala: From Myth to Symbol," in *Kalevala, 1835–1985: The National Epic of Finland* (Helsinki: Helsinki University Library, 1985), p. 1.

14. *Kalevala: The Land of Heroes,* trans. W. F. Kirby (London: J. M. Dent, 1907); repr. 1961, canto 2, pp. 10–11. The meter of the poem was adopted by the American poet, Henry Wadsworth Longfellow in his *Song of Hiawatha* of 1855. Apparently, Longfellow had read the *Kalevala* in a German translation in 1854, and found an affinity between the American wilderness and Pohjola. See *The Complete Poetical Works of Henry Wadsworth Longfellow* (Boston and New York: Houghton Mifflin, 1893), p. 113.

15. Gallen-Kallela's tempera, *Joukahainen's Revenge* (1887), Turku Art Museum, places the hapless man, his eye fixed on the horizon, against a background of snow and furrowed tundra.

16. Even contemporary foreign critics identified the "young Finnish architecture" at the beginning of the twentieth century as the confluence of these two strains. "The new architecture is little based on its Finnish predecessors and stands in radical and violent opposition to them. Its vigorous development is thus striking; but this is understandable, given that it did not have to fight any deeply rooted tradition." Etienne Avenard, "La Jeune Architecture Finlandaise," *Art et Décoration* (January 1908), p. 18. For a thorough discussion of Sonck's architecture, see Pekka Korvenmaa, in *Lars Sonck, Architect: 1870–1956* (Helsinki: Museum of Finnish Architecture, 1981), trans. English Centre; and idem, *Innovation versus Tradition: The Architect Lars Sonck, Works and Projects 1900–1910* (Helsinki: Suomen Muinaismuistoyhdistys, 1991), trans. Jüri Kokkonen.

17. Schildt, *Early Years,* p. 126.

18. See Henrik O. Andersson, "Swedish Architecture around 1920," in Simo Paavilainen, ed., *Nordic Classicism, 1910–1930* (Helsinki: Museum of Finnish Architecture, 1982), pp. 123–135.

19. Cited in Simo Paavilainen, in "Nordic Classicism in Finland," in ibid., p. 79.

20. Granite itself possessed nationalistic overtones for the Finns—literally the bedrock of society—and was a favored material of national romantic architects such as Sonck. See Sixten Ringbom, *Stone, Style & Truth: The Vogue for Natural Stone in Nordic Architecture, 1880–1910* (Helsinki: Suomen Muinaismuistoyhdistyksen Aikakauskirja, 1987).

21. The farm buildings, originally set on a lakeshore, date from as early as 1770 (the sauna), and include a chimneyless main room (*tupa* in Finnish) from the mid-ninteenth century. The buildings, which served an extended family of two legal entities, were moved to Seurasaari in 1909 for the opening of the outdoor museum there. See *Seurasaari Open-Air Museum Visitor's Guide* (Helsinki: National Board of Antiquities and Historical Monuments, 1980), pp. 12–16; and István Rácz and Niilo Valonen, *Seurasaari Ulkomuseo* (Helsinki: Otava, 1973), pp. 20–21. For a general discussion of Finnish folk architecture, see Alfred Kolehmainen and Veijo A. Laine, *Suomalainen talonpoikaistalo* (Helsinki: Otava, 1980); on the detached storage building (*aitta*), see idem, *Suomalainen aitta* (Helsinki: Otava, 1983).

22. On his last visit to Aino and Alvar Aalto's house in Munkkiniemi of 1935–36, just before he committed suicide, Strengell stated: "I have just been to Seurasaari … to see the Niemelä farm. Now I should like to see the modern Niemelä farm once more." Göran Schildt, *Alvar Aalto: The Decisive Years,* trans. Timothy Binham (New York: Rizzoli, 1986), p. 130. In actual disposition, Elissa and Alvar Aalto's "experimental" summer house at Muuratsalo of 1952–53 more closely resembled the farm cluster now at Seurasaari. One cannot attribute Aalto's manner to sources in vernacular architecture alone; the collage and other forms of modern

art, which suggested an order far from the classical ideal, should be considered as well.

23. Alvar Aalto, "Architecture in the Landscape of Central Finland," *Sisä-Suomi* (June 28, 1925); quoted in Schildt, *Early Years*, p. 210.

24. Richard Weston, *Alvar Aalto* (London: Phaidon Press, 1995), p. 102. For an overview of the theme of Aalto and Italy, see Enrico Maria Ferrari, ed., *Alvar Aalto: Il Baltico e il Mediterraneo* (Venice: Marsilio Editori, 1990).

25. Aalto, "Landscape of Central Finland," in Schildt, *Early Years*, p. 207.

26. Alvar Aalto, "Motifs from Times Past," *Arkkitehti* (1922); repr. in ibid.

27. Schildt, *Sketches*, pp. 1–2.

28. No doubt Aalto's phrase is satirical. See Alvar Aalto, "Kuk-kosh-khaa, Tutankhamen's Favourite Wife," *Sisä-Suomi* (January 1, 1924); quoted in Schildt, *Early Years*, p. 128. "Jyväskylä is often called 'The Athens of Finland,'" wrote Satu Mattila, "but Alvar Aalto seems to have pictured the town more as 'The Nordic Florence.'" Satu Mattila, *Alvar Aalto ja Keski-Suomi* [Alvar Aalto and Central Finland] (Jyväskylä: Alvar Aalto Seura, 1985), p. 21; trans. Alan Robson and Tony Melville.

29. These included an unexecuted proposal to add three dignified squares, a colonnaded market hall, and a formally planned garden to central Jyväskylä. See Schildt, *Early Years*, pp. 281, 286. For a more detailed analysis of these projects, see Paul David Pearson, *Alvar Aalto and the International Style* (New York: Whitney Library of Design, 1978), pp. 44–48.

30. While the half-cylindrical apse has Italian precedents, it appeared in exaggerated form in Erik Gunnar Asplund's Lister County Courthouse in Sölvesborg, Sweden, of 1917–21. Aalto's building for the Civil Defense Corps in Seinäjoki of 1924–29 employed virtually the same geometrical organization.

31. The other competitors were Kauno Kallio and Armas Lindgren.

32. Alvar Aalto, "Jämsä Church Competition Statement" (1925), Alvar Aalto Archives, Helsinki, p. 1. Kallio's winning scheme, in contrast, sought its inspiration in the cruciform and domed wood churches of the early nineteenth century, such as Carl Ludwig Engel's church in Lapua of 1827.

33. See Schildt, *Early Years*, p. 288. Aalto's entry received only a purchase prize; Hilding Ekelund's winning entry was constructed with an agitated facade that compares unfavorably today with Aalto's restrained, if heroic, elegance.

34. Aalto, "Landscape of Central Finland," in ibid., p. 210.

35. Alvar Aalto, "From Doorstep to Living Room," *Aitta*, Special Christmas Issue (1926), pp. 63–69; trans. Kenneth Lundell and Marc Treib. The work in question may be Fra Angelico's fresco, *The Annunciation* (c. 1440–50), in S. Marco, Florence.

36. Ibid., p. 64.

37. Ibid., pp. 64–65.

38. Ibid., pp. 66–67.

39. Ibid., p. 68.

40. Ibid.

41. Elias Cornell explored the theme of roof and sky in Asplund's architecture in his essay, "The Sky as a Vault …," a title borrowed from a note in one of Asplund's sketchbooks. The appreciation of the sky often occurs in Asplund's project descriptions. On the Puck restaurant at the 1930 Stockholm Exhibition, he wrote: "Let in the twilight, the deep blue night sky and the thousand shades of light and their charm will seem to reach in to those who are dancing or just sipping their drinks. People do not want to abandon their closeness to nature, least of all in summer." Quoted in Claes Caldenby and Olof Hultin, eds., *Asplund* (Stockholm: Arkitektur Förlag, 1985), p. 31. See also Stuart Wrede, *The Architecture of Erik Gunnar Asplund* (Cambridge, Mass., and London: MIT Press, 1980).

42. Göran Schildt has remarked on the links between Asplund and the somewhat junior Aalto. They are said to have met at the Skandia Cinema in 1923, and the continuing flow of ideas across the Gulf of Bothnia heightened when Aalto lived in Turku at the close of the 1920s. See "Asplund och Aalto—berättelsen om en ömsesidigt berikande vänskap," in *Asplund 1885–1940*, Årsbok 1985 (Stockholm: Sveriges Arkitektur Museet, 1986), pp. 51–66.

43. Kristian Gullichsen has added yet another interpretation, assigning to the human body the origin of Aalto's curve: "Aalto's famous curving line, which is also found in the Villa Mairea, is usually interpreted as a metaphor for the shoreline of a Finnish lake. I think rather, that its origin is in the human body: it is the contour of the hip, so often used in painting, whether in a manner figurative or abstract, as, for example, the guitars of the cubist still lifes. Seen in this way, the origin of Aalto's line is especially international. Several masters of modern art have used the free-form as a means of expression and the line that Aalto liked so much doesn't have any mysterious meaning. It has clearly sensuous meaning and plays a precise role in the composition." Kristian Gullichsen, "Villa Mairea," in Pirkko Tuukkanen-Beckers, ed., *En contact avec Alvar Aalto* (Jyväskylä: Alvar Aalto Museum, 1992), p. 65; trans. Marc Treib and Dorothée Imbert. For Le Corbusier, the sinuous line was a common motif in buildings and even urban schemes, given theoretical underpinning by his interpretation of the natural meander. Le Corbusier, *Precisions: On the Present State of Architecture and City Planning* (1930), trans. Edith Schreiber Aujame (Cambridge, Mass.: MIT Press, 1991).

44. "Aalto himself characterized his New York pavilion as 'a building with the facade inside.'" Schildt, *Decisive Years*, p. 173. For a comprehensive discussion of the pavilion and its design, see Peter B. MacKeith and Kerstin Smeds, *The Finland Pavilions: Finland at the Universal Expositions, 1900–1992* (Tampere: Kustannus,

1993), pp. 135–150; and Schildt, *Decisive Years*, pp. 162–180.

45. Aino and Alvar Aalto, "Mairea," *Arkkitehti*, no. 9 (1939). "We [Maire and Harry Gullichsen] told him [Aalto] that he should regard it as an experimental house; if it didn't work out, we wouldn't blame him." Maire Gullichsen, quoted in Pearson, *Aalto and the International Style*, p. 168.

46. Aalto, "From Doorstep to Living Room," p. 66.

47. For a further elaboration of this metaphor, see Marc Treib, "The Ship in the Woods: The Villa Mairea," paper presented at the Annual Meeting of the Association of Collegiate Schools of Architecture, New Orleans, March 1986.

48. Demetri Porphyrios, *Sources of Modern Eclecticism: Studies on Alvar Aalto* (London: Academy Editions, 1982), p. 57.

49. For reproductions of Aalto's studies for the Villa Mairea, see Göran Schildt, ed., *The Architectural Drawings of Alvar Aalto*, Vol. 10 (New York: Garland Publishing, 1994), esp. fig. 84/380, p. 89.

50. Karl Fleig, ed., *Alvar Aalto* (Zurich: Verlag für Architektur, 1963), p. 164; trans. William B. Gleckman.

51. Alvar Aalto, "Chapel and Cemetery Competition Statement" (1952), typescript (Alvar Aalto Archives, Helsinki).

52. Eeva Maija Viljo, "Alvar Aalto's Design for the Main Building of the College of Education [Pedagogical Institute] at Jyväskylä as an Experiment in Primitivism," in Marja Terttu Knapas and Åsa Ringbom, eds., *Icon to Cartoon: A Tribute to Sixten Ringbom* (Helsinki: The Society for Art History in Finland, 1995), p. 324.

53. Juhani Pallasmaa, "Du tectonique au pictural en architecture," in Tuukkanen-Beckers, *En contact avec Alvar Aalto*, p. 40; trans. Marc Treib.

54. Alvar Aalto, "Main Building of the Institute of Technology," *Arkkitehti*, no. 4 (1966), p. ii.

55. "The halls have indirect sunlight, the series of windows also creating an exterior theatrical increase in height: moreover, this is the principal motive for the central square of the campus, which will automatically become the place where the students gather." Ibid.

56. Alvar Aalto, text fragment, c. 1926 (Alvar Aalto Archives, Helsinki); quoted in Schildt, *Decisive Years*, p. 13.

57. Schildt, *Mature Years*, p. 208.

58. At the project's presentation some days later: "The queen was most impressed by the design and declared that it should be used as the basis for construction." Ibid., p. 210.

59. Göran Schildt, "Alvar Aalto," in Fleig, *Alvar Aalto*, p. 16.

60. "The whole complex of buildings is dominated by the fire that burns at the center of the patio and that, from the point of view of practicality and comfort, serves the same purpose as the campfire in a winter camp,

where the glow from the fire and its reflections from the surrounding snowbanks create a pleasant, almost mystical feeling of warmth." Alvar Aalto, "Experimental House, Muuratsalo," *Arkkitehti,* no. 9–10 (1953), p. 159; repr. in Schildt, *Sketches,* p. 116.

61. Erik Kråkström et al, eds., *Pohjoismaista Arkkitehtuuria, 1950–1954* (Helsinki: Nordic Building Congress, 1955), p. 162.

62. Schildt, *Mature Years,* p. 275.

63. On the use of materials in these villas, see Ritva Tuomi, "On the Search for a National Style," in *Abacus* (Helsinki: Museum of Finnish Architecture, 1979), pp. 57–97; and Marc Treib, "Gallen-Kallela: A Portrait of the Artist as Architect," *Architectural Association Quarterly,* vol. 7, no. 3 (1975), pp. 3–13.

64. Aalto, "Experimental House," in Schildt, *Sketches,* p. 116. Aalto was unsuccessful in his bid for tax deductions based on the work at Muuratsalo, an experimental architectural site. See Schildt, *Mature Years,* p. 267.

65. Schildt, *Decisive Years,* p. 26.

66. Alvar Aalto, quoted in Schildt, *Mature Years,* p. 47.

67. Alvar Aalto, "The Trout and the Mountain Stream," *Domus* (1947); repr. in Schildt, *Sketches,* p. 98.

68. Alvar Aalto, "The Arts," in Karl Fleig, ed., *Alvar Aalto: Volume II, 1963–1970* (Zurich: Éditions d'Architecture Artemis, 1971), p. 12.

69. In Finland, competition entries are identified using a motto or pseudonym, rather than an entry number. Aalto's winning entry was labeled "Curia" (the seat of the Roman senate), demonstrating his attachment of civic space to the cultural landscape of classical times. See Richard Weston, *Town Hall, Säynätsalo* (London: Phaidon, 1993).

70. Cut-and-fill refers to earth either removed or added. Ideally, site work will only redistribute the contour of the existing slope; no soil will be carted away, and none will be added.

71. Schildt, *Mature Years,* p. 158.

72. Aalto had sought additional dimensions for the corridor element as early as 1926, when he asserted that it "offers undreamed-of aesthetic potential, as it is a natural coordinator of inner rooms, and permits the use of a bold, monumental linear scale, even in small buildings." Aalto, "From Doorstep to Living Room," p. 63. Seen in this light, the grand openness of the auditorium lobbies of the Pedagogical Institute at Jyväskylä can be taken as the apotheosis of Aalto's idea of the corridor space.

73. It may also stem, in part, from the considerable part of the program given over to residential functions, including the caretaker's apartment and units presumably for official guests.

74. The scale of the building is also deceptive. Before the more complete pictorial coverage offered by recent publications, the town hall was known only from a handful of black-and-white images taken shortly after occupancy. Photos of the town hall gave the impression that it was a part of a developed urban entity, which at the time, Säynätsalo definitely was not. Presumably, the building also provided the town's citizens with a civic identity, as Aalto had intended.

75. Literally, "City Building According to Artistic Principles." For a recent translation and extensive background study of Sitte's book, see George R. Collins and Christiane Crasemann Collins, *Camillo Sitte: The Birth of Modern City Planning* (New York: Rizzoli, 1986).

76. Gustaf Strengell, *Staden som konstverk* (Helsinki: Holger Schildts Förlagsaktiebolag, 1922). Although trained as an architect, Strengell was more an art and cultural figure, publishing numerous articles and several books, among them *Byggnaden som konstverk* [The Building as a Work of Art] (1928) and *En Bok om Boken* [A Book on the Book] (1931).

77. For information on Saarinen as planner, see Marc Treib, "Eliel Saarinen as Urbanist: The Tower and the Square," *Arkkitehti,* no. 3 (1985), pp. 16–31; and idem, "Urban Fabric by the Bolt: Eliel Saarinen at Munkkiniemi-Haaga," *Architectural Association Quarterly* (January–June 1982), pp. 43–58.

78. Aalto described how his first encounter with the work of Eliel Saarinen—in publications—convinced him to become an architect: "But from the effect those architectural drawings had on me, I can say that a new architect came into the world that morning." Alvar Aalto, "Foreword," in Albert Christ-Janer, *Eliel Saarinen: Finnish-American Architect and Educator* (Chicago: University of Chicago Press, 1950), p. xiv. After Saarinen's immigration to the United States in 1923, Otto-Ivari Meurmann inherited Saarinen's mantle as Finland's leading authority on city planning. In 1947, K. J. Gummerus published his *Asemakaavaoppi* [Planning Theory] (Jyväskylä); it was reprinted in 1982 by Rakkenuskirja, Helsinki, and retains a considerable following.

79. Aalto, "Landscape of Central Finland," in Schildt, *Early Years,* p. 209.

80. Porphyrios, *Sources of Modern Eclecticism,* pp. 88–89. This conclusion follows from Porphyrios's identification of the "autonomous room" in Aalto's architecture, pp. 20–22.

81. Alvar Aalto, in *Casabella* (1954); cited in Schildt, *Mature Years,* p. 214.

82. Schildt, *Mature Years,* pp. 176–177.

83. Quoted in Schildt, *Decisive Years,* p. 148.

84. Juhani Pallasmaa, "The Art of Wood," in *The Language of Wood: Wood in Finnish Sculpture, Design, and Architecture* (Helsinki: Museum of Finnish Architecture, 1989), p. 16.

85. Ibid.

86. For an extended discussion of resonance (in relation to the work of San Francisco architect Stanley Saitowitz), see Marc Treib, "Resonant Geography: The Architecture of Stanley Saitowitz," *de Architect* (March 1997), pp. 34–43

87. Schildt, *Early Years,* p. 34.

88. "Infinity has a tendency to fill the mind with that sort of delightful horror, which is the most genuine effect, and truest test of the sublime." Edmund Burke, *A Philosophical Enquiry into the Origin of Our Ideas of the Sublime and Beautiful* (1757) (Oxford: Oxford University Press, 1990), p. 67. Obviously, it was never Aalto's intention to build a fearful dimension into his architecture. But the sense of the unfathomable accompanies his complex formal manner.

89. Yves-Alain Bois introduced a hybrid term, *picturesque sublime,* to qualify *Clara-Clara,* a 1983 sculpture by Richard Serra. See "A Picturesque Stroll around *Clara-Clara,*" *October,* no. 29 (1984), pp. 34–62.

90. Porphyrios, *Sources of Modern Eclecticism,* p. 63.

91. Christian Norberg-Schulz, in *Arkkitehti,* nos. 7–8 (1976), p. 51. The English architect Maxwell Fry shared this interpretation of Aalto: "Unlike Mies, for whom America was the opportunity to do what he knew he had to do, Aalto was still in transit for the time when the true amalgam of his character would declare itself, coming well down, when the time came, on the earthy, woody side for the release of his creative genius for volume and form in materials, native to his country, that, feeling deeply for, he could re-use for new ends, robustly and as delicately." Maxwell Fry, "Man of the Month," *Architectural Design,* no. 2 (1968); repr. in *Arkkitehti,* no. 2 (1968), p. 61.

92. Alvar Aalto, "The Architect's Conception of Paradise," lecture given at a meeting of Swedish city planners in Malmö, 1957; repr. in Schildt, *Sketches,* pp. 157–158.

93. Alvar Aalto, cited in Kirmo Mikkola, "Aalto the Thinker," *Arkkitehti,* nos. 7–8 (1976), p. 23.

Aalto and Finnish Industry

Pekka Korvenmaa

Transporting logs on a river,
southwestern Finland. c. 1930s

MANY OF THE WORKS that brought Alvar Aalto international fame originated from commissions within Finnish industry. The Toppila Pulp Mill, the Sunila Pulp Mill and Housing, the Standard Terrace Housing at Kauttua, the prefabricated A-House Standard Houses, Villa Mairea (plates 110–124, 155–171), the Enso-Gutzeit headquarters, Helsinki, and even the pioneering regional plans for the Kokemäenjoki River Valley (pages 85, 86) and Imatra (plate 289), just to mention a few, resulted from the numerous contacts Aalto had with the leaders of the industrial-economic power structure of his country. Even though the artifacts, buildings, plans, and unexecuted schemes are already evident from numerous studies, books, and exhibitions of his work, the web of Aalto's relationships and modes of operation within Finnish industry is perhaps less well known. Thus, the purpose of this inquiry is to illuminate the nature of this collaboration, especially before and during the economically critical years of World War II.

The focus will be on the prewar period of the early 1930s through the crucial mid-1950s, on Aalto himself, and on the strategies applied both by him and his clients that resulted in a network of mutual interdependence. The buildings themselves are given less attention here; their analysis as architectural objects calls for different approaches, which can be found elsewhere in this volume and in the plethora of existing Aalto studies as well as those to come.

This essay will explore the nature of Aalto's relationships to the leading industrialists in Finland, with particular attention to the origins of these ties and Aalto's own initiatives in formulating the interaction of architecture, industrial capital, and production technology. It will touch on the architectural profession in Finland and Aalto's role and influence within it as a leading innovator in both the conceptualization and implementation of modernization within the parameters of technology, standardization, and serial production.

This brief foray into one specific aspect of Aalto's voluminous output and sphere of activity should be read against the broad spectrum of information contained in the essential four-part monograph on Aalto by Göran Schildt, as well as the work by others on Aalto's role in product and furniture design.[1] The reader is advised to use these sources to obtain a fuller understanding of the collaboration sketched here through a study of the physical evidence of the artifacts themselves—the buildings.

Forests, Industry, and Architecture in Finland

Until World War II, Finland was predominantly an agrarian society, operating at a remarkably low level of industrialization and urbanization compared to most other European countries. The existing Finnish system of production and corporate capitalism in the first decades of the twentieth century, when Aalto began to win commissions from this sector, was entirely dominated by the abundant forest resources of the nation.[2] Sawmills, cellulose plants, and paper and cardboard factories were located near water supplies—lakes, rivers, or river deltas by the sea (figure 1). This was vital in two ways: it provided pure water for the industrial process and supplied transport routes for lumber, the raw material upon which the industry was based. Products were shipped around the world directly from the principal mill sites, at Sunila, Varkaus, and Summa.

These geographical and economic factors came to affect, to a large degree, the nature of the commissions Aalto was to receive for the industrial plants themselves and for the communities around them. In the larger context, they provided the background for the vast regional plans around major water sites and concomitant industrial routes ultimately exemplified by the Kokemäenjoki and Imatra plans. The peculiar, scattered, antiurban character of the forestry industries in Finland, which formed isolated communities in the countryside without the amenities of housing and social services that an urban structure would have provided, offered excellent opportunities for a vast range of planning and design projects unhampered by restrictions from public legislative bodies.

It was the forestry industries and the leaders of their main corporations that formed the most influential group of powerful and wealthy businessmen in the country in the early 1930s. The social and economic power of the state was relatively weak, and in many ways it was the industrialists who led the process of modernizing Finland, both technologically and socially. They invested not only in production facilities but also in the development of services needed by their often remote industrial communities. This included the design of public buildings and housing by the leading Finnish architects of the country, and it was a tradition that had begun well before Aalto's arrival on the scene. By the same token, the patrons of these communities were dependent on a stable and content work force, and housing of a high standard was an important element in the process of social stabilization, especially in the aftermath of the disastrous civil and class war of 1918.[3] This also meant that Aalto, in a concrete

1. A typical view of the Finnish landscape

manner, was to seek answers to the question put forth by Le Corbusier: architecture or revolution?[4]

The system of patronage of this kind had a long tradition, some two hundred years old, which began in Finland during the early industrialization of the iron mills. The industrialist was the omnipotent overlord of his possessions, which included everything from the factory to the daily life and environment of the workers. The nature of the architectural solutions implemented in the first decades of the twentieth century and later, after World War II, changed to some degree the social distribution of space but to a lesser degree the power structure. Of course, the mechanisms of surveillance and differentiation gradually became subtler and more progressive—for the mutual benefit of the owner and the work force.[5]

In the mid-1930s, export based on the forestry industry increased in volume, and to a great extent it was a tightly knit group of family-owned corporations that benefited. Families such as the Serlachiuses, Rosenlews, Kihlmans, and Ahlströms depended on each other and were not only rivals but also partners, shareholders in mutual, large-scale investments such as the cellulose plant at Sunila. Success meant expansion, and expansion required architecture in which to produce returns on investments. An architect who had proven his skills and was trusted by this key group could look forward to a wealth of commissions. Furthermore, this industrial elite had intimate ties with the national power structure of leading politicians, keen on supporting the industrial backbone of the country. As we will see, Aalto became an inside member of this interconnected web of industry and politics—a somewhat paradoxical path for the leading modernist in the Nordic countries, well-known for his leftist sympathies!

The apparently effortless integration of the avant-gardist Aalto and industrial capitalism is best understood via a brief excursion into the nature of the architectural profession in Finland. A collegial body of modern architects had formed in Finland around the turn of the century, and through such leading figures as Eliel Saarinen the profession had achieved a high cultural and artistic status. Simultaneously, as visible participants in the process of nation building, which led to the advent of political independence from Russia in 1917, architects were able to achieve positions nationally as members of the professional class and become socially equal to, and even integrated with, the leading financial circles. Architects were able to act in several areas during a time of heightened national optimism, from the visual and aesthetic to the rational engineer-like control of urban planning, with its concomitant issues of transport and commerce. Architects became respected leaders in the transition to nationhood, launched before independence, continued with new vigor in the 1920s and 1930s, and were of critical importance after World War II, which required rebuilding of a different sort. Typically, they came to a great degree from middle-class groups such as civil servants and the clergy, as did Aalto himself. The profession at large had a strong sense of integrity, a desire to expand its relevance, and shared the belief inherent in modernism that society could be enhanced through a well-designed environment. Furthermore, when architects campaigned for the exclusive privilege to building design around 1900 they also proclaimed their hegemony over city planning, thus removing it from the domain of civil engineers. This field of professional activity later became extremely important, especially for Aalto, when major decisions were made for the planning of whole regions before, during, and after World War II.[6]

In becoming an architect, Aalto inherited the legacy of a well-organized professional body with high social status that governed the design of the built environment. Aalto's rise to national and then international fame occurred in a country where the cultural and political climate was dominated by right-wing nationalism and the propagation of agrarian values. International modernism, in the vein of the Bauhaus, was generally regarded as leftist, even Bolshevik, in Finland around 1930, not only among established architects but also by the cultured middle and upper classes, that is, the main private patrons of architecture. In the late 1920s, Aalto himself had become an ardent disciple of the social program of modernism, or functionalism, as it became known in the Nordic countries. His intimate ties with the Congrès Internationaux d'Architecture Moderne (CIAM)—the avant-garde movement associated with Le Corbusier, founded in 1928 to promote the cause of modern architecture internationally—and his personal friendships with modernists such as Walter Gropius and László Moholy-Nagy, not to mention a young generation of Scandinavian colleagues such as Sven Markelius and Erik Gunnar Asplund, fortified his ardent devotion to the modernist program. Given the conservative political climate among the representatives of large-scale industry, it is curious to see how rapidly Aalto rose to prominence among the supporters of the status quo and anti-leftist values. Aalto was the foremost Finnish advocate of an architectural idiom and ideology that originated in a hotbed of revolutionary aesthetic and political ideas but yet became one of the most trusted architects of his country's corporate capitalists.[7]

Modernity Through Industry and Architecture

The first large-scale commission Aalto received from the industrialists was for the Toppila Pulp Mill, a sulphate cellulose plant in Oulu, of 1930–33 (figure 2; plates 110–112). It was given to him by Gösta Serlachius, the director of the Serlachius Corporation. Aalto was careful in handling the project with precision, and the result satisfied both the client and fellow architects. It was published in *Arkkitehti* (*Arkitekten*), the journal of the Finnish Association of Architects.[8] But in spite of this achievement further commissions in this area, as well as almost any other projects, had to wait until the economic situation in Finland began to improve. When the

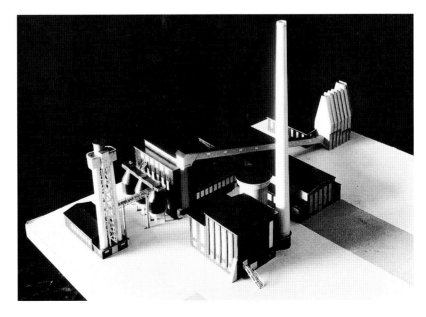

2. Alvar Aalto. Toppila Pulp Mill, Oulu, Finland. 1930–33. Model

boom started, after the economic slump of the early 1930s, it was unexpectedly strong and lasted until the 1939–40 Winter War between Finland and the Soviet Union.[9] The forestry industries and their exports were the dynamic force in this recuperation. Around the middle of the 1930s, plans were made for new mills to pour out sawn lumber, pulp, and paper for many locations. Aalto had proven his capacity for solving industrial problems efficiently and set out to secure his share of commissions.[10]

Before discussing Aalto's designs for industry in the mid-1930s and later, we should address certain conventions within architectural modernism and its buildings for industrial facilities. In the symbol-laden hierarchy of functional building categories, the actual shelters for production, the factories, occupied the lowest level. As devices for the optimization of investments made in machinery and the work force, the buildings for production were often either designed by construction engineers alone or with an architect expected merely to give the final touches to the outward appearance of the structure. Residential buildings and corporate headquarters were something else, with aspirations for representation or ideological links to historical analogies of power. Among architects designing predominantly for large-scale industry, Albert Kahn is one of the best examples of this dualism and typologization of functional categories (figure 3).[11] With Continental, and soon Nordic, modernism all this changed. Modern production technology and industrial processes came to epitomize the all-pervading rationalism and efficiency of modernity. The new architecture (*Neues Bauen*) was meant to be all-embracing, dissolving the differences in the outer characterization of buildings for different uses. In many ways the factory became the paragon when Henry Ford's and Frederick W. Taylor's systems of serial production and employee management were transferred from industrial production into other domains of everyday life.[12]

3. Albert Kahn. Ford Motor Company, River Rouge Plant, Dearborn, Michigan. Begun 1917. Aerial view

At the Toppila Pulp Mill the chief engineer, L. Nyrop, was responsible for the layout of the functional units, the placement of the machinery, and the design of the concrete structures, which were provided by an outside specialist. Aalto's task as architect was to characterize the outer shell, decide on the colors, and reshape some window openings. In describing the project, Aalto admitted that his influence on the whole was restricted to the expression of the facade and, generally, "the outer shaping of a project already designed in advance."[13] For example, the much-illustrated chip container with the "expressive" roof correctly and economically followed the outer shape of the equipment inside. This is not to underestimate Aalto's role in giving the whole a proper architectural appearance but to outline the restricted sphere of operations given to architects in the design of the actual production facilities. It was there that the major investments were made, and no risks were to be taken regarding the optimal functioning of the process. This was also more or less the case with the commissions Aalto received later in the decade. It was not the factories but the accompanying buildings, such as the directors' residences, company headquarters, and housing, where architectural freedom was allowed. There the risks were smaller, functions simpler, and the aspects of production more concerned with keeping the work force content.

In a description of the Toppila mill, the chief engineer stressed the fact that the managing director, Serlachius, paid serious attention to the "outer shaping" of the factory, that is, the contribution of Aalto. But this was not a pioneering example of a Finnish industrialist wholeheartedly promoting controversial modernist architecture, since, in the same years, Serlachius built himself a traditional stately residence at the company's main location in Mänttä. This building consciously harked back to baroque manor houses of the time when Finland was a part of Sweden. In this, as well as in the design of the company headquarters, he used architects of an older generation.[14] But in the sphere of basic production, without regard for the symbolic representation of power, the modern, rationalist, and seemingly nonassociative idiom was allowed.

Before Aalto's next significant industrial commission, the Sunila Pulp Mill and Housing at Kotka of 1936–38 (plates 113–119), several relationships converged in a manner that ultimately had a crucial impact on the scope of his prospects for the future. He not only gained important com-

4. Harry Gullichsen and Alvar Aalto, c. 1938

missions but also found a leading industrialist who became a full-fledged patron and sponsor of modernist architecture. This was Harry Gullichsen, the young general director of Finland's largest private corporation, A. Ahlström (figure 4). The relationship of Aalto and the Gullichsens, Harry and his wife Maire (née Ahlström), the principal heiress of the corporation, has been described at length by Göran Schildt.[15] This fruitful convergence of patronage and friendship covered a major part of Aalto's professional activity in the late 1930s, including, but not limited to, Sunila, the glassworks in Karhula, the Kauttua Master Plan, Artek Corporation, Villa Mairea (the House for Maire and Harry Gullichsen), and the Koke-mäenjoki River Valley Regional Plan. The following will concentrate on the cooperation between Aalto and the A. Ahlström Corporation, although he served other companies simultaneously.

Aalto first met Maire Gullichsen in 1935, when the Artek company was founded to promote modern art and interior design, mainly through the marketing of Aalto's already famous furniture (see plates 59, 63–65, 107, 137, 154). Shortly after Aalto formed a close friendship with the Gullichsens, a decision was made in 1936 to build a major sulphate cellu-lose plant with adjoining housing at a location where one of the major rivers, and thus industrial arteries, of the country flowed into the sea on the southern coast of Finland. Sunila was a joint venture of several major paper producers along the Kymijoki River that needed cellulose for production and export. Gullichsen was appointed director of the Sunila building enter-prise by the consortium, and Aalto was summoned to be the architect. In addition to Gullichsen's backing, he had the Toppila project with which to show his experience of industrial, and especially cellulose-plant, design. When Sunila was completed with great success and publicity in 1938, one

of the shareholders, Tampella Corporation, had already entrusted the archi-tectural design of a major paper factory with housing in Anjala, also in the Kymijoki River Valley, to Aalto (figure 5). At the same time, Aalto became almost a company architect to Ahlström, making both town plans and building designs for the company's sites at Kauttua and Varkaus, as well as one of his masterpieces, the director's residence, Villa Mairea, in Noormarkku, where the firm had its headquarters (plates 155–169).[16]

By the end of the 1930s, Gullichsen was a leading figure in Finnish industrial politics. He was a major player in state politics as well, with national influence in important decisions regarding industrial policies, export, and the course of agrarian, urban, and industrial development. He represented an apolitical, technocratic force—a modern industrialist free of both agrarian backwardness and actual party politics. He held the view that modernization could be achieved through the leadership of industry, since industrialists, unlike politicians, were not bound by voters or old-fashioned public regulations. Aalto represented a professional status comparable to those of doctors and lawyers, also unfettered by statesmanship, and found Gullichsen's vision analogous to his own desire to bring to realization a modern built environment much broader in scope than a few isolated buildings. In 1939 Gullichsen and Aalto were members of an informal association of top politicians and industrialists who met to discuss the future of the country. His bond with Gullichsen had brought Aalto into contact with the core group of national decision makers. This was to give

5. Alvar Aalto. Anjala Paper Mill, Inkeroinen, Finland. 1937–38

him unexpected weight and freedom of operation during and after the coming wars.[17]

Thus, in only ten years, Aalto changed from an outspoken avant-garde opponent of the establishment into an expert deeply entangled with industrial capitalism and national strategies. In order to truly understand this apparent dilemma, it is vital to remember that he saw the alignment of industry and modern technology as a dynamic force for the advancement of the modernization of society, in which modernist architecture served as an instrument for improving everyday life. He believed that social, even radical, renewal was possible without regarding industry or its representatives and the working classes as antagonists in society. Progress and modernism were allied. It had become possible for Aalto to operate on a large scale through Gullichsen, who, in turn, found in Aalto an expert of his own generation capable of giving an outer form to his and his wife's aspirations for an aesthetic renewal to accompany technological advancement and social reform within the working environment. Hence the powerful industrialist strengthened the architect, and the famous architect gave cultural tools and a modern profile to his client. In 1939 Aalto explained: "In the construction of the industrial and productive infrastructure in the country a large amount of socialist ideas have in all peace been integrated with those of capitalism. This has led to an all-embracing, generally accepted social mode of thinking."[18]

Industrial development in the country, his own growing reputation, and especially the trust of the Gullichsens in the late 1930s opened a vast field of possibilities for Aalto: Sunila, Standard Terrace Housing at Kauttua, and Varkaus. The Sunila cellulose-plant project, covering both industrial facilities and residential areas for all strata of the work force, from the director downward, has justly been regarded as one of Aalto's key achievements prior to World War II. The first building stage, from 1936 to 1938, comprised the overall community plan, the plant, a central heating unit, and housing.[19] The result, in a Finnish context, was a coherent and convincing demonstration of the possibilities of modern architecture in the hands of an enlightened industrial client. Never again was Aalto to experience at this scale such freedom regarding land use or functional and formal solutions.

Without discussing the building types as such, some words regarding the character of the whole in relation to industrial building are in order. At Sunila, as at Toppila, Aalto was again restricted in the design of the production facilities by parameters of existing machinery and efficiency studies, and by the engineers' input into the layout of the whole and of the individual concrete structures, around which the whole enterprise turned.[20] This makes it difficult, in retrospect, to extract from Aalto's rhetoric after its completion his actual influence on the shape of the factory itself. Very often solutions with pragmatic reasons have been given a heroic aura; ordinary elements have been known to be raised into spheres of higher cultural meaning through contrived analogies with antiquity or

6. Alvar Aalto. Sunila Pulp Mill, Kotka, Finland. 1936–38. West facade

the Mediterranean.[21] At any rate, it seems as if Aalto was able to persuade the engineers to leave the existing bedrock formations to serve as the foundation for the facilities, rather than blast the entire site to level it off (figure 6). The result added visual drama to the whole and ensured the possibilities of giving the design a sculptural nature, somewhat constructivist or Neo-Plasticist in character. This, of course, hampered the functional aspects of production; a one-level principle would have been more efficient. The red-brick and white-plaster envelopes for the different units naturally have their aesthetic merits, and it was precisely for this that architectural expertise was employed in the factory design.

The Sunila Pulp Mill and Housing project, in spite of its innovative nature, did not come out of a void and can be related to earlier developments in Finnish industrial building. Only one year before the design of Sunila was begun, the largest cellulose factory in Europe had been completed at Kaukopää, in eastern Finland (figure 7). It was designed by Väinö Vähäkallio in a modernist idiom, with bold simple forms in red brick. The project even included housing, also modernist and situated in a pine forest just as Aalto was to do in Sunila. Aalto's own ideas were not directly derived from this grand example of industrial architecture, but

7. Väinö Vähäkallio. Cellulose Factory, Kaukopää, Finland. 1934–35

8. Alvar Aalto. Sunila Pulp Mill and Housing, Kotka, Finland. 1936–38. Workers' row houses with standardized wood houses in the distance

there was a close relationship on a basic level of engineering. The technical manager of Sunila, the civil engineer, Aulis Kairamo, with whom Aalto worked intimately, had been in the team planning and then running Kaukopää. The layout of the two factories is thus very similar. In Sunila, as at Kaukopää, the division of the program into isolated units was dictated by the process rather than the architect's individual intentions.[22]

Although the design of production facilities offered Aalto only limited freedom, it was in the design of the housing that he was able to display his full intentions regarding the use of the site, social divisions, functional novelties, and formal solutions. It has to be borne in mind that at Sunila Aalto operated in virgin territory. Virtually no older layers of building existed, no city planning restrictions were to be obeyed, and only the needs of one investing client had to be fulfilled. The whole was to be handed to the users—the work force—without their involvement in the decision making. The result became significant in terms of both Aalto's future work and Finnish town planning in general.

At Sunila Aalto experimented with several types of housing. Some of them, such as two-story row, or "chain," houses, he had already used at the Paimio Tuberculosis Sanatorium of 1929–33. Now he used the slope of the terrain to achieve multistory solutions with a minimum amount of interior stairs. The three-story row houses, probably the most illustrated part of the project, were based on this ingenious feature. Also in 1937, Aalto designed for Sunila an unbuilt prototype of the terraced multistory houses without any internal stairs; these were realized in Kauttua by A. Ahlström a year later (plate 124). Even though the white-plastered, flat-roofed concrete-and-brick volumes are the ones that made the Sunila housing famous, the project also included a series of single-family, hip-roofed, standardized wood houses (figure 8). This solution for company housing, which was

simultaneously tested in Varkaus by Ahlström, was to have far-reaching consequences once it was developed further for serial production in the early 1940s.

The free-form distribution of buildings without any attention to axiality, geometrizing, or normative city-planning devices has justly been appreciated as an innovative solution, a forerunner of the so-called forest suburbs of postwar Finland. Nevertheless, it should be remembered that the many villa towns designed in pre–World War I Finland applied similar planning methods.[23] Attention should also be paid to the fact that the Sunila units were served by a central heating plant, which certainly affected the layout of the whole.[24] But what interests us here is the "industrial" character of the whole and how, if at all, it renewed the long tradition of designing single-company industrial communities in Finland.

Sunila is mainly nonhierarchical in the traditional sense; there is no clear division of the upper and lower strata of the work force in the form of fences, parks, or other evident instruments of the social ordering of space. Still, the heating plant, around which the plan rotates, divides the whole. The houses for the director (figure 9) and the engineers (plates 118–119) were placed advantageously by the sea, with access to the beach. Aalto was to repeat this in his plan for Kauttua in 1943, where the dwellings of the upper strata of employees were on the lakeshore. The director's residence is not overtly opulent, but it is the only one that is separated from the rest with a fence. (It should be noted that the local director in Sunila was a representative of managerial capitalism and not the owner of the production facilities, as at traditional single-company communities, but a paid director obeying the rules laid down by the actual owners.) The level of privacy given at the various strata of the hierarchy also acts as a subtle social divider, beginning with the director's isolation and the fenced gardens of the engineers' row houses, proceeding down to the balconies in the slope houses, and finally to the workers' housing where the common yard and the forest were enough.

In Sunila, as later in a more modest way in Kauttua, Aalto was able to maintain the continuity of the terrain without fences cutting off separate lots. This visual and spatial unity apparently stressing an equal, democratic right to the grounds was made possible precisely through the hegemony the company had over the whole. With a single owner, no property division was needed. Sunila certainly represented a new concept of a company housing area: by implementing enough segregation to please the owners and the upper levels of the local hierarchy, Aalto was able to introduce several innovative solutions regarding both his own development and the future of Finnish industrial communities in general. The progressive role of modern industry, integrated with an equally modern manifestation of its built infrastructure, epitomized the idea of industry as the beacon of enlightenment that Gullichsen and Aalto shared.

The experiences gained in the design "laboratory" at Sunila were immediately put to use at Kauttua, an Ahlström site, located in the southwestern part of the country (plates 120–124). The production volume and hence the work force of the existing paper factory there were growing rapidly, and the situation called for housing policies similar to those at Sunila. The result was the town plan of 1938, of which only a fragment— one building—was realized in the 1930s. Here the situation differed from Sunila in that the community already had layers of buildings dating back to the eighteenth century.[25] Aalto's scheme left the old core untouched and utilized the unusual drama of the local terrain by placing the required group of houses on a steep hill, overlooking the river valley of the site and the factory.[26]

The Kauttua building program, with many alternative sketches, was ambitious, utilizing the row-shaped slope houses of Sunila, terraced houses (of which one was built), and a huge multistory block at the crest of the hill (figure 10). The social program included a school, a "neighborhood center," and a public sauna. The aspirations for *Licht, Luft, und Sonne* imbedded in the reform program of modernism could be maximized because of favorable natural conditions. Here Gullichsen offered a field where Aalto could test solutions meant to be examples for the future building program of the whole corporation at its various production sites.[27] During these years, terms such as *laboratory* and *research* begin to appear with growing frequency in Aalto's texts, which also stressed biological and psychological factors. Even though the actual architecture in Kauttua, as demonstrated by the four-story "house without stairs," stands visually in stark contrast to surrounding nature, it had become increasingly vital for Aalto to integrate his design with the given topography and vegetation.[28]

In the Kauttua plan the need for housing was concentrated on the middle strata of the work force. The local director already had his secluded residence, and workers' housing is not indicated in the 1938 plan.

9. Alvar Aalto. Sunila Pulp Mill and Housing, Kotka, Finland. 1936–38. Director's house

10. Alvar Aalto. Standard Terrace Housing, Kauttua, Finland. 1937–38

The roomy terraces of the stepped house were intended for office workers and mid-level engineers, not for the socially opposite poles of the community. Regarding the planning principles of the whole, the situation was simpler than in Sunila owing to the already existing infrastructure of services and natural demands of the topography. At any rate, the scheme was a serious investment in the possibilities of modern architecture to solve the problems of building in industrial communities. And, of course, according to the views of both Gullichsen and Aalto, the ideas realized through a private venture would then radiate into society at large. The outbreak of the Winter War in 1939 halted realization of the 1938 Kauttua plan (plate 122), and when Ahlström again required Aalto's services in Kauttua a few years later in 1943 the building program had taken an altogether new direction. No more terraced houses with costly concrete frames and foundations were built, only the small and light single-family wood houses that were developed in Varkaus simultaneously with the Kauttua experiment (plate 170).

Ahlström had its largest industrial complex—sawmill, sulphate cellulose plant, and paper factory—at Varkaus, in eastern Finland near the great lakes and with access to the sea via a channel system. Concurrently with the planning of Sunila, Aalto was asked in 1936 to enlarge the plan of the city. Varkaus differed significantly from Sunila and Kauttua in its size and clearly urban character. It was a company town but at the same time an urban center for the surrounding countryside. It already had a grandiose plan, from the second decade of the century, built on classical axiality and elaborated further during the 1920s. Aalto took the axiality as his starting point and highlighted the urban character of the city center with a mixed-use complex, serving more than just the needs of local industry.[29] New suburban areas were planned with individual lots, to be built with single-family wood houses based on standardized types drawn up by Aalto (figure 11). This was the start of the most intimate relationship Aalto was ever to have with serial industrial production and standardization in architecture, making these rather modest examples of company housing of great importance nationally when compared with the bold but limited gestures at Sunila and Kauttua.

The traditional system of building in wood in Finland, applied in both agrarian and urban contexts, was based on the solid timber wall of horizontal logs with outer clapboarding to allow for architectural character. For reasons of climate, the abundance of forests, and the cost of labor, this technique was not seriously challenged before the 1930s. From then on the solid wall became increasingly supplanted by a frame construction of pre-sawn lumber. The forestry industry had by then developed insulation materials that made the frame house viable in the harsh climate of the country.[30] Along with this, both the state authorities and private enterprise began to regard typification and standardization as tools for solving the problems of housing: the state's concern was focused on the countryside, and industry had an acute need for cost-efficient housing in its own communities.[31]

11. Alvar Aalto. Standard A-House, Varkaus, Finland. 1937

For the newly planned districts in Varkaus a simple, low-cost frame house with a hip roof and horizontal boarding was designed. The first of these were erected simultaneously with the ones in Sunila in 1937. Ahlström or, if not the company board, at least Maire and Harry Gullichsen wanted to raise the standard of workers' housing by providing lots and type drawings in order for modern architecture to meet the masses and in a very tangible form: the workers would build their homes themselves, using the lumber and designs provided by the local sawmill. Only a few Aalto type houses were erected at this stage. Our point here is the interaction of the industrialist, the production facilities providing the building material, the local needs, a closed marketing system, and finally the role of the architect: Aalto, turning toward the core unit of habitation, the single-family shell, and wood, the most traditional material of the foremost national industry.

Although the focus here is on the A. Ahlström Corporation and the association with Gullichsen, Aalto worked for other major companies as well. For instance, Tampella used him extensively at Anjala and Inkeroinen in the Kymijoki River area. The commissions ranged from the elevations of a 300-meter-long paper mill, finished in 1938 (see figure 5), to town

12. Alvar Aalto. Anjala Paper
Mill, Inkeroinen, Finland.
1937–38. Chief engineer's house

planning and housing for various professional groups in Inkeroinen. Even
though the buildings as such are of interest and merit, this relationship differed fundamentally from the one with Ahlström. The Tampella company
directors did not envision modernist or social utopias but simply had a
need for housing in order to attract and maintain a qualified work force. It
remains to be argued if this is one of the reasons behind the altogether different outer character of the hipped-roof Inkeroinen houses for the chief
engineer (figure 12), engineers, and foremen, which were conceived
simultaneously with the modern stepped housing of the Kauttua project.

In addition to the instances discussed here, Ahlström had use for
Aalto elsewhere, such as its Karhula glassworks, and especially in designing
the ideal private environment for the couple whose faith in modernization
at all levels of human life also supported Aalto: the Gullichsens' home,
Villa Mairea, in Noormarkku (plates 155–169). Although this most intimate and lavish testimony to the patronage of modernism and of the ideal
interaction between architect and client certainly belongs to the subject of
building for industry, I will omit a detailed description of it here, as so
much has already been written about it. But to relate it to the simultaneous, modest single-family homes in Varkaus at the other end of the
corporate hierarchy, I would like to stress the manifesto-like character of
Villa Mairea as a profound statement of the Finnish industrial elite, which
demarcated the attitudes of the older and younger generations within
Finnish industry by expressing the internationalism and modernity of the
new, technocratic group of decision makers. The merits of the house itself
match in importance its symbolic modernist character.

As of the critical year 1939, there can be no doubt about the fact
that Aalto, more than any of his Finnish colleagues, had succeeded in

implementing both the ideological and formal aspects of modernism,
aided significantly by large-scale industry and, more precisely, the patronage of the Ahlström company and the Gullichsens. As a national figure,
Gullichsen had also been instrumental in securing commissions from other
companies for Aalto. The boom years of the late 1930s and the role of the
forestry industries in their making were brilliantly manifested in the
Finnish Pavilion at the New York World's Fair of 1938–39. In the pavilion (plates 145–154), the triumphant Aalto stressed the role of the forests
in the culture and national economy of Finland.[32] However, soon the cur-
tain fell tragically before these national and personal successes. First the
Winter War of 1939–40, then the Continuation War of 1941–44, and
finally the Lapland War in 1945 exhausted the Finnish nation to its limits.[33] The war and postwar years were a time of scarcity and pressing social
and economic conditions. The close links between Aalto and industry,
and with the Gullichsens, saved his practice during this period, kept his
office working, and prevented his own mobilization at the front.

Technology and Standardized Housing

Aalto was one of the most prolific writers among modern architects in
Finland, especially from the mid-1930s to the late 1940s,[34] a time of particular interest with regard to the interaction of Aalto, the national war
economy, and the private industrial sector. His own statements on the role
of technology and industrial production in architectural design and actual
construction followed in the vein of modernist rhetoric of the late 1920s,
with its idioms of rationalism, standardization, and industrial production.
Nordic functionalism was strongly linked to German developments.
Historically, it had been Germany that had provided Finland with technological and architectural know-how. Quite soon Aalto began to distance
himself from both German rationalism and the increasingly doctrinaire
statements of CIAM.[35] Simultaneously, he became aware of the British
cultural climate, which leaned toward empiricism, and, in the last years of
the 1930s, of American writers on culture and architecture, such as Lewis
Mumford.[36] This marked a difference from the German idolatry of the
engineering approach, which had been dominant in the new German
architecture around 1930. Analogies with the machine became increasingly
supplanted by psychological and later by biological aspects, which became
even more important. The needs of man, the shelter surrounding him, the

placing of these in the landscape, and design and production parameters guiding this process are evident in Aalto's writings of the late 1930s. His views on the processes of natural variation gradually developed into analogous ideas in architecture. The ambiguous term *organic* became one of the core concepts by which Aalto explained his biomorphic principles concerning the larger environment, the allotment of functional categories in large-scale planning, and on the human and personal level as related to the design of the individual home and its artifacts.

Aalto did not regard variation and organicism as antithetical to modern technology and the industries implementing its innovations. Where the analogy of Fordism had excited the early modernists, Aalto included, it was now the next stage of "humanizing technology" that would make modern industry the true servant of man.

This brought Aalto to the key issue of standardization, which had been one of his main areas of interest from the beginning of his conversion to modernism. His work with industry and his thorough knowledge of wood-based factory processes had given him practical insight into serial production. In furniture design, he had already tested the problems of types and their variations, but he was interested in figuring out how industrial production, based on types and standards, could encompass psychological and formal richness, flexibility and variation, instead of a homogenization. Aalto had elaborated these issues in a lecture delivered in conjunction with his exhibition at The Museum of Modern Art in New York in 1938, and in the lectures at Yale University in the spring of 1939, which included the topics "humanizing architecture" and "humanizing standardization."[37]

In the early 1940s Aalto found a chance to test his ideas in both the private and public spheres.[38] Ironically, it was war that provided the ideal environment for his humanist experiments. Aalto's efforts in reconstruction through architecture had two main phases. The first covered the period during and after the Winter War, between 1940 and 1941, before the next war broke out; the second, on a broader scale and with deeper consequences, reached its peak in 1942–43. After this Aalto withdrew into the background and let others continue the work he had been instrumental in initiating. All of this coincided with the first of his two stints as a professor at the Massachusetts Institute of Technology (MIT) in Cambridge, Massachusetts, in 1940 and with his deep involvement in the launching of house manufacturing on an industrial scale by the A. Ahlström Corporation. These activities are inextricably interwoven, and it is clear that in many ways Aalto acted as prime mover in the integration of domestic and international variables to devise strategies for housing in a worldwide crisis economy.[39]

The devastating results of the scorched-earth policy on the building stock of his country (figure 13) led Aalto to produce plans of strategic dimensions for the coming reconstruction in housing. The Finnish Winter War of 1939–40 was, like the Spanish Civil War a year earlier, one in

which massive air raids against the infrastructure of the country and the civilian population were used to break down operations and morale. Large cities with strategic production facilities suffered greatly, as did the territories at the front and the eastern border. The peace treaty shifted the eastern border significantly to the west, and the population of the ceded territory was evacuated to Finland. Thus, the acute need for housing in spring 1940 was caused both by bombing and relocation. The core unit was to be the single-family wood house, serving both the countryside and the semi-urban areas. According to Aalto, reconstruction in Finland would be an experimental laboratory, where architectural research could be carried out in actual practice. Aalto had stressed the importance of research, in conjunction with industrial production methods, with growing frequency in the years immediately before the war. In the summer of 1939, during the New York World's Fair, he gave a talk in New York in which he stressed the urgency of an "International Institute of Architectural Research." This reflected the ideas voiced in an informal meeting at the office of the American architect William W. Wurster in Berkeley, California, a few weeks earlier, where Aalto suggested Finland as the location for a "small institute for research on [the] small wooden house."[40] To convince those present, he stated: "Modern architecture [is] becoming [a] fad in Finland. Businessmen find it pays."[41] Again in the United States in March 1940, he returned to the same issue on several occasions, directing his mission straight to eventual funding and educational resources, the Rockefeller Foundation and MIT.

A May 1940 memorandum by Aalto suggests a research laboratory at MIT, with this remark included: "Research as an important instrument in education can be carried on only in direct connection with real life."[42] Aalto indicated here the use of Finnish reconstruction as an international laboratory, the results of which could have global significance in meeting

13. Ruins of a village in eastern Finland destroyed in the Winter War, 1940

the housing problems caused by wars or natural catastrophes. The concrete formulation of this was his program for "An American Town in Finland" of 1940 (figure 14). This scheme was not just a visionary idea but a surprisingly careful and detailed working program, in which the types and amount of buildings together with the division of land were specified and included cost estimates. Here industrial house production would be of central importance.[43] The Rockefellers, with whom Aalto had a positive relationship, were on the verge of backing this project, with humanitarian goals extending beyond the example to be built in Finland.[44] A consortium was established to carry the project further, interacting with a charitable organization called "For Finland." Aalto also approached eminent American industrialists, such as Henry Ford, with his booklet on reconstruction and the experimental model town.[45] While this was in preparation, Aalto was appointed a research professor at the Albert Farwell Bemis Foundation of MIT. This foundation was the center for expertise in the rational development of low-cost housing units for single families. Prefabrication in wood was regarded as the most viable technical solution. Aalto, of course, had abundant experience in the problems of the modern usage of wood and of housing type planning through his collaboration with Ahlström. In September 1940, the "Working Program for Division of Architectural Research at MIT" took the small, single-family wood house as its prime subject for investigation. At this point, Aalto's tenure at MIT had only a couple of months more to go, but he had gained firsthand insight into the problems of industrial prefabrication in the country where this sector of industry was already of real significance. With this knowledge, he returned to Finland to implement house production at the Ahlström sawmill in Varkaus using the latest methods. Even though the role of individuals should not be overly stressed in a web of interactions of a technological, economic, and cultural nature, such as the relationship of American production technology and Finnish conditions in 1940, Aalto can with good reason be regarded as the single most important vehicle for the transfer of innovation at a moment when dire need was met with appropriate expertise.

Before he tackled the problems of serial house production on a significant scale, Aalto already had experience of the partial prefabrication of housing and the design of industrially produced objects. An early commission, the Tapani Standard Apartment Block in Turku of 1927–29 (page 27), had been an attempt to follow the Continental practices of achieving efficiency in the process of building by using precast concrete elements.[46] In 1934 Aalto proposed for the forestry-based Enso-Gutzeit Corporation a series of experimental houses where the concrete frame would be filled in with prefabricated, insulated wood panels.[47] In terms of industrially produced objects, Aalto had worked from 1928 on with the factory of Otto Korhonen, Huonekalu- ja Rakennustyötehdas Oy [Furniture and Construction Factory, Ltd.], on a highly successful line of furniture in curved laminated wood and plywood.[48] This "Aalto line" formed the nucleus of the Artek marketing organization, founded in 1935.

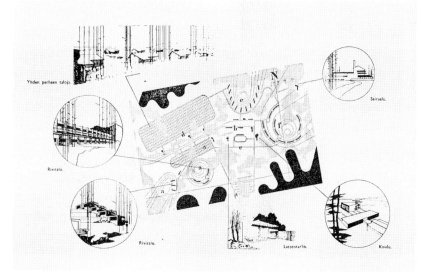

14. Alvar Aalto. "An American Town in Finland." Project, 1940

In 1937 Aalto's wood type houses were made for the A. Ahlström Corporation, which had access to its own forest resources, transport systems, and sawmills. An immediate market was created by the work force at the corporation's various locations. The houses would either be erected and offered for use or could be built by the workers themselves from the set of elements delivered by the factory at a low price (figure 15). This basically answered the problem of company housing for Ahlström, and was preferred to the costly and topography-bound solutions tried out in Kauttua. As a logical extension of the project, it was felt that the houses could also be aimed at the open market. All that was needed was a link between on-site erection based on type drawings and serial production, thus ensuring rapidity and the lowest cost possible. The Ahlström-owned Varkaus housing factory, based on the idea of industrial prefabrication, started operations in 1940.[49]

The launching of this new production line within a company already making a multitude of forest-based items and materials was preceded by careful calculations of the costs, estimates of raw-material flow, and testing of the performance of the wall panels. The National Laboratories of Materials Testing were consulted to achieve optimum endurance with minimum cost. The factory started by producing a few models Aalto had designed before his experience at MIT.[50] Upon his return to Finland, Aalto was put in charge of the whole enterprise. This signified the reorganization of production and especially of a selection of housing components with a wide range of internal variables. The result was known as the AA-System (*AA-järjestelmä*), a broad and flexible array of types serving as

15. Construction of a standard wood A-House. 1940

the basis for those actually produced under the brand name, A-House (*A-talo*) (plates 170–171).[51]

The actual output of the housing factory can be compared with the detailed, partly programmatic, and partly practical memorandum Aalto wrote for the revised working scheme of the factory.[52] This document started with a critique of the Fordism analogy of replication and proceeds to point out the errors made in the United States, for example, by the Gunnison House Company.[53] After stressing the biologically diverse tasks of a house, he concluded that the production of houses should not be based on centralized standardization but exactly the opposite: it should not strive toward a certain type but toward an opposite of unlimited richness in forms and functions. This could be achieved through so-called flexible standardization. According to him, this required a system broad enough from the outset to allow for a multitude of combinations from a limited set of prefabricated panels. Aalto referred to the experiences he had gained at MIT and stressed that the conceptual basis of the system is its most important aspect. Houses of different volume and shape could then result from the specific requirements of the client.[54]

Even if the production of houses for the work force and the open market satisfied the industrialists, this was too narrow a vision for Aalto. He proposed that an experimental area be built with a large selection of all the possible combinations of elements in the system. This would serve as a laboratory, an open-air testing ground for long-term research based on documentation of the changes in the usage and endurance of the buildings. This Finland-based proposal did not materialize. And, in spite of initially positive reactions among the American sponsors of the "American Town in Finland" plan, the scheme remained unrealized. The financial backing anticipated by Aalto ultimately was not forthcoming; what had seemed possible in 1940 was curbed by the changes in the geopolitical status of Finland in a world on the threshold of global war.[55]

Although Aalto's seminal role in reconstruction work during the

Continuation War of 1941–44 does not directly belong to the sphere of relationships with industry, it was tangential to it. When the new war broke out Aalto began to evoke initiatives within his profession regarding the role architects should have in coordinating the reconstruction of the territories regained from the Soviet Union. Accordingly, a Reconstruction Bureau managed by the Finnish Association of Architects was formed in 1942 to direct the planning and building of damaged territories. This was an important strategic move for the whole profession: the architectural office worked directly under the national office for the war economy. This ensured for architects an important role in the many tasks of reconstruction during and immediately after the war. In the beginning, Aalto directed the work and was able to arrange the return of two of his former office architects, Aarne Ervi and Viljo Revell, from the front to serve the bureau.[56] In housing design, reconstruction aid focused on type drawings for single-family wood houses. A factor that was to have far-reaching consequences for the whole development of Finnish architecture after the war was the Standardization Institute which worked as a unit in the Reconstruction Bureau. Even though the immediate reason for a rapid start for standardization was to be found in crisis, the idea from the beginning was that this activity would lead to an overall standardization of Finnish building after the war. Under these exceptional circumstances, Aalto was able to achieve something that he had not succeeded in doing with private industry, the implementation of a nationwide program of flexible standardization.[57]

The war had halted virtually all private construction in Finland, and most architects served at the front, in the war cabinet, or in the Reconstruction Bureau. But in Aalto's office, a steady flow of commissions from industry ensured continuous activity, now maintained overwhelmingly by women architects. That women served as architects was not unusual, as Finland was one of the first countries in the world to train women architects and had a strong tradition of independent women architects with their own offices (as well as those together with men). Aino Aalto is a good example. During the war the role of women increased in Aalto's office and elsewhere. This was typical of all levels of production in Finland: women were employed in large numbers in factories, and they even took care of anti-aircraft artillery installations. The multitude of commissions was possible because industries were needed in the war effort; both Ahlström and Tampella belonged to this area. Ahlström actually expanded during the war; for example, in Kauttua this led to the building of a whole new district with A-House Standard Houses and several distinctive projects, designed according to a new enlarged plan for the community prepared by Aalto in 1943.

Paradoxically, it was the war and the industrial production of paper-based substitute products for the German *Wehrmacht* that caused an expansion in the work force and thus ensured work for Aalto's office. In a wartime letter to the officials at the War Industries Department, Aalto listed six major companies using his services at that time, many of them at several locations, such as Ahlström.[58] In many ways, the relationship with the Gullichsens still supported Aalto. Harry Gullichsen had been in a central position when the Winter War reconstruction schemes were made, and during the next phase he belonged to the strategic core of decision makers of the war economy.[59] After the war, industry again provided Aalto with work, even though the projects were not of the same grand scale as before the war.

The Postwar Industrial Recovery

The armistice with the Soviet Union in 1944 and finally the end of World War II in 1945 did not engender a long-awaited flourishing of Finnish architecture. Wartime restrictions remained in force, and private as well as public construction picked up slowly. Industry again dominated and was given exceptional benefits in the recovery period. The postwar years brought an expansion and broadening of the capacity of Finnish factory production (figure 16). The country had to pay war reparations to the Soviet Union, mainly through forest-based industrial products but also from the heavy-metal and electrical industries. This also signified a shift in Aalto's client base.[60]

Aalto's fruitful collaboration with Ahlström became less important in the mid-1940s, but his contacts with the Tampella mechanical works and the Strömberg Corporation electrical-engineering works rose in significance. These companies expanded rapidly because of war-reparation deliveries and needed buildings for production and for their workers.[61] These commissions resulted in housing clusters at several locations—Helsinki, Tampere, and Vaasa—but none of them bore the same imprint of a commitment to values and ideas beyond the ordinary, as had those before the war. Only in Vaasa, in the Strömberg housing area with its two-story wood row houses of 1945–46, did Aalto elaborate on the conceptual basis of the whole (figure 17).[62] This was understandable in the aftermath of the war and amid hectic expansion activity, but it also signified a profound change in the relationship between Aalto and industry, as he became increasingly critical of modern technological systems in the use of mass production. His postwar experiences in the United States fortified these tendencies.[63] Aalto's enthusiasm before the war turned into criticism of the materialism of postwar America, where unforeseen prosperity resulted in material abundance but little cultural or individual distinction. What had been a dynamic force for renewal in the 1930s now appeared as an overriding homogenizer. Aalto shared the postwar Existentialist pessimism about technology commonly felt in Europe. Also his personal development, career, and age affected this. He was now in his fifties, the banner of enthusiasm for technology was left for the younger generation of architects, such as Aarne Ervi and Viljo Revell.

A further and important factor for the diminishing significance of industrial commissions in the profile of Aalto's office was the recovery of the public sector in Finland in the late 1940s. The time had come for

16. Alvar Aalto. Sawmill, Varkaus, Finland. 1944–45 (demolished)

17. Alvar Aalto. Workers' Row Houses, Vaasa, Finland. 1945–46

municipalities to erect town halls (Säynätsalo Town Hall of 1948–52), for the state to invest in higher education (Helsinki University of Technology, Espoo [Otaniemi], of 1949–66), and for public organizations to erect office buildings (National Pensions Institute, Helsinki, of 1948–57). It was in projects of this kind that Aalto's ambition was now invested (plates 196–214, 240–276). Simultaneously, with the conscious construction of the welfare state in Finland, the public sector became seriously committed to the problems of housing, which diminished the previous responsibilities of industry in this category of building. Both the state and individual municipalities made serious legislative and organizational efforts to bring decent housing within the reach of all. Prices, rents, and bank-loan interest rates were monitored to assure aid to new construction and prevent speculation.

Nevertheless, after the war, there was one company with which Aalto had a more profound relationship that ensured him commissions ranging from the design of the interiors of ocean liners to regional plans. Enso-Gutzeit was a state-owned enterprise based on the forestry industries with which Aalto had already been in contact in 1932, participating in a competition for a weekend cottage, and again in 1934, when proposing the previously cited experimental building with wood panels. In addition to the undisputed expertise Aalto had gained in industrial commissions, there was a subjective reason behind the relationship with the company. From 1945, the director of Enso-Gutzeit was Aalto's former schoolmate, William Lehtinen, who was on the jury of the 1932 weekend cottage competition and was involved, as his country's consul general, in realizing the Finnish Pavilion at the New York World's Fair in 1939.[64] Lehtinen channeled projects to Aalto from the early 1950s until his retirement in 1962 and was able to crown his own career with the Enso-Gutzeit corporate headquarters of 1959–62 by Aalto in Carrara marble on the Helsinki waterfront (figures 18 and 19).

The projects for the company started with an annex to a paper mill in Kotka in 1951 and continued with a production unit of similar nature in Summa, near Kotka, in the industrial region where Sunila and Inkeroinen were also located. The Summa project came to include a carefully conceptualized, ambitious Master Plan for Industrial Community of 1954 (plate 290) with housing for officials and workers in the later years of the decade: of these the site manager's residence is an interesting counterpart to the one at Sunila executed over twenty years previously. It is functionally and hierarchically identical to the one in Sunila but formally altogether different, echoing the approach Aalto used at the Maison Carré in Bazoches-sur-Guyonne, France, of 1956–59 (plates 307–314). As in Sunila, Aalto was here able to plan on virgin ground, and the comparison of these two community plans testifies to the changed role of traffic systems, among other things. In Summa the housing is strictly apart from the main arteries; a system of pedestrian walkways through nature ensures an individual sheltered access to the work place.[65] But, even given the quality of the Summa project and the great quantity of factories, hydroelectric plants, housing, country clubs, and offices Aalto designed for for Enso-Gutzeit, these still do not measure up to the project of largest consequence commissioned by Lehtinen: the Imatra Master Plan of 1947–53 (plate 289).

In order to understand it, we must return to the earlier collaboration of Aalto and Gullichsen in 1940–41. The Kokemäenjoki River is a major water course leading to the coast of the Gulf of Bothnia where the port city of Pori was the major industrial center, as the delta of the Kymijoki River, where Sunila is located, was on the south coast. The Ahlström company, which had forest resources by the river and a major sawmill on the coast, in addition to investments in industry in Pori, had an interest in

18. The Enso-Gutzeit board of directors, with William Lehtinen (third from left) and Alvar Aalto (third from right), reviewing the design for their new headquarters, 1959

19. Alvar Aalto. Enso-Gutzeit Corporation Headquarters, Helsinki. 1959–62

rationalizing communication, future land use, and production along the river to form an integrated route from raw materials to shipping. In 1940 Gullichsen was able to persuade the agrarian districts and the city of Pori to join in this venture of creating a regional plan, comprising the territories of several municipalities. Gullichsen's double strategy linked the benefits of private industry with those of society. In Finland there was no tradition for planning on this scale, and naturally the question of the proper expertise for the task arose. Not surprisingly, Gullichsen requested Aalto to be the expert professional to realize the scheme. Aalto, in turn, had a strong interest in the nature of the project. This regional plan came to him at a time when he was addressing the problems of reconstruction and spoke for the legitimate right of architects to decide large-scale questions of land use, the division of agrarian, urban, and industrial areas, and the distribution of building. Thus, the Kokemäenjoki River Valley Regional Plan could be used to prove the capabilities the profession in this field (figure 20).[66]

An unpublished background statement for the Kokemäenjoki River Valley Regional Plan by Aalto, of 1940, offers a glimpse of his ideas on future Finnish urbanism. According to him, plans like the Kokemäenjoki would enrich the rural areas with small-scale industries, and thus the boundary between cities and farmland would be partly dissolved. At the same time, Aalto envisioned the fragmentation of the existing cities, their peripheries becoming a synthesis of nature and habitation. In this way, the country would have an "organic," interwoven structure of communities, industry, farming, transportation routes, and untouched nature. The character of the Finnish forestry industries' interaction with surrounding rural society had already pointed Aalto in this direction. The plan was received with great interest by the press and was published thoroughly in the journal *Arkkitehti*. When it was launched in Helsinki, the president of Finland was there along with leading politicians and industrialists. After the experiences and successes of the Kokemäenjoki River Valley Regional Plan, Aalto was asked in 1942 to act in a similar vein in connection with the Kymijoki River area, probably the most vital industrial river route of the country, with several of the major companies we have already seen as commissioning parties for Aalto's services.[67]

The Imatra Master Plan, a decade later, gave Aalto a chance to work on the largest possible scale. The commission, initiated by Lehtinen and funded by Enso-Gutzeit, had its background in the changes that the war had made to the country's eastern border. Before the war, the Vuoksi River basin had been one of the most densely concentrated areas of industry, the "Ruhr of Finland," with hydroelectric power plants and large production facilities at Kaukopää and Enso, owned by Enso-Gutzeit. In dictating the new border in 1944, Stalin was careful in ensuring that all the modern plants, excluding Kaukopää, came to the Soviet side. This called for a serious restructuring of industry and the communities serving it along the Upper Vuoksi area still belonging to Finland. As in the Kokemäenjoki River Valley Regional Plan, a major corporation wanted to maximize its

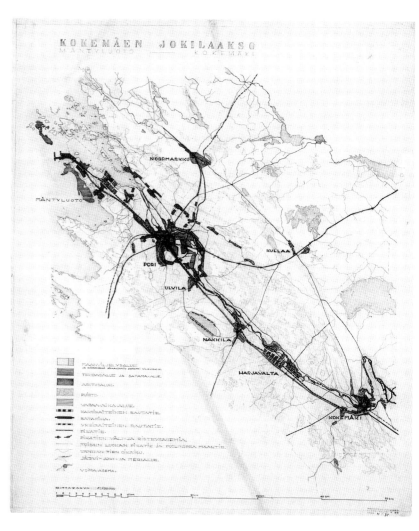

20. Alvar Aalto. Kokemäenjoki River Valley Regional Plan, Kokemäenjoki River Valley, Finland. Project, 1940–41. Alvar Aalto Foundation, Helsinki

production but needed the cooperation and integration of the surrounding communities. The result was a master plan where several communities were united under one municipality running nearly twenty miles north-south and some ten miles east-west. Most of the inhabitants were to depend directly or indirectly on the heavy industry of Enso-Gutzeit. In addition, Aalto affected the daily life of the local inhabitants through his Church of the Three Crosses in Vuoksenniska, Imatra, of 1955–58 (plates 291–306). In a way, the result was a company town of monumental scale but with the appearance of scattered communities in forest and park land. Aalto had seen the fusion of the urban, industrial, agrarian, and natural as the future for Finnish habitation when outlining the Kokemäenjoki River Valley Regional Plan in 1940. This had now become reality to a certain degree. In the preface of the 1953 publication presenting the Imatra plan, Lehtinen concluded that all the planning devices in the scheme, enriching the well-being of the people and making their daily lives as smooth as possible would result "in a harmonious, pleasant whole and via this also in the growing efficiency of the productive sector."[68]

Conclusion

In focusing on Aalto's role in Finnish industry within the context of broader issues, the perspective is easily misunderstood with regard to the architectural profession as a whole because his role was by any standard—Finnish or international—atypical. Of course, other Finnish architects profited from the industrial boom of the 1930s as well as from the postwar reconstruction.[69] But Aalto was exceptional in the way in which he was able to formulate his visions through the maze of technology, industry, and politics, and integrate them for the societal and cultural advancement of the nation. To a certain extent it can be claimed that a cultural aura was given to rather pragmatic forces of productivity. But this cannot be said of the programs regarding industry's role in reconstruction and in regional plans, for here the verbalizations had a real importance that matched the quality and significance of the actual designs. Aalto also had sheer good luck, for example, in his relationship with the Gullichsens and in his connections in the United States. These were crucial to the reconstruction effort in the postwar period and in forming the artistic and intellectual foundations of the standard housing systems. Also exceptional was his ability to remain free from active service during the war and to maintain his contacts with the Finnish national and industrial decision-making apparatus throughout the war. This ensured a continuing office practice. And, of course, the whole process by which Aalto reached this position was rare, even in a country where architects traditionally enjoyed a high social and cultural status.

But Aalto's professional activity had a dual character; it was both singular and communal. Being a master in manipulating and convincing people, he ensured for himself all the benefits that collaboration with big business can bring to an architect. This would not have been possible without a high level of professional expertise, and Aalto was always able to meet the risks he spurred his clients to take. But Aalto was also a spokesman for the concerns of the Finnish architectural profession. His strategy with regard to the regional plans, reconstruction, and industrial housing manufacture was always aimed at strengthening the mandate of his colleagues in determining the country's planned and built infrastructure. Thus, his links with industry also consolidated and widened the scope of operations for other architects. This also occurred on a formal level: his ability to implement a modernist vocabulary in projects such as Sunila, Kauttua, Villa Mairea, and elsewhere gave prominent status to the builders and respectability to the modernist idiom.

Aalto's initial success with Finnish industry had begun at a rather grim moment for international modernism, which had seemed triumphant only a couple of years earlier. It suffices to remember the fate of modernism in Germany from the closing of the Bauhaus in 1933, the bleak opportunities of the modern masters (Ludwig Mies van der Rohe, Walter Gropius, László Moholy-Nagy, and Eric Mendelsohn) before their exodus to the United States, the demise of modernism in the Soviet Union, and the dashed hopes of architects there, such as Ernst May and Hannes Meyer.[70] Not many of Le Corbusier's designs were realized, and the few modernists in Britain could only dream of the opportunities being offered to Aalto.

Aalto's unique opportunities for fulfilling the much-awaited goal of unifying modern architecture with modern industrial production were far greater than those of any of his modernist colleagues in other countries, especially during the war. Much space to operate was given to him by the powers that decided on the politics of cultural production. Of course, this assessment of Aalto's position depends on what is meant here by the unification of modern architecture with industrial production, the outward modernity of buildings or the process of fabricating them. In the first case, it is evident that Aalto was highly successful in formal terms. By comparison, Le Corbusier had only a partial chance to realize the ideas expounded in his voluminous writings on industrial building—at Pessac in 1924—but otherwise he searched in vain for an important industrialist fully committed to his cause.[71] In Germany, it was the municipalities of the 1920s, not industry, that favored the modern idiom. In the Soviet Union, state-sponsored modernism and industrialism flourished together for only a brief moment, with the erection of the new industrial communities in the 1920s. At other locations, some one-company industrial towns applied a modernist approach, as demonstrated in the case of the Bata factory community in Szlin, then in Czechoslovakia.[72] But in the 1930s it was the Nordic countries, their industries and public sectors, that commissioned functionalism on a broad scale. In this way, Aalto and his Scandinavian colleagues were able to work according to the modernist principles adopted in the late 1920s without totalitarian interruptions. Nevertheless, even within this context, Aalto was an exception, owing, as we have seen, to the wealth of opportunities open to him through his connection with Harry Gullichsen.

Concerning the methods and techniques of production with regard to the projects discussed here, it can be stated that Aalto always kept abreast of the newest methods of construction and applied the concrete frame with success, as in the Kauttua stepped houses; the Tapani block and the Enso experimental houses were attempts to utilize industrially produced components for on-site construction. But it was in the conceptualization, production, distribution, and erection of the modest wood A-House Standard Houses that serial factory production was properly applied. The outer appearance of these houses was a mixture of modernist and traditional elements. But it was their nature as industrially produced goods for anonymous consumers that made their conceptualization akin to product design,

such as that of furniture. In designing generic houses, the architect was neither concerned with a specific client nor with a certain lot with distinct
topography. They were intended to work as solutions for housing that
could be transported to any location where a demand for the product was
found. In Finland in the early 1940s these houses were rather radical, but
they were not so in a Scandinavian, Continental, or American context as
far as their mode of production was concerned. But as designs by a leading
modernist with a profound architectural and technological program as their
basis, the AA-System and the A-House were rare examples of the triumphant unity of modernism and industrial production. By comparison,
the failure of the ambitious project for a modernist prefabricated house
involving Walter Gropius and Konrad Wachsmann in the United States at
the same time as Aalto was elaborating his AA-System poses an interesting
lesson.[73] The AA-System, more than any other project, demonstrated how
variables involving architecture, social issues, national resources for production, and modes of production themselves gained momentum in Finland
around 1940 and how Aalto, together with the industrialists, was among
the first to take advantage of this extraordinary circumstance.[74]

In conclusion, it seems appropriate to allow Aalto himself to express
how he perceived Finnish, if not international, industrial architecture, on
which he made a lasting impression. In 1951, when postwar austerity was
about to turn into prosperity and when Aalto himself began to concentrate
on issues other than those of an industrial character, he wrote: "This living
interest in architecture found among our industries is an exceptional phenomenon where even the leading industrial countries lag behind
Finland.... It has given such a field of work for our architects that it is to
be envied by colleagues elsewhere. Along with developing their production facilities, our industries have offered the indisputably best field of
experimentation within housing in our country, hereby demonstrating a
growing concern for social issues linked to increasing actual production."[75]

Notes

1. Göran Schildt, *Alvar Aalto: The Early Years,* trans. Timothy Binham (New York: Rizzoli, 1984); idem, *Alvar Aalto: The Decisive Years,* trans. Timothy Binham (New York: Rizzoli, 1986); idem, *Alvar Aalto: The Mature Years,* trans. Timothy Binham (New York: Rizzoli, 1991); and idem, *Alvar Aalto: The Complete Catalogue of Architecture, Design and Art,* trans. Timothy Binham (New York: Rizzoli, 1994). The bibliographical notes in this last volume give an overview of previous Aalto writing. See also William C. Miller, *Alvar Aalto: An Annotated Bibliography* (New York: Garland Publishing, 1984), which also covers articles on and by Aalto, although with ominous gaps regarding Scandinavian and Finnish material. On furniture, see Juhani Pallasmaa, ed., *Alvar Aalto Furniture* (Cambridge, Mass.: MIT Press, 1984). Aalto's involvement with Artek is described in Pekka Suhonen, *Artek* (Helsinki: Artek, 1985). On glass, see Timo Keinänen, *Alvar and Aino Aalto as Glass Designers* (Iittala: Iittala Glass Museum, 1996).

2. For specifics on the development and nature of the industrial infrastructure and modes of production in other countries (especially in the United States), which was vital to Aalto's later activity in house production, see David A. Hounshell, *From the American System to Mass-Production, 1800–1932* (Baltimore: Johns Hopkins University Press, 1984). To place Finnish industry in a broader context, see Alfred Dupont Chandler, Jr., *Scale and Scope: The Dynamics of Industrial Capitalism* (Cambridge, Mass.: Belknap Press of Harvard University, 1990). For an overview on the industrialization of Finland, see Timo Myllyntaus, *The Gatecrashing Apprentice: Industrializing Finland as an Adopter of New Technology,* Communications, Institute of Economic and Social History, University of Helsinki, Vol. 24 (Helsinki, 1990); On the specific development of forest industries, see Markku Kuisma, *Metsäteollisuuden maa: Suomi, Metsät ja Kansainvalinen Järjestelmä, 1620–1920* [Green Gold and Capitalism: Finland, Forests and World Economy, 1620–1920] (Helsinki: Suomen Historiallinen Seura, 1993); English summary.

3. In the twelfth century, Finland was invaded by the Swedes, who ruled the country until 1809, when Sweden was forced to cede Finland to Russia. In 1917, Finland declared itself independent; this was approved by the new Soviet Bolshevik regime. This precipitated a civil war in 1918 between the "Reds," influenced by the Soviet Union, and the "Whites," supporting the status quo and finally backed by imperial Germany.

4. Le Corbusier, *Vers une architecture* (Paris: Éditions G. Crés, 1923), p. 225.

5. This is exemplified by the Kauttua industrial community; see Pekka Korvenmaa, *Kauttua: Tuotanto ja ympäristö, 1689–1989* [Kauttua: Production and Environment, 1689–1989] (Uusikaupunki: A. Ahlström, 1989); English summary.

6. On the formation of the Finnish architectural profession, see Pekka Korvenmaa, ed., *The Work of Architects: The Finnish Association of Architects, 1892–1992,* trans. Jüri Kokkonen (Helsinki: Finnish Association of Architects, 1992). See also Riitta Nikula, *Armas Lindgren 1874–1929: Architect* (Helsinki: Museum of Finnish Architecture, 1988); Renja Suominen-Kokkonen, *The Fringe of a Profession: Women as Architects in Finland from the 1890s to the 1950s* (Helsinki: Suomen Muinaismuistoyhdistys, 1992); Pekka Korvenmaa, *Innovation versus Tradition: The Architect Lars Sonck, Works and Projects 1900–1910* (Helsinki: Suomen Muinaismuistoyhdistys, 1991); Eeva Maija Viljo, *Theodor Höijer: En arkitekt under den moderna storstadsarkitekturens genombrottstid i Finland från 1870 till sekelskiftet* (Helsinki: Suomen Muisaismuistoyhdistys, 1985), English summary; Riitta Nikula, ed., *Erik Bryggman, 1891–1955: Architect* (Helsinki: Museum of Finnish Architecture, 1991); and Timo Tuomi, ed., *Hilding Ekelund, 1893–1984: Architect* (Helsinki: Museum of Finnish Architecture, 1997).

7. It should be stressed that what at the time was regarded as Bolshevik in Finland was everything from social democratic liberalism to the left, and that geopolitical imperatives aggravated this reaction to anything like socialism. Nordic modernism/functionalism was closely linked to the rise of the Social Democrats and reform politics, especially in Sweden. This was also the program of Aalto spiced with Continental sources, such as the Bauhaus and CIAM.

8. The project was published, with photos by Aino Aalto, in *Arkkitehti,* no. 12 (1931), pp. 188–193. The odd timing of the project, amid a global economic crisis, can be explained by the fact that the investor was foreign. *Arkkitehti,* the official journal of the Finnish Association of Architects, was started in 1903 in Swedish as *Arkitekten.* In 1919, after a short break in publication, it was re-founded as *Arkkitehti/Arkitekten,* a journal appearing in two identical versions, one in Finnish, the other in Swedish. For the notes in this essay I have used whatever edition was available; but as the versions are identical, the citations have all been given under the Finnish title for consistency. During the 1930s, the journal appeared monthly and was numbered one through twelve; as there was no volume number, each year begins anew with the number one.

9. The Winter War between Finland and the Soviet Union lasted from late fall 1939 to March 1940. The Soviet Union had, for some time, complained about the "militaristic threat" of Finland and finally accused Finland of shooting over the border with cannons; this (invented) offense gave them an excuse to attack. The reason for the war was largely strategic: the Finnish border as well as its second largest city, Viipuri, was very near the port and city of Leningrad. To Stalin's surprise, the Red Army was unable to invade Finland and suffered great losses. Nevertheless, in the peace treaty Finland lost most of the eastern province of Karelia and the city of Viipuri. In the Continuation War, Finland regained the pre-1940 borders but lost the eastern territories again in the ensuing peace treaty to that conflict.

10. Some background figures: the production of cellulose rose from 170,000 tons in 1920 to 1,500,000 tons in 1939; that of paper from 160,000 tons to 600,000 tons. Between 1933 and 1937 the annual growth of Finnish industrial production was 15 percent and that of the work force 10 percent; this explains the increased activity in both industrial architecture and housing.

11. On Albert Kahn and his design approaches, see Federico Bucci, *Albert Kahn: Architect of Ford,* trans. Carmen DiCinque (New York: Princeton Architectural Press, 1993).

12. On the relationship of modern industrial production and architectural modernism, see Lisa Brunnström, *Den rationella fabriken: Om funktionalismens rötter* [The Rational Factory: On the Roots of Modernist Architecture] (Umeå: Dokuma, 1990); English summary. On the relationship between the United States and Europe, see Thomas P. Hughes, *American Genesis: A Century of Invention and Technological Enthusiasm, 1870–1970* (New York: Viking, 1983), chs. 6, 7; and Terry Smith, *Making the Modern: Industry, Art and Design in America* (Chicago: University of Chicago Press, 1993), pt. 1.

13. See *Arkkitehti,* no. 12 (1931), pp. 188–193; trans. Pekka Korvenmaa.

14. The Serlachius residence of the early 1930s was by Jarl Eklund (1876–1962). For the corporate headquarters, Serlachius used the office of Jung & Jung (Bertel Jung, 1872–1946; Valter Jung, 1879–1946).

15. Schildt, *Decisive Years,* pp. 139–144.

16. The facts on the history of A. Ahlström Corporation and on the Sunila project are taken from Per Schybergson, *Työt ja päivät: Ahlströmin historia, 1851–1981* (Helsinki: A. Ahlström, 1992).

17. Gullichsen's role as an industrialist, promoter of modern architecture for strategic reasons, and national figure has been sharply analyzed in Terttu Nupponen, "Parhaalla tavalla ja kaukonäköisesti: Tapaustutkimus Kokemäenjokilaakson aluesuunnitelman viriämisestä ja intresseistä 1940-luvun alussa." [In the Best Way and with Foresight: A Case Study on the Initial Interest in the Kokemäenjoki River Valley Regional Plan at the Beginning of the 1940s] (Licentiate thesis for Jyväskylän yliopisto, Sosiologian laitos, 1992), esp. p. 197.

18. This statement is from a memorandum attached to documents regarding a program for *The Human Side,* an international magazine of culture and society, under preparation in fall 1939 but never published. See Schildt, *Decisive Years,* pp. 182–186; and "Propaganda 1939–40," Alvar Aalto Archives, Helsinki (hereafter: AAA, Helsinki); trans. Pekka Korvenmaa.

19. On Sunila, see the many references in the Aalto literature; the list of works in Schildt, *Complete Catalogue;* and Alvar Aalto, in *Arkkitehti,* no. 10 (1938), pp. 145–160; and Paavo Alava, *Sunila, metäjättïen yhtiö: Sunila Oy 1938–88* (Jyväskylä: Sunila, 1988).

20. For a full account of the specialists behind the production facilities, see ibid. Here the construction engineer, L. Nyrop, who had been behind the Toppila plant, was joined by his colleague Magnus Malmberg. He was to be of key importance in many future projects by Aalto.

21. This is not to neglect the obvious and strong impulses Aalto took from antiquity, for example, Greek theaters, or from Italian architecture. His earlier work, and especially the monumental postwar edifices, testify to this. What is meant here is that Aalto was a master of rhetoric, particularly in explaining the design intentions of already executed buildings.

22. Kaukopää is situated near Imatra and dates from 1934–35 in its original form. Even though the housing,

stratified in three social and professional layers, is modernist, it is organized in straight rows as in examples of German modernism of the 1920s. The plant was part of the Enso-Gutzeit company, for which Aalto worked after the war, even expanding the Kaukopää housing area. See Jorma Ahvenainen, *Enso-Gutzeit, 1872–1992* (Jyväskylä: Enso-Gutzeit, 1992).

23. The independent villa towns that sprang up in the vicinity of Helsinki in the first years of the twentieth century, such as Kulosaari and Kauniainen, combined influences from the British garden-city movement and the legacy of Austrian architect and planner Camillo Sitte. These, together with the tenets of modernism exemplified by the Weissenhof layout, are some of the ideas behind the Sunila plan.

24. After the first stage of Sunila had been completed in 1938, Aalto gave a lecture at the Nordic Building Conference in Oslo in which he used Sunila as an example of how much modern systems of heating influence the disposition of buildings, especially when, as in Sunila, the heating and hot water is distributed from a central unit. Regarding Finnish conditions, this was innovative and made possible the unusually high standard of the apartments, equipped with hot water and bathtubs. The heating plant was thus the focal element of the plan, visually as well as functionally. See Alvar Aalto, "Rakenteitten ja aineitten vaikutus nykyaikaiseen rakennustaiteeseen" [The Influence of Construction and Materials on Modern Architecture], *Arkkitehti*, no. 9 (1938), pp. 129–131.

25. See Korvenmaa, *Kauttua*, 1989.

26. For sketches and plans for the grouping of the buildings, see AAA, Helsinki. The scheme usually published has four terraced houses, public buildings, and a sauna by the river. The larger scheme, to which the previous belonged, comprised eleven terraced houses and seven multistory row houses of the Sunila slope type; other designs for the whole exist. Because the function of the buildings for other purposes than housing is not sufficiently indicated in the various designs, it is difficult to point out the relationship of the houses to the central heating plant, but it is to be assumed that the latter would have been the building on the highest part of the hill, since the slope would have helped in the distribution of the hot water.

27. Alvar Aalto, in *Arkkitehti*, nos. 11–12 (1939), pp. 161–163.

28. In Aalto's building instructions for the construction site, he strongly stressed that all trees outside the perimeter of the foundations must be saved and protected with clapboarding during construction (Memorandum on the Kauttua stepped house, AAA, Helsinki). Aalto elsewhere noted: "Only those sites with a maximum amount of biological and psychological advantages" should be chosen for housing; at the same time, he presented a case for national economy: by using hillside housing, land suitable for farming could be saved from urban development (*Arkkitehti*, nos. 11–12 [1939]).

29. See plans in Schildt, *Complete Catalogue*, pp. 12–14.

30. This development was catalyzed by American technology and investments. The Insulite company of Finland, which started producing building insulation sheets in Kymi in 1930, was founded and owned by the Minnesota and Ontario Paper Company in the United States.

31. See Pekka Korvenmaa, "The Finnish Wooden House Transformed: American Prefabrication, War-Time Housing and Alvar Aalto," *Construction History*, vol. 6 (1990), pp. 47–61; and idem, "From House Manufacture to Universal Systems: Industrial Prefabrication, the Utopias of Modernism, and the Conditions of Wood Culture," in *Timber Construction in Finland*, (Helsinki: Museum of Finnish Architecture, 1996), pp. 162–175.

32. On this and also the Finnish Pavilion Aalto designed for the Paris International Exhibition of 1936–37, see Kerstin Smeds, "The Image of Finland at the World Exhibitions, 1900–1992," in Peter B. MacKeith and Kerstin Smeds, *The Finland Pavilions: Finland at the Universal Expositions, 1900–1992* (Tampere: Kustannus, 1993).

33. See note 9. In Finland, World War II consisted of three phases. First, the Winter War of 1939–40 against the Soviet Union was foreplay for the global war and part of the so-called Ribbentrop deal between Stalin and Hitler regarding occupation of Finland and the Baltic states. In the Continuation War of 1941–44, Finland was allied with, but not part of, the Axis forces. After an armistice with the Soviet Union, Finland promised to clear the country of German forces, mainly to be found in northern Finland. The Lapland War against the former allies took place in 1945. The retreating Germans burned down the whole of Lapland and its major town, Rovaniemi. In 1945 the country had to start from scratch; the eastern border moved westward, and with it about 400,000 Karelian refugees. Nevertheless, Finland was never occupied during this period, which was a rare exception in Europe.

34. For Aalto's writings, see Miller, *Annotated Bibliography*. A selection of important articles is translated in Göran Schildt, ed., *Sketches: Alvar Aalto*, trans. Stuart Wrede (Cambridge, Mass., and London: MIT Press, 1978).

35. In his lecture at the annual meeting of the Swedish Society for Arts and Crafts in Stockholm in 1935, Aalto related the benefits and problems of industrial production with psychological and biological nature. He linked standardization to the organicism of nature and considered artifacts as "cells" in the "tissue" of human life. See Alvar Aalto, "Rationalismen och människan" [Rationalism and Man], *Form* (Stockholm), no. 7 (1935). See also Schildt, *Sketches*, pp. 47–51.

36. The success of Aalto's furniture in Britain introduced him to several key persons in the country. British cultural influence, well established at the turn of the century, had been overshadowed by the Nordic and German sphere, and also by Le Corbusier. Britain, however, was Finland's main country for export, and also the awareness of British thinking, exemplified by Herbert Read, began to exert renewed influence from the mid-1930s onward. It is difficult to know how much the writing of Lewis Mumford of the mid-1930s affected Aalto in his critique of the dominating technosystems, but in the last years of the decade they became acquainted. For a recent presentation of Mumford's thinking, see Robert Wojtowicz, *Lewis Mumford & American Modernism: Utopian Theories for Architecture and Urban Planning* (Cambridge and New York: Cambridge University Press, 1996).

37. See document outline of the Yale lectures, spring 1939, AAA, Helsinki; and Alvar Aalto, "The Humanizing of Architecture," *Technology Review* (November 1940), pp. 14–16.

38. In the 1938 Oslo lecture already cited in note 24, Aalto discussed standardization at length, concluding that nature's own standardization, "will result in millions of flexible combinations with no formality; it will also result in a great richness and in a never-ending variation of organically grown forms. This has to be the route also for architectural standardization." (Trans. Pekka Korvenmaa.) The need for architectural, empirical, and laboratory-type research was brought forward in Aalto, "Humanizing of Architecture," 1940.

39. On these events, see Schildt, *Mature Years*; Korvenmaa, "Finnish Wooden House Transformed," for American prefabrication and Aalto; and idem, *The Work of Architects*, pp. 122–127, for an overview of Finnish architects and World War II. Aalto wrote numerous articles on the problems of reconstruction, several of them in English: see Alvar Aalto, "Post-War Reconstruction," *Magazine of Art* (June 1940), pp. 362, 382; idem, "Research for Reconstruction: Rehousing Research in Finland," *Journal of the RIBA* (March 17, 1941), pp. 78–83; and the booklet, idem, *Post-War Reconstruction: Rehousing Research in Finland* (New York: [private printing], 1940). For a general genealogy of type-planned houses in Finland, see Kirsi Saarikangas, *Model Houses for Model Families: Gender, Ideology and the Modern Dwelling. The Type-Planned Houses of the 1940s in Finland* (Helsinki: Suomen Historiallinen Seura, 1993). Also, in an article published in Sweden in 1941, Aalto proposed the idea that an expandable, elastic system of building in wood, based on the elaboration of a traditional method of adding functional units to the core farmstead volume, would play an important role in the future of rebuilding in Finland. Alvar Aalto, "De krigshärjade städerna och byarna" [The War Damage in Cities and Villages], in *Finland: Från krig till krig 1939–1940–1941* (Stockholm: Saxon & Lindströms Fotogravyranstalt, 1941).

40. Notes on a meeting, June 1, 1939; Alvar Aalto, with Ernest Born, Thomas Church, Timothy Pflueger, and William W. Wurster (William W. Wurster Archive, Berkeley, Calif.) See also Marc Treib, ed., *An Everyday Modernism: The Houses of William Wurster* (San Francisco: San Francisco Museum of Modern Art; Berkeley, Los Angeles, and London: University of California Press, 1995).

41. Ibid.

42. Typescript, May 31, 1940, AAA, Helsinki.

43. See correspondence, memoranda, and cost estimates on the project in "Propaganda 1939–40," AAA, Helsinki.

44. John E. Burchard, the director of the Albert Farwell Bemis Foundation, drew up a memorandum of a meeting with Aalto and the Rockefellers on June 27, 1940. After stating, "Even hating housing as they do in a sense all of the sons seem convinced that they owe something to the housing problem," Burchard wrote that, even though the Rockefeller Foundation was interested in Aalto's proposal to build a town in Finland, they were more excited about Aalto's scheme in general, especially if something in that direction

could be realized in the United States. Aalto and Burchard then elaborated the plan according to this idea. MIT was to be the center for the project and the research needed (John E. Burchard Papers, Institute Archives, MIT, Cambridge Mass.).

45. Letter from Alvar Aalto to Henry Ford, September 24, 1940 (AAA, Helsinki): "I appeal to you as the man who has solved a great human technical problem by harmonizing technical standards and the social human need and economy."

46. See Schildt, *Early Years,* p. 291; and idem, *Decisive Years,* pp. 22–23. Even though the building worked well, the time for concrete prefabrication was not yet ripe in Finland, mainly owing to the individualized building in the cities and the low level of urbanization. Not until the 1960s, in conjunction with rapid suburbanization, did the industrial mode of building in concrete become dominant.

47. On the so-called Enso experimental houses, see drawings and descriptions (AAA, Helsinki). Aalto had apparently approached the Enso-Gutzeit company, a leading producer of insulation panels, with this idea himself; see letter of September 1933 from the company to Aalto inviting him to come and present his ideas (AAA, Helsinki).

48. See Pallasmaa, *Alvar Aalto Furniture*; and Suhonen, *Artek.* Aalto's famous glass designs of the 1930s, such as the Savoy Vase, do not belong to the domain of industrial serial production, being at that time handblown and therefore crafted. It was the pressed glass by Aino Aalto that belonged to the sphere of industrial conception; see Keinänen, *Glass Designers.*

49. This factory was the first of its kind in Finland, but it was part of a broader movement. Wood type houses intended for serial production had already been displayed in a major housing and home exhibition in fall 1939 (*Asuntonäyttely 39*) in Helsinki. When Sweden granted prefabricated homes to Finland after the Winter War, their market potential was widely recognized. In 1941 twenty producers of wood houses were active under the collaborative marketing organization, Puutalo, to which A. Ahlström Corporation did not belong.

50. This selection was advertised in the brochure "A-talo: tulevaisuuden talo" [A-House: The House of the Future], of 1940 (AAA, Helsinki).

51. The Varkaus house factory has been mentioned in the following writings: for a narrative, see Schildt, *Mature Years,* pp. 52–62; for a case study, American innovations, and a bibliography, see Korvenmaa, "Finnish Wooden House Transformed"; and for housing in Varkaus, see Mervi Savolainen, "Tehtaan huoneista omaan kotiin: Teollisuuden asuntoarkkitehtuuria Varkaudessa 1910–1940, luvuilla," (Thesis, Department of Archi-tecture, Helsinki University of Technology, 1993). Materials in AAA, Helsinki, include memoranda, brochures, and drawings, such as the memorandum preceding the decision to start production of 1939 and the brochure "Warkauden tehtaan omakotitoiminta," of 1944, describing the housing program of the company at Varkaus and the role the A-House had in this, which actually presents several alternatives for the workers in deciding upon the construction of the house they intend to erect on lots provided by the company. (In the end the arguments give the A-House as the only viable solution.) Although Aalto's office produced the first type drawings, soon a local drawing office was installed at the factory, with the Swiss-born architect Paul Bernoulli from Aalto's office in charge. The local office used Aalto's ideas but also produced designs of its own.

52. Typed 33-page memo, "Taloteollisuuden luonnetta koskevia kysymyksiä" [Questions Concerning the Nature of Industrial House Production] (AAA, Helsinki).

53. For a general reference on American factory housing, see Peter S. Reed, "Enlisting Modernism," in Donald Albrecht, ed., *World War II and the American Dream: How Wartime Building Changed a Nation* (Washington, D.C.: National Building Museum; Cambridge, Mass.: MIT Press, 1995).

54. See 1941 memorandum and parallel document, "Yhteenveto toimenpiteistä talotehtaan järjestelmän ja talokokoelman aikaansaamiseksi" [Summary of the Actions to Be Taken to Achieve System and Selection of Houses for the Factory] (AAA, Helsinki).

55. The idea of a research laboratory appears in ibid. American isolationism, the new war in Europe, and Finland's joining the Axis alliance rapidly changed the previously positive situation of Finland as a target for humanitarian help into an area of political and economic risk. Although the laboratory was never realized, the built examples of the A-House in Kauttua, for example, are still, after fifty years of use, in good condition.

56. For a broader picture of this highly important event, see Korvenmaa, *The Work of Architects*; and idem, "The Crisis as Catalyst: Finnish Architecture, Alvar Aalto, and the Second World War. A Case of Strategic Decision-Making," in *The Architecture of the Essential,* Proceedings of the 6th International Alvar Aalto Symposium, Helsinki, 1995.

57. The Standardization Institute soon showed results: the first exhibition for foreign guests was held in December 1942. See the special issue of *Arkkitehti,* nos. 5–6 (1943), devoted to the topic; and the programmatic publication, *Rakennustaide ja standardi: Jälleenrakentamisen ydinkysymyksiä* [Architecture and Standardization: Core Problems of Reconstruction] (Helsinki: Reconstruction Bureau, 1942). The basic text by Aalto was polished by the author Mika Waltari. For a comparison of how the war accelerated the development of building and of the role of architects within the wartime power structure, see Albrecht, *World War II and the American Dream,* 1995. For a personal perspective regarding the duties of architects, see William Lescaze, *On Being an Architect* (New York: G. P. Putnam's Sons, 1942), chs. 7, 8. For the United States and reconstruction in Europe, see Jean-Louis Cohen, *Scenes of the World to Come: European Architecture and the American Challenge, 1893–1960* (Montreal: Canadian Center for Architecture; Paris: Flammarion, 1995), ch. 7.

58. Undated letter from Aalto to state officials (AAA, Helsinki).

59. Gullichsen actually took a deep interest in the problem of housing for the people in eastern Finland, traveling there on a bicycle tour with his wife and apparently being shocked by what he saw. Aalto cited Gullichsen's plea for decent housing in a letter to Herbert Hoover in Palo Alto, August 1940; Maire Gullichsen also described these events in a letter to Aalto, then at MIT, August 6, 1940 (AAA, Helsinki).

60. The war reparations Finland had to pay to the Soviet Union in 1945–52 were greater per capita than the ones Germany had to pay the Allies after World War I. During the Continuation War, Finland had been allied with the Axis forces. When the United States implemented the Marshall Plan to aid European recovery, Finland was not excluded because of its Axis alliance (nor were Germany, Austria, or neutral Sweden); it was the Soviet Union that dictated that Finland was not to benefit from this massive rescue program. Thus, Finland had to pay war reparations, which were never less than six percent of the annual national production and went as high as sixteen percent. As reconstruction proceeded, Finnish industrial production expanded; in 1945–48 the industrial work force grew by 50,000 persons, at the same time that the birth rate was the highest in Europe.

61. This is not to say that Ahlström ceased to employ Aalto, but the intense relationship changed character to become a more usual client-architect relationship. After the war, the Strömberg Corporation was mainly owned by Ahlström and by Tampella, which to a certain degree explains the use of Aalto.

62. See the descriptions attached to the drawings (AAA, Helsinki). The project is well represented in Schildt, *Complete Catalogue,* pp. 236–237.

63. See Alvar Aalto, "Kulttuuri ja tekniikka" [Culture and Technology] (1947), in Schildt, *Sketches.*

64. See Schildt, *Complete Catalogue,* pp. 123–124; and Smeds, "The Image of Finland."

65. See Aalto's description of the principles of the plan (AAA, Helsinki).

66. The area covered in the plan is about 70 kilometers long, running east-west along the river valley, and some 30 kilometers wide north-south. The majority of the region is agricultural, with seven parishes and with the city of Pori at its western end. The plan was intended to serve the rural communities in their future expansion and to make a coherent transportation system in the form of a railway and a functionally differentiated road network. Simultaneously, it was intended to consolidate the Ahlström interests in western Finland by binding together the route of log transport, the river, the industries in the city of Pori, the sawmill on the coast, and the harbor of Pori. The site of the corporation's headquarters at Noormarkku, where the director and his wife resided in Villa Mairea, was integrated into the plan. Located 25 kilometers from Pori, it was connected to the city by road and railway. In relating the plan to national strategies, two factors should be mentioned. First, a new major hydroelectric plant ready to serve industrial expansion had recently been finished in Harjavalta, along the river. Second, after the Winter War serious consideration was given to the issues of the possibly negative industrial future of the regions next to the eastern border. Therefore, to ensure the industrial future of the nation, the western parts grew in significance.

67. The Kokemäenjoki project, and the strategies of both Gullichsen and Aalto, are discussed at length (in Finnish) in Nupponen, "Parhaalta tavalla ja

kaukonäköisesti"; for a condensed version, see idem,
"Professional Control and National Reconstruction:
Modern Urbanism, Planning Technologies and
Professional Strategies of Finnish Architects in
Wartime," *Proceedings of the XIII World Congress of
Sociology* (Bielefeld, Germany), July 1994. Aalto wrote
a detailed description of the project, "Kumo älvdal,"
Arkkitehti, nos. 1–2 (1943), pp. 6–11; and a 25-page
brochure, *Kokemäenjoen laakson aluesuunnitelma* (Pori:
Satakunnan kirjateollisuus, 1943). Aalto's background
statement for the defense of the initiative is undated
but is most probably from 1940 (AAA, Helsinki). On
the Kymijoki plan, see Schildt, *Complete Catalogue,*
pp. 16–17. Aalto was consulted in 1942, but the war
stopped the planning. The information given in the
publication on the final plan of 1956 differs from
Schildt's information (according to which Aalto was
still employed on the project), but the 1956 publication states that suggestions were requested in 1943
from several architects, Aalto included, and Carolus
Lindberg was chosen. See *Kymenlaakson aluesuunnitelma*
(Kotka: Kymenlaakson aluesuunnitelma r.y., 1956).
These regional plans based on river arteries were analogous to the American endeavors of a similar nature of
the late 1930s, such as the Tennessee Valley Authority
(TVA). Aalto was fully aware of American efforts, such
as the TVA and the New York Regional Plan, but he
does not mention them explicitly when describing the
background for the Kokemäenjoki plan. See Aalto's
presentation in *Arkkitehti*, no. 1 (1942), and the
brochure by him on the same issue; the plan and its
possible connections to the United States are also mentioned in Schildt, *Mature Years,* pp. 59–60, where
Schildt refers to a research paper by Jussi Rautsi of
1984 (but does not specify it in the text).

68. William Lehtinen, *Imatran yleiskaava*, (Helsinki: Enso-
Gutzeit, 1953); trans. Pekka Korvenmaa. A variety of
contracts, memoranda, and program papers concerning
the master plan exists in AAA, Helsinki; according to
them, the contract for the project was made in
October 1947. The regional planning initiated by
industry had several offspring: in 1950 Aalto was asked
to work on a vast plan for the whole of Lapland, and
at the same time his friend, professor Päiviö Oksala, in
Jyväskylä asked him to think about a regional plan for
central Finland (see reply from Aalto to Oksala,
1950–51, in AAA, Helsinki). Aalto also wrote on the
issue of planning on a national scale: "Valtakunnansuunnittelu ja kulttuurimme tavoitteet" [National
Planning and the Goals of Our Culture], *Suomalainen
Suomi*, no. 5 (1949), pp. 261–265; trans. Pekka
Korvenmaa.

69. For an overview of the situation between 1930 and
1950, see the illustrated book, *Suomen teollisuuden
arkkitehtuuria* [Industrial Architecture in Finland]
(Helsinki: Finnish Association of Architects, 1952).

70. For many recent accounts of art and architecture under
totalitarian rule, see Jan Tabor, ed., *Kunst und Diktatur:
Architektur, Bildhauerei und Malerei in Österreich,
Deutschland, Italien und der Sovjetunion, 1922–1956,*
2 vols. (Baden: Verlag Grasl, 1994).

71. On Le Corbusier and industrialism, see the seminal
study by Mary McLeod, "'Architecture or Revolution': Taylorism, Technocracy and Social Change,"
Art Journal, vol. 43, no. 2 (summer 1983), pp. 132–147.

72. On Bata and Szlin, see Jane Pavitt, "The Bata Project:
A Social and Industrial Experiment," *Twentieth Century
Architecture*, no. 1 (summer 1994), pp. 31–44. The
Soviet development regarding industrial towns still
needs to be explored in full.

73. See Gilbert Herbert, *The Dream of the Factory-Made
House* (Cambridge, Mass.: MIT Press, 1984).

74. The concept of momentum is here applied in the sense
in which Thomas P. Hughes has elaborated it within
the history of technology and regarding large systems
of production and distribution. The Ahlström company was a good example of the full "vertical integration" of capacity, ranging from its forests down to the
end user. See Chandler, *Scale and Scope,* chs. 1, 2.

75. Aalto's promotional statement of 1951 on publishing
Suomen teollisuuden arkkitehtuuria [Industrial Architec-
ture in Finland]; typescript, AAA, Helsinki; trans.
Pekka Korvenmaa.

Alvar Aalto and the New Humanism of the Postwar Era
Peter Reed

Regardless of which social system prevails in the world or its parts, a softening human touch is needed to mould societies, cities, buildings, and even the smallest machine-made objects into something positive to the human psyche, without bringing individual freedom and the common good into conflict. These forces have assembled around architecture to such an extent that we can now speak of a new, broader purpose for architecture, encompassing the whole world and its cultural crisis. We might also say: We have now reached the stage when architecture has regained the status it had in the Classical civilizations of the past.

—Alvar Aalto[1]

IN THE YEARS IMMEDIATELY FOLLOWING World War II, with much of Europe in ruins and American technological prowess triumphant, architects, critics, and historians fervently debated what proper role monumentality, history, technology, and human values would play in postwar rebuilding. Architects and city planners were expected to provide architectural expressions for a world desperately in need of a humane, aesthetic, and modern architecture that would restore dignity to a world scarred by extraordinary inhumanity. In the postwar rebuilding and expansion, Alvar Aalto's work provided compelling examples. His buildings and projects—for Scandinavia, Germany, and the United States—embodied a new humanism in which architecture balanced the pragmatic and functional elements of building with formal variety, social and psychological issues, history, and innovation. Aalto's harmony of functional and romantic ideas, his rich palette of materials, and a design strategy predicated on emotive and associative content provided a modern alternative to the functionalist International Style, to industrialized standardization, and to the politically suspect classicism favored by the Nazi and Soviet empires.[2] Moreover, the

Alvar Aalto. Säynätsalo Town Hall, Säynätsalo, Finland. 1948–52. View from the west

shocking brutality of war coupled with the defeat of the Nazis and rise of Soviet power across Finland's new eastern border created a climate especially receptive to a modernism that emphasized the "humanizing factor."

Aalto's lofty claim, in 1950, of a golden age for contemporary architecture on a par with the classical past seems prescient, for it was in his work then on the drawing board and in ensuing projects that he responded so brilliantly to the world's cultural crisis. In this extraordinarily prolific period, Aalto was awarded numerous competition prizes and commissions for cultural and civic centers, universities, housing, office buildings, churches, and auditoriums. It was a time of rebuilding and expansion, and Aalto enjoyed an international reputation; his designs were considered aesthetically expressive and socially responsive. Much of Aalto's international success can be attributed to an architecture that was contemporary yet embodied preindustrial values (what others have called a kind of international regionalism)[3] that found currency in the years immediately before the war and in the decades of rebuilding.

Aalto's rise to international prominence came in 1937 at the Paris International Exhibition, where the bombastic Soviet and Nazi pavilions on the right bank of the Seine, dominated the international pavilions of the forty-two participating nations (figure 1). In their severe monumental classicism and heroic figural sculpture the two pavilions confronted each other across the exhibition's main concourse in the shadow of the Eiffel Tower. Amid this unabashed display of power, which foreshadowed the international political crisis unfolding in Europe, Aalto's Finnish Pavilion was repeatedly noted by leading critics as one of the few examples of architectural merit (plates 131–139). A writer for *Cahiers d'art* claimed there were only five pavilions worthy of individual mention, those of Czechoslovakia, Finland, Japan, Spain, and Sweden.[4] British architect Serge Chermayeff, writing for *The Architectural Review*, singled out Aalto's pavilion, as did the American historian and critic, Henry-Russell Hitchcock, when he wrote of "the Finnish Pavilion, the work of the greatest individual architect represented in the Exposition."[5]

The overall effect of the largely timber structure, which sidestepped the existing trees on the slope of the Trocadero, must have been enchanting. The different wood columns from rough-cut birch trees, slender columns in entasis with applied ribs suggesting fluting, and a decidedly orientalizing cluster of bamboolike poles lashed together with a basketmaker's skill added to the rustic effect, creating a multivalent order that prized variety over homogeneity. Even Amédée Ozenfant, the Purist painter and former collaborator of Le Corbusier, noted: "It is perhaps in the timber structures (Japan, Finland above all) that the most ingenious constructive ideas are to be found...the mastery of wood and steel shown by these architects and engineers is on a level with that of their Gothic precursors."[6] The art and industry exhibits inside the pavilion complemented the architecture in their originality and progressive spirit. Among them were displays of Aalto's bentwood furniture, produced by Artek, and the world

1. Albert Speer. German Pavilion, Paris International Exhibition, Paris. 1937

premier of his colorful glass vases, manufactured by Karhula-Iittala and distinguished by asymmetrical curvilinear shapes (plates 138, 140, 142), all of which demonstrated a fresh, organic quality that owed more to nature and individual creativity than to historical typologies or formal systems. Even the exhibit of Finland's social statistics charted progressive democratic ideals, such as the increasing number of women in the workplace (plate 139). The prevalence of wood in the pavilion—birch and plywood furniture, the paper and pulp industry, birch-bark columns, wood cladding, and photographs of the pristine Finnish landscape—powerfully identified Finland with nature, and this also assumed a political dimension. "Nature," Aalto later explained, "is, of course, freedom's symbol. Sometimes it is even nature that creates and maintains the concept of freedom."[7] The sharp contrast between the portrayal of Finland and other European countries made an indelible impression on many who visited the fair.

A year after the Paris fair, The Museum of Modern Art in New York presented an exhibition of Aalto's architecture and furniture, and published the first book on his work.[8] In 1939, Americans experienced his architecture firsthand in the Finnish Pavilion at the New York World's Fair (plates 145–154). In one of the twentieth century's most astonishing interiors, a three-tiered, undulating wood wall served as a backdrop for large photomurals and product displays. In assessing the impact of the design nearly two decades later, Reyner Banham offered this appraisal: "No other architect in the world, let alone Finland, could have produced at that moment anything quite so spectacular, so appropriate, and so completely original as that great disquieting, irregularly planked wall of wood sagging wavily out over the visitors to the pavilion."[9] In explaining his intentions, Aalto described the need to evoke atmosphere and instinct in order to convey an impression of Finland to the visitors: "Objects by themselves can hardly give a convincing picture of a country; it can only arise out of the atmosphere created by the objects and constitutes, in other words, a totality that can only be grasped instinctively."[10] The design was a synthesis of forms derived both from the Finnish landscape and practical considerations. The architecture, predicated on atmosphere and instinct (with its inherent appeal to the subconscious), paralleled the ideas presented in his talks and writings. Among the themes he emphasized was the need to humanize architecture, which later became the core of virtually all his later talks and writings. To achieve his goal, Aalto spoke of the "psychological" aspects of architecture, meaning, in part, one's emotional response.[11] His position challenged the technological clarity of the International Style as well as the robotic consumer wonders of the Westinghouse and General Motors presentations at the New York fair. In Aalto's view, modern architecture of the last decade was too overtly rational, lacking psychological and empathetic dimensions. The term *mystery* began to appear in his vocabulary. In "My Frank Lloyd Wright," an unpublished tribute composed in 1940 for The Museum of Modern Art's exhibition *Frank Lloyd Wright: American Architect*, Aalto referred to rational and romantic elements in architecture and nature that appealed to his "mental and emotional being."[12] In his appreciation of Wright, Aalto objected to modern architecture where "every element is visible, every corner's function and construction can be explained. There are many tendencies in the new architecture toward a more complete and clear mechanism than the human being itself. Never so with Frank Lloyd Wright. His works have always, without a single exception, the limitations of the human being.... There is always something which reminds us of the unknown depths of our own being."[13]

In developing his ideas for an architecture that derived from the creator's instinct and the notion of empathy, Aalto was clearly inspired by the Finnish philosopher Yrjö Hirn and the architect Henry van de Velde. At the turn of the century, Hirn espoused a theory of play in the creative process, which Aalto interpreted architecturally as a necessary reconciliation between technology, economy, and artistic intuition.[14] Aalto also enjoyed a long friendship with van de Velde (of the same generation as Wright). In a famous debate on the occasion of the first great Deutscher Werkbund exhibition in Cologne in 1914, van de Velde challenged Hermann Muthesius who advocated greater standardization. Van de Velde vehemently proclaimed the virtues of the creative artist: "So long as there are still artists in the Werkbund and so long as they exercise some influence on its destiny, they will protest against every suggestion for the establishment of a canon and for standardization. By his innermost essence the artist is a burning

idealist, a free spontaneous creator."[15] Aalto clearly considered himself an inheritor of van de Velde's theoretical legacy, which he believed was responsible for leading architecture in a more cultivated direction. In his 1957 eulogy for van de Velde, Aalto described him as "the European continent's grand old man in terms of revitalizing the arts...one of the earliest links in the chain of development which has led to architecture's creative role in our social system.... Let it be said simply that his personal influence has penetrated deeply into the Nordic countries."[16]

The sense of mystery and emotional content revealed in Aalto's postwar work satisfied a widespread cultural longing for symbolic content and meaning, without the extremes of either totalitarian classicism or overly rationalized functionalism. Divorced from political vicissitudes, his postwar oeuvre thus became emblematic of social democratic ideals. For Aalto, technology was subservient to form, and, while he exploited technology and occasionally explored unusual structural systems, it was never his chief interest. Material, light, space, form, and atmosphere were primary. His ideas of flexible standardization, which permit some degree of individuality and freedom, were conceived to avoid the overwhelming uniformity of machine production. As the architect Edward Ford has observed, Aalto was "the enemy of rigid and arbitrary standards, responding with sensitivity to the most minute of functional concerns, softening the harshness of industrialization."[17] While serving as a visiting professor at the Massachusetts Institute of Technology (MIT) after the war, Aalto reflected on the shortcomings of American culture, which, in his opinion, was too enamored of technology and lacked depth: "America is in any case the country that shows us the whole cultural future of the world, mistakes and all. In America's industrial culture lies not only its whole future development, but its own reflection."[18]

Aalto was not alone in his reservations about the pervasiveness of technology. In 1947, he and approximately sixty leading architects and designers attended a seminar, titled "Planning Man's Physical Environment," at Princeton University (on which occasion Aalto, Wright, and New York city planner Robert Moses received honorary degrees) where they contemplated the central issues of the time: "How can one subdue a machine without destroying it, how can one preserve industry without 'industrializing' man?"[19] The purpose of the conference was not to draft a resolution but to explore ideas about the psychological, philosophical, visual, and social aspects of the environment. Predictably, Aalto claimed that the architect's responsibility was to maintain a human quality in architecture. By way of example, he described Finland's recent wartime success in achieving variety and flexibility with prefabricated wood-frame houses.

Paralleling the debate on industry, technology, and human values, an important discussion among modern architects, critics, and historians centered on the idea of monumentality in postwar architecture. As early as 1944, Sigfried Giedion, Louis I. Kahn, and others addressed the issue in a publication edited by Paul Zucker, which included a section called "The Problem of a New Monumentality."[20] They demanded an architecture that

2. Alvar Aalto. Baker House, Senior Dormitory, Massachusetts Institute of Technology, Cambridge. c. 1947. Comparative studies. Alvar Aalto Foundation, Helsinki

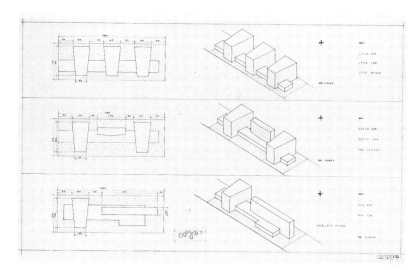

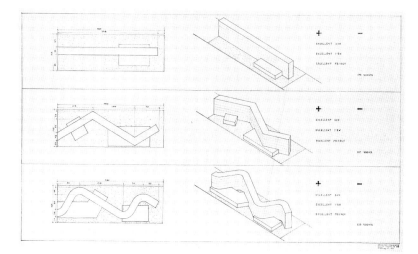

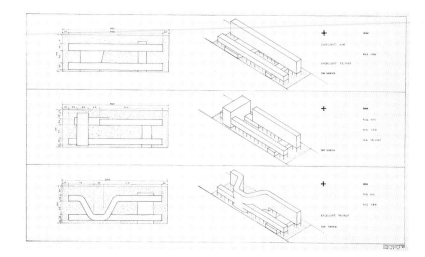

would embody the eternal need for spiritual and symbolic expression.[21] Giedion fervently pursued the idea, and his lecture, "The Need for a New Monumentality," presented at the Royal Institute of British Architects in London on September 26, 1946, generated wider debate, mainly in *The Architectural Review*. Historians, critics, and practitioners grappled with definitions of monumentality, even questioning its appropriateness and relevance at mid-century.[22] The American critic, Lewis Mumford, contributed a particularly thoughtful essay to this discussion, although he was quick to avoid the term *monumentality* because of its dangerous connotations with recent totalitarian architecture. His essay, "Monumentalism, Symbolism and Style," expanded Giedion's position. Mumford observed a new, healthy interest in the expressive element in architecture, aesthetics, and civic dignity.[23] Modern architecture, he argued, had evolved to the point of greater complexity and choice, "choices in form, choices between ponderosity and lightness, between magnificence and humility, between complexity and simplicity: choices which are ultimately not practical and technical, but aesthetic, ethical, personal."[24] In advocating a richer expression in postwar modernism and pleading for a "broader, more human viewpoint that embraces the technical in the regional and organic," he cited Frank Lloyd Wright and Alvar Aalto as two architects who were leading modern architecture in this direction.[25]

While contemplating these issues on technology, monumentality, and humanism in architecture, Aalto had the opportunity to demonstrate his ideas in Baker House, the new Senior Dormitory at MIT, one of the earliest commissions among America's postwar university and college campus expansions (plates 181–195).[26] A brilliant design that demonstrates Aalto's desire to avoid an institutional character, the six-story dormitory is situated on a long narrow site along Memorial Drive overlooking the Charles River. Its form contrasts with the neoclassical domed and colonnaded main buildings of the MIT campus, but its unconventional undulating facade, metaphorically evoking its riparian context, had practical and functional advantages over more conventional modern building types. As preliminary studies show, the design evolved from a scheme of staggered blocks aligned diagonally to the unique, sculptural expressionist composition of the final building.[27] In a series of comparative studies prepared for the building committee, Aalto demonstrated the pros and cons of other, more typically functionalist schemes, evaluating them for sun, view, and privacy (figure 2). His unique design fulfilled the program to house 353 students in single, double, and triple rooms, while providing nearly every room with a river view and ample sunlight. In the double-curve solution, a greater variety of idiosyncratic room types was achieved—wedge-shaped rooms (some nearly triangular, others trapezoidal), which students subsequently nicknamed "coffins, pies, and couches"[28]—all furnished by Artek.[29]

The variation in room types was further reflected on the facade in the subtle changes in fenestration. The two contrasting facades also mitigated against uniformity: the campus facade, where the main entrance is located, is distinguished by its saw-tooth plan, echoed in a remarkable cascading staircase unfortunately sheathed in stucco rather than tile, as Aalto originally specified.[30] The decision to use tinted stucco sacrificed the textural richness Aalto had envisioned. Two staircases, cantilevered from the main body of the building, rise in opposite directions from the main entrance, and at each landing common rooms are arranged behind them.

Aalto's didactic comparative studies seem to have been intended for the client's benefit and as a criticism of modern architecture generally. Indirectly, they also differentiate his design from that of another leading modernist, Walter Gropius (then head of the Department of Architecture at neighboring Harvard University). While Aalto was designing Baker House, Harvard announced plans for a new graduate student center to be designed by Gropius and The Architects Collaborative (figure 3). It was to house twice as many students on a much larger site than MIT's narrow strip of land and comprised eight buildings, none more than four stories high, arranged in a series of small quadrangles. While the plan relied on a traditional college typology, the buildings reflected a Bauhaus aesthetic. A general uniformity of the buildings and bedrooms was indicative of the pragmatic, overly rational approach of *Existenzminimum*, which created the institutional monotony that Aalto deliberately sought to avoid in his irregular plan.[31]

Baker House is one of the first demonstrations of Aalto's new interest in brick, which seems to have been inspired as much by New England architecture as by his new friend Frank Lloyd Wright. Aalto later recounted hearing Wright proclaim the virtues of the lowly brick: "Brick is an important element in the creation of form. I was once in Milwaukee together with my old friend Frank Lloyd Wright. He gave a lecture that began, 'Ladies and gentlemen, do you know what a brick is? It is a small, worthless, ordinary thing that costs 11 cents but has a wonderful quality. Give me a brick and it becomes worth its weight in gold.' It was the first time I had heard an audience told so bluntly and expressively what architecture is. Architecture is the turning of a worthless stone into a nugget of gold."[32] Aalto lavished much attention on the varied patinas of the brick and on the manner in which it was laid to achieve the desired imperfections and historical resonance, rather than machined perfection: "The bricks were made of clay from the topsoil, exposed to the sun. They were fired in manually stacked pyramids, using nothing but oak for fuel. When the walls were erected, all bricks were approved without sorting, with the result that the colour shifts from black to canary yellow, though the predominant shade is bright red."[33] The brick was

3. Walter Gropius and The Architects Collaborative. Harkness Commons, Harvard Graduate Center, Harvard University, Cambridge, Mass. 1948–50

to be laid so that the horizontal joints were gouged more deeply than the vertical.[34] While the building was under construction Aalto's friend, William W. Wurster (dean of the School of Architecture and Planning), reported on its progress in the summer of 1948: "It is very beautiful. The brickwork is *just* right. It is wonderfully free of any smooth thin feeling. It honestly makes me think of Florence. I hope you like it that I should feel so. I do not think it needs any trellis at the face of the two inner curves, but this, appropriately, must be as you wish. It is a very great building."[35] The historical associations Wurster perceived in the brickwork increased in much of Aalto's subsequent work. The trellis, a favorite motif of Aalto's, was depicted in several drawings (plate 186) but never realized.

Despite his success and popularity in the United States, Aalto did not pursue a postwar career in America. A series of spectacular competition successes and commissions in Finland, coupled with Aino Aalto's death in 1949 after a long illness, focussed his work at home, where two highly significant projects prefigured new directions in his postwar architecture. Both had been designed in 1944 in collaboration with the Stockholm architect Albin Stark: the Avesta Civic Center (plates 176–180) and the Johnson Institute, also in Avesta, Sweden (figure 4). While Finland was still at war, Sweden remained neutral, wealthy, and able to plan impressive new civic structures. The brief partnership with Stark, a competent and respected architect, provided Aalto with an effective outlet for his creative energies at a time when building was largely curtailed in most of Europe.[36] In their form, historicism, civic symbolism, and public spaces, the Avesta projects foreshadowed Aalto's more renowned civic centers in Finland—Säynätsalo, Seinäjoki, Alajärvi, and Rovaniemi—as well as university campuses for Helsinki and Jyväskylä. Moreover, they mark Aalto's exploration of new typologies.[37]

Avesta, a small city dominated by Axel Axelson Johnson's industrial ironworks, had anticipated building a new city hall as early as 1941, when the city architect prepared a site plan for the large rectangular block in the existing town grid. These documents were sent to Stark's office in Stockholm in early 1944, and over the summer Aalto and Stark prepared plans (signed and dated September 1944).[38] They proposed a group of connected buildings surrounding a piazza. The multifunctional civic center included a city hall, auditorium, library, hotel, workers' club, and ground-floor shops surrounding a courtyard that was open at one corner. The six-story city hall dominated the composition by virtue of its height, and the 700-seat auditorium, with its sloping curved roofline (suggesting its acoustic function) and nascent fan-shaped plan, contrasted with the surrounding prismatic forms. These main elements were linked by a three-story pitched-roof structure draped in vines (for the hotel, workers' club, and adult-education center) that also formed the principal facades of the courtyard. A skylit library was placed off to one corner and connected to the auditorium by a pergola. The idea of grouping together buildings for different functions into one complex was intended to create a prominent civic focal point, whose aggregate was greater than the sum of its parts.

Aalto and Stark observed that a typical modern city hall was virtually indistinguishable from many office buildings and that, in today's society, the city hall was no longer the undisputed center of civic life. By combining many functions into one complex, the architects could more effectively focus the city's public activities and further attract civic life than if the individual elements were scattered about the city. The plan itself, cranked slightly off the axis of the existing grid, was also intended to call attention to the town center. It was unusual in its picturesque asymmetry, and inspired by medieval and ancient architecture and town planning, but a more immediate source was Ragnar Östberg's Stockholm City Hall, completed in 1923, with an asymmetrical courtyard plan (figure 5).[39] Aalto and Stark wrote a lengthy description of their proposal that acknowledged its underlying historical inspiration: "One often finds that old castles, churches, and other dominant buildings in ancient towns occupy a special position within the modern town that has grown around them. They are generally at an angle to the surrounding square blocks, without a common axis. This produces a charming contrast which powerfully underlines the predominance of the ancient and venerable. A modern town centre can be accentuated by analogous means, forming a distinctly dominant feature in the townscape."[40] The manner in which this description was written recalled Camillo Sitte's influential texts on the art of city building, published in 1889 (*Der Städtebau nach seinen kunsterlischen Grundsätzen*). The architects also called attention to the Greek character of their composition: like the Athenian Acropolis, different buildings are grouped to form a continuous entity while preserving their individual character.[41] The rich mixture of materials also contributed to the distinct civic presence. The proposed yellow brick with red roof tiles was fairly traditional in Sweden,

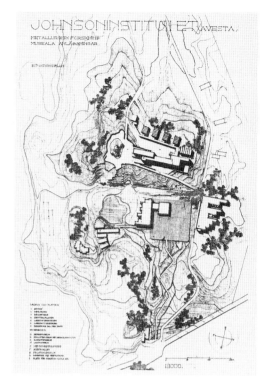

4. Alvar Aalto and Albin Stark. Johnson Institute, Avesta, Sweden. Project, 1944. Site plan. Whereabouts unknown

but the city hall was to be distinguished by its copper cladding, reflecting one of Avesta's main industries and "giving it a distinct identity among all the world's town halls."[42] The colorful palette marked a departure from Aalto's more typical, white functionalist architecture in favor of a decidedly more contextual approach.

The amassing of public functions around a piazza-like courtyard was central to Aalto's ideas of civic architecture. Taken together, these buildings are capable of doing what none of them can do individually: become a dominant feature in the city's life, in effect, the city crown, and concentrate civic life in such a way that it becomes a symbol of individual loyalty, while introducing the citizens of Avesta to civic life in a practical way.[43] The civic plaza, as the architects referred to the courtyard, was itself intended as a protected space with "an intimate and embracing character."[44] As a venue for various public gatherings, its possibilities included open-air theatrical performances and a cinema (the rear wall of the auditorium stage could be opened to the plaza). Such functional flexibility reappeared in later projects, such as the Kuopio Theater competition of 1952 and Siena Concert Hall of 1966, and retractable partition walls were used, most notably, in the Church of the Three Crosses at Vuoksenniska (plate 301).

Concurrent with the civic-center project, Axel Johnson commissioned an idealistic laboratory campus on a hilly site overlooking his ironworks. The institute included a variety of physics and chemistry research laboratories, museums for mining and seafaring, an exhibition showroom, an auditorium, an open-air theater, and housing.[45] The laboratories and museums were grouped around a courtyard enclosed on three sides, not

1

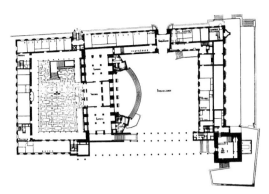

5. Ragnar Östberg.
Stockholm City Hall,
Stockholm. 1913–23.
Ground-floor plan

unlike the quintessential American campus plan by Thomas Jefferson for the University of Virginia at Charlottesville. The fan-shaped auditorium nestled into the hillside, and the "Greek" outdoor amphitheater conformed to the sloping landscape, constituting one of the earliest of many such theaters that appeared in his designs. This ambitious project was never realized owing to changes in Johnson's fortunes at the end of the war.[46] Perhaps Aalto already anticipated his new design for the Helsinki University of Technology, whose main building in downtown Helsinki had been destroyed by Soviet bombs in the Winter War of 1939–40. In his 1949 winning competition entry (and in its realization 1953–66) for a new suburban campus on the site of an old estate at Otaniemi, the crowning auditorium, in the form of an amphitheater, is sited at the head of an open courtyard from which classrooms and a library stretch across the gently sloping site (plates 259–274).

While designing the Avesta projects, Aalto had begun work on a master plan, initially commissioned in 1942, for the small industrial community of Säynätsalo, near Jyväsklyä, in central Finland.[47] Aalto developed the plan as time and staff permitted during the war; a final plan was completed toward the end of the decade. It entailed housing for nearly 5,000 people and a small town center with a series of buildings arranged in a stepped pattern flanking an open space (plates 197, 199). Then, in early 1948, Aalto was asked to develop sketches for a town hall, but the proposal was deferred. In July 1949, the community decided to proceed, and three architects were invited to compete: Alvar Aalto, Seppo Hytönen, and Veikko Raitinen. Aalto was declared the winner shortly after the deadline of December 15, 1949.[48] A sketch drawn on the copy of the master plan and a related preliminary study (plates 198–199) indicate the most significant changes from the master plan to the competition scheme: the series of stepped buildings in the master plan now terminated in an enclosed elevated courtyard and with a towering council chamber. In his written statement accompanying the competition drawings and model (plates 200–202, 204–205, 207, 209), Aalto elaborated on these two chief design elements and invoked historical analogies similar to those in his description of the Avesta Civic Center to explain his entry's bearing the rather grand motto,

"Curia," which referred to the seat of the Roman senate: "I used the enclosed courtyard as the principal motif because in some mysterious way it emphasizes the social instinct. In government buildings and town halls, the courtyard has preserved its primal significance from the days of ancient Crete, Greece, and Rome through the Middle Ages and the Renaissance."[49] Whereas the Avesta Civic Center site was flat, the gentle slope at Säynätsalo provided Aalto with an opportunity for a more dramatic section. The elevated courtyard is approached in two ways, by terraced grass-covered steps or by a granite staircase. This emphasizes the ceremonial nature Aalto intended for the court. Like Avesta, the building was designed to serve several purposes, but here multiple functions are zoned so that the administrative and cultural offices are arranged around the courtyard and the shops are on the ground floor—a kind of separation of the sacred and profane, or at least the civic and commercial.[50]

The courtyard appeared frequently in Aalto's other projects at this time, for example, even in a project for his own backyard. Upon Aino's untimely death on January 13, 1949, Aalto designed a courtyard wall to shelter their joint grave, which would have perpetuated her memory in the garden behind the house and studio and created greater architectural unity between the house and yard (plate 216).[51]

The council chamber at Säynätsalo, crowned by a pitched roof, dramatically rises an entire story above the courtyard. Rather than design a very practical single three-story building (as proposed by architects Hytönen and Raitinen), Aalto divided the various levels and rather matter-of-factly defended the design for its flexibility (it could be built in stages), variety, and sense of monumentality befitting a civic structure.[52] The architectural promenade—from the ground up the outdoor stairs to the inner courtyard, into the sunlit corridor, and up the inner staircase to the lofty chamber with its open wood trusses—is one of the most brilliant sequences in modern architecture. It fully achieves the monumentality and sense of importance and ceremony that Aalto intended, while maintaining an intimate scale.

The chamfered profile of the council-chamber roof drew upon several sources. The most immediate was Aalto's winning entry in the Helsinki University of Technology competition of April 1949 (plate 259), where the auditorium (later redesigned to resemble a Greek amphitheater) dominates the staggered arrangement of classroom buildings. Another likely source, noted by the architect and author, Stuart Wrede, was Asplund's Crematorium for Skövde, Sweden, of 1937–40 (figure 6),[53] where Asplund exposed the wood roof trusses to the chapel below, effectively eliminating the ceiling altogether and, thereby, creating a taller, more airy space. This became a popular Scandinavian motif, and Aalto used it effectively in his Malmi Funeral Chapel of 1950 and the Central Cemetery and Funeral Chapel, Lyngby-Taarbaek, Denmark (with Jean-Jacques Baruël), of 1951–52 (plates 217–225). The analogy to medieval town halls, especially Siena's, has also been noted by Aalto's biographer, Göran Schildt, and further underscores

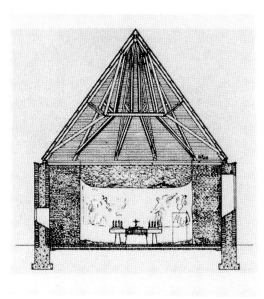

6. Erik Gunnar Asplund.
Skövde Crematorium,
Skövde, Sweden. 1937–40.
Section

the historical links Aalto forged.[54] Aalto's inventive wood truss, an honest display of the structure, also seems to symbolize the upholding of democratic ideals of a nation that had suffered much damage but maintained its independence and resisted succumbing to the sphere of Soviet power.

One of the first postwar competitions won by Aalto—the National Pensions Institute in Helsinki in 1948—projected an even more ambitious sense of urban monumentality than the Säynätsalo Town Hall. His winning entry bore the evocative Latin motto "Forum redivivum" (Forum revived) and was notable for its urban design and principal interior skylit space (plate 240).[55] The design was a conscious effort to define a new monumentality. The original site overlooked Töölö Bay, roughly a kilometer from the city center (figure 7). Aalto took full advantage of the gently sloping site and picturesque street layout, envisioning buildings of varying heights surrounding several squares on different levels seamlessly linked by broad staircases and pedestrian paths. As he did in the Avesta Civic Center, Aalto combined buildings of varying functions in a slightly angled composition. To achieve the desired sense of civic monumentality, Aalto explained that a complete separation of pedestrian and automobile traffic was essential.[56] Thus, in this modern forum, the market squares and terraced open spaces are deliberately small and human-scaled to contrast with the tall surrounding buildings.

Aalto's preliminary sketches depict the figure-ground relationship between the buildings and open spaces in the slightly skewed plan. The oblique view of the tall office towers and the banking hall crowned with prismatic skylights suggests the informal order and importance of hierarchy and spatial sequence in achieving the desired sense of monumentality (plates 241–243). He favored this scenographic device to frame views in

other contemporary projects around that time as well. For example, it is evident in sketches for the Helsinki University of Technology (plates 260–261) and in the approach to the Säynätsalo council chamber, framed by the ceremonial terraced entrance (plate 206; page 94). Whereas the council chamber at Säynätsalo and the auditorium at Otaniemi were the most important symbolic architectural elements, their equivalent at the Pensions Institute was the principal interior space: a four-story hypostyle hall crowned by crystalline skylights and ringed by balconies and offices. An early sketch suggests that Aalto initially considered a single, enormous glacial skylight to cover the atrium, surrounded by tiers of offices (figure 8; see also plate 241). The resemblance between Aalto's section sketches and Bruno Taut's visionary *Alpine Architecture* of 1919 (figure 9) is remarkable, even in the way the crystal mountain rises from the stepped sides of the foreground chasm. In Aalto's final competition scheme, the single monitor was replaced by a grid of smaller crystalline skylights, covering the atrium and supported by a forest of cruciform columns with outwardly tapering ribs that echoed the angled forms of the crowning skylights and evoked arboreal metaphors. The crystalline shapes mark a significant development not only in the design of Aalto's skylights—heretofore usually cylindrical, as in the Viipuri City Library and Baker House lounge (plates 108, 194–195)—but they also reflect a further development in Aalto's expressionistic forms, which increased dramatically in the following decade. He adapted the design most

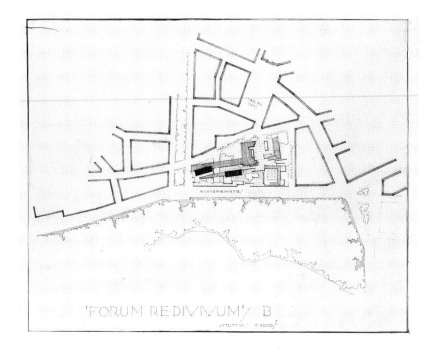

7. Alvar Aalto. National
Pensions Institute, Helsinki.
Competition, 1948. Scheme
B: site plan

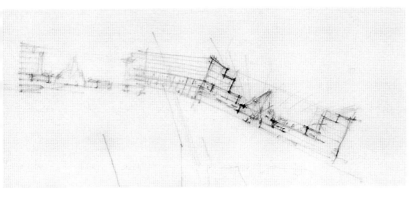

8. Alvar Aalto. National
Pensions Institute, Helsinki.
Study for competition, 1948.
Skylight sketch (detail).
Alvar Aalto Foundation,
Helsinki

effectively in the realized building (plates 250–252) and in later projects, such as the Academic Bookstore in Helsinki of 1961–69. Typically, in his own statements about the project, he rather laconically explained the functional advantages of steep skylights designed to shed rain and snow, and he defended the atrium workspace (surrounded by balconies with more conventional offices) as allowing for flexibility. But these pragmatic remarks disguised the heroic artistic expression of the generous interior public space so appropriate for the harsh northern climate, with its limited daylight hours throughout much of the year.

The parallel with Taut could also be extended beyond formal similarities to include the expressionistic philosophy that developed after World War I. Taut's ideal and fantastic vision embodied an apolitical socialism that transcended national boundaries—a symbolism echoed by Aalto when he projected an architecture not beholden to specific social systems. Such a philosophy complemented Aalto's desire to reverse the decline in public buildings by making suitably monumental institutions for a classless society (Finland's social welfare state), epitomized by the National Pensions Institute, a social insurance institution in the nation's capital, and the Säynätsalo Town Hall for a small industrial community. But, for Aalto, such a social system did not mean an end to artistic expression in public buildings. On the contrary, Aalto suggested that the public buildings in a community should be as important as the vital organs of the human body "if we want to prevent our communities from becoming psychologically repugnant and physiologically destructive to their citizens."[57] The admonition was directed toward mundane designs that merely solved the practical problems of housing a bureaucracy.

The historicism underlying Aalto's work of the 1940s and early 1950s, coupled with the human qualities that he advocated, generally

began to assume greater significance and interest among other architects. The philosophical and theoretical change in direction of the Congrès Internationaux d'Architecture Moderne (CIAM) at mid-century is highly illustrative of this juncture. Although Aalto had been active in CIAM in the late 1920s and early 1930s, his architecture and thinking eventually departed from CIAM's Functional City, as exemplified by the Athens Charter of 1943.[58] But, by the eighth CIAM conference, in 1951, the rational analysis of the city had softened. The theme was "The Heart of the City: Towards the Humanisation of Urban Life."[59] The principal subject was the core of the city, which had particular relevance in the rebuilding of Europe, and architects examined with new eyes the great, historic civic piazzas and pedestrian spaces of European cities. Their statements echoed Aalto's ideas about the relevance of ancient and medieval civic buildings and spaces, and the emphasis placed on "humanisation" shows the extent to which their thinking now centered on Aalto's chief concerns, which he had attempted to explore in the aborted publication, *The Human Side*, in 1939.[60]

Although Aalto did not attend CIAM conferences after the war and is not even mentioned in the published proceedings of the 1951 conference, his significance was acknowledged indirectly by his friend Sigfried Giedion, who had recently (in 1949) added a chapter about Aalto to the eighth printing of the second, enlarged, edition of his seminal work, *Space, Time and Architecture*. Giedion provided the concluding remarks at the CIAM conference: "Today [architectural] evolution is no longer confined to one nucleus—to Europe or the U.S.A. Today it emerges from the furthest

9. *The Crystal Mountain,*
from Bruno Taut, *Alpine
Architecture* (1919)

regions: in Finland and Brazil the level of creative architecture is higher than in England, Switzerland or Sweden."[61] What further characterized the contemporary period, he observed, was a change of attitude toward the past in relation to the future: "Ever since Bergson we have realized that history is not something static and dead, but something that ceaselessly 'gnaws into the future.'"[62] History, he explained, served not only as a storehouse of forms to imitate but also as a priceless container of human knowledge and experience. For Giedion and others, history was considered central to the idea of humanizing architecture. An indication of the significance that this played in the eighth CIAM conference can be gleaned from the profuse and varied entries indexed in the proceedings under the topic "Human."[63] This was the climate in which architects began to rebuild Europe. The acceptance of the past was for Aalto, as for other architects, central to the meaning and significance of their architecture. The role of the materials, the symbolic city crown, and the courtyard, for example, were essential components in his civic architecture. For Aalto, the courtyard symbolized and fostered the social instinct in its embrace of space, and he acknowledged its primal significance since Minoan civilization.

All of these elements are present in one of Aalto's most significant, albeit private, postwar projects: the Experimental House, a summer house built for himself and his second wife, Elissa, in 1952–53 on Muuratsalo Island near Säynätsalo (plates 226–231). The sloping profile of the dwelling's white exterior courtyard walls appears ruinlike, as the house sits perched on a granite outcropping in a dense forest. Two great gaps in the walls frame spectacular views of Lake Päijänne. The atrium, which had originally captivated Aalto on his first trip to Italy in 1924, was forcefully revived in the imaginative and idiosyncratic courtyard. The floor and walls of the courtyard, with a fire pit in the center, are laid in playful patterns of brick and tile; the overall effect resembles something like a patchwork quilt. Aalto explained that the house "was built to give the architect a chance to play purely for pleasure's sake. But it has also been done for serious experimental purposes, essentially to deal with problems that the architect cannot get involved with on ordinary building projects.... The building complex at Muuratsalo is meant to become a kind of synthesis between a protected architectural studio and an experimental center where one can expect to try experiments that are not ready to be tried elsewhere, and where the proximity to nature can give fresh inspiration both in terms of form and construction."[64] The walls around the patio are divided into approximately fifty panels composed of varying patterns and shapes of bricks and glazed ceramic tiles, as though a brick manufacturer's samples had been woven together in a playful aesthetic composition. The summer house was a spectacular retreat from the everyday world and provided a unique setting for contemplation and experimentation.

One of the tasks Aalto set for himself there was to "develop a type of standard brick or standard element so that it becomes possible to make walls in a capricious curved form without having to change the standard

pieces."[65] Recognizing an inherent tension between a free-form architecture and standard elements, he needed to invent a brick to allow the desired flexibility. "It must be possible to find a form for a brick wall that is round, concave, right-angled, everything."[66] He fulfilled this goal at the House of Culture in Helsinki, commissioned by the Finnish Communist Party in 1952 and completed in 1958 (plates 280–288).[67] The main part of the complex is a large auditorium with curvilinear contours radiating from the stage. For the broad convex exterior walls, he designed a specially manufactured wedge-shaped brick to accommodate the free-form curves. Moreover, the nearly square profile of the brick mitigates against either a horizontal or vertical directional emphasis.

Parallel to Aalto's renewed interest in the courtyard, ruins, materials, and their historical associations, he also further developed an expressionist, sculptural formal vocabulary, which was evident in Baker House and the House of Culture. Much of his work reflects a synthesis of these interests, which all contribute to the monumental and humanist character of his oeuvre. In the 1950s, his architecture became increasingly expressionistic, and, in his 1955 lecture, "Between Humanism and Materialism," he acknowledged the importance of formal expression as a means of tempering industrial cultures by its empathic power: "*The architect's task is to restore a correct order of values....* It is still the architect's duty to attempt to humanize the age of machines. But this should not be done without regard for form. Form is a mystery that defies definition but gives people a feeling of pleasure totally different from anything accomplished with government aid."[68]

In 1955, Aalto began to design the Church of the Three Crosses at Vuoksenniska, one of his most expressive and sensual buildings, and one in which his "mysterious" sense of form and light is most apparent. The church and parish house were commissioned for a forest community in Imatra developed after the war under the auspices of the Enso-Gutzeit company, for which Aalto had just completed a master plan (plate 289). The postwar rationing of concrete had been lifted, and the medium was well suited for the sculptural character of Aalto's design. Viewed from the main approach, the sloping roof profile unites the wall of the nave with the roof in a seamless vaultlike transition (plate 298). The white concrete walls and black metal roof complement the palette of the surrounding birch forest, and the tall bell tower deliberately echoes the smokestacks of the nearby factories. The general profile recalls the Vallila Church project of 1929 (plate 87), an acoustically expressive form, which Aalto elaborated upon at Vuoksenniska. But unlike Vallila, with its large continuous nave, at Vuoksenniska, even in the earliest sketches, Aalto planned to divide the large nave into a trinity of smaller spaces for practical, as much as acoustical, purposes (plates 291–294, 299).

The approach to the church from the side entrances does not fully prepare visitors for the experience inside, where the plastic qualities of concrete are given even more exuberant expression. The play of light from the clerestory windows and hidden skylight dissolves the white curv-

10. Le Corbusier. Notre Dame du Haut, Ronchamp, France. 1950–54

ing surfaces into an immateriality that belies the massive concrete structure; the brick-red terracotta tiles and the wood floor, pews, and chairs give a warm glow to the sacred space. In contrast to the relatively calm rectilinearity of the entrance area, the nave and the east wall (with its three great windows) take on a lyrical, baroque character (plates 300–303, 306). A single skylight and a hidden side window diffuse light upon the altar and sloping walls of the nave, creating a powerful metaphor for the spirit. The staggered organ pipes in the choir loft and the three convex clerestory windows define the east wall. Each window has a different rhythm of vertical panes; their varying heights evoke in glass the melody emanating from the choir to the rear of the church. The nineteenth-century philosopher Friedrich von Schelling's romantic idea that architecture is frozen music is here given palpable form.[69]

While the apsidal shapes derive partly from their acoustic function, these complex structures with interstices between the inner and outer walls harbor retractable sliding partitions. Massive concrete partitions, pocketed in the outer walls of the church (both on the east and west), slide into place mechanically on a track of steel ball bearings set in motor oil in order to divide the eight-hundred-seat church into three separate rooms (plates 300–302). This flexibility allows the church to host several community functions simultaneously. Each partition is formed of two principal wall sections, which meet at a pier. The ceiling track is flanked by crossbeams that resolve into ribbed fan vaults concealing ventilation ducts where they meet the east wall, one of Aalto's most complex details (plate 306). The exuberance of the white sculpted interior overwhelms the practical advantages of the spatial flexibility. While there is a formal resonance here with German baroque churches, the concrete church bears a more apt comparison with Le Corbusier's Notre Dame du Haut in Ronchamp, France, completed in 1954 (figure 10), which has an even greater sculptural and expressive form than Aalto's Vuoksenniska church. Le Corbusier's postwar architecture was increasingly sculptural, and it contributed much to the neo-expressionist tendency then emerging in European architecture.[70] It is perhaps not surprising, in this regard, that Aalto's work, especially in Germany where he was so successful, assumed even greater expressive form.

Outside Finland, the greatest concentration of Aalto's buildings is to be found in Germany. All were built after the war, beginning in the 1950s,

and there were numerous unbuilt projects as well.[71] In the postwar rebuilding of Germany, shaking off the legacy of the only acceptable architecture under Hitler—totalitarian classicism and *Heimatstil* (a national romantic and traditionalist, often rustic, variation of Art Nouveau)—was the principal challenge for German architects.[72] In seeking an appropriate architectural expression for rebuilding a country in ruins, German architects looked especially to Scandinavia for ideas. Günther Feuerstein described the situation: "There seemed to be an inability or a disinclination to restore the situation of the thirties, because of the deeply rooted suspicion of that period, whose quality was only gradually discovered later. Many of its masters had emigrated, others were dead.... Architects accepted ideas from Scandinavia and Switzerland most readily. The tendency in those countries was to avoid extreme formulas in favor of a pleasant, casual, and humane architecture, which contrasted sharply with the monumental pseudo-classicism of the totalitarian systems."[73] While Scandinavian architecture represented a humane architecture, the other great influence in Germany came from America and was ultimately even more pervasive. American corporate International Style architecture (Ludwig Mies van der Rohe's work, in particular) had an enormous indirect impact on German architecture. It was seen as a universal solution for all kinds of architectural problems.[74] But Aalto's architecture was prized precisely for its fresh expressive quality, in stark contrast to Miesian regularity. Aalto won competitions and received commissions for highly significant buildings that were praised for their originality and represented a wide range of building types: theaters, churches, apartment buildings, cultural centers, and recreational facilities.

Aalto's first project in the former Reich was not actually in Germany but in Austria. In 1952, he was invited to enter a competition for a multiuse sports, congress, and concert hall in Vienna's Vogelweidplatz. The program was immense: an indoor stadium, tennis courts, gymnastics hall, swimming pool and diving area, restaurants, congress hall, parking, and many additional facilities. The city officials seized this opportunity, despite times of economic hardship, to build an ambitious structure that would have far-reaching cultural significance, lift Vienna's image on the world stage, and possibly increase their chances of hosting Olympic games. They also wanted the architecture to reflect a postwar spirit of freedom, humanity, and international cooperation. *Der Aufbau*, a journal that covered Vienna's reconstruction, reported on "this noble competition of which the best solution to this difficult architectural task should serve as an inspiration for all who strive for a new world of individual freedom within the heart of the community."[75] The competition organizers selected architects whom they considered to be the best form-giving architects and engineers—prominent architects with sound building experience. Five European architects were invited to compete with nine Austrians: Alvar Aalto, Robert H. Matthew of Great Britain (one of the architects for the new Royal Festival Hall), and Pier Luigi Nervi of Italy had the greatest international reputations; the others were Karl Egender of Switzerland and Walter Höltje of Germany. The limited competition was announced in September 1952 with a deadline of March 2, 1953. The only foreigner on the jury was also its chairman, Sven Markelius, Aalto's friend and colleague from Stockholm.

All of the competing architects presented modernist visions with technically advanced structural systems that employed various trusses, suspension systems, or parabolic arches. The structural heroics and progressive imagery matched the spirit of the program. The immense program proved challenging: Nervi, for instance, impressed the jury with the beauty of his parabolic scheme, but his stadium was too small, and he omitted several other important requirements, thus disqualifying his design.[76] With Aalto's recently completed Sports Hall (on the new Helsinki University of Technology campus), constructed in time for the 1952 Helsinki Olympics, he had demonstrated structural ingenuity and skill in designing a large sports pavilion of wood trusses (plates 275–276).

Aalto's winning submission was a daring scheme for what would have been one of his largest single buildings (plates 278–279; figure 11). For the principal building, the huge sports hall, Aalto designed a steel-cable suspension structure to achieve a wide span uninterrupted by interior columnar supports. Placed off to one side in a trapezoid-shaped park and, thereby, preserving many of the trees and open spaces, the arena in plan was a large fan-shaped asymmetrical form. The sloping roof profile reflected the structural cable system itself. Like a giant circus tent, as Leonardo Mosso observed, or the irregular topography of a mountain slope, the hall towered above the surrounding grid of apartment buildings.[77] The jury was captivated by the unconventional, individual appearance of Aalto's scheme, which satisfied most of the program requirements in a single structure, rather than divide them among several pavilions (as proposed by the other architects).

Aalto's somewhat free-form structure contrasted with the majority of other entries, which were regular, symmetrical shapes: round, rectangular, or oval. In his written competition statement, Aalto justified his design by explaining its functional merits and emphasizing the flexibility of the program. He questioned the effectiveness of a symmetrical sports hall in terms of the viewers' experience. In round and oval arenas, he argued, the seats all have a different value: the best seats are all on the side of the finish line. Thus, Aalto eliminated seats on both ends, and, in his fan-shaped building, created primary and secondary seating areas: the majority of the seats were arranged on the side of the finish line, and a smaller secondary range of seats was placed directly opposite on the long side of the stadium. This side could also be transformed into a concert stage, or dais, for performances. To take advantage of the vast area underneath the multiple tiers of seating, Aalto congregated smaller exercise rooms, restaurants, tennis courts, promenades, cafés, and foyers—an environment he described as an "interior garden."[78]

The suspension roof was designed primarily to permit functional flexibility. The ceiling was covered by acoustical panels that could be rotated for varying degrees of sound reflection or absorption. The panels also reflected light from windows in the side walls. While Aalto's design satisfied the program requirements and was highly regarded on aesthetic grounds, the proposed structural system proved too uncertain for the client and jury. The jury felt the technical explanations for the roof system were insufficient and too challenging for current technology. The city officials wanted to begin construction in a few months time. Thus, two first prizes

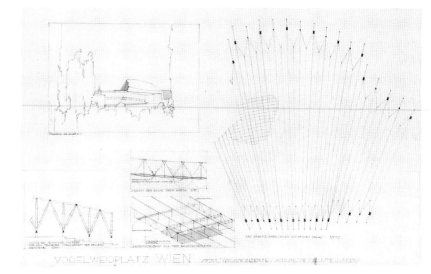

11. Alvar Aalto. Sports, Congress, and Concert Complex, Vogelweidplatz, Vienna. Project, 1952–53. Competition drawing: perspective, roof plan, and structural details. Alvar Aalto Foundation, Helsinki

were awarded, one to Aalto and another to Roland Rainer, a young Austrian architect, designer, and city planner.[79] Rainer's design was ultimately realized because its simpler structural system more closely matched the economical realities and capabilities of the building industry. Vienna was in no mood to take risks with Aalto's innovative and untested structure, which seemed economically uncertain and could have jeopardized the building schedule. The dream of such vast suspension structures for stadiums had fascinated architects since at least the 1920s, when Heinz and Bodo Rasch published their schemes in *Wie Bauen?* (figure 12). Although Aalto did not pursue this technology, suspension structures were further developed by a number of architects, among them the German Frei Otto, and became more prevalent in the 1960s.

The opportunity for Aalto to build in Germany came in 1954 when he and fifty-two other architects, representing fourteen countries, were invited to participate in the Berlin International Building Exhibition, or Interbau, in West Berlin (plates 315–320). The site was the Hansaviertel, a densely populated neighborhood that had been obliterated by a bombing blitz on November 22–23, 1943.[80] Modeled on the famous Weissenhofsiedlung exhibition in Stuttgart of 1927, arranged by the Deutscher Werkbund and directed by Mies van der Rohe, the Interbau buildings were to become permanent housing. The exhibition, which opened in 1957, had a very clear political agenda in a divided Germany. Sponsored by the West Berlin senate, the exhibition was conceived as a countermanifestation to East Berlin's Stalinallee, where the Soviet-style architecture was based on a banal stripped classicism (figure 13).[81]

The massive building campaign in the Hansaviertel (figure 14) was also seen as a way of shedding the legacy of Hitler's classicism and quaint *Heimatstil*. In the exhibition catalogue, Theodor Heuss, president of West Germany, wrote that the new Germany would be modern, not traditional, underscoring its aesthetic and ideological differences from Nazi Germany and the contemporary Stalinallee.[82] Otto Suhr, burgermeister of West Berlin, was bolder about the exhibition's political intentions: "Barely a

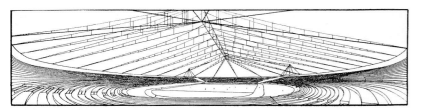

12. Heinz and Bodo Rasch. Stadium with suspension roof structure. Project, 1928. From Heinz and Bodo Rasch, *Wie Bauen?* (1928)

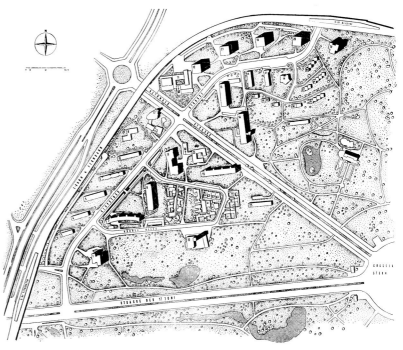

13. Egon Hartmann. Stalinallee, Block B South, East Berlin. c. 1953

14. Interbau Exhibition, Hansaviertel, West Berlin. 1957. Site plan

kilometer away from INTERBAU there begins the other Berlin, another world, separated from us but still belonging to us. The new buildings, from now on, extend toward that boundary and will prove their powers of attraction."[83] In contrast to the aesthetic monotony of the Stalinallee, the individual buildings of the Interbau were situated in a parklike setting and demonstrated architectural variety in the housing types and concomitant buildings, including a church, cinema, and shops. The buildings ranged from single-story row houses to a seventeen-story apartment building.[84]

The exhibition opened in July 1957, fifty years after the Deutscher Werkbund was founded and thirty years after the landmark Weissenhof exhibition. With the exception of Mies van der Rohe, many of the same architects participated in the Interbau as in the earlier, Stuttgart, exhibition. Aalto's apartment building had no parallel in the east or west. The eight-story building was split into two main blocks joined by a centrally located breezeway entrance. Hardly an *Existenzminimum*, each apartment had generous spaces and an atriumlike balcony (page 125). The asymmetry of the overall plan, the slight fanning of the building profile, and the simulated ashlar stonework of the concrete-paneled facade impressed the critics. The impact of the Hansaviertel apartment building was immediate and led to further commissions for Aalto in Germany.

Two months before the Interbau had opened in Berlin, the city of Bremen in northern Germany announced plans for Neue Vahr, the largest social housing project ever planned in the Federal Republic of Germany. It was considered a model for the ideal garden city. Within the next four years 10,000 apartments were built at Neue Vahr, an empty wasteland adjacent to an existing neighborhood. The agency in charge, Gemeinnützige Wohnungsbaugemeinschaft (GEWOBA), was a nonprofit low-cost housing organization that had been established in 1924.[85] A master plan for the ambitious project had been prepared in 1956 by a team of architects and urban planners, led by the renowned German planner, Ernst May (figure 15).[86] The general planning principles were based on neighborhood units. Housing ranged from two to eight stories, reaching a climax in a single twenty-two-story highrise adjacent to the main shopping center and bordering a small man-made lake. In May's plan, the tower (a rather conventional Y-shaped volume) provided Neue Vahr with a city "crown," and it also symbolized GEWOBA's attitude toward innovative architecture.[87] The press quickly claimed the proposed *Hochhaus* (literally, high house) as a new symbol not just of Neue Vahr but of the entire city-state of Bremen. But local opinion also criticized GEWOBA's progressive plans as brutally modern and ridiculed the proposed highrises as depressing and tasteless *Wohnmaschinen* (housing machines).[88] Heretofore, Bremen's architecture had been composed mainly of individual houses and duplexes.

In June 1958, Aalto, who hardly had a reputation for tall-building design, was commissioned to design the new city crown for Bremen. His Berlin building had been widely acclaimed, but GEWOBA was especially attracted to the fact that Aalto did not seek universal solutions in his archi-

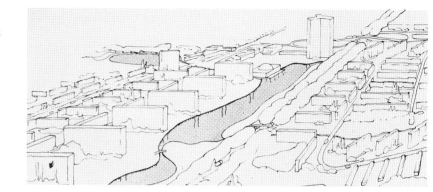

15. Ernst May. Master plan, Neue Vahr, Bremen, Germany. 1956

tecture but searched instead for a new solution for each task.[89] At the same time, the Bremen press praised Aalto's architecture as a realistic "human architecture" that satisfied people's needs. The decision to select a non-German architect with these qualities was a deliberate and clever strategy to appease local controversy.[90] The strategy succeeded.

Ironically, Aalto was generally critical of tall apartment buildings. In writing about his master plan for Nynäshamn, Sweden (1943–46, with Albin Stark), which included "point block" towers, he acknowledged his skepticism of highrises; instead, he preferred low-rise buildings and single-family dwellings in contact with the ground: "The question of a limitation on the height to which one can build, for example, highrise apartment houses, is one of today's most difficult questions. We can say with good reason that the solution has always been a kind of measure of the social level, difficult to define, of different cultural and social organizations. Fundamentally the question is not economic; rather, it is social and psychological factors—often in direct conflict with economic demands—that determine the parameters for housing."[91] Only under certain conditions would he accept the highrise:

> *There are cases in which it is possible to achieve a more advantageous architectural form and greater social and psychological advantages by building real highrise buildings. It is quite possible that a certain number of inhabitants, both families and individuals, belong to a group whose housing problems can be solved in a satisfactory way with highrise apartments, but certainly such a building type cannot satisfy more than 25 percent of the inhabitants. To state my own view, I would say that extra-tall buildings of six or more floors can be defended only where the situation requires such a solution. . . . I would like to point out one cir-*

16. Neue Vahr, Bremen, Germany. c. 1962. Aerial view

17. Ludwig Mies van der Rohe. Glass Skyscraper. Project, 1922. Model. The Museum of Modern Art, New York. Mies van der Rohe Archive

cumstance that is often overlooked when weighing questions of this type. Highrise apartments must be regarded, both socially and architecturally, as a considerably more dangerous form of building than single-family houses or lowrise apartments. The highrise building, therefore, presumes a more stringent architectural standard and greater artistry and social responsibility. A badly planned private house or a less successfully planned block of modest lowrise flats disturbs a housing area much less than a badly planned and constructed group of highrise buildings.[92]

At twenty-two stories, the Neue Vahr tower is Aalto's tallest building, and, by virtue of its height and context, one of his most conspicuous (figure 16; plates 322, 327). His earliest sketches fill pages in which he explored fan shapes, in plan and perspective, studying the most aesthetically pleasing and functional curves (plates 321, 323–325). As the design evolved, he incorporated elements from Baker House and the Hansaviertel apartment building. All of the approximately 200 apartments, each with a balcony contained within the facade (a significant reversal of the projecting cantilevered balconies typical of his functionalist-era buildings), face west for optimal light and sunset views of the old city. Above the ground-floor shops, each floor contains nine small apartments: seven one-room apartments, a one-and-one-half room apartment, and a two-room apartment. By virtue of the nonorthogonal fan-shaped plan, each apartment has a slightly different floor plan, which achieves the variety and sense of individuality so often lacking in tall buildings of more regular shape. Each floor also has a common room; although no longer used, at the time of the building's completion in 1962 it reflected other social realities and a client's generous budget for such amenities.

Aalto's design was received as extremely elegant and ingenius.[93] In its unusual floor plan and expressive character, it bears comparison with Hans Scharoun's "Romeo and Juliet" apartment buildings in Stuttgart (1954–59, with Wilhelm Frank), with their irregular, angular plan. But Aalto's Neue Vahr highrise also functioned as a city crown, and, in this regard, it was exceptional among Germany's tall buildings of the 1950–60s and can only be compared to Mies van der Rohe's Glass Skyscraper project for Berlin of 1922 for its innovative organic form (figure 17). Aalto's tower is hardly a glass curtain-wall structure, but its segmented curves and tapering sharp angles set it apart from the surrounding apartment blocks. The unique, white concrete-paneled and tile-sheathed *Aalto Hochhaus*, as it is now commonly known, symbolizes the dignity and humanity of the new postwar community.

Among Aalto's future German clients who visited the Berlin Interbau was a delegation from Wolfsburg, the industrial city founded by Hitler with the expertise of Ferdinand Porsche in 1937 and dedicated to producing Volkswagens. The new city lacked many basic civic and cultural institutions and, like many of the older German cities and villages, participated in a postwar reconstruction program of "social rearmament." In 1954, a new city hall designed by Paul Baumgarten (a well-known Berlin architect, who had also participated in the Interbau exhibition) was built on Porsche Strasse in the center of the city (figure 18). An adjacent site was earmarked for a new cultural center that would combine a variety of functions. The program for the new center was largely conceived by David Fischer, the director of the school board, who envisioned a single building encompassing commercial

18. Paul Baumgarten, City Hall (left center), and Alvar Aalto, Cultural Center (right center), Wolfsburg, Germany. Aerial view, c. 1962

shops, a library, facilities for adult continuing education, auditoriums, art exhibition spaces, a youth center, and hobby and craft rooms in conjunction with the national social program, *Heim des offenen Tur* (Home of the open door).[94] The need for institutions offering diversity in the otherwise mono-cultural industrial community was acute. Life in Wolfsburg revolved around a single activity: producing Volkswagens. With the establishment of the forty-hour work week, people needed suitable activities to fill their free time. The inhabitants of the new town had little in common outside of work; they had come from all over Germany and also included Italian immigrants, who had helped build Wolfsburg. Thus, there was little sense of common ground, and the new cultural center was to provide a communal setting outside the factory. Architecturally, it was to be a significant contribution to the cityscape.

In December 1957, the city was awarded one of six grants from the German government to build a model community center, and the council was free to search for its architect. Initially, Baumgarten was the architect of choice. The council was pleased with the recently completed city hall, and he also enjoyed a reputation as one of Germany's best architects. But the council had also become acquainted with Aalto through Peter Koller, a city planning official whose son was studying architecture and who, apparently, called attention to the Finnish architect. Koller encouraged the council to pursue Aalto, citing Viipuri City Library and the recently completed House of Culture in Helsinki as relevant examples of the architect's outstanding work.[95] Thus, in January 1958, Baumgarten and Aalto were invited to compete. The architects visited the site in February, and entries were submitted in June.[96] On July 1, 1958, Aalto was selected the winner, and his competition entry is remarkably similar to the final building (plates 344–360).

The complicated program, which virtually demanded several buildings in one, was well suited to Aalto. Since the Avesta Civic Center project of 1944, he had designed and advocated civic centers encompassing multiple functions, usually expressed volumetrically and grouped around a central courtyard. But there was no need for a new outdoor piazza at Wolfsburg. Rather, Aalto's building provided an edge to the existing plaza in front of the tall city hall. Its principal northeast facade, although only two stories tall, achieves a remarkable monumental presence. Fan-shaped in plan, five auditoriums, elevated above a ground-floor colonnade of copper-clad columns, form a sweeping, stepped facade that reaches a crescendo in

the largest auditorium. As drawn in elevation (plate 346) the rhythm provides a counterpoint to the gently sloping contours of the background landscape, a strategy Aalto had adopted several months earlier for the North Jutland Art Museum in Aalborg, Denmark, of 1958–72, designed with Elissa Aalto and Jean-Jacques Baruël (plate 343). Contextually, the sweeping profile of the Wolfsburg structure also forms a subtle transition from the street to the city-hall tower. The size of the complex is relatively intimate, but the sense of scale lends an indisputable monumentality, which is reinforced by the materials and historical references. The windowless facade of the auditoriums is sheathed in Carrara marble with alternating bands of Pamir syenite,[97] which, Schildt has noted, was a direct borrowing from the Cathedral of Siena and its campanile.[98] This was the first time Aalto used marble as exterior cladding, and it became a favorite medium in his late civic work.

Shops and offices aligned along the main street behind a colonnade conceal a vast array of rooms within—the auditoriums, the keystone-shaped library, an outdoor roof terrace, and several arts-and-crafts studios. While most of the principal rooms have irregular, complex shapes, some of the secondary rooms were regularized in the final plan. The idea of an interior landscape in Aalto's work is seen, especially, in the main entrance lobby, with its tiled columns and walls, and in the library, with its vast sunken pit. Skylights abound throughout the building in an extraordinary variety of shapes and sizes: they are more numerous and complex here than in any other building by Aalto (plates 353–360). The inventive designs range from a constellation of skylights that seems to float over the library to small openings that punctuate each entrance to the auditoriums. The subtle modulation of light, with such emphatic and elaborate means, in Aalto's buildings of this period—Church of the Three Crosses at Vuoksenniska, National Pensions Institute, Helsinki University of Technology auditorium, and North Jutland Art Museum—was unparalleled. Not since the baroque and rococo periods had an architect shown such a keen interest in light effects that were not a matter of merely increasing transparency. The roof terrace provides a protected outdoor play area and is surrounded by sun-filled rooms and hallways. Abutting its south end, a group of workshops and studios adjoin a small atrium with a large chimneyless firepit. The sheltered atrium can be transformed into another open-air space by opening a sliding glass wall and retracting the movable skylight ceiling. The memory of Muuratsalo's sylvan courtyard hearth is here transported to an urban cultural center so that industrial workers can enjoy atavistic pleasures while pursing life-enriching interests. The success of the cultural center led to other commissions in Wolfsburg: the Heilig Geist Church and Parish Center of 1960–62 and St. Stephanus Church in the suburb of Detmerode, completed in 1968.

Another successful competition Aalto was invited to participate in was that for the Essen Opera House of 1959–88, one of the most prestigious building types in postwar Germany (plates 361–366). German theater design had been very experimental in the 1920s, as exemplified by Walter Gropius's and Erwin Piscator's Total Theater project of 1927, notable for its flexible seating and stage arrangements. Such radical experiments were not taken up in the postwar era. New theaters and opera houses became cultural status symbols for the new affluent society, and, in their appeal to a sense of civic pride, their designs generally adhered to more conventional types. According to one critic: "The wish for splendidly prestigious buildings with a 'segregated' stage on which the world portrayed was presented to a public in the auditorium accorded with the Economic Miracle and the feeling of 'We count again.'"[99]

During the postwar reconstruction, several cities in the industrial Ruhr River Valley (such as Bochum, Düsseldorf, and Münster) built new theaters. Essen had ambitions of becoming a new cultural center in the region, and theater and music were increasingly popular. Essen could claim only one principal theater, the Stadttheater (originally built in 1892, destroyed in 1944, and rebuilt in 1950). Thus, a committee to oversee the project for a new theater was formed in 1955, and a site was chosen: a small park in the Stadtgarten. Eventually, the committee announced plans for the "ideas" competition on December 12, 1958, with a deadline for entries on July 1, 1959. They sought an outstanding example of modern architecture, well integrated into the city's urban context. There were thirty-three entries in the competition, which was open to all architects from Essen. Additionally, several other German architects and three foreigners were paid to participate.[100] Aalto had previously demonstrated his skill in theater design in the House of Culture in Helsinki (plates 280–288). Neither Gropius nor Mies van der Rohe, who had submitted designs for the Mannheim National Theater competition in 1953 (figure 19), nor

Hans Scharoun, who had recently designed the Berlin Philharmonic Concert Hall (figure 20), were invited.

The free-form massing of Aalto's composition seems, to some extent, derived from the organic motifs of the park landscape, itself irregular in plan and contour. The sculptural form evokes associations of a monolithic mountain rising from the surrounding green park. It is clearly a freestanding building, somewhat isolated in the park and, consequently, divorced from the surrounding urban context. A compelling interpretation offered by Aalto's colleague, Harald Deilmann, suggested that the combination of mountain imagery with an auditorium recalled the symbolism of Delphi, where Aalto had traveled and sketched several years earlier in 1953 (page 56).[101] Not surprisingly, his competition entry also envisioned a small outdoor amphitheater nestled against two sides of the building. In this picturesque composition, the entrance is not particularly conspicuous and is placed at the corner of the building, a convenient location for vehicular access and underground parking. The drama and excitement occur in the interior, which echoes the free form of the exterior. The impressive airy lobby with wide stairs, permitting a stately promenade to the three tiers of balconies with park views, is a grand setting that matches the city's civic ambitions. The white palette is rendered in a rich variety of materials: Carrara marble, tile, and brass highlights. The auditorium, with its unusual asymmetrical shape, recalling the House of Culture plan, is an intense, vibrant indigo blue with shallow white balconies that seem suspended in space. (Aalto had proposed a similar design for New York's Lincoln Center during its initial planning in 1956.)[102] The theater was neither experimental nor avant-garde in character, but it fully satisfied its symbolic and artistic role in the city.

The jury, comprising various city representatives and several senior German architects, the best-known being Egon Eiermann, announced the results on August 18, 1959. They were unanimous in awarding Aalto first prize, and, to underscore their decision, no second and third prizes were given. Aalto's entry apparently rendered the jury speechless, and they proclaimed it the strongest artistically and most unusual in its individuality. To appreciate the winning design that overwhelmed the jury, it is worthwhile to consider some of the other competition entries. The majority of schemes called for a rectangular building mass with an interior designed for flexibility. Some of these schemes relied on triangular, hexagonal, and octagonal planning modules, which the jury deemed either too restrictive or technically problematic in their efforts to create flexible spaces. Others demonstrated sound planning but were artistically lackluster. Their inspiration seems to have been the kind of universal space and clear sense of order proposed by Mies van der Rohe in his Mannheim National Theater plan. Aalto's theater was virtually unique among the competing designs in its organic expression and imagery. Only Scharoun's Berlin Philharmonic Concert Hall, one of the German expressionist's greatest works, rivals Aalto's in its inventive plan.

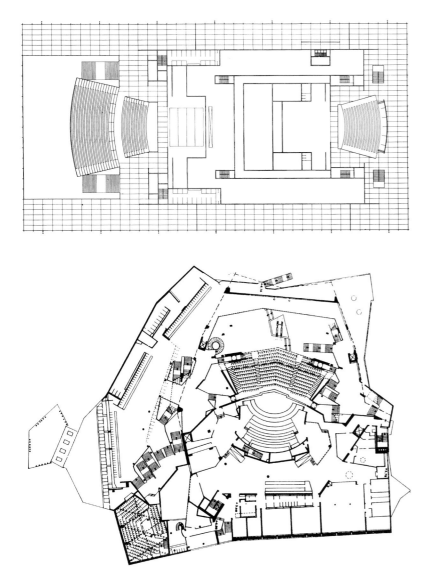

19. Ludwig Mies van der Rohe. National Theater, Mannheim, Germany. Project, 1953. First-floor plan. The Museum of Modern Art, New York. Mies van der Rohe Archive

20. Hans Scharoun. Berlin Philharmonic Concert Hall, Berlin. 1956–63. Plan

In 1963, four years after the competition, Aalto was ordered to proceed with developing the plan. But not until 1983, seven years after his death, was Essen prepared to commence construction. The 1,100-seat theater was finally completed in 1988 by Elissa Aalto in association with Harald Deilmann. Numerous modifications were made, especially in the enlargement of the back-of-house facilities and in some of the details. But the general massing, lobby, and auditorium reflect Aalto's intentions.

In 1959, the same year as the Essen competition, Aalto was commissioned to develop a plan for the area around Helsinki's Töölö Bay. Since the turn of the century, the location had been the focus of new development, including the National Museum, the Parliament Building, and, more recently, the initial site of the National Pensions Institute. Concomitantly, there had been a series of unimplemented urban plans, the most recent from 1954. Aalto's plan, initially presented and approved by the city council in 1961, focused on two main areas: a business district and bus station, and an entirely new group of cultural institutions strung along the shore of the bay, including a concert hall, opera house, Museum of Finnish Architecture, Finnish Academy, library, and museums (plates 392–393).[103] This grand gesture for Finland's capital city rivals any American "City Beautiful" plan in scope.[104] It was as if the ancient Greek traveler, Pausanias (who had dismissed a city of the Phocians as hardly worthy to be called a city, because it had no government offices, no gymnasium, no theater, no market, and no piped water supply),[105] had declared Helsinki unfit for its capital status, and Aalto responded with a plan symbolic of ideological values of individual liberty and freedom of expression in the Western world.

The plan underwent numerous revisions in the following decade, and only Aalto's Finlandia Hall (plates 394–408), a new concert and congress hall, was ever realized.[106] In the early studies, the concert hall closely resembled the Essen Opera House in its overall massing. But, as the program and design evolved, the vast complex, with two concert halls, meeting rooms, and foyers, assumed a more angular shape. Set on a gently sloping site, the building has two main entrances: one for pedestrians along the principal thoroughfare, Mannerheim Street, and the other for arrival by car on a lower level along the bay. The sequence of staircases and foyers to reach the double-height lobby and balconies overlooking Töölö Bay is a spectacular promenade befitting the monumentality of the complex. As with many of his later institutional and religious works, Finlandia is clad in Carrara marble panels, a decision that has had disastrous consequences. Unfortunately, the effectiveness of marble cladding was never tested at Aalto's Experimental House in Muuratsalo. Warping like butter curls, the marble panels have not survived the extreme temperatures of the northern climate. But visually and aesthetically, the whiteness of the marble created a far more compelling and startling image than dark, native granite cladding. The dramatically chamfered roof of the large concert hall rises like a craggy snow-covered mountain from the horizontal mass of the main building, crowning the new hall and providing a new city crown to that part of Helsinki and a counterpoint to the adjacent tower of the National Museum by Gesellius, Lindgren, and Saarinen of 1902–12 (plate 408; page 49).

Aalto's greatest ambition was to create a new heart for the capital city. In his opinion, an individual building was an insufficient reflection of a culture, which could only be assessed in the broadest terms:

> *There is a great deal of interest in art in our society.... There are those who consider collecting some type of art work all that is necessary to be taking an active part in cultural affairs.... For a person with this attitude it is naturally of no consequence how the organic structure that surrounds him evolves: he does not care what his home village looks like, how the city he lives in is structured or functions, if it improves on or destroys nature, if the traffic flows smoothly or if it is a free-for-all, just to name a few examples.*
>
> *And yet the true sign of culture is the ability to create a balance in the whole environment of cities, villages, traffic arteries, nature, and other elements that form the framework of our lives, and only in this totality can one include true art and the refined types of technology that serve man in a proper way.*[107]

When examined in its totality, Aalto's lifelong effort to shape the built environment—from a three-legged stool to housing, cultural institutions, and entire regional plans—reflects a profound desire to create an ethical, life-affirming culture. Since the 1937 Paris International Exhibition, when the Finnish Pavilion so captivated the critics and launched Aalto's international career, his architecture has had enormous appeal in Finland and much of the postwar Western world. Throughout his mature work, as he had in much of the output of his brilliant youth, Aalto did not seek universal solutions and formulas. His subtle manipulation of materials, respect for their natural and historical associations, utilization of a formal vocabulary that favored free form over regularity, and his profound and acute understanding of the individual site and circumstance created an original architecture that was designed to appeal on many levels, not the least of which were its sensory, visceral, and ultimately humane qualities.

Notes

1. Alvar Aalto, [Eulogy for Eliel Saarinen] (1950); repr. in Göran Schildt, *Alvar Aalto: The Mature Years*, trans. Timothy Binham (New York: Rizzoli, 1991), pp. 168–169.

2. See Demetri Porphyrios, *Sources of Modern Eclecticism: Studies on Alvar Aalto* (London: Academy Editions, 1982); and Colin St. John Wilson, *The Other Tradition of Modern Architecture: The Uncompleted Project* (London: Academy Editions, 1995).

3. Porphyrios, *Sources of Modern Eclecticism*, p. 81. See also Kenneth Frampton, "Towards a Critical Regionalism: Six Points for an Architecture of Resistance," in Hal Foster, ed., *The Anti-Aesthetic: Essays on Postmodern Culture* (Port Townsend, Wash.: Bay Press, 1983), pp. 16–30.

4. "Souvenirs de l'Exposition," *Cahiers d'art*, nos. 8–9 (1937).

5. Henry-Russell Hitchcock, "Paris 1937," *Architectural Forum*, no. 67 (September 1937), p. 160.

6. Amédée Ozenfant, "Notes of a Tourist at the Exhibition, 1937," in John Willett, ed., *Art and Power: Europe under the Dictators 1930–45* (London: Hayward Gallery, 1995), p. 116.

7. Alvar Aalto, "Valtakunnansuunittelu ja kulttuurimme tavoittet" [National Planning and Cultural Goals], *Suomalainen Suomi* (1949); repr. in Göran Schildt, ed., *Sketches: Alvar Aalto*, trans. Stuart Wrede (Cambridge, Mass., and London: MIT Press, 1978), p. 102.

8. [John McAndrew, ed.], *Aalto: Architecture and Furniture* (New York: The Museum of Modern Art, 1938).

9. Reyner Banham, "The One and the Few: The Rise of Modern Architecture in Finland," *The Architectural Review*, no. 723 (April 1957), p. 247.

10. Alvar Aalto, "Maailmannäyttelyt: New York World's Fair/The Golden Gate Exposition" [World's Fairs: The New York World's Fair and the Golden Gate Exhibition] *Arkkitehti* (1939); repr. in Schildt, *Sketches*, p. 64. On Aalto's Finnish pavilions for Paris and New York, see Peter B. MacKeith and Kerstin Smeds, *The Finland Pavilions: Finland at the Universal Expositions, 1900–1992* (Tampere: Kustannus, 1993).

11. See, for example, Alvar Aalto, "Outline of Series of Lectures at Yale University—Spring 1939" (William W. Wurster Archive, Berkeley, Calif.).

12. Alvar Aalto, "My Frank Lloyd Wright," unpublished manuscript, 1940, Registrar's files, exhibition 114, The Museum of Modern Art, New York. The Museum had planned a *Festschrift* in honor of Wright, but he objected to the content of an essay by Walter Curt Behrendt and threatened to cancel the exhibition, on view November 13, 1940–January 4, 1941, if the book were published. Ultimately, Henry-Russell Hitchcock's *In the Nature of Materials: The Buildings of Frank Lloyd Wright, 1887–1941* (New York: Hawthorn Books, 1942) was published with Wright's cooperation. The book, Hitchcock explained in his preface, was intended as "a sort of ex post facto catalogue of the exhibition." Ibid., p. xxvii.

13. Aalto, "My Frank Lloyd Wright."

14. Alvar Aalto, "Experimental House, Muuratsalo," *Arkkitehti–Arkitekten* (1953); repr. in Schildt, *Sketches*, p. 115. See also Göran Schildt, *Alvar Aalto: The Decisive Years*, trans. Timothy Binham (New York: Rizzoli, 1986), pp. 77–78.

15. Henry van de Velde, in Ulrich Conrads, ed., *Programs and Manifestoes on 20th-Century Architecture*, trans. Michael Bullock (Cambridge, Mass.: MIT Press, 1975), p. 30.

16. Alvar Aalto, "Henry van de Velde in Memoriam," *Arkkitehti–Arkitekten* (1957); repr. in Schildt, *Sketches*, p. 143. Aalto also recognized his friendship with van de Velde on other occasions, in his 1953 essay, "Experimental House, Muuratsalo," ibid., p. 115. In an exhibition of their work in Zurich in 1948, Aino and Alvar Aalto dedicated a bentwood experimental design to van de Velde, with the following remarks: "The great pioneer of the architecture of our times, the first to envisage the revolution in the techniques of wood." Karl Fleig, ed., *Alvar Aalto* (Scarsdale, N.Y.: Wittenborn, 1963), p. 73.

17. Edward R. Ford, *The Details of Modern Architecture*, Vol. 2 (Cambridge, Mass., and London: MIT Press, 1996), p. 119.

18. Alvar Aalto, "Kulttuuri ja tekniikka" [Culture and Technology], *Suomi-Finland–USA* (1947); repr. in Schildt, *Sketches*, p. 94.

19. Ibid., p. 95. Aalto was specifically referring to the Princeton conference in this passage. See also "Planners' Platform," *Architectural Forum*, no. 86 (April 1947), pp. 12–14; and "On Planning Man's Physical Environment," *Architectural Record*, no. 101 (April 1947), pp. 98–100.

20. Paul Zucker, ed., *New Architecture and City Planning: A Symposium* (New York: Philosophical Library, 1944), pp. 547–604.

21. Louis I. Kahn, "Monumentality," in ibid., pp. 577–588. See also David B. Brownlee and David G. De Long, *Louis I. Kahn: In the Realm of Architecture* (New York: Rizzoli, 1991), pp. 42–43.

22. For more on the discussion and literature of monumentality, see Christiane C. and George R. Collins, "Monumentality: A Critical Matter in Modern Architecture," *Harvard Architecture Review*, no. 4 (1984), pp. 14–35; and William J. R. Curtis, "Modern Architecture, Monumentality and the Meaning of Institutions: A Reflection on Authenticity," in ibid., pp. 64–85.

23. Lewis Mumford, "Monumentalism, Symbolism and Style," *The Architectural Review*, no. 105 (April 1949), pp. 173–180.

24. Ibid., p. 173.

25. Ibid., p. 175.

26. The associate architect was the Boston firm of Perry, Shaw, and Hepburn.

27. In several studies, Aalto also flirted with a hexagonal module for the library, which was ultimately eliminated from the program. Such modular planning devices are rare in Aalto's work. Instead, he tended to favor organic asymmetrical shapes that obscure any apparent module underlying the design.

28. Deborah Poodry and Victoria Ozonoff, "Coffins, Pies and Couches: Aalto at MIT," *Spazio e societa*, no. 5 (June 1982), pp. 104–123.

29. Drawings for the furnishings are in the Artek company archive, Helsinki.

30. Stucco was substituted at the request of the client to expedite the construction process. See J[ames]. R. Killian, Jr. (president of MIT), letter to Alvar Aalto et al., November 18, 1948 (Alvar Aalto Archives, Helsinki [henceforth AAA, Helsinki]). Killian said he would accept tile only if it would not delay the completion of the building.

31. For a critical comparison of Gropius's Graduate Center and Aalto's Baker House, see St. John Wilson, *The Other Tradition of Modern Architecture*, pp. 93–102.

32. Alvar Aalto, "Between Humanism and Materialism," lecture, Central Union of Architects, Vienna, 1955; repr. in Schildt, *Sketches*, p. 133.

33. Alvar Aalto, quoted in Schildt, *Mature Years*, p. 159.

34. See the minutes of a job meeting with Aalto, April 9 and 10, 1947 (AAA, Helsinki).

35. William W. Wurster, letter to Alvar Aalto, August 16, 1948 (AAA, Helsinki).

36. For Aalto's association with Stark, see Schildt, *Mature Years*, pp. 72–84. Stark's archive is now at the Swedish Museum of Architecture, Stockholm, and contains drawings and written documents. The archive had not been fully catalogued during the researching of this essay.

37. Up to this time, Aalto's experience in designing a city hall, or similar building type, was limited to a school assignment, his competition entry for the Finnish Parliament (1923–24), and sketches for the League of Nations competition (1927). The schools he and Aino had designed were the Inkeroinen Elementary School, two kindergartens, and the unsuccessful competition for the enlargement of Helsinki University (1931).

38. Sketches and final drawings are in the Stark Archive, Swedish Museum of Architecture, Stockholm. I was unable to find a program for the new building, only the architects' description.

39. For a further discussion of the impact of Östberg's architecture, see Stuart Wrede, *The Architecture of Erik Gunnar Asplund* (Cambridge, Mass., and London: MIT Press, 1980), pp. 2, 11; and Porphyrios, *Sources of Modern Eclecticism*, pp. 8, 28.

40. Alvar Aalto and Albin Stark, quoted in Göran Schildt, *Alvar Aalto: The Complete Catalogue of Architecture, Design and Art*, trans. Timothy Binham (New York: Rizzoli, 1994), p. 32. The architects' full description was originally published in *Arkkitehti*, no. 10 (1944).

41. Alvar Aalto and Albin Stark, "Stadscentrum i Avesta," p. 3 (Stark Archive, Swedish Museum of Architecture, Stockholm).

42. Quoted in Schildt, *Complete Catalogue*, p. 32.

43. Aalto and Stark, "Stadscentrum i Avesta," p. 2.

44. Ibid., p. 3; trans. Kjersti Board.

45. The architects' description is in the Stark Archive, Swedish Museum of Architecture, Stockholm.

46. Schildt, *Complete Catalogue*, p. 83.

47. See the correspondence between Aalto and Dr. Hilmer Brommels of the Parviainen company (later bought by Enso-Gutzeit), the principal client (AAA, Helsinki).

48. Architect members of the jury included Aulis Blomstedt and Yrjö Lindegren. (See a letter from Alvar Aalto to the Säynätsalo municipality, October 10, 1949, regarding the competition and changes in the program [AAA, Helsinki].) The final drawings, completed in March 1950, a few months after the competition, basically reflect the competition scheme.

49. Alvar Aalto, quoted in Schildt, *Complete Catalogue*, p. 130; the complete descriptions for the competition entry can be found in AAA, Helsinki.

50. The idea was that the municipal services could expand into the shops and apartments if more space was needed.

51. For Aalto's ideas on the unity between house and garden, see his 1926 essay, "From Doorstep to Living Room," in Schildt, *Early Years*, pp. 214–218.

52. In this regard, see Aalto's competition statement. Aalto's proposal exceeded the size specified in the competition program, and, in the course of the competition, Aalto petitioned for more space. See the letter from Aalto to the Säynätsalo municipality, October 10, 1949 (AAA, Helsinki).

53. Wrede, *Architecture of Erik Gunnar Asplund*, pp. 216–217; n. 141, p. 240.

54. Schildt, *Mature Years*, p. 158.

55. For a further description of this project see Schildt, *Complete Catalogue*, pp. 137–140; and Paul David Pearson, *Alvar Aalto and the International Style* (New York: Whitney Library of Design, 1978), pp. 211–216.

56. Excerpts from Aalto's competition statement (AAA, Helsinki) are in Schildt, *Complete Catalogue*, p. 138. A section of Aalto's statement is subtitled, "The Concept of Monumentality in the Pensions Building."

57. Alvar Aalto, "The Decline of Public Buildings," *Arkkitehti–Arkitekten* (1953); repr. in Schildt, *Sketches*, p. 112.

58. Le Corbusier, *The Athens Charter*, trans. Arthur Eardsley (New York: Grossman, 1973); originally published as *La Charte d'Athènes* (1943).

59. International Congresses for Modern Architecture, 8th Congress, Hoddesdon, England, 1951. Papers delivered at the congress were published in J. Tyrwhitt, J. L. Sert, and E. N. Rogers, eds., *The Heart of the City: Towards the Humanisation of Urban Life* (New York: Pellegrini and Cudahy, 1952).

60. Aalto planned this publication with Gregor Paulsson. See Schildt, *Decisive Years*, pp. 180–186.

61. Tyrwhitt, Sert, and Rogers, *The Heart of the City*, p. 162.

62. Ibid.

63. Among the entries were: "HUMAN/Humanity/ Human Being/Human Nature, HUMAN ACTIVI-TIES/Affairs/Experience/Life, HUMAN ASPECTS/ View/Respect/Spirit/Will, HUMAN NEEDS/ Desire/Contact/Friendliness, HUMAN SCALE/ Human Measure, HUMAN VALUES/Significance/ Factors/Traditions, HUMANISATION/Humanising." Ibid., p. 180.

64. Aalto, "Experimental House, Muuratsalo," pp. 115–116.

65. Ibid., p. 116.

66. Aalto, "Between Humanism and Materialism," p. 133.

67. According to Schildt, Matti Janhunen, who represented the Finnish Communist Party and was formerly the head of the Pensions Institute, was acquainted with Aalto from the National Pensions Institute competition; see Schildt, *Mature Years*, p. 185.

68. Aalto, "Between Humanism and Materialism," pp. 131, 133.

69. Friedrich von Schelling, *Die Philosophie der Kunst*, ed., K. F. A. Schelling (Stuttgart, 1859); in English, *The Philosophy of Art*, trans. Douglas W. Stott (Minneapolis: University of Minnesota Press, 1989), p. 164.

70. On Le Corbusier's relationship to the neo-expressionist tendency in postwar architecture, see, for example, Rosemarie Haag Bletter, "Expressionism and the New Objectivity," *Art Journal*, no. 43 (Summer 1983), pp. 108–109.

71. There are six buildings and seven projects. As Schildt noted, by the late 1960s Aalto was revered in Germany: "He would no doubt have been fully employed in Germany for the rest of his life if he had chosen to focus his practice there.... Hans Scharoun, who was head of the Berlin Academy of the Arts, arranged a major Aalto exhibition there, which later travelled to Wolfsburg, Hamburg, and Essen. In 1969 he became a member of the order *Pour le Mérite*, which was founded by Frederick the Great." Schildt, *Mature Years*, p. 198.

72. Günther Feuerstein, *New Directions in German Architecture*, trans. Thomas E. Burton (New York: George Braziller, 1968), p. 10.

73. Ibid., p. 11.

74. Ibid., p. 12.

75. "Internationaler Wettbewerb 1952 Sporthalle Wien," *Der Aufbau*, no. 8 (September 1953), p. 433; trans. Peter Reed.

76. Ibid., pp. 433–465.

77. Leonardo Mosso, "Il Vogelweidplatz di Alvar Aalto," *Marmo*, no. 4 (1966), pp. 7–51.

78. Alvar Aalto, project description (AAA, Helsinki).

79. For more on Rainer, see *Roland Rainer: Arbeiten aus 65 Jahren* (Salzburg and Vienna: Residenz Verlag, 1990).

80. Ulrich and Marianne Baumgarten, "Eindrücke aus der 'INTERBAU,' 1957, in Berlin," *Werk*, no. 44 (1957), p. 205.

81. Anders Åman, *Architecture and Ideology in Eastern Europe during the Stalin Era: An Aspect of Cold War History*, trans. Roger and Kerstin Tanner (New York: Architectural History Foundation; Cambridge, Mass., and London: MIT Press, 1992); originally published in Sweden in 1987. See especially Chapter 12: "How the Other Side Built—Interbau in West Berlin."

82. Ibid., p. 232.

83. Otto Suhr, quoted in ibid., p. 233.

84. Because of its size, Le Corbusier's Unité d'Habitation was located outside the Hansaviertel near the Olympic Stadium.

85. For a history of GEWOBA and Neue Vahr, see Hans-Joachim Wallenhorst, *Die Chronik der GEWOBA 1924 bis 1992* (Bremen: GEWOBA, 1993); and the exhibition catalogue, *Modell Neue Vahr* (Bremen: GEWOBA, 1993).

86. Other planners included Max Säume, Günther Hafemann, and Hans Bernhard Reichow.

87. Wallenhorst, *Die Chronik der GEWOBA*, p. 236.

88. Ibid., p. 243.

89. *Modell Neue Vahr*, p. 61.

90. Wallenhorst, *Die Chronik der GEWOBA*, p. 250.

91. Alvar Aalto, "Rakennuskorkeus sosiaalisesa kysymyksenä" [Building Heights as a Social Problem], *Arkkitehti* (1946); repr. in Schildt, *Sketches*, p. 92. "Point block" towers are highrise apartment buildings in which the central core contains staircases and elevators, and the flats fan out from that center.

92. Ibid., p. 93.

93. Wallenhorst, *Die Chronik der GEWOBA*, p. 253.

94. Fischer and his colleagues investigated various cultural centers and youth homes, including those in Ludwigshafen, Duisberg, and Heidelberg. Information regarding the competition and background of the program can be found in the Wolfsburg City Hall Archive, "Das Kulturzentrum," pp. 19–21.

95. Ibid.

96. Aalto's competition drawings are dated June 10, 1958.

97. Schildt, *Complete Catalogue*, p. 95.

98. Schildt, *Mature Years*, p. 193.

99. Andreas Rossmann, "What Kind of Theatre for What Kind of Theatre?" *Kultur Chronik*, no. 6 (1988), p. 10.

100. The invited architects were Aalto, Otto Appel (Frankfurt), Fritz Bornemann (Berlin), W. Frey and J. Schader (Zurich), Prof. Graubner (Hannover), David Helldén (Stockholm), Prof. Dr.-Ing. Schwippert (Düsseldorf), and Prof. Weber (Munich and Frankfurt). On the competition, see the exhibition pamphlet, *Ideen-Wettbewerb für den Neubau eines Opernhauses in Essen* (Essen: Museum Folkwang, 1959); and Jürgen Joedicke, "International Theater Competitions Dusseldorf and Essen," *Architektur Wettbewerbe*, no. 29 (1960), pp. 202–297.

101. Harald Deilmann, "Vom Entwurf zur Ausführung," in Dietmar N. Schmidt, ed., *Das Theater von Alvar Aalto in Essen* (Essen: G. D. Baedeker Verlag, 1988). Deilmann was the architect of the Münster Theater.

102. See Schildt, *Complete Catalogue*, p. 103.

103. For a summary of Aalto's plan, see ibid., pp. 33–35; and Alvar Aalto, "New Centre for the Town of Helsinki," *Arkkitehti*, no. 3 (1961), pp. ii–iv, trans. Fred A. Fewster.

104. The City Beautiful movement, or American Renaissance, refers to the period from approximately 1876–1917, when large-scale plans for civic improvement drew inspiration from Baron Haussmann's Paris and classical civilization. The majority of new civic institutions were designed in an American Beaux-Arts architectural style. See *The American Renaissance, 1876–1917* (Brooklyn: Brooklyn Museum, 1979).

105. Lewis Mumford, *The City in History: Its Origins, Its Transformations, and Its Prospects* (New York and London: Harcourt Brace Jovanovich, 1961), pp. 133–134.

106. The area continues to be the subject of study today, and, in the fall of 1997, Helsinki sponsored a competition for the area at the foot of Töölö Bay.

107. Alvar Aalto, "Taide ja tekniikka" [Art and Technology], lecture, Finish Academy, October 3, 1955; repr. in Schildt, *Sketches*, p. 127. The Helsinki plan in its entirety attempted to bring just such a holistic vision to the city.

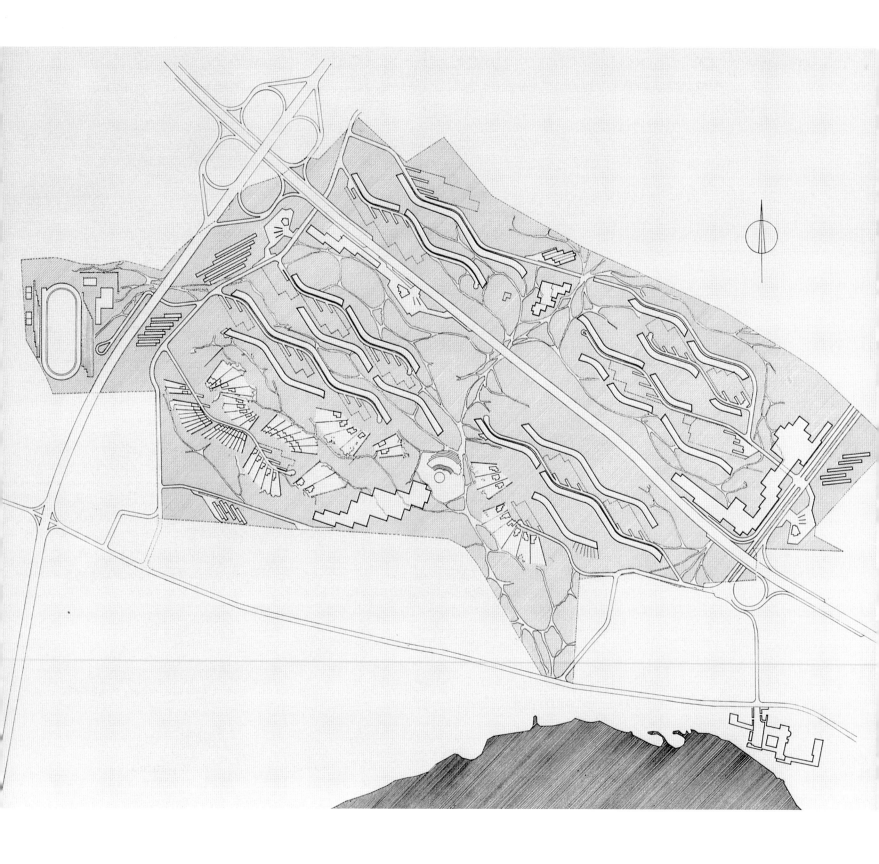

The Legacy of Alvar Aalto: Evolution and Influence

Kenneth Frampton

The structures which were means to create a new architecture have been wrested from us and turned into commercialized decorative ends in themselves with no inner value. There was a time when a misconstrued, lifeless traditionalism was the chief enemy of good architecture. Today its worst enemy is the superficial decorative misuse of the means acquired during the breakthrough. . . . The contrast between deep social responsibility and decorative "surface effects" is perhaps the oldest and certainly the most topical issue in the debate on architecture. Please do not think that I wish to disparage beauty in rejecting decorativeness. Architecture must have charm; it is a factor of beauty in society. But real beauty is not a conception of form which can be taught, it is the result of harmony between several intrinsic factors, not least the social.

—Alvar Aalto[1]

Alvar Aalto. Housing, Patricia, Pavia, Italy. Project, 1966–68. Site plan. Alvar Aalto Foundation, Helsinki

THE VIEW THAT THE FINAL SIGNIFICANCE of an architect's career must ultimately depend upon his or her long-term influence is one that is at variance with the contemporary cult of the star. It stems from the conviction that, in architecture, the creative capacity of the culture as a whole is of more consequence than the contribution of any particular individual—a sentiment that Aalto himself endorsed when he accorded credit, as he did on many occasions, to the "anonymous," highly experienced architects who had assisted him over the years. This acknowledgment gives priority to the social cultivation of the art rather than emphasize the presence of any singular talent. Thus, irrespective of Aalto's indisputable status as a master architect, a position of which he was fully aware, of greater import in the last analysis, both for him and for the culture of this century, was and still is the more general implication of his contribution at both a practical and theoretical level.

As Demetri Porphyrios has shown in his revealing study, *Sources of Modern Eclecticism* (1982), Aalto's architecture after 1934 was a total antithesis to the *homotopia* of western European rationalism. Whereas the homotopic model was based on order, regularity, symmetry, recurrence, and familiarity, irrespective of whether this assumed a neoclassical or a functionalist format, Aalto's *heterotopic* approach was one that favored fragmentation, layering, multiplicity, and a more-or-less continual state of organic growth. Porphyrios characterized this approach as one in which order arises haptically out of juxtaposition, rhythmic repetition, and asymmetrical inflection without any evident unifying or universal principle. As Porphyrios put it: "If the homotopic mind set out to establish frontiers of an uninterrupted continuity, heterotopia was to destroy the continuity of syntax and to shatter predictable modes of the homogenous grid."[2]

Some forty years younger than Frank Lloyd Wright and approximately a decade younger than the generation of Le Corbusier and Ludwig Mies van der Rohe, Aalto may be seen as being doubly fortunate in terms of the place and the date of his birth, in the first instance, because he inherited the rich cultural tradition of Finnish national romanticism just as it was entering its decline and, in the second, because he came upon the modern movement when its pioneers had already established a zero-degree functionalism against which he could react in humanist and organic terms.

As the architect Colin St. John Wilson has written, Aalto may be seen as having expanded modern functionalism to include within its rubric a psychoneurological response to different levels of stimuli arising from a single cause, as filtered simultaneously through the visual, aural, and tactile senses.[3] In this sense, in an age in which we are overwhelmed by ephemeral images of every kind, we may justly see him as an architect whose oeuvre was totally antithetical to the reduction of building to modular spatial arrangements largely determined by proximal or productive considerations, or to provisional assemblies predominantly conceived to provide a spectacular image—the cult of the "decorated shed" against which he reacted throughout his life. While this did not render him immune to the picturesque in European culture, Aalto's predisposition for asymmetrical compositions was always qualified by a deep concern for an appropriately organic aggregation of the parts and for the integration of the resultant assembly into the site.

Aalto belonged to that "existential" generation of northern European intellectuals in which, to put it in terms of Martin Heidegger, "building, being, dwelling and cultivating"[4] were seen as part and parcel of the same socio-organic response to the conditions of existence. And while he was too democratic and realistic to have anything to do with the chauvinistic politics that were fatally associated with this view, Aalto's ecological propensity brought him nonetheless close to Hugo Häring's *Neues Bauen* movement, that is to say, to that alternative line in modern architecture identified by St. John Wilson as "the other tradition."[5] This tradition, loosely associated with northern European expressionism, would be more precisely defined through the work of Häring and Hans Scharoun and, above all, perhaps through Häring's famous Gut Garkau farm complex of 1924, which came closest to anticipating Aalto's heterotopic syntax.

The work of Aalto is of critical import at the end of the twentieth century because, while he was by no means antithetical to the manifest advantages of modern technoscience and industrial production, he was, simultaneously, far from sanguine about the tendency to regard technological advance as an end in itself rather than as a means to a liberative end. He thought that the habitat in general, should be able to respond easily and freely to cyclical life changes and to fluctuations in the daily pattern of existence, particularly as these affected psychic mood as well as physical well being. Like the Franco-Irish architect Eileen Gray, he thought that "a window without a shutter was like an eye without an eyelid"[6] and that the interior of the living volume should, within limits, be freely modifiable by the occupant. On these grounds, like Giancarlo de Carlo, he was opposed to the very notion of cheap housing.

As de Carlo put it in 1968 in his pamphlet *Legitimizing Architecture*: "We have a right to ask 'why' housing should be as cheap as possible and not, for example, rather expensive; 'why' instead of making every effort to reduce it to minimum levels of surface, of thickness, of materials, we should not try to make it spacious, protected, isolated, comfortable, well equipped, rich in opportunities for privacy, communication, exchange and personal creativity."[7] A decade earlier Aalto had already pursued a similar line of reasoning in bitterly ironic terms. Thus, in 1957 he argued:

> *Then there is our old enemy the speculator in real estate. That is the enemy number one of the architect. But there are other enemies too who may be even more difficult to defeat. For instance, we have in my country . . . the theoretical line of building economy, which is popularly stated in this way: "What form of house is most economical? . . . How deep should it be? How long? What is the cheapest way we could give people badly needed houses?" Of course, this may be called science. But it is not. The answer is very, very simple—the deepest house is the cheapest. That is clear. One can go further and say that the most inhuman house is the cheapest, that the most expensive light that we have is daylight— let us eliminate that, and then we will get cheaper housing. . . .*
>
> *Real building economy cannot be achieved in this ridiculous way. The real building economy is how much of the good things, at how cheap cost, we can give. . . . It is the same in all economy—the relationship between the quality of the product and the price of the product. But if you leave out the quality of the product, the whole economy is nonsensical in every field.*[8]

However, Aalto's concept of building economy was not restricted to housing. It extended, as we shall see, to the economy of the built environment as a whole. Thus, elsewhere in the same speech of 1957, we find him stating: "The most expensive thing is fresh air, because it is not only a question of ventilation, but also a question of city planning. Fresh air for human beings costs acres of ground and good gardens and forests and traffic and meadows."[9] In short, he cited everything that cannot be readily achieved in dense urban environments, which are fed by the carcinogenic automobile and other equally polluting late-modern technologies.

For Aalto, building culture was to be given the widest possible interpretation rather than be narrowly understood in a classical or modern avant-gardist sense. Hence, despite his lifelong attachment to Italy, he displayed no interest whatsoever in humanistic proportional systems or, for that matter, in any radically hermetic intellectual proposition. And, while he was not averse to employing organizing grids and modules, and indeed would frequently do so, he was totally opposed to the use of modular systems as ends in themselves. His intuitive, biomorphically inspired approach to environmental design caused him to place an enormous emphasis on the capacity of built form to modify equally both the landscape and the urban fabric. In this regard he would have been sympathetic to the architect Mario Botta's slogan, "building the site."[10] All of Aalto's sites were built in this topographical sense, and his achievements as an architect cannot be separated at any stage of his career from his capacity as a designer of landscapes.

From Constructivism to Organicism

Aalto's mature career seems to break down into two interconnected but distinct episodes: on the one hand, the early *constructivist* work that he designed and realized in Turku in close collaboration with Erik Bryggman, such as the Turku 700th Anniversary Exhibition and Trade Fair of 1929 (plates 77–84), and, on the other, the shift toward *organicism*, as this was first unequivocally expressed in his own house and studio, completed in the Helsinki suburb of Munkkiniemi in 1935–36 (plates 125–129).[11] In retrospect, it is clear that the laconic character of Finnish constructivism derived from its origin in the severity of Nordic classical form.[12] In Aalto's case, this is at once evident in the Southwestern Finland Agricultural Cooperative Building in Turku of 1927–30 and in the different phases of his competition entry for the Viipuri City Library of 1927–35 (plates 89–109), wherein one may witness the gradual evolution of classical norms into constructivist tropes. However, unlike the extravagant engineering forms adopted by the Russian Constructivists, Aalto eschewed the technological rhetoric of the Soviet avant-garde in the name of an objective propriety. This much is at once clear when one compares the main elevation of Aalto's Turun Sanomat Building of 1928–30 (plate 42) to the Vesnin brothers' project for the *Pravda* newspaper building in Moscow of 1923, with which Aalto was surely familiar. We find the same singular display device in both, namely the projection of the front page of their respective newspapers onto a large glass wall facing the street. While the Russians augmented this ultramodern gesture with all sorts of technological paraphernalia, from transparent elevator cabins to digital clocks, the large display window of Aalto's building was simply juxtaposed with sober, steel-framed ribbon windows, typical of a functionalist facade of the late 1920s.

Aalto's gradual recasting of neoclassical tropes into the sobriety of the *Neue Sachlichkeit*[13] may be readily perceived if we not only follow the stages of the Viipuri City Library but also if we observe the development of the Southwestern Finland Agricultural Cooperative Building at the level of its interior detailing, particularly the treatment devised for its 500-seat theater (page 26). While the first version of this auditorium was a Nordic classic essay after the manner of Erik Gunnar Asplund's Skandia Cinema in Stockholm of 1922–23 (page 25), the second was an objective, prismatic volume of similar proportions, wherein discrete technical components assumed the space-modulating role that had been previously afforded by the classically romantic mural depicted in the initial perspective. Where the mural had previously articulated the wall surface and the volume into upper and lower zones, this division now depended upon the virtual plane established by Poul Henningsen's light fittings, hung in a U-formation around the sides of the auditorium. A similar functional articulation, in ornamental terms, is evident in the retractable footlights that pop out of the stage and in the severe reveals of the vomitoria leading into the hall.

The subtle shift that occurred in Aalto's work at this time, as he passed from the neoclassical formality of Nordic classicism to the "product-form" of the *Neue Sachlichkeit*, was never more evident than in the Tapani Standard Apartment Block in Turku of 1927–29 (figure 1; p. 27). Commissioned by Juho Tapani of the Tapani Construction Company, this block was constructed out of standard precast, light-weight concrete units, namely 50-cm-wide beams and 30-cm-thick wall units, both components being hollow in order to lighten their weight and accommodate mechanical services within the void. Of the technologically progressive character of this work, Göran Schildt has written:

> *The building has shops on street level and three stairways, with lifts to the five residential floors. The structural principle of transverse bearing walls between non-load-bearing facades was borrowed from Mies van der Rohe's house at Stuttgart's Weissenhof exhibition in 1927, and provides flexible variation of secondary walls and windows, allowing for varied apartment size, from studio flats to three-room apartments with kitchen and servant's room. Some apartments contain a living room which can be partitioned in various ways. When the building was completed in 1929, Aalto furnished one of the flats with high-quality standard furniture, some of it made by the Thonet company, some designed specially by Aino Aalto. This model apartment was exhibited to the public during the Turku 700th anniversary exhibition.*[14]

Immediately after completing this building, the Aalto office began to produce a series of standard drawings, featuring normative solutions for windows, doors, and a wide range of other components, with the ostensible aim of reusing these solutions in future work. Thus, while Aalto's typological approach had its roots in Nordic classicism, it became technologically focused through the work of the German and Dutch left-wing functionalists with whom he became familiar between 1929 and 1932. As Elina Standertskjöld has shown, the effects of this influence are particularly evident in Aalto's emerging sense of the creative potential of the typical object in the evolution of modern environmental culture.[15] Aalto's interest in perfecting quasi-industrial prototypes was stimulated further by his decision to attend the second Congrès Internationaux d'Architecture Moderne (CIAM), held in Frankfurt in 1929. Aside from the ingenious solutions he devised for light fittings, handrails, and doors, together with the standard signs that he developed for both the Turun Sanomat Building of 1928–30 (page 34; plates 42–51) and the Paimio Tuberculosis Sanatorium of 1929–33 (plates 52–72), Aalto also evolved standard solutions for prototypical casement and sliding double-glazed windows, in both timber and steel, which were subsequently exhibited at the Frankfurt congress.

This preoccupation with norms reached its apotheosis with the Stockholm Exhibition of 1930, held under the auspices of the newly constituted Swedish welfare state. Aalto wrote of this exhibition with great enthusiasm and perspicacity on two separate occasions. In May 1930, he wrote:

> *I see it as a very positive manifestation that the artist is in a sense denying himself by going outside of his traditional sphere of work, that he is democratizing his production and bringing it out of a narrow circle to a wider public. The artist thus steps in among the people to help create a harmonious existence with the help of his intrusive sensibility, instead of obstinately upholding the conflict between art and nonart which leads to acute tragedies and a hopeless life.*
>
> *The biased social manifestation which the Stockholm Exhibition wants to be has been clad in an architectural language of pure and unconstrained joy. There is a festive refinement but also a childish lack of restraint to the whole. Asplund's architecture explodes all the boundaries. The purpose is a celebration with no preconceived notions as to whether it should be achieved with architectural or other means. It is not a composition in stone, glass, and steel, as the functionalist-hating exhibition visitor might imagine, but rather is a composition in houses, flags, searchlights, flowers, . . . and clean tablecloths.*[16]

In a second article, he adopted a more critical attitude, discriminating between the evolutionary character of a refined material culture, as opposed to the pursuit of superficial radicalism as an end in itself. This was already an articulation of the ethical position that he would assume throughout the remainder of his career.

The international socialist challenge to provide decent minimum residential accommodation for all was patently the inspiration behind Aino and Alvar Aalto's 60-square-meter, one-bedroom apartment designed for the *Rationalization of the Minimum Dwelling* exhibition staged in Helsinki in 1930

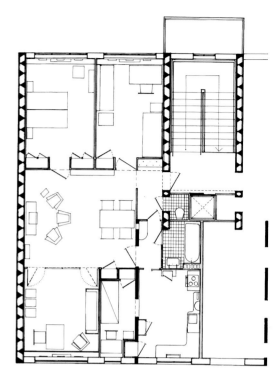

1. Alvar Aalto. Tapani Standard Apartment Block, Turku, Finland. 1927–29. Apartment plan

(page 29). In addition to modern furnishings, this exhibition featured a range of prototypical products pioneered by Finnish manufacturers, including rubber and linoleum floor finishes and the Enso-Gutzeit company's standard plywood doors, which served as the prototype for the plywood doors that Aalto installed in Paimio. Aalto's first plywood and tubular-metal chair, the so-called Hybrid Chair, also dates from this time, making its debut in the furnishing of Paimio. His general preoccupation with standardized serial production at this time led finally to the development of the Paimio Chair of 1931–32, made entirely out of bent, laminated plywood (plates 63, 65). This chair, with its cantilevering organic form, was poised on the dividing line between Aalto's early constructivism and the organicism of his later career.

Aalto's next attempt at an organic inflection of structural form came with his "bent-knee" leg of 1933, which was the key to the production of his famous three-legged, stackable stool, first shown in London that year (plate 107).[17] This leg was produced by inserting slivers of wood into a series of saw cuts and then bending and gluing it into position. With this diminutive "column," as the architectural critic Gustaf Strengell termed it, Aalto was able to transform not only his furniture but also his entire architectural syntax, even though he continued to design the occasional piece in tubular steel, such as the convertible sofabed, specially designed for Sigfried Giedion's *Wohnbedarf* furniture store in Zurich in 1932. From this date onward however, Aalto's furniture tended to be exclusively of wood, with an ever-expanding repertoire of birch pieces, ranging from the triangular, laminated bookshelf brackets to the so-called sledge tea trolley of 1937.

In his 1940 essay, "The Humanizing of Architecture," Aalto returned to his rationale for abandoning tubular steel as an appropriate material for the production of furniture: "The tubular steel chair is surely rational from technical and constructive points of view: It is light, suitable for mass production, and so on. But steel and chromium are not satisfactory from the human point of view. Steel is too good a conductor of heat. The chromium surface gives too bright reflections of light, and even acoustically it is not suitable for a room. The rational methods of creating this furniture style have been on the right track, but the result will be good only if rationalization is exercised in the selection of materials which are most suitable for human use."[18]

Viipuri City Library, as completed in 1935 in what is now Vyborg, Russia, testifies to a similar transposition in a shift from the classical ashlar of the main entrance to the constructivist character of the steel-framed glass doors set back from the stone front and braced by welded, tubular struts (plates 99–100). Similarly, the vestigial neoclassicism of the top-lit reading rooms (see Asplund's Stockholm Public Library of 1926) are enriched throughout by a number of carefully inflected details, from the familiar conic lantern lights first pioneered in the Turun Sanomat Building to the serpentine, double-scaled, biomorphic character of the timber stair rails that lead down into the lending area, together with the plywood-faced checkout counter centrally situated between the main reading room and the lending section (plate 108). At the same time, despite the Asplundian functionalist character of the detailing, it would be hard to imagine a more organic element than the undulating acoustical timber ceiling suspended within the orthogonal prism of the Viipuri auditorium (plates 101, 103–105; page 20).

A comparable concern for ergonomic inflection had been evident in the inclined splash-backs of the washbasins in the Paimio Tuberculosis Sanatorium, which were angled to minimize the noise of water discharging into the basin, the patients' rooms being doubly occupied (plates 67, 69). He adopted an equally nuanced attitude toward the quality of the artificial light so as not to expose the recumbent patient to direct illumination. A similar concern for the modulation of natural light led him to crank up the floor slab at an angle close to the window to provide a transitional zone between the glare of the window surface and the softer light of the room. While the angled soffit obviated the effect of glare at the ceiling, the cranked floor at the window afforded a place for the installation of radiant heating below a continuous top (plate 68).[19]

Aalto extended these biorealist concerns to the design of the minimum dwelling, wherein he linked them to the issue of flexibility. His 1930 essay, "The Dwelling as a Problem," which was his prompt response to the idea of *Existenzminimum*, as this had been posited by the *Neue Sachlichkeit* architects at the 1929 CIAM conference. To this end, we find him writing, with the Stockholm Exhibition still fresh in his memory:

No family can live in one room, not even two, if they have children. But any family can live on an equivalent area if this area is divided up with particular attention to this family and its members' lives and activities. A dwelling is an area which should offer protected areas for meals, sleep, work, and play. These biodynamic functions should be taken as points of departure for the dwelling's internal division, not any out-dated symmetrical axis or "standard room" dictated by facade architecture.

Modern man—and the family—are more mobile than before. This is reflected in furniture's mechanical characteristics. Sixty square meters—and morning exercise for the whole family: this assumes furniture can be easily moved and folded up. . . .

Moveable and foldable furniture enlarge a minimal dwelling. And in fact, the whole method of designing the interior that I have mentioned aims at enlarging the dwelling by developing its use possibilities.

In and of themselves, large dimensions are no advantage, but rather a drawback. If we take a minimal dwelling as our point of departure and strive to increase the use possibilities of its various parts with the purpose of psychologically making the dwelling appear roomier, then we arrive at a concept, no longer of a minimal dwelling, but of a universal dwelling—a dwelling which in its characteristics is better and more correct than the one where an emotional handling of the space has led to an unorganic totality.

The biological conditions for human life are, among others, air, light, and sun. Air does not have to do with the size of the rooms or their number. It is an independent concept. We can surely build a dwelling with a large cubic footage of air without using the floor area uneconomically and affecting the ceiling height. The air space is a question of ventilation. On the other hand one must give a great deal of consideration to the air's quality. And this is a question that is dependent on the city's internal organization, the town plan.[20]

While Aalto had by no means relinquished the idea of standardization at this stage, one cannot help remarking on his pejorative use of the term *standard* in this text. By the mid-1930s, Aalto tended to value standardization only at a relatively small and incremental scale. As far as the larger whole was concerned, particularly in respect to housing, he moved away from the *Zeilenbau* row-house pattern of the *Neue Sachlichkeit* to adopt a more organic, aggregated dwelling form. He now tended to favor fan-shaped housing clusters rather than east-west rows of terraces of the same height, width, and length set a standard distance apart. After 1932 he tended to regard such orthogonal east-west orientation as being overdetermined by normative criteria, not to mention its excessive optimization of cross ventilation.

Thus, despite his continued sympathy for the socially-committed functionalism of the Swedish *acceptera* group,[21] Aalto distanced himself from both the formalist and materialist wings of the international avant-garde, particularly during the first half of the 1930s, when he was completing the first three canonical works of his career: the Turun Sanomat Building, the Paimio Tuberculosis Sanatorium, and the Viipuri City Library (plates 42–72, 89–109). By 1935 he had begun to question the techno-scientific and productive criteria that were still being insisted upon by materialist architects and intellectuals. In a lecture, "Rationalism and Man," given in that year, he once again sought to extend the concept of rationality into the psychophysiological domain:

> We can say that one of the ways to arrive at a more and more humanely built environment is to expand the concept of the rational. We should rationally analyze more of the requirements connected with the object than we have to date. . . . As soon as we include psychological requirements, or, let us say, when we can do so, then we will have already expanded the rational method to an extent that has the potential of excluding inhuman results. . . .
>
> A standard article should not be a definitive product; it should on the contrary be made so that the form is completed by man himself according to all the individual laws that involve him. Only in the case of objects that have a neutral quality can standardization's coercion of the individual be softened and its positive side culturally exploited. There is a civilization that, even in its traditional phase, its handicraft era, showed enormous sensitivity and tact towards the individual in this regard. I mean parts of the Japanese culture, which, with its limited range of raw materials and forms, inculcated a virtuoso skill in creating variations and almost daily recombinations. Its great predilection for flowers, plants, and natural objects is a unique example. The contact with nature and its constantly observable change is a way of life that has difficulty getting along with concepts that are too formalistic.[22]

It is remarkable that someone who had never been to Japan and who, as far as we know, had little contact with Japanese culture,[23] should turn to the Orient for a model in his passage from the functionalist emphasis of constructivism to the critical potential of an organic architecture, in which a more flexible range of forms could be recombined according to the metabolic needs of everyday life. Henceforth, the principles of combination and recombination were to be the main qualifying factors for Aalto as far as standardization was concerned. Thus, as he put it in a lecture at the Nordic Building Conference in Oslo in 1938: "In nature standardization appears, above all and almost exclusively, only in the smallest units, the cells. This results in millions of elastic combinations in which there is no trace of formalism. Furthermore this gives rise to the enormous wealth of organic growing shapes and their eternal change. Architectonic standardization must follow the same path."[24]

At the same time, there was nothing willfully antirational in Aalto's organicism, for, as he wrote in 1960: "It is not the rationalization itself that was wrong in the first and now past period of modern architecture. The wrongness lies in the fact that the rationalization has not gone deep enough."[25]

There is no single work in Aalto's long career that is more synthetically symptomatic of his critical response to all these issues than his Apartment Building for the Interbau Exhibition in the Hansaviertel, Berlin, of 1954–57 (plates 315–320), for it is here, perhaps more than anywhere else, that he brought together two ostensibly opposed impulses. On the one hand, there was his lifelong recognition that the most urgent problem confronting the species was some satisfactory solution to the perennial social problem that Friedrich Engels had identified as the "housing question"; on the other hand, there was his growing conviction that the vernacular in general and the Finnish vernacular, in particular, embodied within its form a key to the solution of this crisis. As far as Aalto was concerned, this potential stemmed from the fact that the Karelian agrarian tradition was quintessentially additive in character and, therefore, perennially open to the process of agglutinative growth. He returned to this theme in the midst of the Continuation War of 1941–44, when eastern Karelia was occupied by Finnish troops, in an essay simply titled "Architecture in Karelia":

> The first essential feature of interest is Karelian architecture's uniformity. There are few comparable examples in Europe. It is a pure forest-settlement architecture in which wood dominates, . . . in most cases naked, without the dematerializing effect that a layer of paint gives. In addition, wood is often used in as natural proportions as possible, on the scale typical of the material. A dilapidated Karelian village is somehow similar in appearance to a Greek ruin, where, also, the material's uniformity is a dominant feature, though marble replaces wood. By making this comparison I am not in any way trying to fan some kind of Finnish chauvinism; it is a purely instinctive association whose justification experts surely could recognize.
>
> Another significant special feature is the manner in which the Karelian house . . . is in a way a building that begins with a single modest cell or with an imperfect embryo building, shelter for man and animals and which then figuratively speaking grows year by year. "The expanded Karelian house" can in a way be compared with a biological cell formation. The possibility of a larger and more complete building is always open.[26]

From this, he went on to argue that the inevitably tight economic constraints governing the period of postwar reconstruction would, by definition, necessitate a similar additive approach. As he put it:

> The task presupposes an architectural system according to which houses can grow and be enlarged over the years. We cannot accomplish our work with the conventional cultural loans or the "technocratic" rationalism and buildings that have been dominant in Europe in recent

times. The system must be created here and must take our own circumstances into consideration; but certain features in the Karelian building system that I have just mentioned can give us some excellent help in finding the right system, at least to the extent that larger population groupings, thanks to this architecture, become accessory to the necessary self-confidence and feeling that we are not taking the wrong path.[27]

With these words, Aalto categorically rejected the technocratic rationalism of the early modern movement as unacceptably reductive, while recognizing that without the popular support of society one cannot achieve anything of lasting consequence as far as the habitat is concerned. This Karelian thesis evidently implied some form of topographically inflected, low-rise, high-density housing, such as Aalto had already demonstrated in the Sunila Pulp Mill and Housing of 1936–38 and the Standard Terrace Housing in Kauttua of 1937–38 (plates 118–124). Thus, while he was not totally opposed to highrise construction, it is clear that for him, as for Frank Lloyd Wright, the preferred line was horizontal, since, as he put it in 1946: "Highrise apartments must be regarded, both socially and architecturally, as a considerably more dangerous form of building than single-family houses or lowrise apartments."[28] Last, but not least, there was the clear implication that the key to ecologically responsible housing production in the future lay in the "ready-made" model of the Finnish vernacular, just as this had once served as the point of departure for the Finnish national romantic architects of the 1890s. It was just this Finnish tradition that led Aalto back to the L- and U-shaped plans of the English Arts and Crafts house, and to type plans that, in their turn, had been derived from vernacular forms. As we have noted, his own house in Munkkiniemi signaled this return as early as 1935, and this would find further elaboration in the adjacent timber ambulatory and courtyard that was designed to receive Aino Aalto's grave after her premature death in 1949 (plate 216).

It is virtually the same Finnish vernacular paradigm that resurfaced with full force in his highrise Hansaviertel apartment building of 1954–57. In this instance, each apartment is, in effect, a small single-story patio house (figure 2), and we may say that their syncopated aggregation creates the semblance of a diminutive village on each floor. The basic apartment is an assembly of three bedrooms, plus a bathroom and a kitchen, grouped around three sides of a central living room that opens directly to the exterior through a generously proportioned terrace partially inset into the corpus of the building. Each terrace is shielded from the next, and from the ground, by virtue of the way it is incorporated into the staggered plan of the block. A galley-kitchen gives direct access to this terrace for the purposes of eating outdoors, while the kitchen is directly accessed from a generously proportioned internal foyer. Acoustical and visual privacy is facilitated throughout by a pattern of circulation that serves the flanking bedrooms while being partially screened from the central living volume. This carefully modulated arrangement is matched by the generosity of the

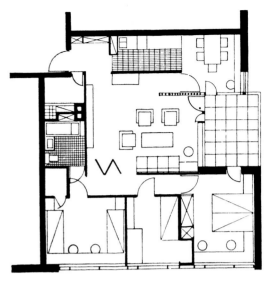

2. Alvar Aalto. Apartment Building, Interbau Exhibition, Hansaviertel, Berlin. 1954–57. Apartment plan

glazed elevator hall, which is wide, naturally lit, and well-ventilated. It is a room, rather than an access corridor in the usual sense. In ergonomic terms, this apartment layout plan is one of the most brilliant, middle-class apartment plans invented in the entire span of the twentieth century, and the mystery is that neither Aalto nor anyone else would have the occasion or the desire to replicate its form or develop a further variation of its patio organization.[29]

While Le Corbusier displayed comparable ingenuity in the development of his typical highrise dwelling units, these were invariably too spartan to be accepted at a popular level or, alternatively, where luxurious, were too expensive to be made available to society at large. Hence, the fundamental limitations of his heroic Unité d'Habitation in Marseilles of 1948–54 (figure 3), which, while occupied today, was never fully available for either working-class or lower-middle-class accommodation.

The virtues of Aalto's Hansaviertel prototype do not end with the units themselves, for the modular rhythm of the block, established through its precast concrete, modular wall system, sets up a significant interplay with the inset terraces that are automatically incorporated into its form. These terraces are rhythmic at another scale in that the raised soffits above the living rooms impart a "noble" identity to each apartment. Furthermore, the gray concrete panels, cast from steel formwork, are rhythmically jointed, so as to create a coursed effect reminiscent of stone facing on a gigantic scale—the merest hint, one might say, of a latent Nordic classical sensibility. At the same time, the partially protruding terraces, opening toward the south and thereby imparting a direction to the massing, serve to distance the overall form from any sense of classical propriety, except for the entry portico, which, framed by a peristyle of concrete columns, imparts a classic touch to the entrance (plate 316). Aalto's intention in

3. Le Corbusier. Unité
d'Habitation, Marseilles,
France. 1948–54.
Axonometric

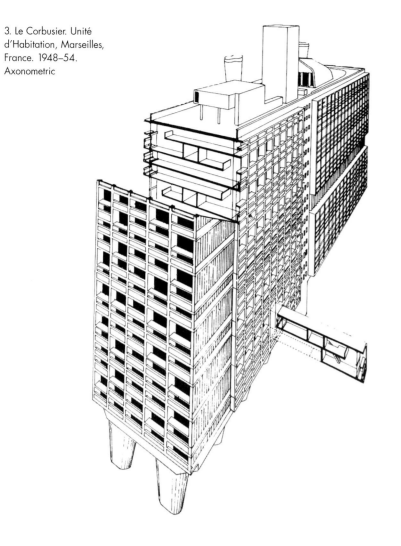

developing this apartment type and block formation is confirmed by the description that appears in the first volume of his complete works, published in 1963:

> *The conventional apartment house is a sort of collective dwelling; it can never possess the same qualities as, say, a private house, which has a direct relation to the landscape. Nevertheless, the private house, which is often placed as a box in a small garden without a protected interior court, has its negative sides, while, on the other hand, the apartment block can present some positive advantages. Therefore an attempt should be made to combine, in an ideal manner, the specific advantages of an apartment block with the merits of the individual house. . . .*
>
> *The conventional small corridor-like balconies were here transformed into patios around which the rooms of the apartments were grouped. This grouping around the open-air room created an intimate, private atmosphere.*[30]

This cluster organization entailed the provision of balconies, which, by virtue of the manner of their enclosure, ensured both privacy and a sense of being in the open air. At the same time, their chevron formation implied a biomorphic organization similar to that analyzed in D'Arcy Thompson's *On Growth and Form* of 1917.[31] Unlike the modular cubic character of Le Corbusier's Pavillon L'Esprit Nouveau, at the Exposition Internationale des Arts Décoratifs et Industriel Moderne in Paris of 1925 (which was also designed as a prototypical highrise dwelling), Aalto's Hansaviertel apartments could have been readily adapted to form clusters of single-story houses at grade, aggregating into picturesque assemblies with each house stepping down to follow the contours of the site, much like the format that Jørn Utzon adopted in his Kingo Housing, completed near Helsingør in Denmark in 1956.

Aalto's Influence

Despite the essential Nordic character of Aalto's architecture, its influence has extended well beyond the confines of his native Finland. One may think of it as radiating out a series of fronts, first influencing those close to home, especially his Finnish apprentices of the immediate postwar years, then widening out to affect Scandinavia, and finally spreading further afield to touch the work of architects practicing in England, Spain, Portugal, and North America, to cite only those countries where his influence has been explicit. However, the constantly widening influence of his practice did not diminish his impact at a theoretical level, particularly as it emerged in a series of essays in which he was continuously engaged in a critique of the modern movement.

The impact of Aalto's work on Finnish practice has been as fertile as it has been extensive and no matter how one reinterprets the history of the recent past there is hardly a Finnish architect of caliber in the second half of the twentieth century who has not been profoundly influenced by his work. Thus, irrespective of whether one is following the organicist or the constructivist line in Finnish architecture, his influence is always present. It is particularly evident when one takes into consideration the trajectory of Aalto's industrial architecture and the way in which such remarkable works as the Anjala Paper Mill of 1937–38 (page 75), the chemical fertilizer plant for Typpi Oy at Oulu (1950–1960s), or the Enso-Gutzeit Pulp Mill in Kotka of 1951 are reinterpreted in the brilliant industrial plants designed by Erkki Kairamo in the 1980s and, above all, in the pulp mill he realized at Lohja in 1980 in collaboration with Jaako Sutela.

The dualistic character of Aalto's career as a modern architect presages the dichotomous scope of his impact on Finnish architecture. I am referring not only to his later, and more familiar, organic manner but also to the way in which his early constructivist work seems to have served as an inspiration for subsequent Finnish practice. Indeed, one may retrospectively argue that Aalto's Finnish followers divide broadly into two groups: on the one hand, there is the constructivist line in which we may count such architects as Aarne Ervi, Viljo Revell, Aarno Ruusuvuori,

Erkki Kairamo, Kristian Gullichsen, and Juhani Pallasmaa, together with the work of two more recent firms, that of Markku Komonen and Mikko Heikkinen and that of Pekka Helin and Tuomo Siitonen; on the other hand, there are the architects who were clearly influenced by the more organic aspects of Aalto's production, among them, Kaija and Heikki Sirén, Reima Pietilä, Juha Leiviskä, Georg Grotenfelt, and, at one time, the partnership of Kapy and Simo Paavilainen. In terms of the constructivist following, one may cite such canonical pieces as Aarne Ervi's power stations at Pyhäkoski of 1942–46 and Seitenoikea of 1961, Viljo Revell's housing, realized in Tapiola in the 1950s (page 38), and Pallasmaa's prototypical timber vacation housing of 1971–72 at Rånäs and Vänö Island. With regard to this prefabricated housing system, we have to acknowledge the influence of Aalto's rival Aulis Blomstedt, who was Pallasmaa's teacher. The work of Blomstedt surely lies within the constructivist camp, although it can be said that his architecture displayed a greater affinity for the work of Erik Bryggman than for that of Aalto. Within this same hard line, however, we need to recognize the important achievements of Ruusuvuori, above all, his Weilin and Göös Printing Works in Tapiola of 1964–66, and his equally constructivist Sauna Bonsdorff Kellosalmi of 1985, although this last, like Gullichsen's Pieksämäki Poleeni Civic Center of 1983–89, seems to be situated, ambiguously, between two poles—in part organicist, in part close to the sobriety of Bryggman and Blomstedt.

Within the organicist line, we may single out such exceptional pieces as Kaija and Heikki Sirén's Student Dormitory in Otaniemi of 1950–54 (figure 4), designed on the eve of their leaving the Aalto office, or their university chapel for the same campus dating from 1957. To these works, we must surely add Reima Pietilä's Dipoli Student and Conference Center in Otaniemi of 1961–66, which represents the organicist line taken to tectonically irresolvable extremes. And, for greater balance, we may look to Simo Paavilainen's Olari Church and Congregation Center in Espoo of 1981 or, in a more lyrical vein, to Juha Leiviskä's churches, above all, those built in Kirkkonummi, Männistö, and Myyrmäki (figure 5), between 1980 and 1992. At the same time, we should not fail to note the influence of Neo-Plasticism on Leiviskä's architecture nor the fact that his earlier masterwork, the Kouvola City Hall of 1964–68, achieved a remarkable synthesis between Nordic classicism, organicism, and details of a decidedly objective, *sachlich*, rigor.

In acknowledging the degree to which constructivist and organicist impulses have become mixed in Finnish architectural production, it becomes clear that the number of latter-day architects who appear to be inspired by Aalto begins to proliferate to such an extent that one would be hard-pressed to find any other country in the world where there has been such a strong homogenous culture of architecture and yet, at the same time, one in which there has been such diversity and quality. The exhibition, *An Architectural Present—7 Approaches*, at the Museum of Finnish Architecture in Helsinki in 1990, made this exceptionally clear in such

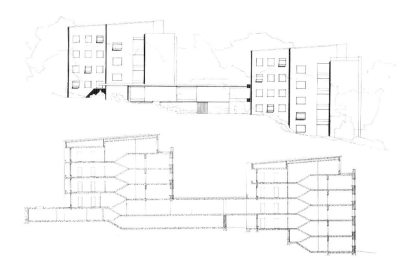

4. Kaija and Heikki Sirén. Student Dormitory. Helsinki University of Technology, Espoo (Otaniemi), Finland. 1950–54. Elevation and section

5. Juha Leiviskä. Myyrmäki Church and Parish Center, Vantaa, Finland. 1980–84

projects as Kari Järvinen's and Timo Airas's Siiskonen House in Mikkeli of 1985, and their Suna School of 1987, as well as Pekka Helin's and Tuomo Siitonen's Ylätuvanpolku Apartment Buildings in Helsinki of 1981 or Helin's remarkable Experimental Housing, Hestra, in Borås, Sweden, of 1993 (figure 6), an undeniably constructivist work but still referential to Aalto's Standard Terrace Housing, the stepped slab blocks designed for Kauttua of 1937–38 (plates 120–124).[32] Last, but not least, one cannot overlook the hypersensitive work of Georg Grotenfelt, such as his Notterkulla House of 1990, which reminds us at once of the rustic syntax employed in the Villa Mairea.[33]

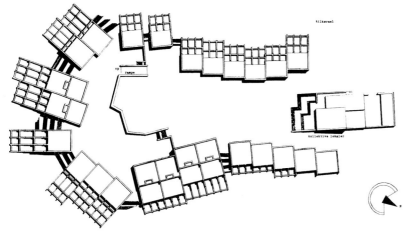

6. Pekka Helin. Experimental Housing, Hestra, Borås, Sweden. 1993

7. Jørn Utzon. Housing, Birkehøj, North Zealand, Denmark. 1960. Site plan

Aalto's Scandinavian influence outside Finland has been minimal, in fact, far less than one might expect. With the exception of Sigurd Lewerentz's Crematorium, Eastern Cemetery, in Malmö of 1943, and Sverre Fehn's Nordic Pavilion, Biennale di Venezia of 1962, there are relatively few non-Finnish Scandinavians who have been directly touched by his work. Among his Danish followers, one may surely cite Jørn Utzon and Arne Jacobsen, above all, the staggered pattern of the latter's postwar Søholm Terraced Housing in Klampenborg, near Copenhagen of 1950–55, although this staggered housing pattern was by no means typical of his manner. Tobias Faber may also be counted as a Danish acolyte, above all, for his early partnership with Utzon, of whom one may argue that no other architect with such a distinct manner has been so deeply influenced by Aalto. This transfer seems to have taken place at two levels: first, Utzon responded directly to Aalto's emphasis on topography as the indispensable point of departure for any architectural endeavor, and, second, he adopted in a more systematic way Aalto's additive approach toward the rationalization of building production, seeing it as a strategy for the spontaneous generation of incremental form.[34]

As I have already suggested, this additive principle was the fundamental precept informing Utzon's Kingo and Fredensborg housing schemes of 1956 and 1962–63, respectively, and it is equally evident as a town-building paradigm in Utzon's project for a settlement in Odense, dating from 1967. But perhaps no work of Utzon's is so unequivocally indebted to Aalto as his unrealized project of 1960 for a low-rise housing scheme in Birkehøj in North Zealand, Denmark (figure 7), wherein clustered blocks of stepped housing, reminiscent in section of Aalto's Kauttua Standard Terrace Housing of 1937–38, are built up around a tumulus-like earthwork that accommodates communal facilities.

For both Aalto and Utzon, the additive principle was also capable of operating at a more tectonic scale, as Aalto would demonstrate with great skill in the early 1950s. This dimension appears particularly forcefully in two exceptional works: his Glassworks Warehouse for the A. Ahlström Corporation in Karhula, Kotka, of 1948–49 (figure 8), and his athletics hall for the Helsinki University of Technology campus in Otaniemi of 1950–52 (plates 275–276). In both instances, the repetition and serial permutation of laminated timber trusses constitute the tectonic means whereby the roofwork of the building is established. In the Karhula warehouse, it was a question of a series of three shallow-pitched, laminated-timber trusses, set side by side, bearing on concrete columns; in the Otaniemi athletics hall, a series of parallel, laminated-timber trusses, of progressively diminishing span and rise, roof over the tapering plan of the running track. In Karhula, the additive formation of the trusses is asymmetrically inflected by the superimposition of monitor lights (imparting a rhythmical impetus to the building as a whole); in Otaniemi, through repetition and an incremental increase in the width of wide-span, laminated-timber trusses, Aalto generated the stepped "elliptical" plan-profile of the athletics hall as it rose within the forest site as the core of an

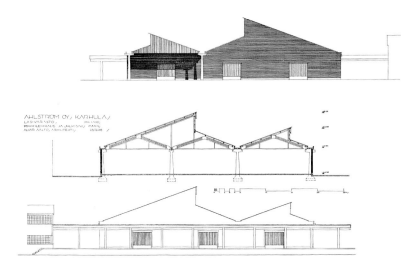

8. Alvar Aalto. Glassworks Warehouse for the A. Ahlström Corporation, Karhula, Kotka, Finland. 1948–49. Elevations and section

9. Jørn Utzon. Sydney Opera House, Sydney, Australia. 1957–73. Aerial view

10. Colin St. John Wilson. British Library, London. 1975–98. Aerial view

adjacent assembly of ancillary buildings. Utzon made comparable use of the additive principle in his Sydney Opera House of 1957–73 (figure 9), conceived as a set of exfoliated vaults suspended over an earthwork, which thereby established a dialogical opposition between "pagoda" and "podium." What is ultimately Aaltoesque about the concrete shell vaults in Sydney is the way in which they are incrementally assembled out of a set of reiterated precast-concrete components.

In England, Aalto's organicism engendered a decisive following in the second half of the 1950s, particularly at Cambridge University, where Sir Leslie Martin was named professor of architecture in 1956. It is hardly an accident that Aalto was awarded the Gold Medal by the Royal Institute of British Architects in 1957, with Martin presiding over his investiture. Around this time, Martin entered into private practice with Colin St. John Wilson, who would later serve as architect of the new British Library, now scheduled for its official opening in 1998, after more than twenty-two years in the making (figure 10). A subaltern, but key, figure in the evolution of Martin's Cambridge practice was Patrick Hodgkinson, who had worked for Aalto an entire year in the early 1950s while still a student at the Architectural Association School of Architecture in London. Under the aegis of Martin and Wilson, Hodgkinson served as the main designer and job captain for the Harvey Court Residence, completed in Cambridge in 1962 as a new dormitory for Gonville and Caius College (figure 11). This work, like Hodgkinson's subsequent house for Lord Adrian of 1962–64,[35] synthesized in an unexpected way elements drawn from both Aalto and the American

11. Martin and Hodgkinson. Harvey Court Residence, Gonville and Caius College, Cambridge University, Cambridge, England. 1957–62. Model

12. Louis I. Kahn. Alfred Newton Richards Medical Research Building, University of Pennsylvania, Philadelphia. 1957–61

architect, Louis I. Kahn; a similar, if different, conjunction of the same two influences may be detected in the early work of James Stirling and James Gowan, particularly their project for Selwyn College, Cambridge, of 1959, and their canonical engineering laboratories, built at Leicester University in 1959–63. While the lecture halls in Leicester clearly owe a good deal to Aalto, the servant-and-served articulation of the entire complex evidently derives from the work of Kahn. In the first instance, it is a question of the canted, cantilevered brick-faced form of the raked halls and the furnishing of the same; in the second, the Kahnian presence makes itself felt in the freestanding brick-faced elevator and stair towers that clearly echo the use of very similar towers in Kahn's Alfred Newton Richards Medical Research Building at the University of Pennsylvania in Philadelphia of 1957–61 (figure 12). At the same time, the most unequivocal Aaltoesque work of the Stirling and Gowan practice was Andrew Melville Hall, their dormitory complex for the University of St. Andrews, Scotland, of 1964–68 (figure 13), evidently influenced by Aalto's 1957 competition entry for the Town Hall and Administrative Offices of Marl, Germany (figure 14). As far as Harvey Court is concerned, we may say that the asymmetrical block, U-shaped in plan, and the chevron formation envisaged for its subsequent growth owe much to the additive principle we find in the work of Utzon and Aalto, whereas the reiterative brick piers running around the external perimeter of the block are indebted to Kahn.

The production of the Martin office was consistently Aaltoesque throughout the duration of its existence, as one may judge from its designs for the new Group of Library Buildings at Oxford University (1959–64), with St. John Wilson, or its Center for Modern Art, Gulbenkian Foundation, designed in 1979 with Ivor Richards and completed in Lisbon four years later. However, unlike Stirling, Martin found himself caught between the project of evolving a normative, brick-faced, organic architecture, suitable for the British climate, and the demands then being made for a new scientific rationalism in architecture, particularly as this might be applied to the modular design of laboratory buildings.[36] This swerve back toward technocratic rationality could hardly have been more removed from Aalto's late organic manner, particularly as he reintroduced neoclassical tropes into his characteristic heterotopic approach, in such works as his Enso-Gutzeit corporate headquarters in Helsinki of 1959–62 (page 85) and Finlandia Hall of 1962–71 (plates 394–408), both clad in marble revetment. Despite this schism, Aalto's free style took root in England, in part because it afforded a means for resolving difficult briefs on irregular sites, as we may judge from works as diverse as the Wolfson Institute, Royal Postgraduate Medical School in London by Lyons, Israel, Ellis, and Gray of 1961, or Wilson's diminutive dormitory tower, the William Stone Building for Peterhouse College, Cambridge University, of 1964.

Among the more surprising aspects of Aalto's legacy is the considerable impact he exercised on the architecture of Spain and Portugal. This influence seems to date from Aalto's official visit to Barcelona in 1951 just before the formation of Grupo R under the auspices of Josep Maria Sostres and Oriol Bohigas.[37] Despite this contact, no work influenced by Aalto surfaced in Spain until a decade later, and then not in Catalonia but in the Castile region—Antonio Fernando Alba's El Rollo Monastery, completed outside Salamanca in 1962. All in all, the one Spanish architect who seems to have been the most consistently influenced by Aalto is Rafael Moneo. Educated in the Madrid Escuela Téchnica Superior de Arquitectura under Alejandro de la Sota and Xavier Saenz de Oiza, and thereafter briefly apprenticed to Utzon, when the latter was developing the Sydney Opera House in the early 1960s, Moneo first revealed himself as an architect of exceptional caliber in his brick-tiled Bankinter, designed in collaboration with Ramón Bescós in Madrid in 1973–76. In this medium-rise office building Moneo engaged in a unique, hybrid organic expression as much influenced by Utzon, Asplund, and Wright as by Aalto. Despite this broadly eclectic palette, elements drawn specifically from Aalto have continued to surface in Moneo's work, from his National Museum of Roman Art in Mérida of 1980–84 to his Pilar and Joan Miró Foundation in Palma de Mallorca, Spain, of 1987–92 (figure 15). It is clear from the first of these works that Moneo, like Stirling and Martin, would be as much influenced by Kahn as by Aalto, although the resulting synthesis seems to be more subtly integrated than what had been achieved in England three decades earlier. The Miró Foundation is a particularly organic work inasmuch as the building is inlaid into an irregular, heavily contoured site. Aalto persists as a discernible influence on Moneo, even in the latter's larger civic works, such as the twin auditoriums designed for the Kursaal site in San Sebastien in 1990 or the stepped form of his L'Illa block, realized in Barcelona in 1994 as the result of a collaboration with the urbanist Manuel de Solà-Morales. More minimalist than any building either by Aalto or Utzon, Moneo's twin auditoriums on the Kursaal site, nonetheless, echo in their monopitched form Aalto's Säynätsalo Town Hall of 1948–52 (plates 196–214) and, especially, Utzon's Sydney Opera House (see figure 9), for the way in which their glazed prismatic forms inflect toward the mouth of the river as it sweeps into the ocean. At the same time, these opaque, crystalline masses may be seen as corresponding to Aalto's geological metaphor; that is to say, they aspire to becoming windowless megaliths as in Aalto's House of Culture in Helsinki of 1952–58 (plates 280–288). However, among Moneo's works to date, we may still claim that the Miró Foundation is the most heterotopic and, hence, perhaps the one work that is most intimately connected to Aalto's production.

Equally heterotopic from the outset has been the work of the Portuguese master, Alvaro Siza, who has always openly acknowledged the seminal influence of Aalto on his own organic manner. See, for example, the swimming pool he realized in the Quinta da Conceicão in Matozinhos, Portugal, of 1958–65 (figure 16), the Banco Pinto in Oliveira de Azemeis of 1971–74, and the Beires House in Povoa do Varzim of 1973–76. Aalto's influence has remained a constant, if oblique, reference throughout Siza's career, as we may readily judge from the University of Porto School of Architecture under construction on the banks of the Douro in Porto of 1987 and from the Modern Art Galician Museum that he completed in Santiago de Compostela in 1994.

The arresting, sculptural quality of Siza's work—its abrupt oscillation between classical reminiscences and organic license—seems to be surprisingly presaged by Aalto's later work, such as the Wolfsburg Cultural Center in Germany of 1958–62 (plates 344–360), where converging fan forms

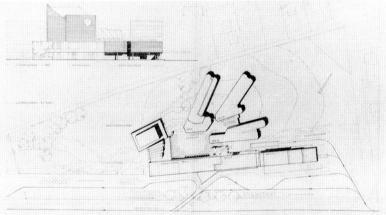

13. James Stirling. Andrew Melville Hall, University of St. Andrews, Scotland. 1964–68. Aerial view and collage

14. Alvar Aalto. Town Hall and Administrative Offices, Marl, Germany. Project, 1957. Elevation and plan. Alvar Aalto Foundation, Helsinki

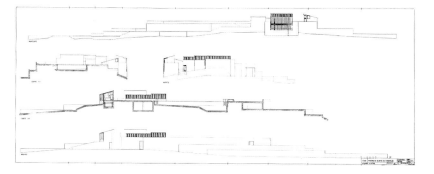

15. Rafael Moneo. Pilar and Joan Miró Foundation, Palma de Mallorca, Spain. 1987–92

16. Alvaro Siza. Quinta da Conceicão, Matozinhos, Portugal. 1958–65. Elevations and sections

erupt out of one end of a low orthogonal courtyard structure, or the *aula magna* of the Helsinki University of Technology at Otaniemi of 1949–66 (plates 267–269), where the monopitched, radial auditorium roof stands out sharply against the sky. If, in some Zeus-like transposition, one were to substitute white rendering for the banded stone-and-brickwork facing of these buildings and thereafter set them down in a Mediterranean landscape, one would have morphological and spatial juxtapositions peculiarly close to the most recent work of the Portuguese master.

Aalto's architecture did not gain a discernable hold over American practice until the 1980s, although there were occasional forays much earlier, above all, in the work of Charles Eames, who, significantly enough, first came in contact with Aalto through that midwestern outpost of Finnish cul-

ture, Eliel Saarinen's Cranbrook Academy of Art in Bloomfield Hills, Michigan, to which the thirty-year-old Eames came in 1938. This contact subsequently led to his collaboration with Eliel Saarinen's son, Eero Saarinen, first on their design for an exhibition of Cranbrook faculty work in 1939 and then their molded plywood chairs, first shown at the exhibition, *Organic Design in Home Furnishings,* at The Museum of Modern Art in 1940. Eames and the younger Saarinen were awarded prizes for their designs. This launched Eames on his international career as a designer of molded furniture in plywood and plastic. These chairs, plus the prototypical bent-plywood splints that they jointly designed for the U.S. Navy in 1942, testify equally to the precedent of Aalto's bent- and laminated-wood furniture. While Eames's early architectural practice in the mid-1940s still displayed something of this Finnish influence, he was soon drawn to the modular rationality of Ludwig Mies van der Rohe's Illinois Institute of Technology Campus, a paradigm that would come to fruition in Eames's Case Study House in Pacific Palisades, California, of 1949.

The evidence now suggests that it was largely the actual presence of the émigré masters of the modern movement—above all Mies and Walter Gropius—that paradoxically emphasized for American architecture the Art Deco/Beaux-Arts tradition and the Pax Americana, postwar cult of structural modularity. This last seems to have circumvented the promise of an inflected, organic modernity, such as that embodied in Aalto's first permanent work in America, Baker House, the Senior Dormitory for Massachusetts Institute of Technology in Cambridge of 1946–49 (plates 181–195). Thus, despite Wright's native organicism, and the Gropius/Breuer involvement with the rough stone and timber cladding characteristic of the New Humanism, technocratic rationalism largely carried the day in a country that played out its Puritan ethos in the normative, transcontinental postwar practice of Skidmore, Owings, and Merrill. Perhaps the only significant exception to this was in Southern California in the late work of Richard Neutra and Rudolf Schindler, and in John Entenza's Case Study Houses, which initially involved Charles Eames and Eero Saarinen.

Aalto's influence returned to the American scene by fits and starts, first on the West Coast in Charles Moore's Condominium I, Sea Ranch, built in Sonoma County, California, on the very edge of the Pacific in 1965 (figure 17; designed with Donlyn Lyndon, William Turnbull, and Richard R. Whitaker); then in Robert Venturi's new Mathematics Building projected for Yale University in 1969; and finally, through the neo-Corbusian work of certain members of the "New York Five," such as in Michael Graves's Rockefeller House, designed for Pocantico Hills, New York, in 1969, where a heavily contoured site began to erode, as it were, the neo-Purist integrity of the house. Soon after, traces of Aalto began to appear in the work of Richard Meier, above all, in his Undergraduate Housing for Cornell University in Ithaca, New York, of 1974, comprising two serpentine dormitory blocks (figure 18), which were clearly derived from Aalto's 1966–68 plan for housing in the Patricia suburb, near Pavia,

17. Moore, Lyndon, Turnbull,
Whitaker. Condominium I,
Sea Ranch, Sonoma County,
California. 1965

Italy (page 118). However, where Graves and Meier were too involved in formalist modes to pursue Aalto's example in any consistent evolutionary way, Moore and Venturi were side-tracked by the sophistry of sceno-graphic populism, the "decorated shed," which Aalto had singled out in the mid-1930s as a particularly seductive and pernicious diversion from the modern project. At the same time, it is clear that Venturi was profoundly influenced by Aalto on an emotional level, as is evident in his 1966 book, *Complexity and Contradiction in Architecture*,[38] and from an appreciation he wrote in *Arkkitehti* after Aalto's death in May 1976:

> *Like all work that lives beyond its time, Aalto's can be interpreted in many ways. Each interpretation is more or less true for its moment because work of such quality has many dimensions and layers of meaning. When I was growing up in architecture in the 1940s and 1950s Aalto's architecture was largely appreciated for its human quality, as it was called, derived from free plans which accommodated exceptions within the original order, and from the use of natural wood and red brick, traditional materials introduced within the simple forms of the industrial vocabulary of the Modern architecture. These contradictory elements in Aalto's work connoted—rather paradoxically it seems now—qualities of simplicity and serenity....*
>
> *I think we can learn timely lessons about monumentality from*

Aalto's architecture because architectural monumentality is used indiscriminately in our time and it wavers between dry purity and boring bombast. Aalto's monumentality is always appropriate in where it is and how it is used, and it is suggested through a tense balance again between sets of contradictions. The auditorium at the Technical Institute at Otaniemi combines collective scale and intimate scale, expressionistic forms and conventional forms, plain and fancy symbolism, and pure order interrupted by inconsistencies planned for the right places.[39]

It is interesting to note how Venturi appreciated Aalto's low-key monumentality as opposed to the rhetorical "new monumentality" that had dominated American commercial and civic architecture since the late 1940s, a syndrome to which Venturi's own work had been an organic, but subversively disjunctive, reaction. It is exactly at this point, however, that we may locate Venturi's conditioned understanding of Aalto, since he ends his homage with the odd claim that Aalto's most endearing characteristic was the fact that he didn't write about architecture. Not only was this patently untrue, as the evidence indicates (despite Aalto's own rhetorical disclaimers), but also one can see how this misreading suited Venturi's own ironic critique, since Aalto's writing so clearly returns us to a consciousness of modernism in all its potential "positive" richness.

Aalto's checkered reception in North America could hardly have been more paradoxical, given the fact that he had realized substantial works in the United States, first in 1938–39 with his Finnish Pavilion for the New York World's Fair (plates 145–154) and then more permanently in 1949, with the completion of Baker House at MIT (plates 181–195). There followed other works, large and small, which, while not particularly well known, were nonetheless evidence of his continuing presence in America: the Poetry Room secreted away in the Lamont Library at

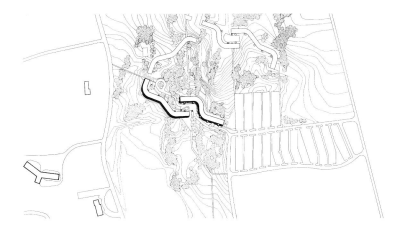

18. Richard Meier.
Undergraduate Housing,
Cornell University, Ithaca,
New York. Project, 1974.
Plan

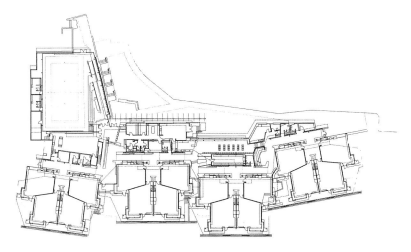

19. Patkau Architects. Strawberry Vale Elementary School, Victoria, British Columbia, Canada. 1992–95. Plan

Harvard University, Cambridge, Massachusetts, of 1948–49; the Kaufmann Conference Room at the Institute of International Education, sponsored by Edgar Kaufmann, Jr. (1961–65); and the Mount Angel Abbey Library in St. Benedict, near Portland, Oregon, of 1964–70 (plates 376–384).

Certain works influenced by Aalto appeared in Canada in the early 1960s—one thinks of John Andrews's Scarborough College in Scarborough, Ontario, of 1962, and of William J. McBain's and Carmen Corneil's Girl Guide Headquarters in Toronto of 1972.[40] But another decade would pass before his organic ethos would surface again, rather indirectly, in the work of the American architect Steven Holl, who would "repatriate" an aspect of his organic spirit to Finland in his Helsinki Museum of Contemporary Art of 1993–98, and, more directly, in the Vancouver practice of John and Patricia Patkau, with their Canadian Clay and Glass Gallery in Waterloo, Ontario, of 1986–88, their Seabird Island School in Agassiz, British Columbia, of 1992, and their Strawberry Vale Elementary School, Victoria, British Columbia, in the suburbs of Vancouver of 1992–95 (figure 19).

Megalopolitan Ecology

Like Ludwig Mies van der Rohe and Ludwig Hilberseimer, both of whom were subject to the influential proto-ecological writings of Raoul Francé,[41] Aalto envisaged a more-or-less continual urbanization of the earth's surface, one in which his all but mythical "forest town" would come to be universally adopted in northern Europe and, to some extent, elsewhere as a kind of regional Gaia System,[42] equally devoted to agrarian and industrial development, the one continuously fusing into the other. Aalto first posited his

concept of the forest town in his 1936 master plan for the industrial community of Sunila, near Kotka, of which he remarked in a lecture of 1956: "The housing is placed wholly on the southern slopes leaving the northern slopes to the forest....Both the housing developments and the factory itself are designed to grow without disrupting their harmony."[43] Here, the heroic monumental Sunila Pulp Mill built for a consortium of major paper producers as a gridded, brick-faced matrix on an island promontory facing the sea was complemented by low-rise workers' housing laid out in a fan formation on an adjacent mainland site (plates 113–119). This terraced housing was integrated into the contours of the undulating ground, as opposed to the orthogonal row-house (*Zeilenbau*) planning principle of the *Neue Sachlichkeit*, which had influenced Aalto's master plan for Ahlström's Varkaus factory projected in the same year. Aalto's subsequent planning work for the A. Ahlström Corporation in the late 1930s (owing to the patronage of Harry Gullichsen) would confirm the distance he had gone from both the row-house tradition and the perimeter-block models of urban development, the one stemming from Otto Häsler's pioneering row-house paradigm, first realized in Celle, near Hanover, in 1926, the other deriving from Eliel Saarinen's plan for Munkkiniemi and Greater Helsinki of 1915. The exclusion of these paradigms from Aalto's urban form is first evident in his Kauttua site plan for the A. Ahlström Corporation of 1938 (plate 122).

Aalto's green-city ideology seems to have been informed by a number of countervailing open-city planning models developed during the first four decades of the century, from N. A. Ladovsky's formalistic planning precepts, which seem to have influenced a prototypical new town, "An American Town in Finland" (page 82), designed by MIT students under Aalto's direction in 1940, to the Anglo-Saxon garden-city model refined by Clarence Stein and Henry Wright in Radburn, New Jersey, and in their green-belt New Towns. Aalto would have become familiar with the latter through his friend Lewis Mumford, whose influential *The Culture of Cities* had been published in 1938. The other primary influence on Aalto's approach to planning at this time was unquestionably the Tennessee Valley Authority (TVA) Regional Plan promulgated under the auspices of Franklin Delano Roosevelt's New Deal after 1933. This was surely the inspiration behind Aalto's Kokemäenjoki River Valley Regional Plan of 1940–42 (page 86), when Harry Gullichsen persuaded several river-based municipalities, from Pori to Kokemaki, to unite in commissioning Finland's first regional plan from Alvar Aalto. For all intents and purposes, this was a linear industrial city at a regional scale, wherein the traditional livelihood of agriculture would be supplemented by timber-related light industry, with a new main road and rail line following the river's course as an efficient transportation spine throughout the length of the region. Of this layered protomegalopolitan plan, Aalto wrote: "The principle governing the housing areas is that they should not be developed into separate, heavy, indivisible entities, but instead grow like star-shaped figures from the existing agglomerations, with belts of farmland, forests, and parks between.... The natural landscape itself is valuable as a means of architectural characterization in the planning of the communities."[44]

Aalto's regional planning strategies had been influenced by the work of Frank Lloyd Wright, particularly in his Usonian phase, above all, surely by Wright's Galesburg Country Homes in Galesburg, Michigan, of 1946–49, which seems to anticipate almost to the letter, the cellular layout of the residential quarters in Aalto's plans for Rovaniemi of 1944–46 (figure 20) and Imatra of 1947–53 (plate 289). Of Imatra, Göran Schildt has written: "Aalto planned for a projected population of 100,000, of whom some 37% were to live in single-family homes and 63% in apartment houses no more than four storeys high. The goal of small, organically integrated residential districts with their own heating plants, day-care facilities, health centres, sports fields, shops, etc., bears witness to Aalto's interest in American neighborhood theories. The plan, completed in 1953, was implemented by and large, but the high cost of land in the densely-built areas led to an undesirable scattering of new construction to peripheral areas."[45]

Aalto's master plan was, in his words, a "formation of trees, planted areas, meadows, and fields, providing a distinctive feature characteristic of Imatra and separating the built-up areas"[46] thereby obviating the need for formal parks of any kind. This diffusion of tended woodland justified the title, "forest town." As Jussi Rautsi has written of the Imatra plan: "There is thus no need to plan artificial parks in the midst of settlement, especially as the forest often penetrates all the way to the central areas. The Finnish character of the parks must be preserved, even further accentuated. The unique beauty of Finnish nature is not based on luxuriant growth or colours or enormous scale. Our nature is marked by a realistic beauty, and should be kept that way."[47]

Aalto justified his forest-town approach in terms that were reminiscent of Bruno Taut's deurbanizing thesis, as set forth in his 1920 publication, *Die Auflösung der Städte oder die Erde eine gute Wohnung* [The Dissolution of Cities]. Thus, we find Aalto writing of the Kokemäenjoki River Valley Regional Plan: "Exactly as the medieval cities once upon a time lost their fortification walls and the modern city grew out beyond them, the concept of the city today is in the process of shedding its constraints. But this time it is happening, not to lead once again to the creation of a larger unit, but rather so that the city will become part of the countryside. The underlying meaning of such regional plans is that they synchronize country and city."[48]

Despite their organic flexible character, Aalto's regional plans remained largely unrealized due to speculation and other economic constraints.[49] Such interests did not prevent the realization of Aalto's smaller civic complexes however, where the geological metaphor assisted him in establishing the identity of the place through the way in which the profile of the built form extends into the site. This is at once evident in the case of Säynätsalo Town Hall of 1948–52, where the municipal structure is the cumulative element of a chevron formation of lowrise structures running through the center of the town (plates 196–214). Here, Bruno Taut's con-

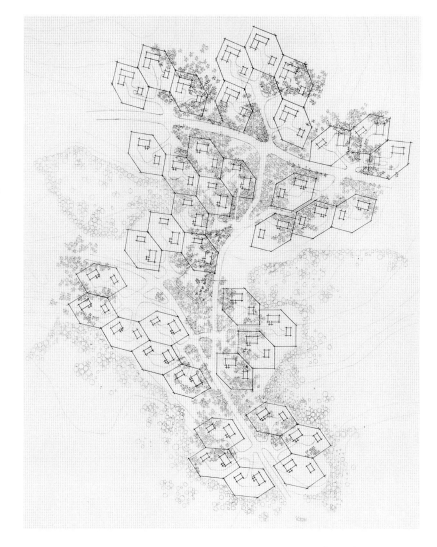

20. Alvar Aalto. Housing, Rovaniemi, Finland. 1944–46. Site plan. Alvar Aalto Foundation, Helsinki

cept of the "city crown"[50] returns in the mono-pitched roof of the council chamber, which rises up as an indicator, so to speak, of the way in which the town ought to grow. A similar roof crowned most of Aalto's later civic centers with the same basic intention, namely, to serve as a symbolic core around which the rest of the municipality would develop.

Resisting closure around either a classical paradigm or a technological norm, Aalto strove for an organic flexibility, wherein function and production would play their appointed roles without being over-determined and where, within the megalopolis, agriculture and industry would interact with nature in such a way as to create an environmental ecology satisfying to fundamental human needs. Aalto's overall sociocultural attitude was close to that of the physician-philosopher, Alexis Carrel, whom he was to cite on more than one occasion. Aalto made explicit reference to Carrel in his 1940 obituary for Erik Gunnar Asplund and again in his essay, "National Planning and Cultural Goals" of 1949.[51] Carrel, a Franco-American research doctor and Nobel Prize winner, was one of the first scientists to mount a full-scale critique of industrial civilization, particularly with regard to the priority given to mass production and consumption at the expense of deeper psychocultural needs. Complex and contradictory, and in some respects profoundly pessimistic, Carrel was a rather atypical figure for Aalto to identify with. For, although he was as preoccupied as Aalto with regional decentralization and with what he called a nominalist mediation of any kind of universal principle, he was, at the same time, elitist and skeptical as to the prospects for democracy. However, like Aalto he was opposed on biological grounds to large areas of glass, regarding overexposure to the sun as debilitating for both mind and body, and, to this end, he wrote with gratifying prejudice for anyone coming from the Baltic: "We must not forget that the most highly civilized races—the Scandinavians, for example, are white, and have lived for many generations in a country where the atmospheric luminosity is weak during a great part of the year."[52] It is interesting to note that Carrel was already part of Aalto's intellectual milieu by the late 1930s, as we may judge from the inclusion of Carrel as a prospective author in the first ten issues of the unrealized Anglo-Swedish magazine, *The Human Side*, which was to have been edited by Gregor Paulsson and Alvar Aalto on the eve of World War II.[53]

It is one of the ironies of the history of the modern movement that while the deurbanizing[54] principle of Aalto's forest town was directly inspired by the regional planning paradigms of the TVA and by the greenbelt New Towns realized in the United States in the 1940s, the full welfare-state potential of these pioneering prototypes was ultimately realized in Finland rather than in North America. The reasons for this are many and complex: on the one hand, the Finns were confronted with a major rebuilding program at the end of the war and, on the other, the country benefited from having a mature government, while America, simultaneously triumphant both from winning the war and overcoming the Depression, in exactly the same period, began to sell the government-financed New Deal, green-belt New Towns back into private ownership.

An additional tragic irony of this moment resides in the fact that Aalto, who had everything to give to the idea of the forest town and who had, in any case, prepared the ground for its coming into being as a generic form of regional urbanism, was almost totally excluded from its actual realization. The ultimate reason for this is suggested by Jere Maula in his article, "The Growing Perspective of Urban Planning," where he argues that the bureaucratic aspect of Finnish social democracy favored Swedish productive norms for its large-scale housing programs to the "neglect of the local tradition," as he put it, by which he surely meant Aalto and the school of Aalto.[55]

Aalto at the Millenium

In June 1977, in the commemorative issue of *L'Architecture d'aujourd'hui* following Aalto's death, the Italian architect, Leonardo Mosso, analyzed the underlying substance and method of Aalto's work in the following profound and moving terms:

> *Each project has a double system of requirements: those that are material and those that are social. Material requirements must absolutely be resolved or else the very reasons for a project's existence are compromised. . . . As for the social requirements, Aalto attempts to solve the material problems of the individual within the framework of social organization, by inserting qualities of sociability into the system of objective requirements. He seeks to overcome man's egoism (in the sense of a primacy of self over others) by combining functions that tend to be more collective than individualistic, while at the same time, he fights against alienating aspects by including insulating and protective qualities. Aalto incorporates physically into his spaces the basic attributes of this dialectic. . . . The aphorism "to achieve Paradise on earth through the sole means of the art of the building" means (as the whole of Aalto's practice demonstrates) the recreating of a unity between urban tissue and natural surroundings. In other words, permitting the entire population to recover urban spaces colonized by capitalist commercialism and profit seeking, by all that destroys the identity of man and of social man.[56]*

Now, twenty years later, on the occasion of the centenary of his birth, we have cause to reassess, in comparable terms, the relevance of Aalto's work to the architecture of the emerging future, above all, because of the fragmented character of contemporary development and the ever-widening domain of the megalopolis in the late modern world. As far as this last is concerned, it is clear that Aalto embraced a critically realistic view in which ecologically tempered tracts of regional urbanization would become the universal norm, however much they may be layered and inflected, as his vision of the forest town implies.

Aside from the general relevance of his ecological critique, it is equally necessary to acknowledge the pertinence of Aalto's heterotopic method, given the fragmented, not to say chaotic, character of urban development as it currently prevails. The way in which this method may serve as a counter principle to rationalism has never been better defined than by Demetri Porphyrios in 1982, wherein he characterized heterotopic principle as achieving cohesion "through adjacency: where the edges touch, where the fringes intermingle, where the extremities of the one denote the beginning of the other, there in the hinge between two things an unstable unity appears."[57] Porphyrios proceeded to argue that it was just this sensibility that enabled Aalto to distance himself from all forms of positivism and from the latter's secret alliance with consumerism inasmuch as rationalized production presupposes the equal but opposite "irrationality" of unbridled consumption. By a similar token, Aalto distanced himself from any kind of vulgar populism and from the perennially romantic myth of individual genius. As Porphyrios put it: "The heterotopic sensibility of Aalto . . . was neither an individual expressionism (that is, a secretly lodged *maniera*), nor a Dionysian irrationalism, and even less a liberating transformation of Modernism."[58] It was, as we have seen, in many respects, a return to the fragmentary aggregational manner of the English Free Style and, hence, to the ethos of Scandinavian national romanticism in all its multifarious forms. This seemingly retrograde move enabled Aalto not only to integrate topographic idiosyncrasies but also to meet the specificity of a brief in an appropriate way without sacrificing either rhythmic drive or functional performance. Above all, it facilitated the realization of buildings that were laid into their surroundings in such a way that one could not discern with certainty where building ended and context began.

While Aalto exploited the sensuous potential of the heterotopic method for what he called its unpremeditated style creating power, the significance of this strategy at the end of the century, resides in its categorical antipathy to building as a proliferation of freestanding objects. Like the comparable architecture of Hugo Häring and Hans Scharoun, with whom, as Colin St. John Wilson reminded us, there was always an affinity,[59] Aalto's buildings were either landscapes in themselves, as in the case of the Wolfsburg Cultural Center of 1958–62 or, alternatively, they extended into the surroundings in such a way as to transform the preexisting ground, as in the case of the Maison Carré of 1956–59 or Seinäjoki Civic Center of 1958–87

(plates 307–314, 344–360, 367–375). Of parallel ontological consequence was the way in which his buildings were constituted as topographic structures rather than as gratuitous sculptural gestures, which, by definition, can never transcend their freestanding isolation. This is the paradox of Aalto's heterotopic legacy, for while it is an idiosyncratic response to the specificity of both site and program, it remains open, almost by design, to the subsequent collective transformation of the work across time. It anticipates, in terms of the larger future, that which is already inherent in the design process itself. It is the precondition, one might say, for Alvaro Siza's insistence that the main task of architecture resides in transformation rather than invention.[60]

Thus, the ultimate significance of Aalto's work for the coming century resides in his conviction that the built work always has to be rendered, in large measure, as a landscape, thereby fusing and *con*fusing both figure and ground, in a ceaseless interplay between natural constraint and cultural ingenuity. This surely is the critical essence of what Aalto leaves to us, as we contemplate a totalizing limitless environment in which we can no longer say where city ends and country begins. And, while the ruthless rapacity of late-modern development takes us further and further from the ecological ethic of Aalto's forest town, the hope remains that all the ill-considered, ill-related, half-abandoned objects of our time may, one day, be redeemed through an ad hoc creation of layered, topographic assemblies, irrespective of whether these be roofworks or earthworks or, as is more often the case, an inseparable mixture of both.

Notes

1. Alvar Aalto, interview in *Pagens Nyheter* (Stockholm), October 28, 1936; repr. in Göran Schildt, *Alvar Aalto: The Decisive Years*, trans. Timothy Binham (Rizzoli: New York, 1986), pp. 202–203.

2. Demetri Porphyrios, *Sources of Modern Eclecticism: Studies on Alvar Aalto* (London: Academy Editions, 1982), p. 2.

3. Colin St. John Wilson, *The Other Tradition of Modern Architecture: The Uncompleted Project* (London: Academy Editions, 1995), pp. 6, 30, 86–90.

4. Martin Heidegger, "Building, Dwelling, Thinking" (1954), in English in Albert Hofstadter, *Poetry, Language, and Thought* (New York: Harper Colophon, 1975), pp. 145–161.

5. St. John Wilson, *The Other Tradition of Modern Architecture,* p. 16.

6. See Jean Badovici and Eileen Gray, "From Eclecticism to Doubt," *L'Architecture vivante* (Autumn 1929). See also St. John Wilson, *The Other Tradition of Modern Architecture*, p. 117.

7. Giancarlo de Carlo, *Legitimizing Architecture* (Milan: Electa, 1968).

8. Alvar Aalto, "The RIBA Discourse: 'The Architectural Struggle,'" speech given to the Royal Institute of British Architects, London, 1957; repr. in Göran Schildt, ed., *Sketches: Alvar Aalto*, trans. Stuart Wrede (Cambridge, Mass., and London: MIT Press, 1978), p. 147.

9. Ibid.

10. See Francesco Dal Co, *Mario Botta: Architetture 1960–1985* (Milan: Electa, 1985), p. 17.

11. The break to a kind of organic collage has been seen, in part, as a return to Finnish national romanticism of the 1890s. This affinity was not missed by Aalto's long-standing friend, the architect and architectural critic, Gustaf Strengell, who, just prior to his tragic suicide, characterized the architect's house as the new Niemelä farm. This referred to a collection of eighteenth- and nineteenth-century timber structures clustered around a central yard and exhibited in close proximity to their original forest setting. See Schildt, *Decisive Years*, p. 130.

12. See Simo Paavilainen, ed., *Nordic Classicism, 1910–1930* (Helsinki: Museum of Finnish Architecture, 1982).

13. The term *Sachlichkeit* had been current in German cultural circles long before 1924, when the art critic G. F. Hartlaub hit upon the phrase *die neue Sachlichkeit* [the new objectivity] to identify a postwar school of anti-Expressionist painting. *Sachlichkeit* seems to have been first used in an architectural context in a series of articles written by Hermann Muthesius for the journal, *Dekorative Kunst*, between 1897 and 1903. These articles attributed the quality of *Sachlichkeit* to the English Arts and Crafts movement, particularly as manifested in the handicraft guilds (such as that founded by C. R. Ashbee) and the application of the craft ethic to early garden-city suburbs. For Muthesius, *Sachlichkeit* seems to have meant an objective, functionalist, eminently yeoman approach to the design of objects, implying the ultimate reform of industrial society itself. In the second half of the 1920s, the term was closely associated with the left-wing functionalist architects of Germany's Weimar Republic, Switzerland, and the Netherlands.

14. Göran Schildt, *Alvar Aalto: The Complete Catalogue of Architecture, Design and Art*, trans. Timothy Binham (New York: Rizzoli, 1994), p. 224.

15. See Elina Standertskjöld, "Alvar Aalto and Standardization" and "Alvar Aalto's Standard Drawings 1929–32," *Acanthus 1992* (Helsinki: Museum of Finnish Architecture, 1992), pp. 84–111.

16. Alvar Aalto, "The Stockholm Exhibition I," summary of interview in *Åbo Underrättelsen* (May 22, 1930); repr. in Schildt, *Sketches*, p. 16. Inspired by the vision of Gregor Paulsson, the leading figures of the so-called *acceptera* faction were the architects Erik Gunnar Asplund, Uno Åhren, Wolter Gran, Sven Markelius, and Eskil Sundahl. They were also the leading designers of the 1930 Stockholm Exhibition. They were closely connected to the socialist *Clarté* movement, which helped develop the program for the exhibition. Gunnar and Alva Myrdal were part of this intellectual circle, while Viola Markelius was the editor of the group's radical journal to which Aalto contributed. See Schildt, *Decisive Years*, p. 49.

17. This exhibition was organized by P. Morton Shand in the London department store, Fortnum & Mason. The success of this show led to the establishment of Finmar, a company that was especially dedicated to the sale of Aalto furniture. See Schildt, *Decisive Years*, pp. 103–128.

18. Alvar Aalto, "The Humanizing of Architecture," *Technology Review* (1940); repr. in Schildt, *Sketches*, p. 77.

19. Aalto's biological turn of mind was very much influenced by his contact with the Hungarian Bauhaus master, László Moholy-Nagy, whom he first met in 1930, the year that Moholy-Nagy's *Von Material zu Architektur* (translated as *The New Vision*) was first published. See Schildt, *Decisive Years*, pp. 70–77.

20. Alvar Aalto, "Asuntomme probleemina" [The Dwelling as a Problem], *Domus* (1930); repr. in Schildt, *Sketches*, pp. 29–30, 32.

21. See *acceptera* (Berlings: Arlöv, 1980), a facsimile of the original 1931 publication.

22. Alvar Aalto, "Rationalism and Man," lecture at Swedish Craft Society, Stockholm, May 9, 1935; repr. in Schildt, *Sketches*, pp. 48–51.

23. The only evidence we have of Aalto having had any direct contact with Japanese culture is what we know of his friendship with the first Japanese ambassador to Finland, Hakotara Ichikawa, and his wife. See Schildt, *Decisive Years*, pp. 107–113.

24. Alvar Aalto, "The Influence of Construction and Material on Modern Architecture," in Bernhard Hoesli, ed., *Alvar Aalto Synopsis: Painting, Architecture, Sculpture* (Basel and Stuttgart: Birkhäuser Verlag, 1970), p. 13. A slightly different version of the same text appears in Schildt, *Sketches*, pp. 62–63.

25. Aalto, "Humanizing of Architecture," in ibid., p. 77.

26. Alvar Aalto, "Karjalan rakennustaide" [Architecture in Karelia]; repr. in ibid., p. 82.

27. Ibid., pp. 82–83.

28. Alvar Aalto, "Rakennuskorkeus sosiaalisesa kysymyksenä" [Building Heights as a Social Problem], *Arkkitehti* (1946); repr. in ibid., p. 93.

29. Aalto did, in fact, deploy the Hansaviertel block type and apartment plan in his unrealized housing projects for Kampementsbacken, Stockholm (1958) and for Björnholm on the southern Finnish coast (1959).

30. Karl Fleig, ed., *Alvar Aalto* (London: Tiramti, 1963), p. 168.

31. See D'Arcy Wentworth Thompson, *On Growth and Form*, ed. J. T. Bonner (Cambridge: Cambridge University Press, 1971). First published in 1917, the book was expanded and revised in 1942.

32. I am referring, in particular, to the stepped section of Helin's Borås A-block, rather than Siitonen's equally experimental but vertical Borås B-block, built on an adjacent site.

33. For all these works, see Marja-Riitta Norri, ed., *An Architectural Present—7 Approaches* (Helsinki: Museum of Finnish Architecture, 1990).

34. Jørn Utzon, "Additive Architecture," *Arkitektur* (Copenhagen), vol. 14, no. 1 (1970), p. 1.

35. For Hodgkinson's house for Lord Adrian in Cambridge, see Douglas Stephen, Kenneth Frampton, and Michael Carepetian, *British Buildings 1960–64* (London: Adam & Charles Black, 1965), pp. 66–70.

36. See Leslie Martin, *Buildings and Ideas 1933–83* (Cambridge: Cambridge University Press, 1983).

37. Grupo R was organized, primarily by Josep Maria Sostres and Oriol Bohigas, as a nationalist cultural movement, oriented toward the recovery of a modern architecture that would be organically inflected. In his article, "Posibilidades de una arquitectura barcelonesa," published in the magazine *Destino*, Bohigas exploited Aalto's visit to Barcelona in 1951 as an occasion on which to argue for an organic Catalan modernism. See Helio Piñón, *Nacionalisme i Modernitat en L'Arquitectura Catalana Contemporània* (Barcelona: Ediciones 62, 1980), pp. 19–39.

38. Robert Venturi, *Complexity and Contradiction in Architecture*, The Museum of Modern Art Papers on Architecture, Vol. 1 (New York: The Museum of Modern Art, in association with the Graham Foundation for Advanced Studies in the Fine Arts, 1966).

39. Idem, "Alvar Aalto," *Arkkitehti* (July–August 1976), pp. 66–67; repr. in *Progressive Architecture* (April 1977), pp. 54, 102; as "Le Palladio du mouvement moderne," *L'Architecture d'aujourd'hui*, no. 191 (June 1977), pp. 119–120; and in idem, *A View from the Campidoglio* (New York: Harper & Row, 1984), pp. 60–61.

40. This building was designed in 1962 soon after Corneil returned to Canada after working for Aalto in the late 1950s.

41. See Fritz Neumeyer, *The Artless Word: Mies Van der Rohe on Building Art* (Cambridge, Mass.: MIT Press, 1991), pp. 102–106. Mies was profoundly influenced by Raoul Francé's protoecological writings. In the mid-1920s, one finds Mies in total accord with Francé's dictum: "The best one can do is to find a compromise between the I and this law (of ecology) and to adjust to it according to the variables of the surroundings." Here we encounter a surprising affinity between Mies and Aalto, particularly concerning their respective attitudes toward regional planning.

42. The name of this hypothesis derives from the Greek goddess of the earth, Gaia. The term was coined by James Lovelock in the 1970s and refers to his hypothesis

that the homeostatic balance of the earth's biomass is regulated by a complex network of interwoven feed-back systems. See James Lovelock, *Gaia: A New Look at Earth* (London: Oxford University Press, 1979) and *The Ages of Gaia: A Biography of Our Living Earth* (New York: Norton, 1995). See also Max Oelschlaeger, *Postmodern Environmental Ethics* (New York: SUNY, 1995).

43. Alvar Aalto, "Problemi di architettura" (1956); repr. in Schildt, *Complete Catalogue*, p. 14.

44. Alvar Aalto, *Arkkitehti*, no. 1 (1942); cited in Schildt, *Complete Catalogue*, p. 16.

45. Ibid., p. 22

46. Alvar Aalto, *Arkkitehti*, nos. 1–2 (1957); cited in ibid.

47. See Jussi Rautsi "Alvar Aalto's Urban Plans 1940–1970," *DATUTOP 13* (Tampere) (1988), p. 52.

48. Alvar Aalto, "Valtakunnansuunnittelu ja kulttuurimme tavoittet" [National Planning and Cultural Goals], *Suomalainen Suomi* (1949); repr. in Schildt, *Sketches*, p. 100.

49. Rautsi, "Alvar Aalto's Urban Plans 1940–1970," p. 55.

50. Bruno Taut, *Die Stadtkrone* (Jena: Diederichs, 1919).

51. For these texts by Aalto, see Schildt, *Sketches*, pp. 66–67, 99–102.

52. Alexis Carrel, *Man, the Unknown*, 2nd ed. (New York: Harper & Row, 1939), p. 214.

53. See Schildt, *Decisive Years*, pp. 182–186.

54. Soviet regional planning theory in the late 1920s was influenced by the debate taking place between the "urbanists" and the "deurbanists," with the former recommending the housing of the people in large communal blocks (*dom kommuna*) and the latter favoring the redistribution of the urban population throughout the countryside. The deurbanists recommended the creation of new settlements out of impermanent, prefabricated, free houses. See Anatole Kopp, *Town and Revolution: Soviet Architecture and City Planning 1917–1935*, trans. Thomas E. Burton (New York: George Braziller, 1970), pp. 168–178.

55. Jere Maula, "The Growing Perspective in Urban Planning," in *Heroism and Everyday Life: Building in Finland in the 1950's* (Helsinki: Museum of Finnish Architecture, 1994), p. 202.

56. Leonardo Mosso, "Aalto: Architect of Social and Cultural Reintegration," *L'Architecture d'aujourd'hui*, no. 191 (June 1977), p. 122.

57. Porphyrios, *Sources of Modern Eclecticism*, p. 3.

58. Ibid.

59. St. John Wilson, *The Other Tradition of Modern Architecture*, pp. 27–35.

60. See Alvaro Siza, "Interview," *Plan Construction* (May 1980). "Architects invent nothing. They work continuously with models which they transform in response to problems they encounter."

Plates

The following plates present a selection of Alvar Aalto's most important designs and buildings, organized, for the most part, chronologically. All works are by Aalto unless otherwise designated.

In the captions, the name of a work is followed by its location and date. If a design is unexecuted, the word *project* appears before the date. Works are dated to reflect the period from design to completion: from the beginning of a competition, commission, or design phase through to completion of the built work (or design process, if unbuilt). A building no longer extant is noted as such. Each illustration has its own plate number followed by a description.

The illustrations are of three types: original drawings (sketches or competition, presentation, or working drawings); redrawn plans, sections, or axonometrics; and photographs of buildings or models.

For original drawings, the description may be followed, in parentheses, by the name of the delineator, if other than Aalto, or the date of the drawing, if it adds information to the overall dates. This information is followed by the medium and dimensions of the drawing. If only a portion of a drawing is shown, the word *detail* is used; if all of the drawing is shown but the edges of the paper have been trimmed, the word *sheet* appears to indicate such cropping. Dimensions for drawings are given in inches, height before width, followed by centimeters in parentheses. (Dimensions of three-dimensional objects, such as models, which appear in photographs, are given in inches and centimeters, height before width before length.) If a drawing has been reproduced from a photograph provided by the Alvar Aalto Foundation, rather than from the drawing itself, the medium and dimensions are omitted.

For redrawn plans, sections, or axonometrics, the date of the drawing and the name of the delineator(s) are given.

For photographs of built works, a description or view is given after the plate number. Sources and credits for photography are given in the Photograph Credits.

Park Café
Project, 1917

1
School assignment (University of Technology, Helsinki): elevation and ground-floor plan. India ink on cardboard, 26 1/16 x 17 3/4" (66.2 x 45 cm). Alvar Aalto Foundation, Helsinki

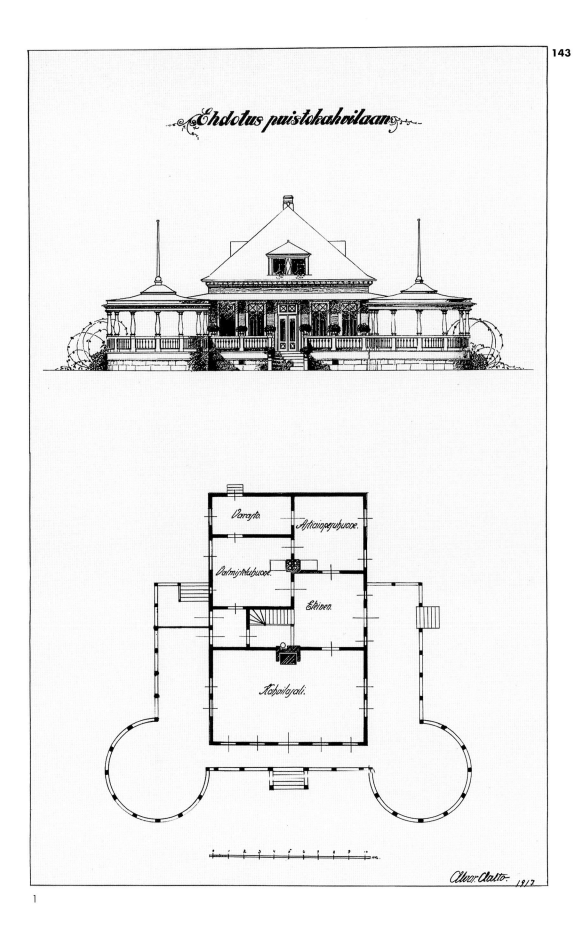

1

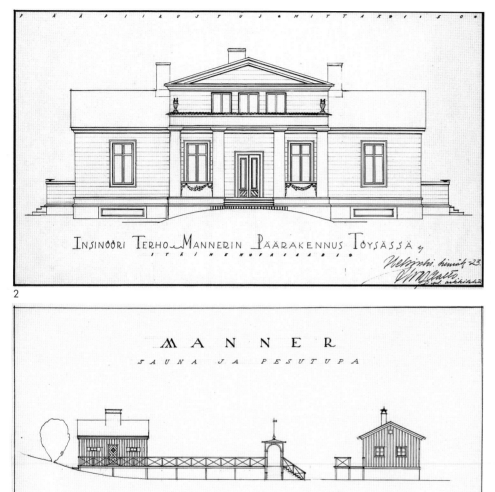

House and Sauna for Terho Manner

Töysä, Finland.1923 (sauna demolished

2
House elevation. India ink
on paper, sheet 16⅝ x 24⅝"
(42.2 x 62.6 cm). Alvar
Aalto Foundation, Helsinki
3
Sauna elevations, plan, and
section. India ink on tracing
paper, sheet 15⅛ x 21⁹⁄₁₆"
(38.5 x 54.8 cm). Alvar
Aalto Foundation, Helsinki

Furnishings for Hämäläis-Osakunta Students' Club
Helsinki. 1924

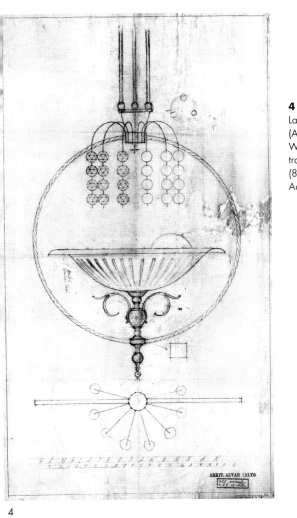

4

4
Lamp for ladies' room
(Aino Marsio Aalto).
Watercolor and pencil on
tracing paper, 34¹⁄₁₆ x 19³⁄₁₆"
(86.5 x 48.7 cm). Alvar
Aalto Foundation, Helsinki

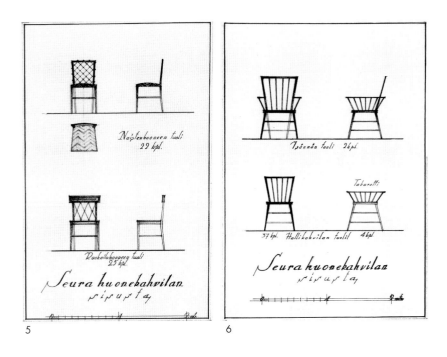

5   6

Furnishings for Seurahuone Café
Jyväskylä, Finland. 1924 (demolished)

5
Chairs for ladies' room and
dining room. India ink,
watercolor, and pencil on
tracing paper, 17⅝ x 11⅞"
(44.8 x 30.2 cm). Alvar
Aalto Foundation, Helsinki

6
Chairs for "master of the
house" and hall café. India
ink and pencil on tracing
paper, 17⅝ x 12" (44.8 x
30.4 cm). Alvar Aalto
Foundation, Helsinki

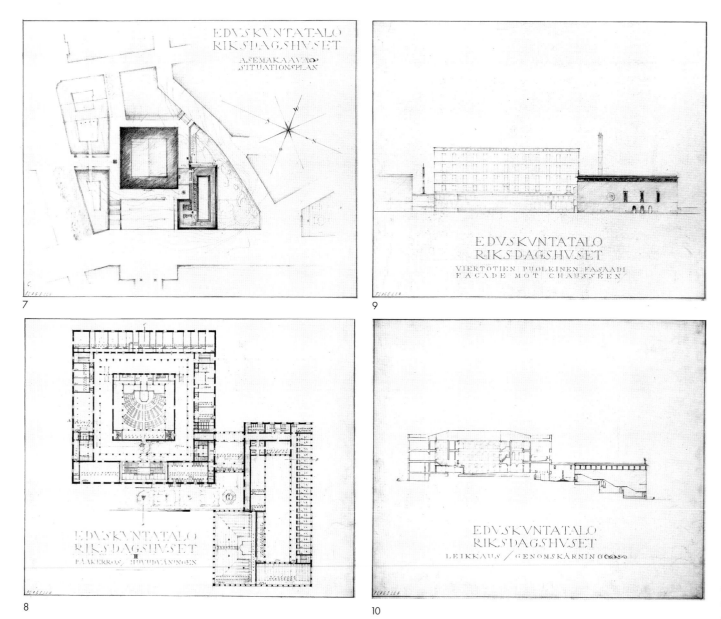

7

9

8

10

Finnish Parliament House
Helsinki. Project, 1923–24

7
Competition drawing: site plan. Pencil on cardboard, 24⅝ x 31" (62.6 x 78.6 cm). Alvar Aalto Foundation, Helsinki
8
Competition drawing: first-floor plan. Pencil on cardboard, 24⅝ x 31" (62.6 x 78.6 cm). Alvar Aalto Foundation, Helsinki
9
Competition drawing: elevation. Pencil on cardboard, 24⅝ x 30⅞" (62.6 x 78.4 cm). Alvar Aalto Foundation, Helsinki
10
Competition drawing: section. Pencil on paper, 24¾ x 31" (62.8 x 78.6 cm). Alvar Aalto Foundation, Helsinki

Seinäjoki, Finland. 1924–29

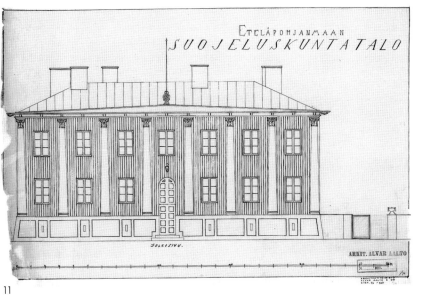

11

11
Elevation. India ink on tracing paper, 14^{13}/$_{16}$ x 22^{9}/$_{16}$" (37.6 x 57.3 cm). Alvar Aalto Foundation, Helsinki

12
Vestibule section. India ink and pencil on tracing paper, 16^{5}/$_{16}$ x 27^{9}/$_{16}$" (41.5 x 70 cm). Alvar Aalto Foundation, Helsinki

13
Site plan (1997; Jari Frondelius and Peter B. MacKeith)

14
Vestibule lamp details. Pencil and color pencil on tracing paper, 28^{15}/$_{16}$ x 19^{1}/$_{16}$" (73.5 x 48.4 cm). Alvar Aalto Foundation, Helsinki

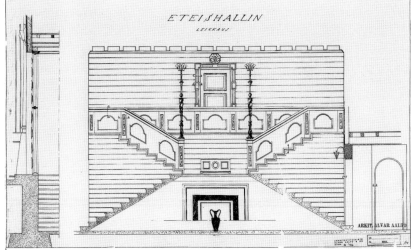

12

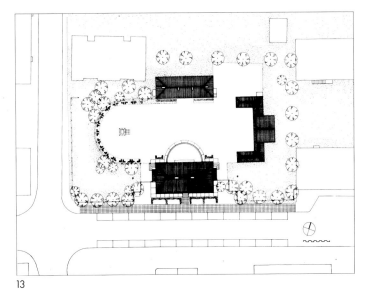

13

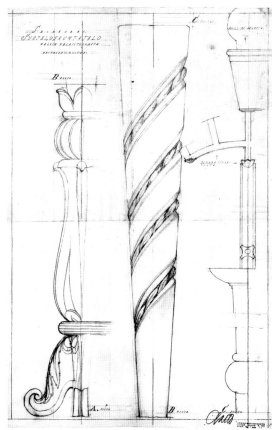

14

Jyväskylä Workers' Club
Jyväskylä, Finland. 1924–25

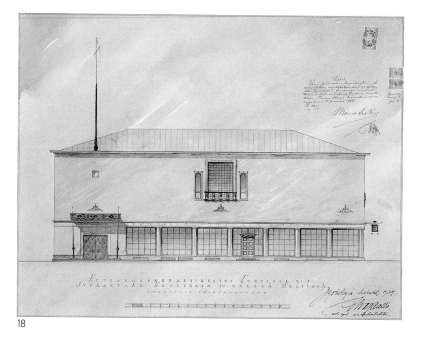

15

16

17

18

15
View from northeast
16
View from southeast
17
North elevation and section. Ink, watercolor, and pencil on paper, 25⁹⁄₁₆ x 19⅞" (65 x 50.5 cm). The Jyväskylä Workers' Society, courtesy Alvar Aalto Museum, Jyväskylä
18
East elevation. Ink, watercolor, and pencil on paper, 19¹¹⁄₁₆ x 25⅜" (50 x 64.5 cm). The Jyväskylä Workers' Society, courtesy Alvar Aalto Museum, Jyväskylä

19
Theater and balcony plans. Ink, watercolor, and pencil on paper, 19¹¹/₁₆ x 25⅜" (50 x 64.5 cm). The Jyväskylä Workers' Society, courtesy Alvar Aalto Museum, Jyväskylä

20
Basement and ground-floor plans. Ink, watercolor, and pencil on paper, 19¹¹/₁₆ x 25⅜" (50 x 64.5 cm). The Jyväskylä Workers' Society, courtesy Alvar Aalto Museum, Jyväskylä
21
Entrance to theater
22
Theater

21

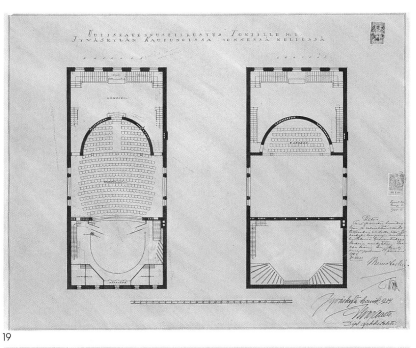

19

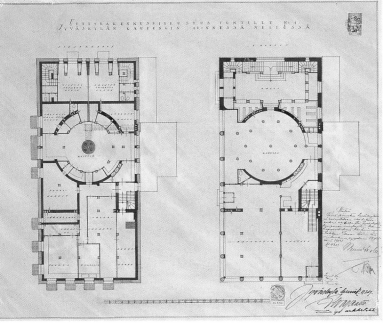

20

22

Funeral Chapel
Jyväskylä, Finland. Project, 1925 and 1930

23

24

23
First version (1925): court-yard perspective. Pencil on paper, sheet 16⅞ x 12¹³⁄₁₆" (41.7 x 32.5 cm). Alvar Aalto Foundation, Helsinki

24
First version (1925): interior perspective. Charcoal on pasteboard, 18⁷⁄₁₆ x 13⅞" (46.8 x 35.3 cm). Alvar Aalto Foundation, Helsinki

25
Second version (1930): perspective and plan. Pencil on paper, sheet 11 x 18½" (28 x 47 cm). Alvar Aalto Foundation, Helsinki

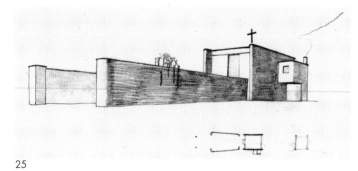

25

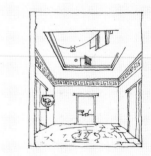

Atrium House for Väinö Aalto
Alajärvi, Finland. Project, 1925

26
Atrium perspective and ground-floor plan. India ink and paint on pasteboard, sheet 9½ x 5⅜" (24.2 x 13.6 cm). Alvar Aalto Foundation, Helsinki

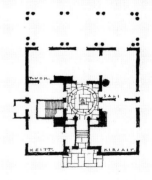

26

27

28

Jämsä Church
Jämsä, Finland. Project, 1925

29

27
Original Jämsä Church,
c. 1826, before fire.
Photograph (1921), 3⁹⁄₁₆ x
5⁷⁄₁₆" (9 x 13.8 cm). Alvar
Aalto Foundation, Helsinki
28
Jämsä Church after fire, with
sketch of new church, 1925.
Pencil on photograph, 3⁹⁄₁₆ x
5½" (9 x 14 cm). Alvar Aalto
Foundation, Helsinki
29
Interior and exterior
perspective sketches.
Pencil on paper, 6⁵⁄₁₆ x 8½"
(16 x 21.6 cm). Alvar Aalto
Foundation, Helsinki
30
Church and existing bell-
tower perspective sketch.
Pencil on paper, 6¹⁵⁄₁₆ x 5¾"
(17.6 x 14.6 cm). Alvar Aalto
Foundation, Helsinki

30

31

31
View from north
32
North elevation. Ink, watercolor, and pencil on board,
25⁹⁄₁₆ x 19⁵⁄₁₆" (65 x 49 cm).
The Muurame Parish,
courtesy Alvar Aalto
Museum, Jyväskylä
33
Plan. Ink, watercolor, and
pencil on board, 26 x 19¹¹⁄₁₆"
(66 x 50 cm). The Muurame
Parish, courtesy Alvar Aalto
Museum, Jyväskylä

Muurame Church
Muurame, Finland. 1926–29

MUURAMEN KIRKKO
POHJOISFASAADI

32

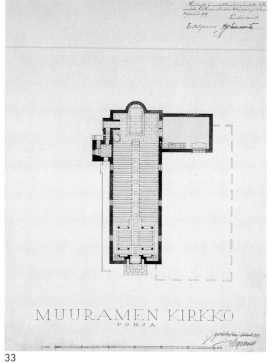

MUURAMEN KIRKKO
POHJA

33

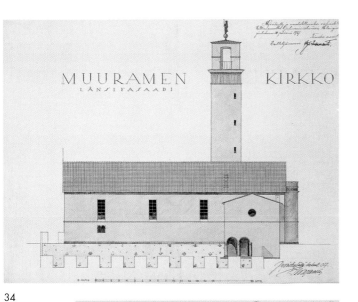

34

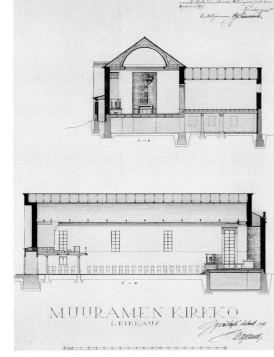

35

34
West elevation. Ink, watercolor, and pencil on board, 19⅜ x 25⅝" (49 x 65 cm). The Muurame Parish, courtesy Alvar Aalto Museum, Jyväskylä
35
Sections. Ink, watercolor, and pencil on board, 25⅝ x 19⅜" (65 x 49 cm). The Muurame Parish, courtesy Alvar Aalto Museum, Jyväskylä
36
Interior

36

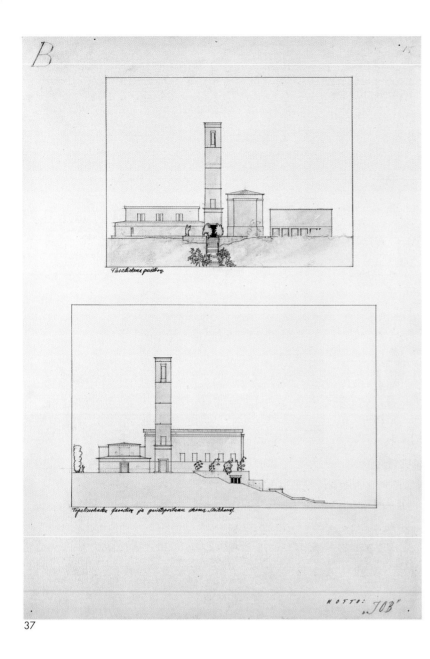

37

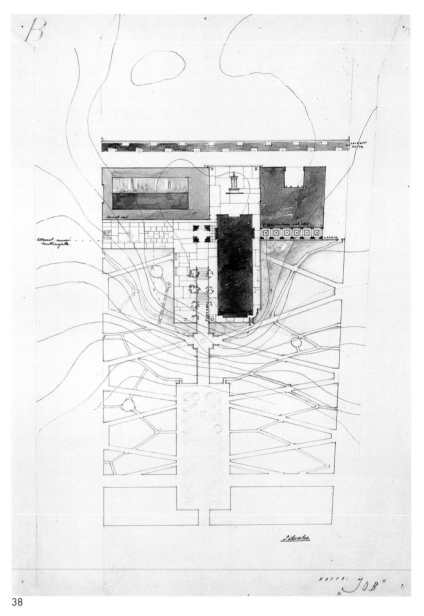

38

Töölö Church
Helsinki. Project, 1927

37
Competition drawing:
elevations. Ink, watercolor,
and pencil on board,
20⅟₁₆ x 14⅜" (51 x 36.5 cm).
Museum of Finnish
Architecture, Helsinki

38
Competition drawing: site
plan. Ink, watercolor, and
pencil on board, 20⅟₁₆ x 14⅜"
(51 x 36.5 cm). Museum of
Finnish Architecture, Helsinki

39
Perspective sketches.
Pencil on paper, 8⅝ x 11"
(22 x 28 cm). Alvar Aalto
Foundation, Helsinki
40
Perspective, plan, and
section sketches. Pencil on
paper, sheet 11 x 8⅝"
(28 x 22 cm). Alvar Aalto
Foundation, Helsinki
41
Elevation and perspective
sketches. Pencil on paper,
sheet 11 x 8⅝" (28 x 22 cm).
Alvar Aalto Foundation,
Helsinki

39

League of Nations
Geneva, Switzerland. Project, 1926–27

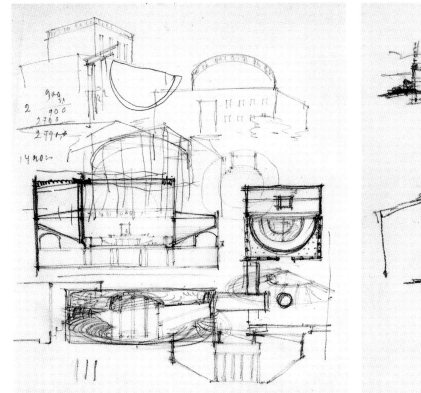

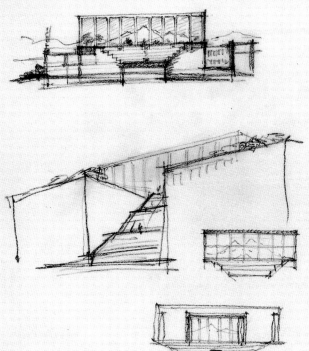

40

41

Turun Sanomat Building
Turku, Finland. 1928–30

42

42
Facade
43
Perspective. India ink on pasteboard, sheet 16 x 18⅝" (40.6 x 47.3 cm). Alvar Aalto Foundation, Helsinki
44
Exploded axonometric (1997; Matti Tapaninen and Peter B. MacKeith)

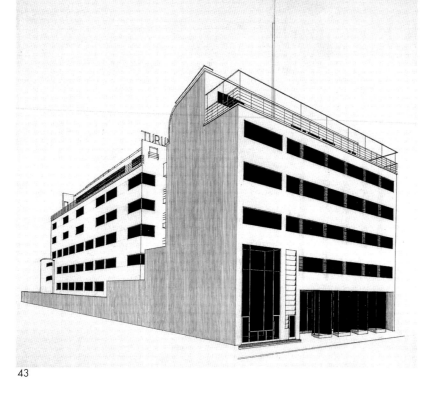

43

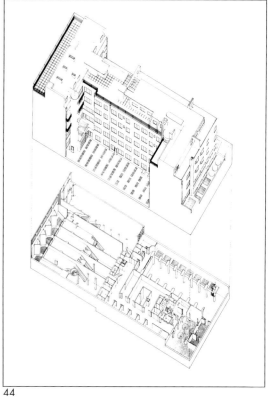

44

45
Display-window and entrance
perspective. Pencil on tracing
paper, sheet 21 1/16 x 19½"
(53.5 x 49.5 cm). Alvar
Aalto Foundation, Helsinki
46
Pressroom

45

46

47

Turun Sanomat Building

47
Ground-floor workroom
48
Conference-room perspective.
Pencil and color pencil on
tracing paper, 9 x 11⁷⁄₁₆"
(22.8 x 29 cm). Alvar Aalto
Foundation, Helsinki

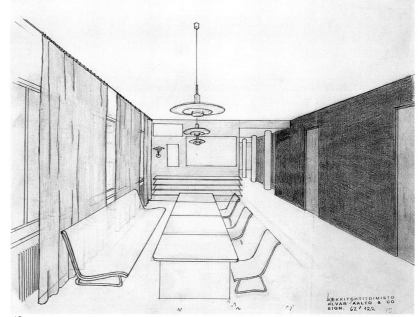

49

49
Stairway
50
Color-sample study (detail).
Painted and color papers,
8⅞ x 14" (22.5 x 35.5 cm).
Alvar Aalto Foundation,
Helsinki
51
Stair-hall perspective.
Ink and watercolor on
pasteboard, sheet 19¹¹⁄₁₆ x
14¹⁵⁄₁₆" (50 x 38 cm). Alvar
Aalto Foundation, Helsinki

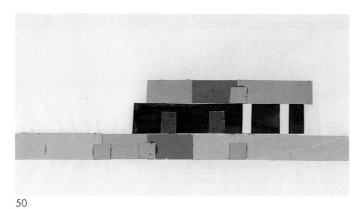

50

51

Paimio Tuberculosis Sanatorium
Paimio, Finland. 1929–33

52
Entrance court
53
Plan, section, and perspective
sketches. Pencil on tracing paper,
22⁷⁄₁₆ x 21¾" (57 x 55.3 cm).
Alvar Aalto Foundation, Helsinki
54
Plan and perspective sketches.
Pencil on paper, 8⅝ x 11"
(21.9 x 28 cm). Alvar Aalto
Foundation, Helsinki
55
Aerial view

52

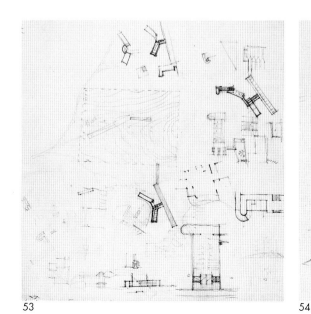

53

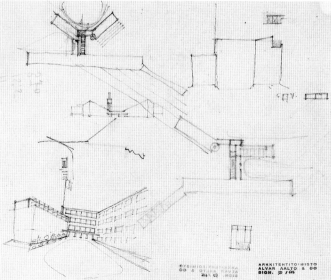

54

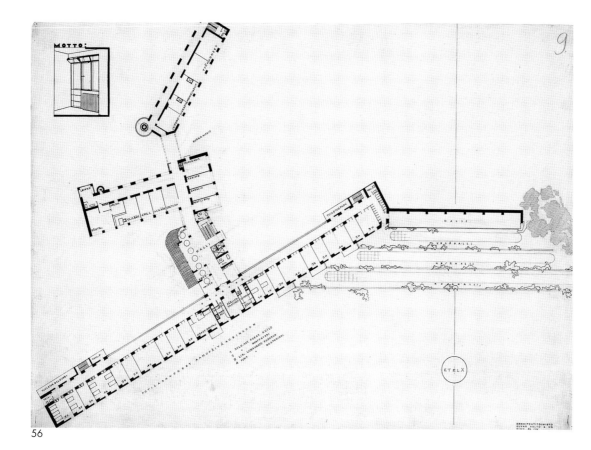

56

56
Competition drawing:
ground-floor plan. India
ink and pencil on card-
board, 20 x 28⅝"
(50.8 x 72.8 cm). Alvar
Aalto Foundation, Helsinki
57
Competition drawing: sec-
tions. India ink and pencil
on cardboard, 20⅟₁₆ x
28⅝" (51 x 72.8 cm).
Alvar Aalto Foundation,
Helsinki

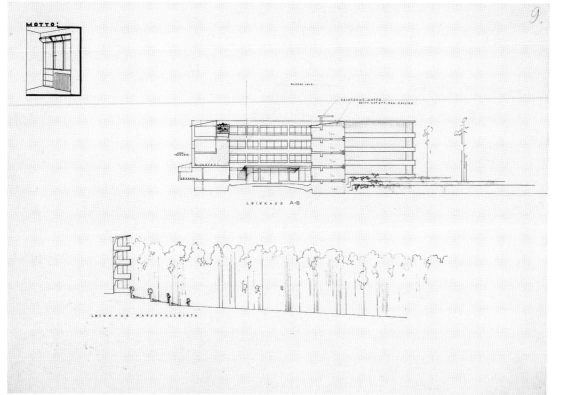

57

58

58
Stairway
59
Stacking Chair, Model 60, 1931–32. Solid and laminated birch, 31¾ x 15½ x 17⅜" (78 x 39.4 x 43.5 cm). The Museum of Modern Art, New York. Gift of Manfred Ludewig
60
Entry waiting area

59

60

61

Paimio Tuberculosis Sanatorium

61
Lounge
62
Dining hall

62

63

64

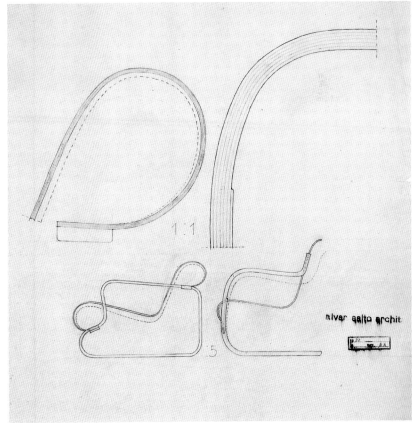

65

63
Paimio Chair, 1931–32. Bent plywood, bent laminated birch, and solid birch, 26 x 24 x 34½" (66 x 61 x 87.6 cm). The Museum of Modern Art, New York. Gift of Edgar Kaufmann, Jr.

64
Armchair (Chair 31), 1931–32. Laminated birch and lacquered molded plywood, 24⅝ x 23¾ x 30¾" (65 x 60.4 x 78 cm). The Museum of Modern Art, New York. Architecture and Design Fund

65
Paimio Chair and Chair 31: sections and wood details. Pencil on tracing paper, 23 x 21⅜" (58.5 x 54.2 cm). Alvar Aalto Foundation, Helsinki

66

67

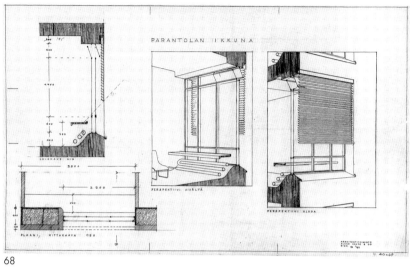

68

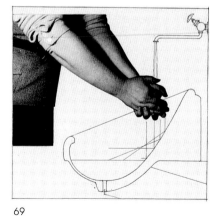

69

Paimio Tuberculosis Sanatorium

66
Patients' room
67
Patients' room
68
Patients' room window:
sections and perspectives.
India ink and pencil on
tracing paper, 14¾ x 25³⁄₁₆"
(37 x 64 cm). Alvar Aalto
Foundation, Helsinki
69
Washbasin section. Ink,
pencil, and photocollage
on board, 9⅝ x 11¹³⁄₁₆"
(24.5 x 30 cm). Alvar Aalto
Foundation, Helsinki

70

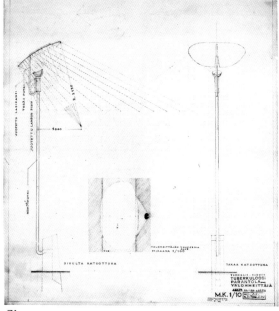

71

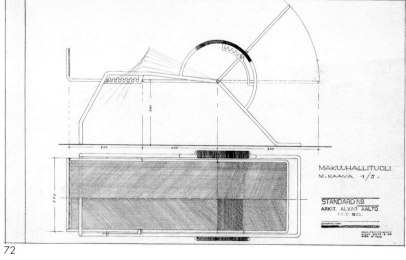

72

70
Balcony
71
Outdoor lamp elevations
(Lars Wiklund). Pencil on
tracing paper, 31³⁄₁₆ x 26⅛"
(79.2 x 66.4 cm). Alvar
Aalto Foundation, Helsinki
72
Chaise longue elevation and
plan. India ink and pencil on
tracing paper, 14¾ x 25³⁄₁₆"
(37.5 x 64 cm). Alvar Aalto
Foundation, Helsinki

"Merry-Go-Round" Summer Cottage
Aitta magazine competition, 1928

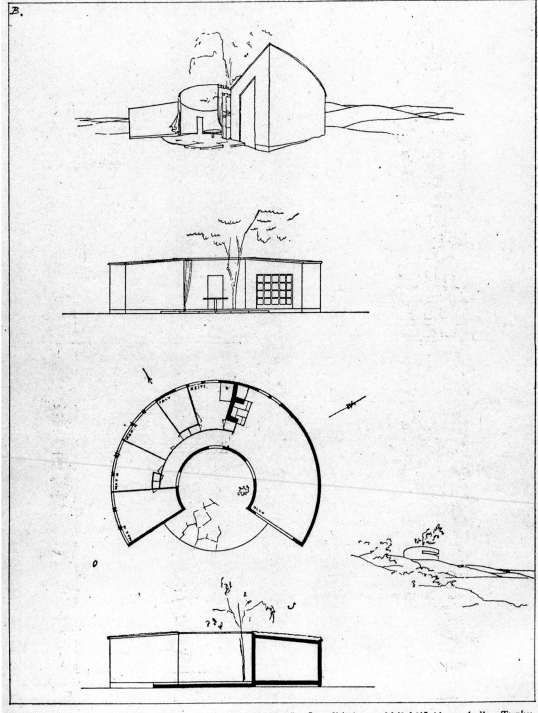

B-ryhmän I palkinto: arkkitehti Alvar Aalto, Turku.

73

73
Page from *Aitta* (May 1928). Perspectives, elevation, plan, and section. Museum of Finnish Architecture, Helsinki

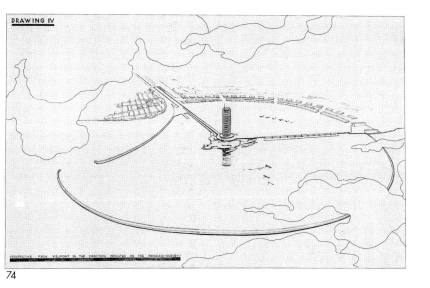

74

Columbus Memorial Light House
Santo Domingo, Dominican Republic. Project, 1929

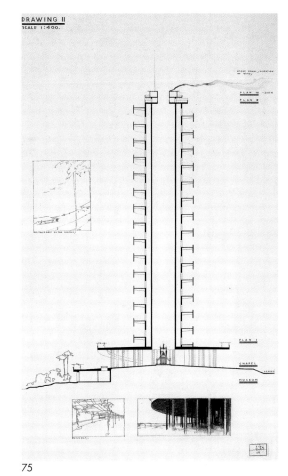

75

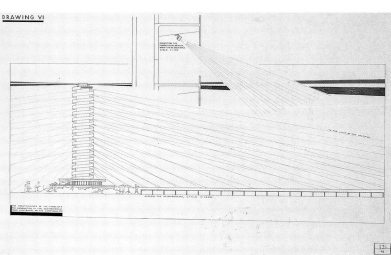

74
Competition drawing: aerial perspective. India ink and color ink on pasteboard, 19¹¹⁄₁₆ x 31⅞" (50 x 81 cm). Alvar Aalto Foundation, Helsinki

75
Competition drawing: section and perspectives. India ink and color ink on pasteboard, 31⅞ x 19¹¹⁄₁₆" (81 x 50 cm). Alvar Aalto Foundation, Helsinki

76
Competition drawing: elevation and section detail. India ink and color ink on pasteboard, 19¹¹⁄₁₆ x 31⅞" (50 x 81 cm). Alvar Aalto Foundation, Helsinki

76

Alvar Aalto and Erik Bryggman:
Turku 700th Anniversary Exhibition and Trade Fair
Turku, Finland. 1929 (demolished)

78

77
Kiosk with advertising pillars: perspective. India ink and color pencil on tracing paper, sheet 19¹¹⁄₁₆ x 14⁹⁄₁₆" (50 x 37 cm). Alvar Aalto Foundation, Helsinki
78
Kiosk with advertising pillar: perspective. India ink and color pencil on tracing paper, sheet 19⅝ x 18" (49.8 x 45.7 cm). Alvar Aalto Foundation, Helsinki
79
Exhibition pavilion perspective. India ink and watercolor on pasteboard, 11⁷⁄₁₆ x 16½" (29 x 42 cm). Alvar Aalto Foundation, Helsinki

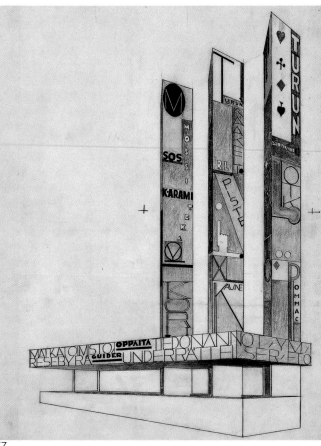

77

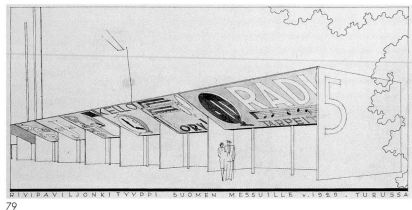

79

80

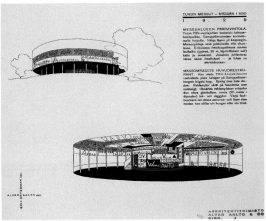

81

80
Kiosk with advertising pillars
81
Restaurant perspectives.
Printed promotional flyer,
7¹⁄₁₆ x 9¹⁄₁₆" (18 x 23 cm).
Alvar Aalto Foundation,
Helsinki
82
General view

82

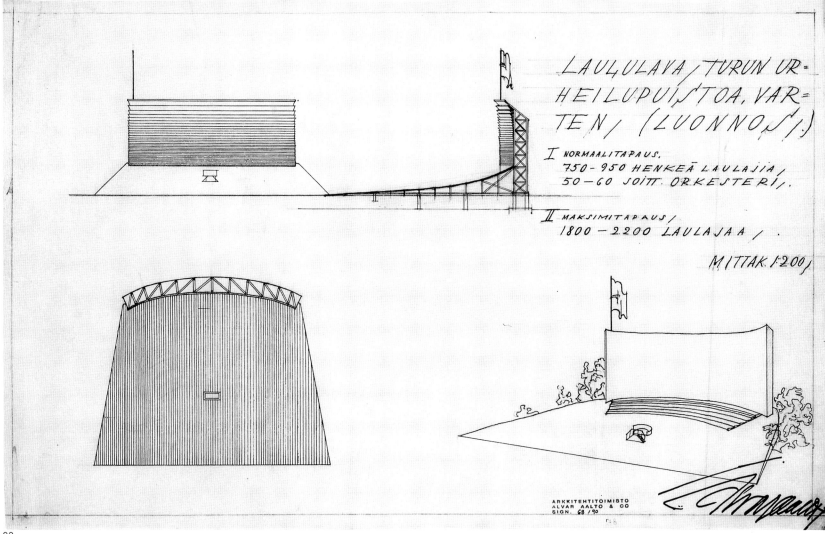

LAULULAVA/TURUN UR=
HEILUPUI/TOA, VAR=
TEN/ (LUONNO/I.)

I NORMAALITAPAUS.
750 - 950 HENKEĀ LAULAJIA,
50 - 60 SOITT. ORKESTERI,.

II MAKSIMITAPAUS/
1800 - 2200 LAULAJAA/.

MITTAK. 1:200/

ARKKITEHTITOIMISTO
ALVAR AALTO & CO
SIGN. 68/90

83

Turku 700th Anniversary Exhibition

83
Choir platform: elevation,
section, plan, and perspective. India ink and pencil on
tracing paper, 12⅜ x 20⅜"
(31.5 x 51.7 cm). Alvar Aalto
Foundation, Helsinki
84
Choir platform

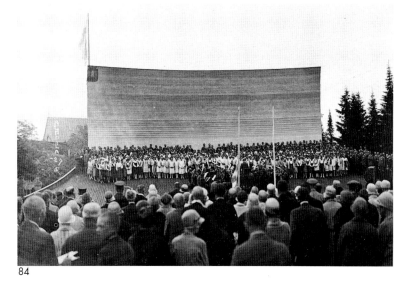

84

Vallila Church
Helsinki. Project, 1929

85
Competition drawing: ground-floor plan. India ink and pencil on pasteboard, 14⅜ x 20⅛" (36.5 x 51 cm). Alvar Aalto Foundation, Helsinki

86
Competition drawing: interior perspective toward chancel. Pencil on pasteboard, sheet 14⅜ x 20⅛" (36.5 x 51 cm). Alvar Aalto Foundation, Helsinki

87
Competition drawing: side elevation. India ink and pencil on pasteboard, 14⅜ x 20⅛" (36.5 x 51 cm). Alvar Aalto Foundation, Helsinki

88
Sections. Pencil on tracing paper, 11 x 18⅜" (28 x 46.5 cm). Alvar Aalto Foundation, Helsinki

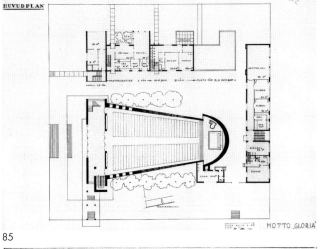

85

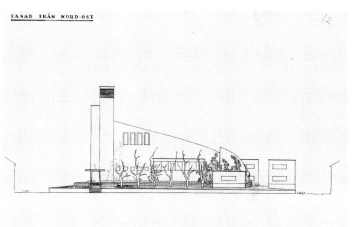

87

86

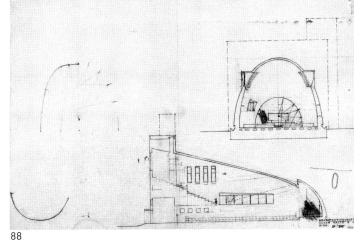

88

Viipuri City Library
Viipuri, Finland (now Vyborg, Russia). 1927–35

89
Study for competition (1927):
elevation, plan, section, and
stair sketches. Pencil on
tracing paper, 21⁷⁄₁₆ x 13⅜"
(54.5 x 34 cm). Alvar Aalto
Foundation, Helsinki

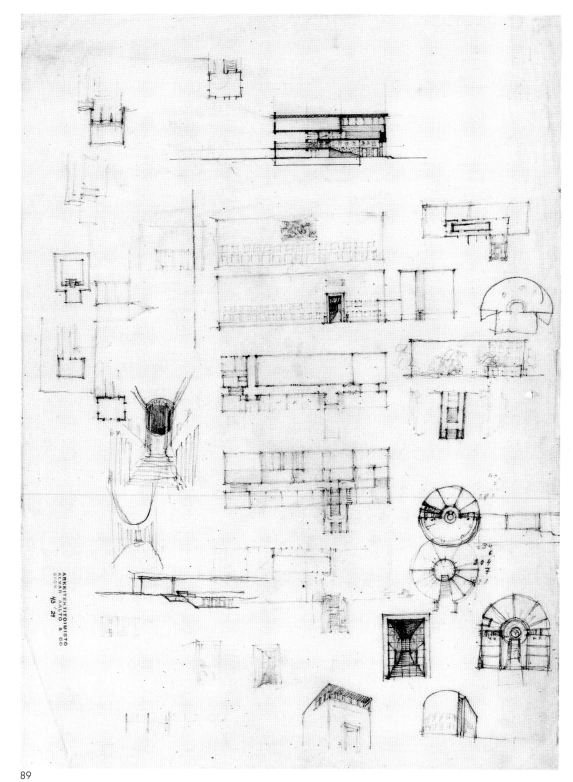

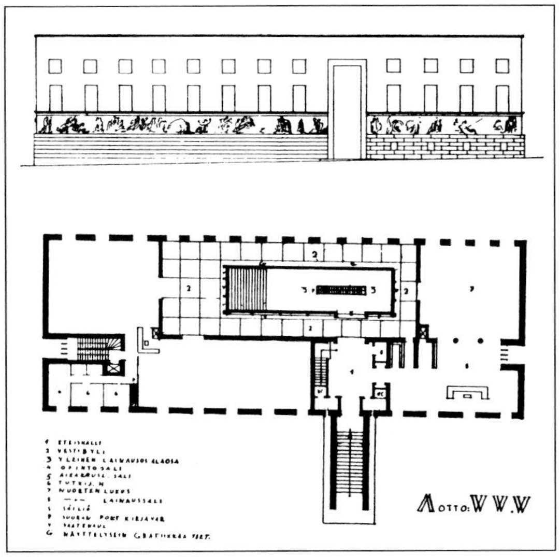

90

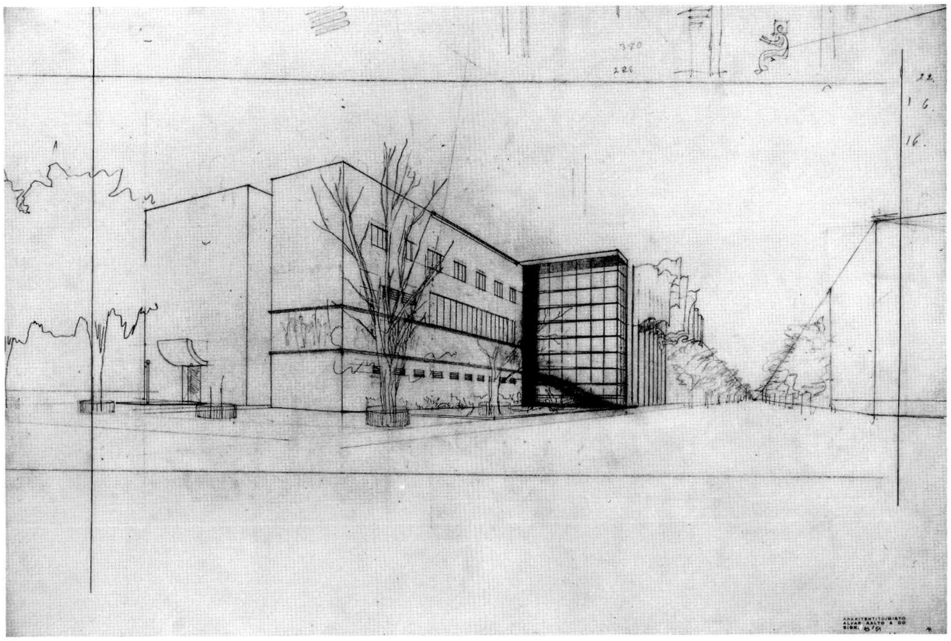

91

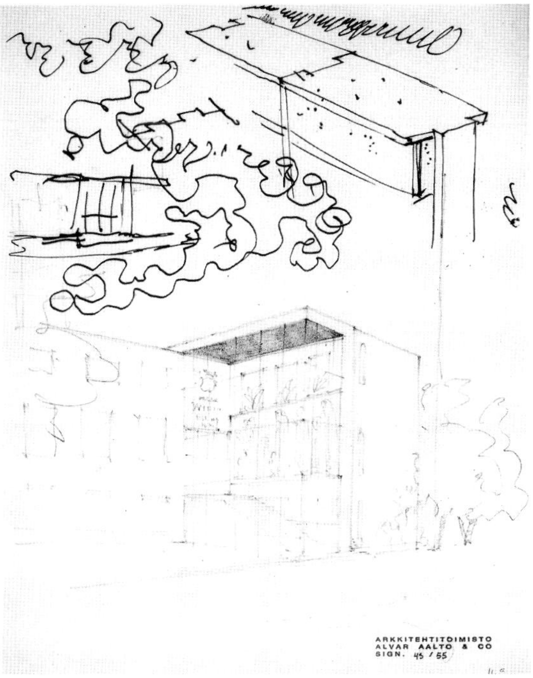

92

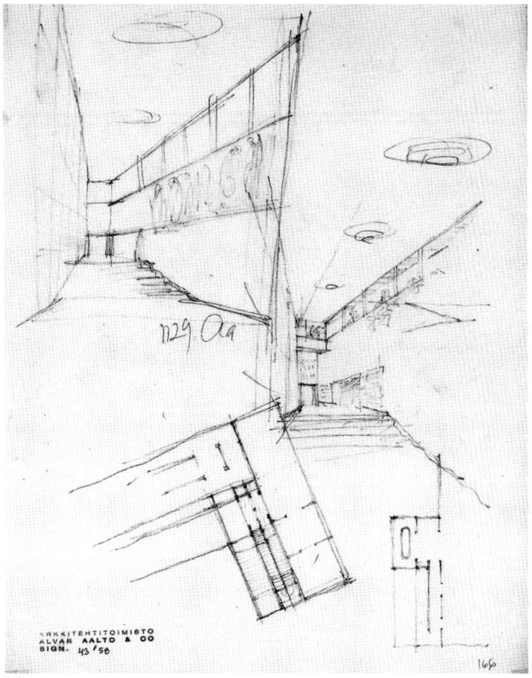

93

90
Competition drawing (1927): elevation and first-floor plan. Alvar Aalto Foundation, Helsinki

91
Second version (1928): perspective. Pencil and color pencil on tracing paper, 17¹³⁄₁₆ x 28⅝" (45.3 x 72.8 cm). Alvar Aalto Foundation, Helsinki

92
Third version (1929): main entrance perspective sketch. India ink and pencil on paper, 11 x 8¹¹⁄₁₆" (28 x 22 cm). Alvar Aalto Foundation, Helsinki

93
Third version (1929): main entrance interior perspective and plan sketches. Pencil on paper, 11 x 8¹¹⁄₁₆" (28 x 22 cm). Alvar Aalto Foundation, Helsinki

Viipuri City Library

94
Aerial view
95
Final version (1933): site
plan. Alvar Aalto
Foundation, Helsinki
96
Final version (1933): upper-
floor plan. Alvar Aalto
Foundation, Helsinki
97
Final version (1933): main-
floor plan. Alvar Aalto
Foundation, Helsinki
98
Final version (1933):
ground-floor plan. Alvar
Aalto Foundation, Helsinki

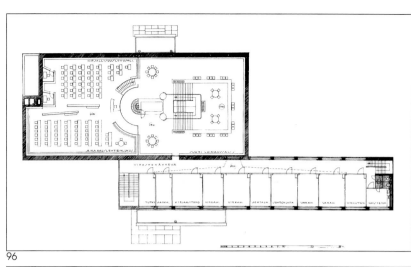

96

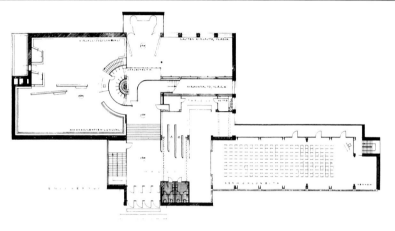

97

94

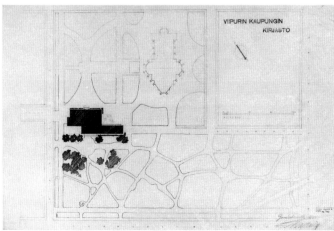

95

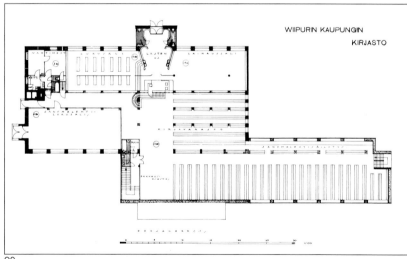

98

99

100

99
Main facade
100
Entrance lobby, with Aarne
Ervi, Alvar Aalto, and Aino
Aalto (1935)

101

Viipuri City Library

101
Auditorium
102
Auditorium entrance

102

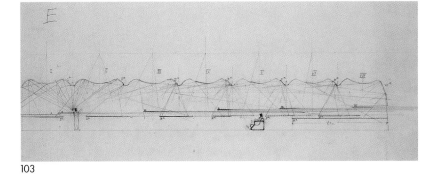

103

103
Final version (1933):
auditorium acoustic study
section. Pencil and color
pencil on tracing paper,
sheet 14 x 25⅜" (35.5 x
64.5 cm). Alvar Aalto
Foundation, Helsinki

104
Final version (1933):
auditorium section details.
Pencil on tracing paper,
26⅞ x 56⁵⁄₁₆" (68.2 x
143 cm). Alvar Aalto
Foundation, Helsinki

105
Auditorium

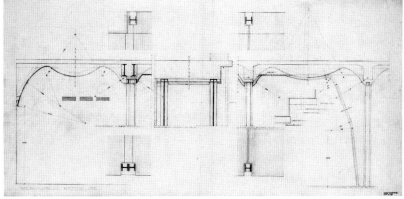

104

105

Viipuri City Library

106

106
Stairway
107
Stacking stools

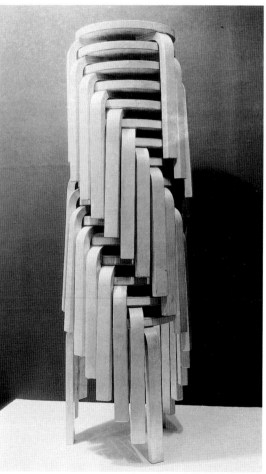

107

108

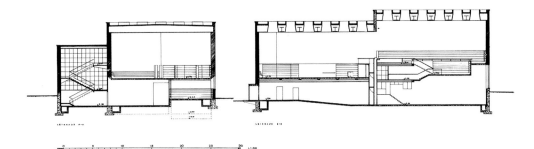

108
Reading room, with
circulation desk and stairway
109
Final version (1933):
sections. Alvar Aalto
Foundation, Helsinki

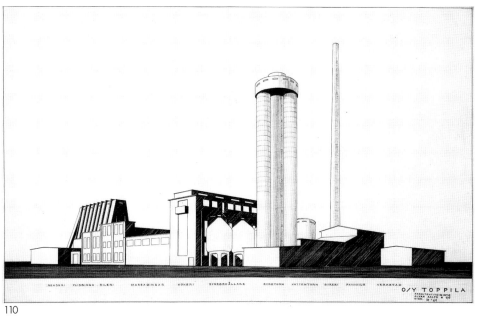
110

111

Toppila Pulp Mill
Oulu, Finland. 1930–33 (partially demolished)

110
Perspective. India ink on
tracing paper, 14⅚ x 24⅜"
(37 x 62 cm). Alvar Aalto
Foundation, Helsinki
111
Water tower and processing
plant
112
Wood-chip container

112

113

Sunila Pulp Mill and Housing
Kotka, Finland. 1936–38

113
Aerial view
114
Site plan. Alvar Aalto
Foundation, Helsinki

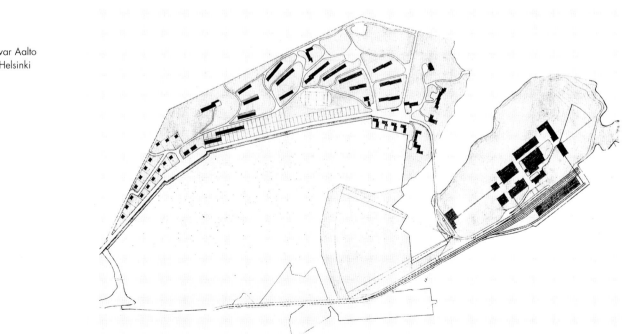

114

115

Sunila Pulp Mill and Housing

116

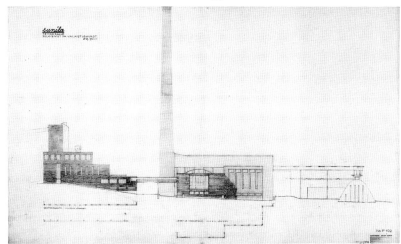
117

115
Site panorama. Photograph,
4¼ x 28½" (11 x 72.5 cm).
Alvar Aalto Foundation,
Helsinki
116
Pulp mill from west
117
Pulp mill west elevation.
Pencil on tracing paper,
32¹¹⁄₁₆ x 57½" (83 x 146 cm).
Alvar Aalto Foundation,
Helsinki

118
Engineering-staff housing
119
Engineering-staff housing:
first- and ground-floor plans.
Pencil on tracing paper,
23⅜ x 33½" (60 x 85 cm).
Alvar Aalto Foundation,
Helsinki

118

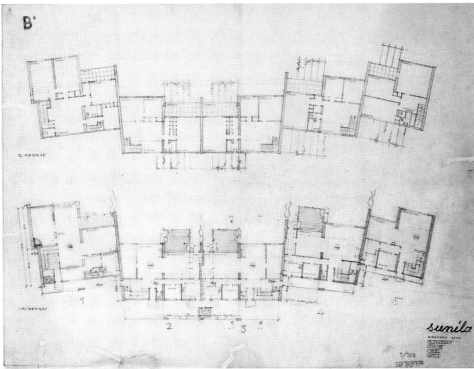

119

Standard Terrace Housing
Kauttua, Finland. 1937–38

120

121

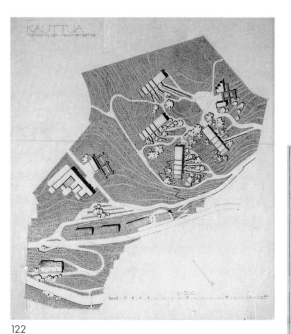

122

123

120
First-floor plan. Alvar Aalto Foundation, Helsinki
121
Ground-floor plan. Alvar Aalto Foundation, Helsinki
122
Site plan. Pencil and color pencil on paper, 30⁵⁄₁₆ x 27¹⁄₁₆" (77 x 68.8 cm). Alvar Aalto Foundation, Helsinki
123
Perspective. Pencil and color pencil on tracing paper, 11⅝ x 16⅜" (29.5 x 41.6 cm). Alvar Aalto Foundation, Helsinki
124
Exterior

House and Studio for Aino and Alvar Aalto
Munkkiniemi, Helsinki. 1935–36

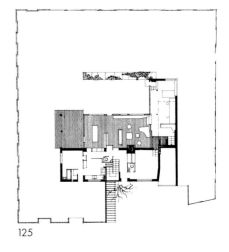

125

126

127

125
Site plan with
ground-floor plan
126
Street facade
127
Living room

128

129

128
Garden facade
129
Studio

Finnish Pavilion, Paris International Exhibition
Paris. 1936–37 (demolished)

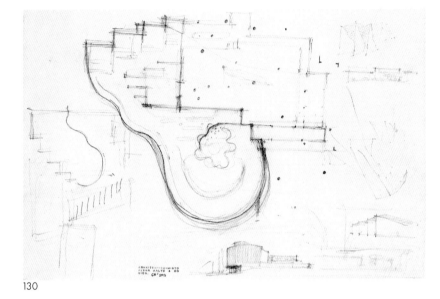

130

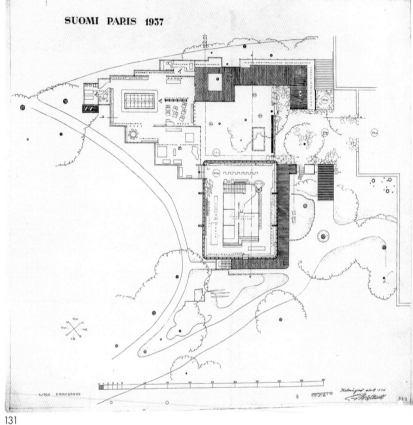

131

132

130
Study for competition
entry: plan and perspective
sketches. Pencil on tracing
paper, 11¹³⁄₁₆ x 18¹⁄₁₆"
(30 x 47.5 cm). Alvar Aalto
Foundation, Helsinki
131
Ground-floor plan. India ink
and pencil on paper, 33¹³⁄₁₆ x
35¹³⁄₁₆" (85.5 x 91 cm). Alvar
Aalto Foundation, Helsinki
132
Facade

133

134

135

133
Courtyard
134
Exploded axonometric
(1992; Antti-Matti Siikala
and Peter B. MacKeith)
135
Atrium

136

Finnish Pavilion, Paris International Exhibition

136
Terrace
137
Exhibit of Aalto's furniture
(by Artek) and architecture
(on far wall)

137

138

139

138
Exhibit of Aalto's glass
vases (by Karhula-Iittala) and
hanging lights
139
Installation design
(business and social
statistics): elevation. Pencil
on tracing paper, 12⅜ x 30½"
(31.5 x 77.5 cm). Alvar Aalto
Foundation, Helsinki

Karhula-Iittala Glass-Design Competition
1936

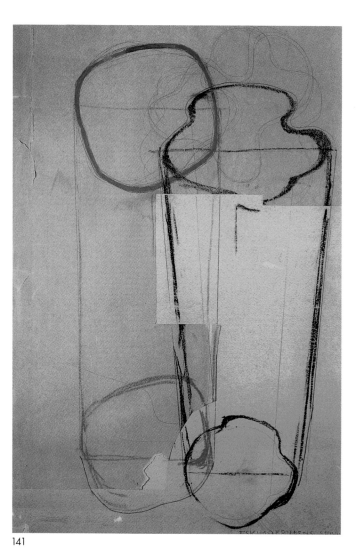

141

140
Vases. Glass, dimensions
variable. Collection
A. Ahlström Corporation
141
Competition drawing: vase
designs. Pencil, chalk,
gouache, and paper on
cardboard, 27½ x 19¾"
(69.8 x 49.3 cm). Iittala
Glass Museum, Iittala,
Finland

Karhula-Iittala
Glass-Design Competition

142
Savoy Vase. Mold-blown glass, 5⅝ x 8⅛" (14.3 x 20.5 cm). The Museum of Modern Art, New York. Gift of Artek-Pascoe, Inc.

143
Competition drawing: vase design. Ink, pencil, gouache, and tracing paper on paper, 27½ x 15¾" (69.8 x 40 cm). Iittala Glass Museum, Iittala, Finland

142

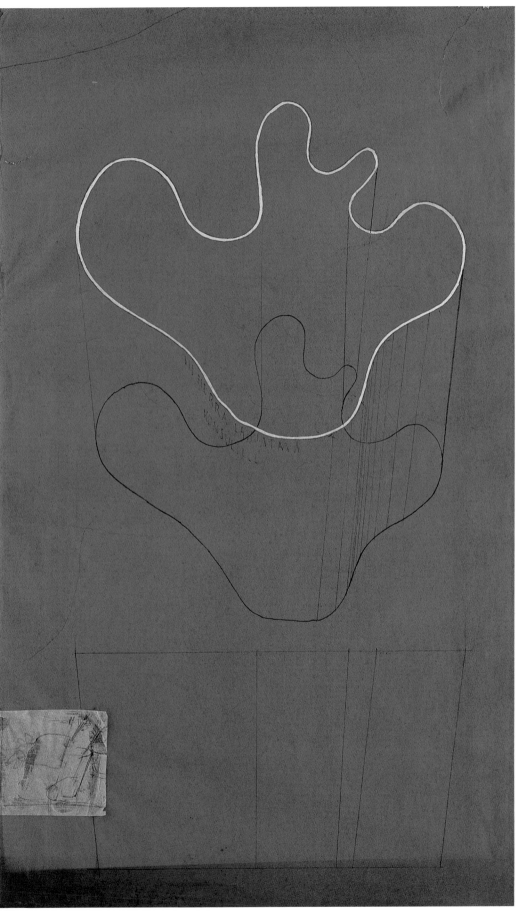

143

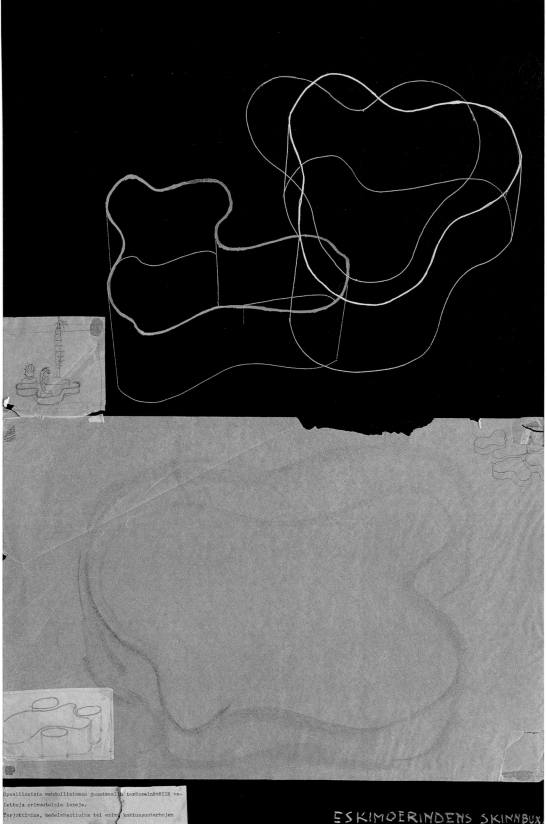

144
Competition drawing: vase
designs. Pencil, chalk,
gouache, and tracing paper
on paper, 25 x 18¾" (63.5 x
47.6 cm). Iittala Glass
Museum, Iittala, Finland

Finnish Pavilion, New York World's Fair
Queens, New York. 1938–39 (demolished)

145

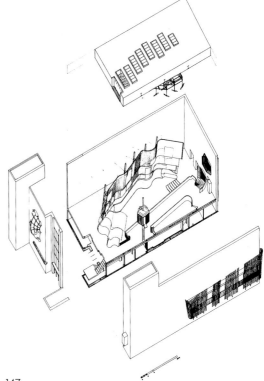

147

146

145
Exterior
146
Interior perspective. India
ink and pencil on tracing
paper, 36⁵⁄₁₆ x 37³⁄₁₆"
(92.2 x 94.4 cm). Alvar
Aalto Foundation, Helsinki
147
Exploded axonometric
(1992; Laura Mark and
Peter B. MacKeith)
148
Interior

Finnish Pavilion, New York World's Fair

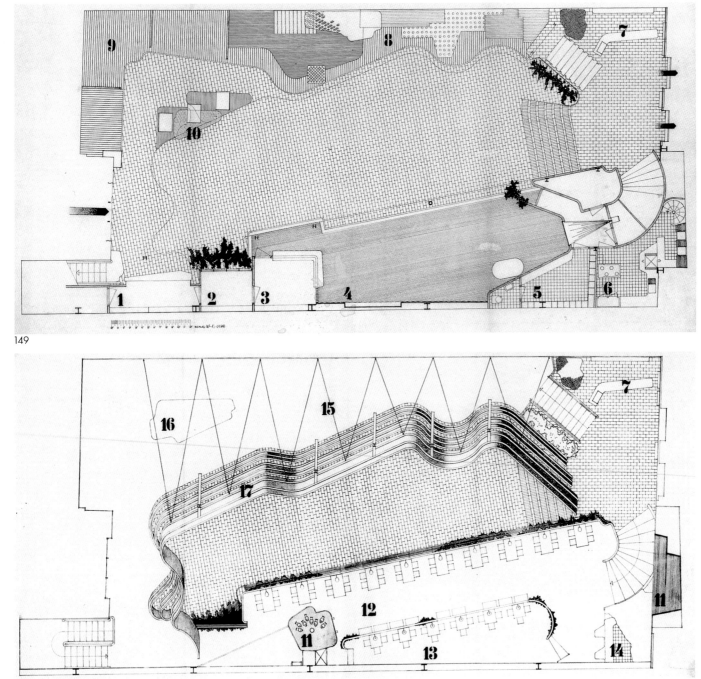

149

150

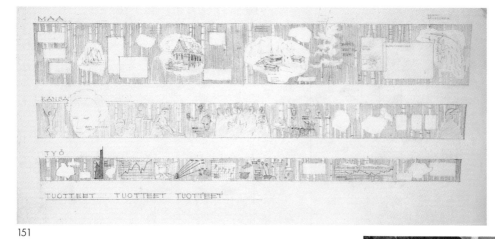

151

153

152

151
Installation design (country, people, and work): elevations. Pencil and color pencil on tracing paper, 16⅜ x 29⁹⁄₁₆" (41.8 x 75.1 cm). Alvar Aalto Foundation, Helsinki

152
Section. India ink on tracing paper, 27⅝ x 33¹⁄₁₆" (70.1 x 84 cm). Alvar Aalto Foundation, Helsinki

153
Restaurant

154
Exhibit of Aalto's furniture (by Artek)

154

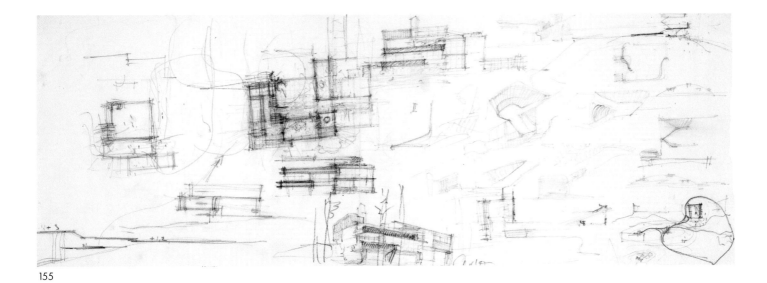

155

Villa Mairea
House for Maire and Harry Gullichsen
Noormarkku, Finland. 1938–39

156

157

158

158
Early version (1938):
south elevation. Pencil
and color pencil on
tracing paper, 17⅜ x 17⅛"
(44.2 x 43.8 cm). Alvar
Aalto Foundation, Helsinki
159
Plan, interior perspective,
and stair sketches. Pencil
on paper, 11¾ x 16¹⁵⁄₁₆"
(29.8 x 43 cm). Alvar Aalto
Foundation, Helsinki

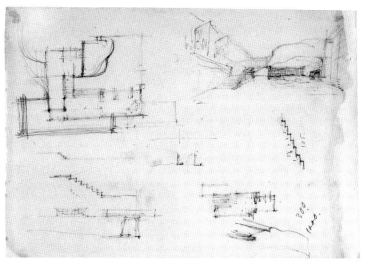

159

Villa Mairea

160
Ahlström family estate site
plan (1997; Teemu Toivio
and Peter B. MacKeith).
1. Villa Mairea 2. Havulinna,
Walter Ahlström House (1901)
3. Isotalo, Antti Ahlström
House (1877)
161
Ground-floor, pool, and
sauna plan. Alvar Aalto
Foundation, Helsinki
162
First-floor plan. Alvar Aalto
Foundation, Helsinki
163
Entrance

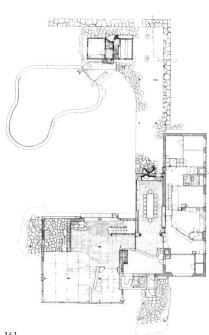
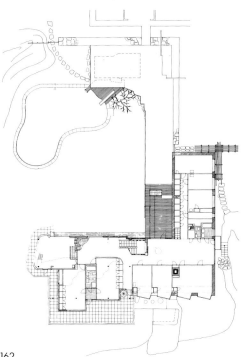

161

162

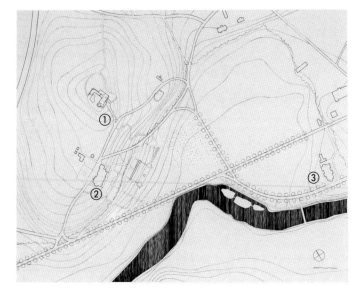

160

163

164

165

164
View from south
165
Garden facade

166

Villa Mairea

166
Living room
167
Living room
168
Library
169
Stairway

167

168

A-House Standard Houses
Begun 1937

170

170
Workers' Housing for
A. Ahlström Corporation,
Kauttua
171
"A hus" pamphlet (c. 1940).
Perspectives, plans, and
elevation. Alvar Aalto
Foundation, Helsinki

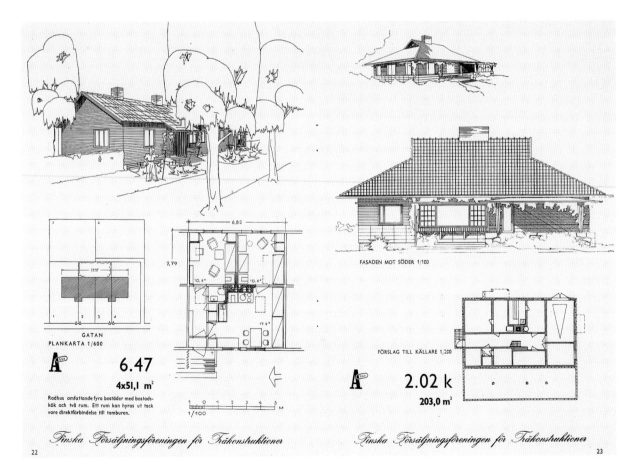

171

172

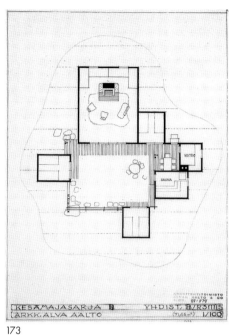

173

AA Standard Summer Cottages
Project, 1941

172
Aerial perspective (series B,
type B/R3). India ink on
tracing paper, 9½ x 12"
(24 x 30.5 cm). Alvar Aalto
Foundation, Helsinki
173
Plan (series B, type B/R3).
India ink on tracing paper,
12 x 9½" (30.5 x 24 cm).
Alvar Aalto Foundation,
Helsinki
174
Plan (series B, type B/2-3).
India ink on tracing paper,
12 x 9½" (30.5 x 24 cm).
Alvar Aalto Foundation,
Helsinki
175
Plan (series B, type B/K).
India ink on tracing paper,
12 x 9½" (30.5 x 24 cm).
Alvar Aalto Foundation,
Helsinki

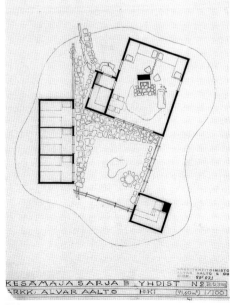

174

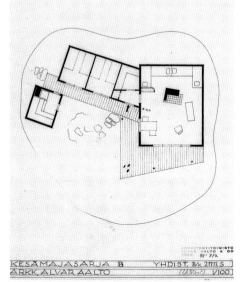

175

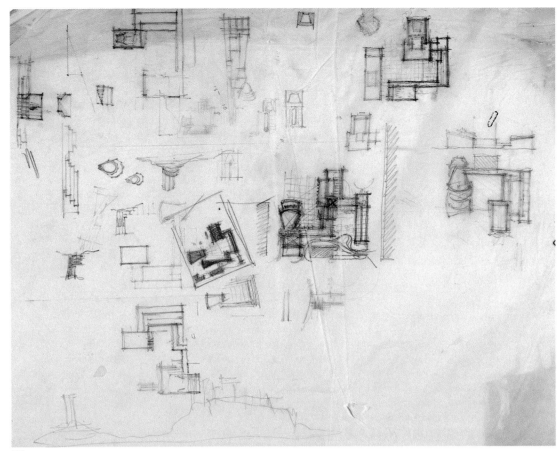

176

Alvar Aalto and Albin Stark:
Avesta Civic Center
Avesta, Sweden. Project, 1944

176
Plan and section sketches.
Pencil and color pencil on
paper, 18⅞ x 24¹³⁄₁₆" (48 x
63 cm). Swedish Museum
of Architecture, Stockholm
177
Elevation. Pencil and color
pencil on paper, sheet 16½ x
30⁵⁄₁₆" (42 x 77 cm).
Swedish Museum of
Architecture, Stockholm
178
Section. Pencil and color
pencil on paper, sheet 16½ x
33⅞" (42 x 86 cm). Swedish
Museum of Architecture,
Stockholm

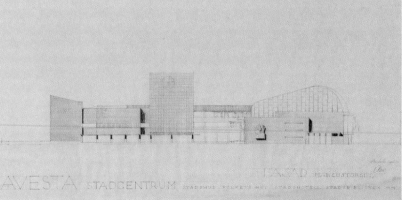

177

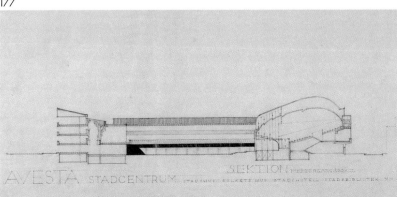

178

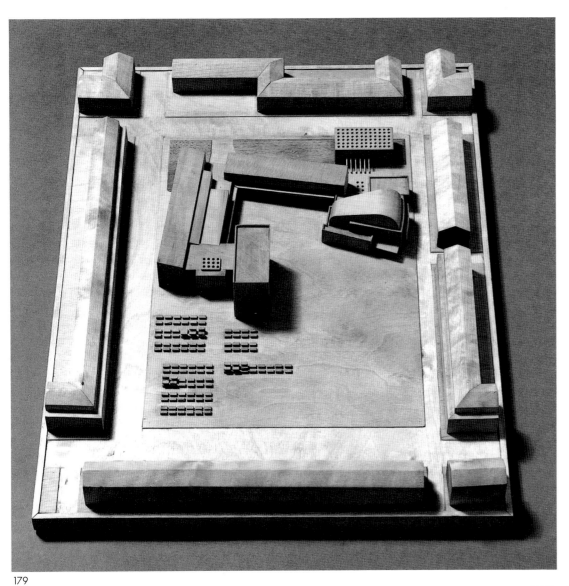

179

179
Site model. Wood, 2½ x
18⅛ x 14¼" (6.4 x 46.1 x
36.1 cm). The Museum of
Modern Art, New York.
Emilio Ambasz Fund, Mr.
and Mrs. Edward Larrabee
Barnes Fund, and Gift of
Alvar Aalto Architects Ltd.
180
Ground-floor plan. Pencil and
color pencil on paper, 27⅜ x
34¹⁄₁₆" (69.5 x 86.5 cm).
Swedish Museum of
Architecture, Stockholm

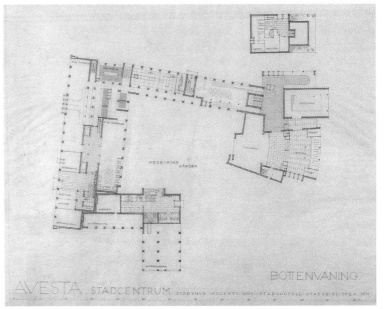

180

Baker House
Senior Dormitory for Massachusetts Institute of Technology
Cambridge, Massachusetts. 1946–49

181
Aerial view
182
Plan and perspective sketches.
Pencil on paper, 8¼ x 8⅝"
(21 x 22 cm). Alvar Aalto
Foundation, Helsinki
183
Plan sketch. Pencil and color
pencil on tracing paper, sheet
8 x 30¹¹⁄₁₆" (20.3 x 78 cm).
Alvar Aalto Foundation,
Helsinki
184
River facade

181

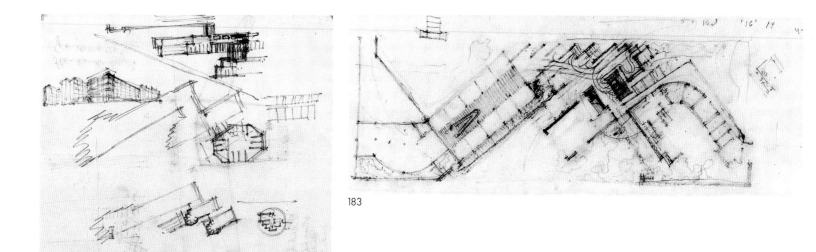

182

183

185

Baker House

185
River facade
186
Perspective. Pencil on tracing paper, 19$\frac{1}{16}$ x 32$\frac{3}{8}$" (48.5 x 82.3 cm). Alvar Aalto Foundation, Helsinki
187
Ground-floor plan

186

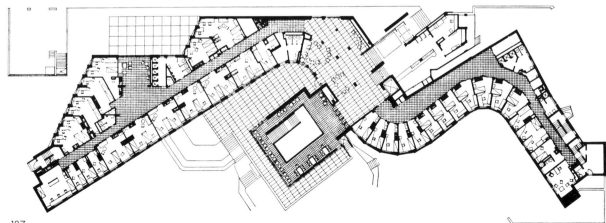

187

188

189

188
Campus facade with main entrance
189
Exterior detail
190
Elevation. Pencil on tracing paper, 17¹⁵⁄₁₆ x 51⁹⁄₁₆"
(45.5 x 131 cm). Alvar Aalto
Foundation, Helsinki

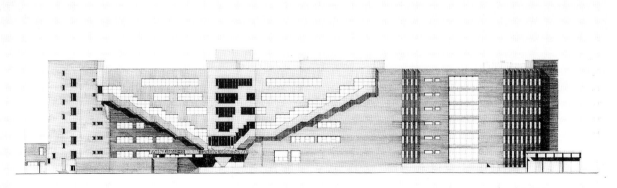

190

191

192

Baker House

191
Student's room
192
Corridor
193
Students' room

193

194

194
Dining hall and lounge
exterior
195
Dining hall and lounge

195

Säynätsalo Town Hall
Säynätsalo, Finland. 1948–52

196

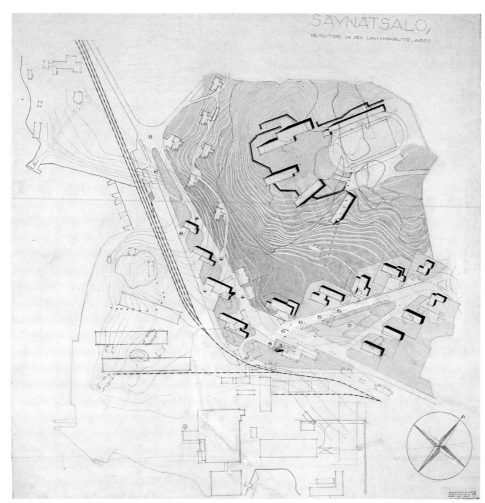

197

196
View from south
197
Säynätsalo Master Plan
(c. 1947). Ink, pencil, and
color pencil on tracing
paper, 33¹¹⁄₁₆ x 32¹¹⁄₁₆"
(85.5 x 83 cm). Alvar Aalto
Foundation, Helsinki

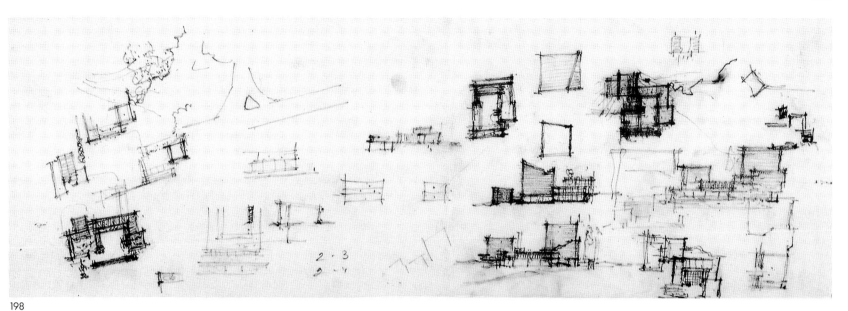

198

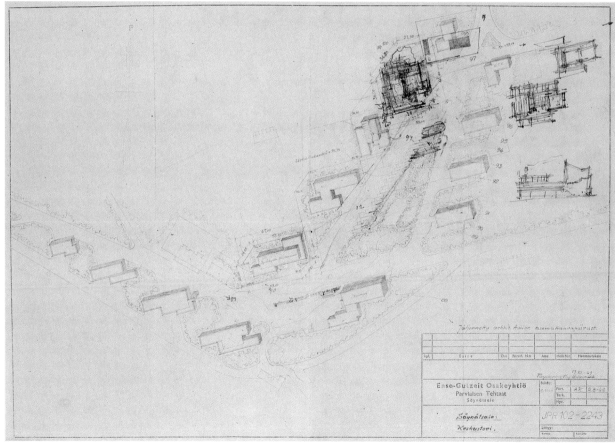

198
Plan and elevation sketches.
Pencil on tracing paper,
9⁹⁄₁₆ x 30⁵⁄₁₆" (24.3 x 77 cm).
Collection Alvar Aalto Family
199
Plan and elevation sketches
on site plan (c. 1949). Pencil
on print, 16½ x 23⅜" (42 x
59.3 cm). Collection Alvar Aalto
Family

199

200

200
Competition model.
Wood, cardboard, and
paint, 3⅛ x 16¾ x 13¾"
(8 x 42.5 x 35 cm). City of
Jyväskylä/Säynätsalo Town
Hall Archive
201
Competition drawing:
ground-floor plan. Pencil and
color pencil on tracing
paper, 19⅛ x 18¾" (48.6 x
47.8 cm). City of Jyväskylä/
Säynätsalo Town Hall
Archive
202
Competition drawing: first-
floor plan. Pencil and color
pencil on tracing paper,
18½ x 18¾" (47 x 47.8 cm).
City of Jyväskylä/Säynätsalo
Town Hall Archive

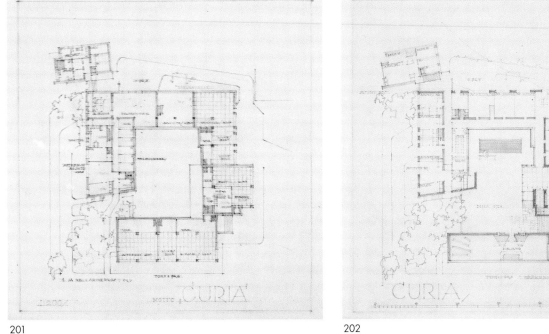

201

202

203

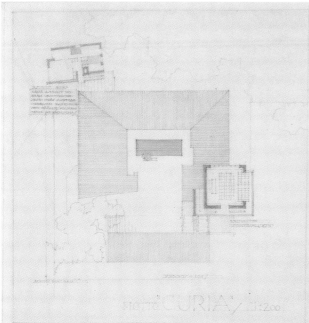

204

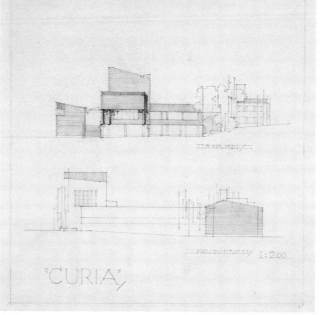

205

206

Säynätsalo Town Hall

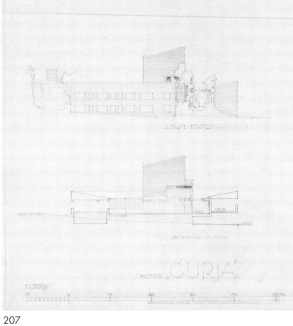

206
View from west
207
Competition drawing: west elevation and section. Pencil and color pencil on tracing paper, 19⅛ x 18¾" (48.5 x 47.8 cm). City of Jyväskylä/ Säynätsalo Town Hall Archive

207

208
View from south
209
Competition drawing: south
elevation and section. Pencil
and color pencil on tracing
paper, 19⅛ x 18¾" (48.5 x
47.8 cm). City of Jyväskylä/
Säynätsalo Town Hall Archive

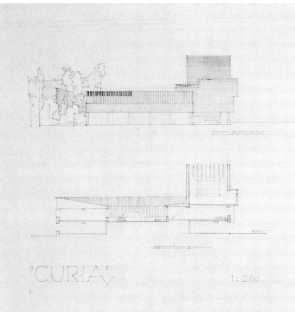

210

210
Courtyard
211
Corridor

211

212

212
Council chamber trusses
213
Council chamber stairway
214
Council chamber

214

213

Gravesite at Aalto's House
Munkkiniemi, Helsinki. Project, c. 1949

215

215
Proposed grave location in garden
216
Site plan with grave. Pencil and color pencil on tracing paper, 22¹⁄₁₆ x 21⁷⁄₁₆" (56 x 54.5 cm). Collection Alvar Aalto Family

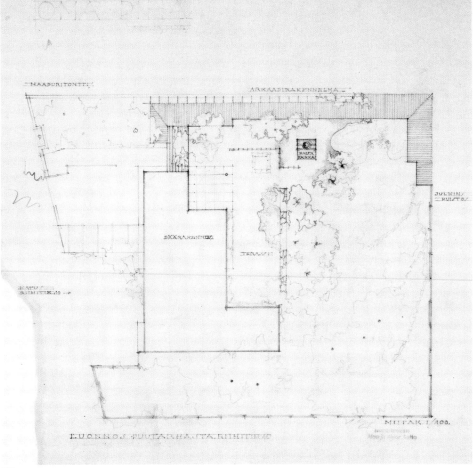

216

Malmi Funeral Chapel
Helsinki. Project, 1950

217

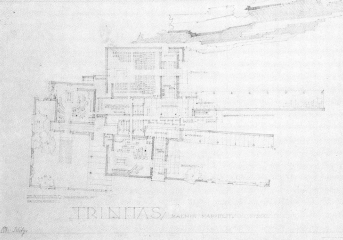

218

217
Competition drawing:
elevation and section. Pencil
and color pencil on tracing
paper, sheet 23¼ x 35⅛"
(59 x 89 cm). Alvar Aalto
Foundation, Helsinki

218
Competition drawing: plan.
Pencil and color pencil on
tracing paper, sheet 24⅝ x
35⅞" (62.5 x 90 cm). Alvar
Aalto Foundation, Helsinki

219
Site-plan sketch. Pencil on
tracing paper, 11¹³⁄₁₆ x 24¹³⁄₁₆"
(30 x 63 cm). Alvar Aalto
Foundation, Helsinki

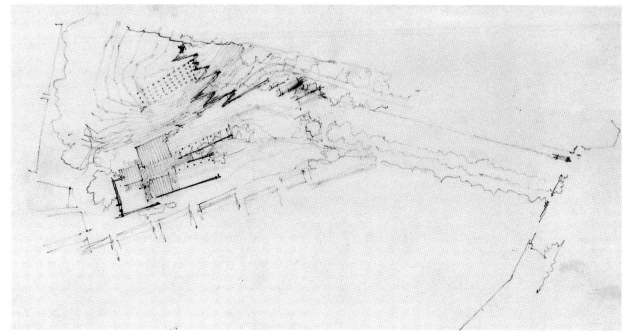

219

220

Alvar Aalto and Jean-Jacques Baruël:
Central Cemetery and Funeral Chapel
Lyngby-Taarbaek, Denmark. Project, 1951–52

220
Competition model. Wood, 5½ x
35¹³⁄₁₆ x 16⅛" (14 x 91 x 41 cm).
Collection Lyngby-Taarbaek
Kommune

221
Competition drawing: site plan.
Pencil and color pencil on paper,
sheet 20⅛ x 28⅜" (51 x 72 cm).
Collection Lyngby-Taarbaek
Kommune

222
Competition drawing: site plan
(alternative scheme). Pencil and
color pencil on paper, sheet
20⅛ x 28⅜" (51 x 72 cm).
Collection Lyngby-Taarbaek
Kommune

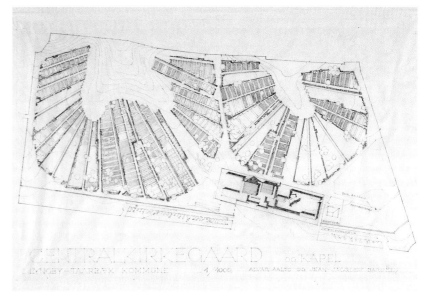

221

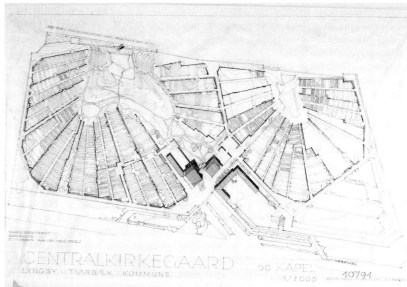

222

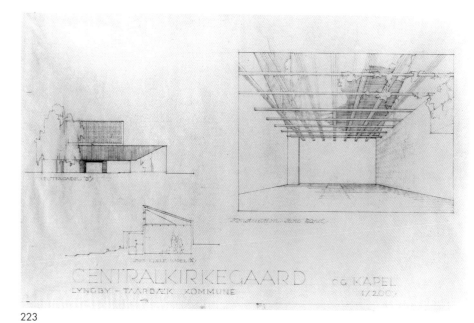

223

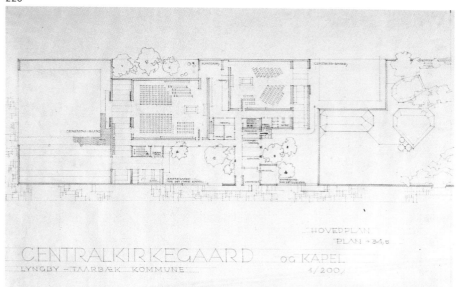

224

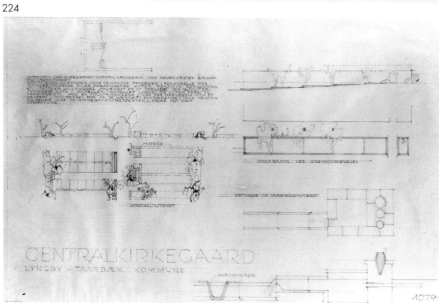

225

223
Competition drawing: west
elevation, large chapel
interior perspective,
and small chapel section.
Pencil on paper, 20⅛ x 28⅜"
(51 x 72 cm). Collection
Lyngby-Taarbaek Kommune
224
Competition drawing: plan.
Pencil and color pencil on
paper, sheet 20⅛ x 28⅜"
(51 x 72 cm). Collection
Lyngby-Taarbaek Kommune
225
Competition drawing:
graveyard watercourse
sections and details. Pencil
and color pencil on paper,
sheet 20⅛ x 28⅜" (51 x
72 cm). Collection Lyngby-
Taarbaek Kommune

Experimental House and Sauna
for Elissa and Alvar Aalto
Muuratsalo, Finland. 1952–53

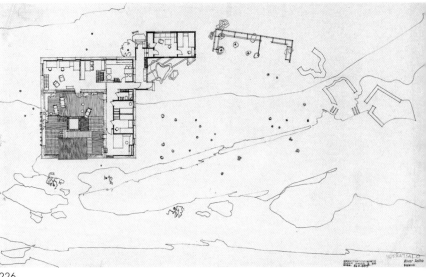

226

227

226
Plan. India ink on tracing
paper, 15½ x 25¹³⁄₁₆"
(39.5 x 65.5 cm). Alvar
Aalto Foundation, Helsinki
227
View from south
228
View from southwest

Experimental House

229
Courtyard wall detail
230
View toward lake
231
Courtyard wall detail

229

230

231

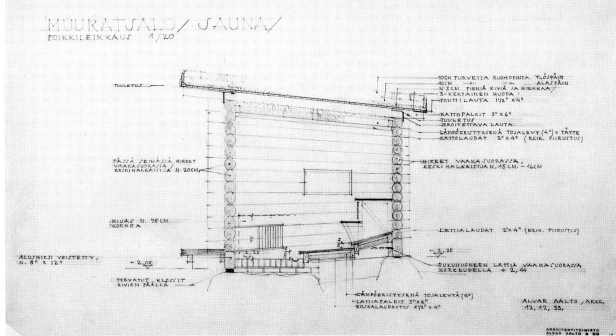

232

233

234

232
Sauna section. Pencil on
tracing paper, 11¹³⁄₁₆ x 23⁷⁄₁₆"
(30 x 59.5 cm). Alvar Aalto
Foundation, Helsinki
233
Sauna
234
Lake Päijänne from sauna

234

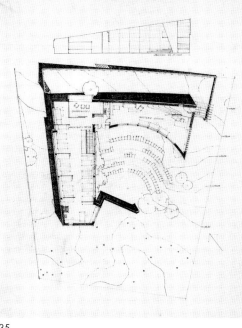

Alvar Aalto's Studio
Munkkiniemi, Helsinki. 1954–56

235
Section and plan. Pencil and color pencil on tracing paper, 25½ x 21⅛" (64.7 x 53.7 cm). Alvar Aalto Foundation, Helsinki
236
Garden court

235

237
Aalto's studio
238
Elevation. Ink on vellum,
13¾ x 26⅜" (35 x 67 cm).
Alvar Aalto Foundation,
Helsinki
239
Studio

237

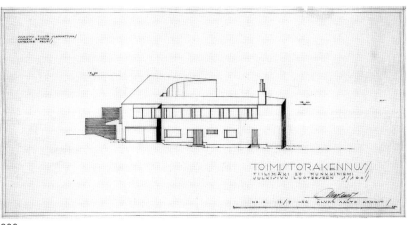

238

239

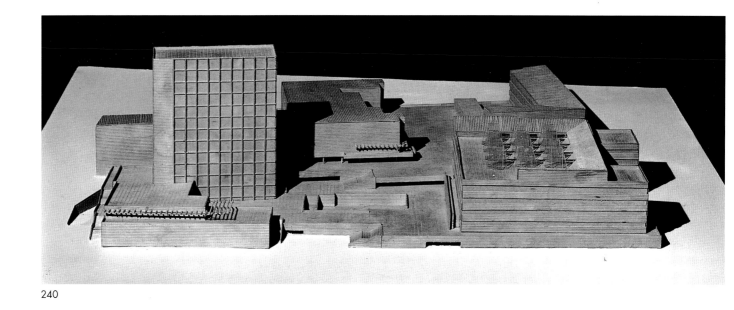

240

National Pensions Institute
Helsinki. Competition, 1948; executed, 1952–57

241

240
Competition model (scheme B).
Wood and plastic, 6¼ x 19 x
24¾" (16 x 48.2 x 62.8 cm).
Alvar Aalto Foundation,
Helsinki
241
Study for competition (1948):
plan and section sketches.
Pencil on tracing paper, sheet
11¹³⁄₁₆ x 25⅜" (30 x 64.5 cm).
Alvar Aalto Foundation,
Helsinki

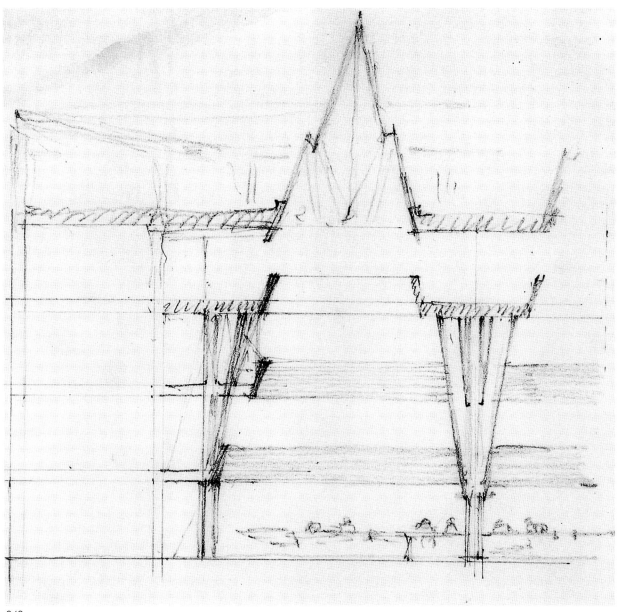

242

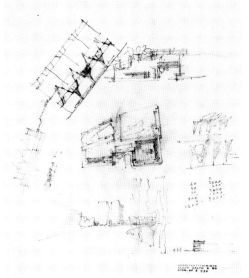

242
Study for competition (1948): hall and skylight section sketch. Pencil on tracing paper, 11¹³⁄₁₆ x 12⅜" (30 x 31.5 cm). Alvar Aalto Foundation, Helsinki
243
Study for competition (1948): section, plan, and perspective sketches. Pencil and color pencil on tracing paper, 13⁹⁄₁₆ x 11¾" (34.5 x 29.8 cm). Alvar Aalto Foundation, Helsinki

National Pensions Institute

244

245

244
Aerial view
245
Final version: site plan. Alvar
Aalto Foundation, Helsinki

246

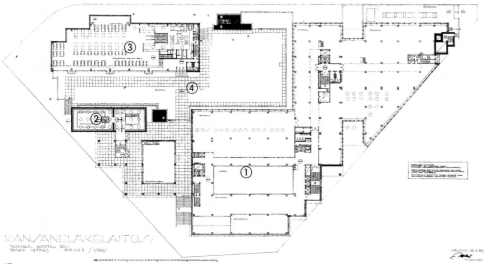

247

246
Main facade
247
Final version: first-floor plan.
Alvar Aalto Foundation,
Helsinki. 1. main hall
2. library 3. dining hall
4. courtyard

248

National Pensions Institute

248
Entry corridor
249
Entrance

249

250

251

250
Skylights
251
Main hall
252
Skylight section

252

253

254

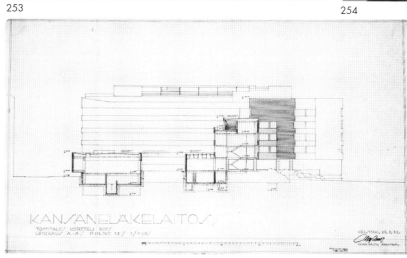

255

National Pensions Institute

253
Courtyard
254
Dining hall
255
Final version: section. Alvar
Aalto Foundation, Helsinki
256
Boardroom

256

257

258

257
Southeast corner
258
Rear facade

Helsinki University of Technology
Espoo (Otaniemi). Competition, 1949; executed,1953–66

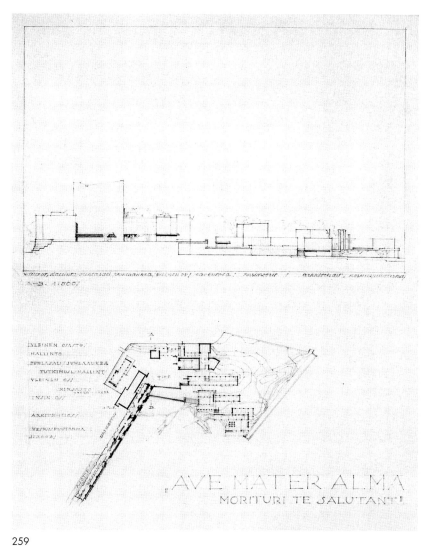

259

259
Competition drawing:
elevation and plan. Pencil on
tracing paper, 22⁷⁄₁₆ x 18⁷⁄₁₆"
(57 x 46.8 cm). Alvar Aalto
Foundation, Helsinki
260
Study for competition:
perspective and site-plan
sketches. Pencil on paper,
sheet 8¼ x 7⅜" (21 x
18.8 cm). Alvar Aalto
Foundation, Helsinki
261
Study for competition:
perspective sketches. Pencil
on paper, sheet 8¼ x 7⅜"
(21 x 18.8 cm). Alvar Aalto
Foundation, Helsinki

260   261

262

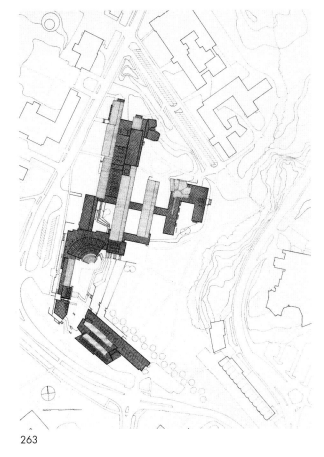

262
Aerial view
263
Site plan (1997; Teemu Toivio
and Peter B. MacKeith)

Helsinki University of Technology

264

264
Exterior
265
Plan and perspective
sketches. Pencil on tracing
paper, 23⁷⁄₁₆ x 29⁵⁄₁₆"
(59.6 x 74.5 cm). Alvar
Aalto Foundation, Helsinki
266
Plan, elevation, and
perspective sketches. Pencil
on tracing paper, 17⁵⁄₁₆ x
23⁹⁄₁₆" (44 x 59.8 cm). Alvar
Aalto Foundation, Helsinki

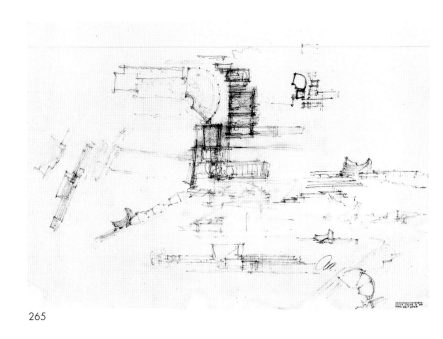

265

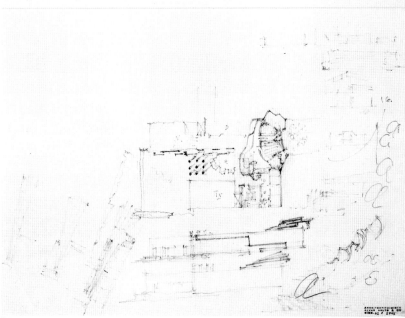

266

267

267
Main building
268
Main building perspective
sketch. Pencil on tracing
paper, sheet 11¹³⁄₁₆ x 17⁷⁄₁₆"
(30 x 44.3 cm). Alvar Aalto
Foundation, Helsinki

268

Helsinki University of Technology

269
Main building
270
Main building section and perspective sketches. Pencil on tracing paper, 19⅞ x 11¹³⁄₁₆" (50.5 x 30 cm). Alvar Aalto Foundation, Helsinki
271
Main building section. Alvar Aalto Foundation, Helsinki
272
Main building east elevation. Alvar Aalto Foundation, Helsinki

269

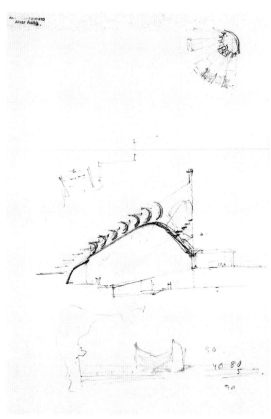

270

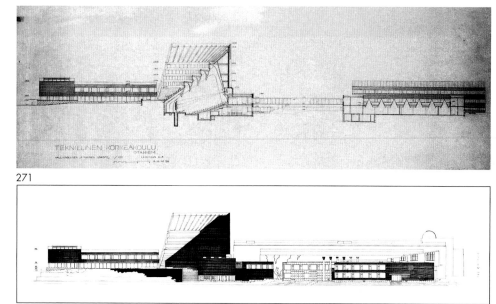

271

272

273

273
Auditorium
274
Auditorium lobby

274

275

276

Helsinki University of Technology

275
Sports hall (1950–52)
276
Sports-hall interior

277

Sports, Congress, and Concert Complex
Vogelweidplatz, Vienna. Project, 1952–53

277
Sketches. Pencil on tracing
paper, 11¹³/₁₆ x 22¹³/₁₆"
(30 x 58 cm). Alvar Aalto
Foundation, Helsinki
278
Competition model. Painted
wood, 5½ x 42½ x 23"
(14 x 108 x 58.3 cm). Alvar
Aalto Foundation, Helsinki
279
Section. Alvar Aalto
Foundation, Helsinki

278

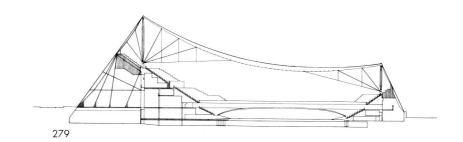

279

House of Culture
Helsinki. 1952–58

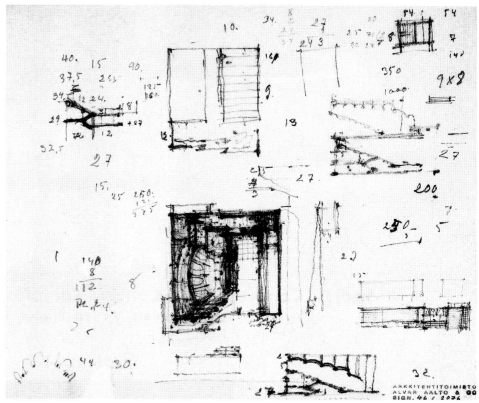

280

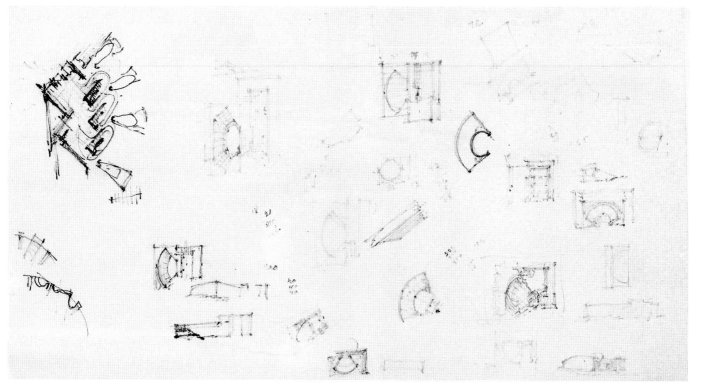

280
Plan and section sketches.
Pencil on tracing paper,
8¼ x 11" (21 x 28 cm).
Alvar Aalto Foundation,
Helsinki
281
Plan and section sketches.
Pencil on tracing paper,
11¹³⁄₁₆ x 22⅝" (30 x 57.5 cm).
Alvar Aalto Foundation,
Helsinki

282

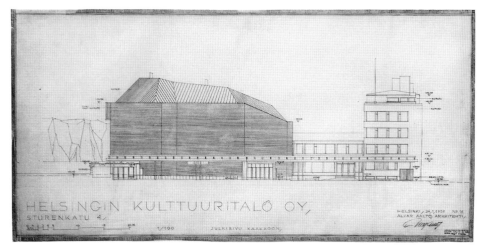

283

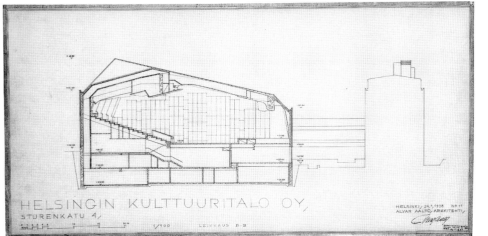

284

282
General view
283
Elevation. Alvar Aalto
Foundation, Helsinki
284
Section. Alvar Aalto
Foundation, Helsinki

285

House of Culture

286

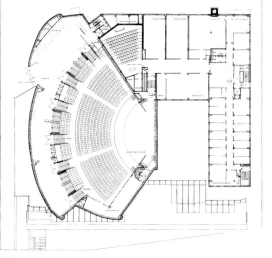

287

285
Auditorium
286
Lobby
287
First-floor plan. Alvar Aalto
Foundation, Helsinki
288
Exterior detail

Imatra Master Plan
Imatra, Finland. 1947–53

289
Plan. Ink on cardboard,
39⅜ x 28¾" (100 x 73 cm).
Alvar Aalto Foundation,
Helsinki

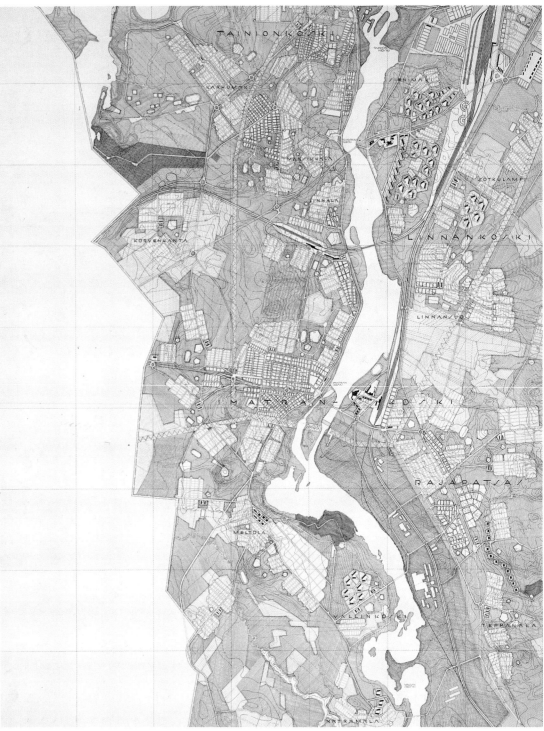

Master Plan for
Industrial Community
Summa, Finland. 1954

290
Plan. Pencil and color
pencil on print, 61¹³⁄₁₆ x 35"
(157 x 89 cm). Alvar Aalto
Foundation, Helsinki

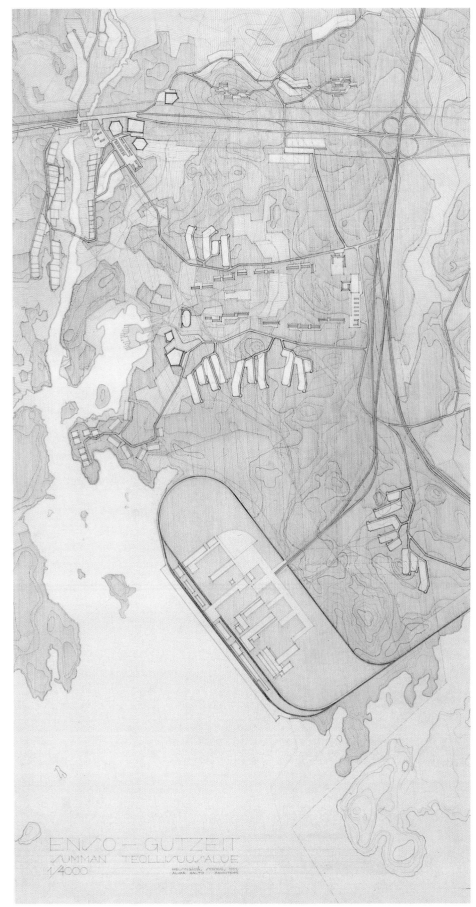

258

Church of the Three Crosses
Vuoksenniska, Imatra, Finland. 1955–58

291
Plan, elevation, and section
sketches. Pencil on tracing
paper, 11¹³/₁₆ x 42¹⁵/₁₆"
(30 x 109 cm). Alvar Aalto
Foundation, Helsinki
292
Plan and elevation sketches.
Pencil on paper, 8¼ x 7¹/₁₆"
(21 x 18 cm). Alvar Aalto
Foundation, Helsinki
293
Plan and section sketches.
Pencil on paper, 8¼ x 7¹/₁₆"
(21 x 18 cm). Alvar Aalto
Foundation, Helsinki
294
Plan sketch. Pencil on paper,
8¼ x 7¹/₁₆" (21 x 18 cm).
Alvar Aalto Foundation,
Helsinki

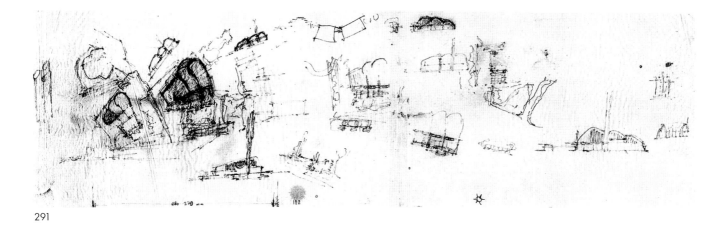

291

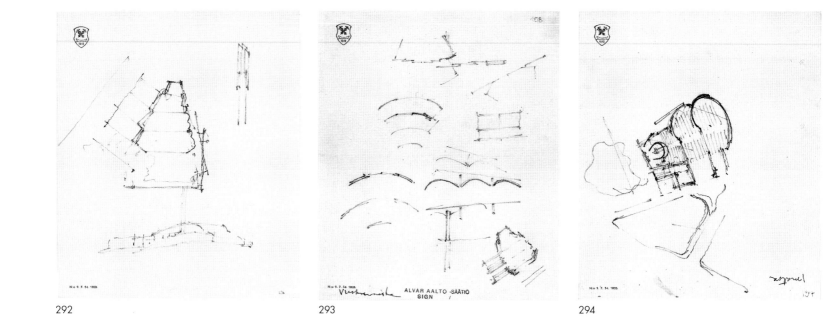

292 293 294

295

295
View from southwest with
pastor's house
296
Site plan. Alvar Aalto
Foundation, Helsinki
297
View from northeast

296

297

Church of the Three Crosses

298

298
View from west
299
Plan and perspective sketches.
Pencil on tracing paper,
11¹³⁄₁₆ x 21¼" (30 x 54 cm).
Alvar Aalto Foundation,
Helsinki

299

300

301

300
Interior with movable
partition walls open
301
Interior with movable
partition walls visible
302
View toward altar

302

Church of the Three Crosses

303

304

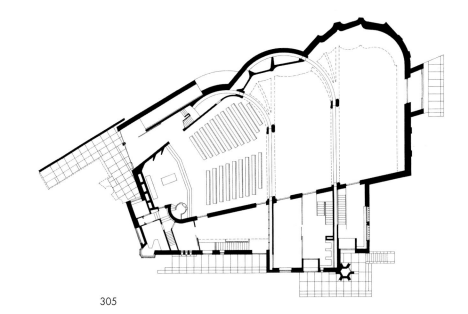

305

303
View from altar
304
Pews
305
Ground-floor plan (1997;
Richard Sturgeon)
306
Interior detail

Maison Carré
House for Louis Carré
Bazoches-sur-Guyonne, France. 1956–59

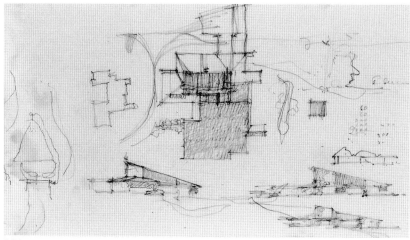

307

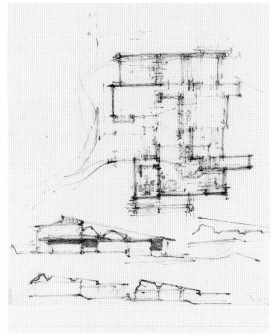

308

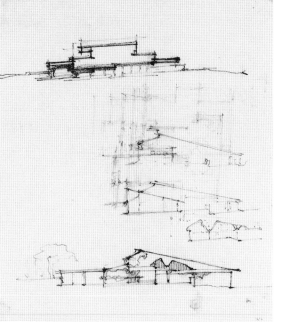

309

310

307
Plan, elevation, and section
sketches. Pencil on tracing
paper, 11¹³⁄₁₆ x 24⅜"
(30 x 62 cm). Alvar Aalto
Foundation, Helsinki
308
Plan and section sketches.
Pencil on tracing paper,
11¹¹⁄₁₆ x 10¼" (29.7 x 26 cm).
Alvar Aalto Foundation,
Helsinki
309
Elevation and section
sketches. Pencil on tracing
paper, 13³⁄₁₆ x 11¹³⁄₁₆" (33.5 x
30 cm). Alvar Aalto
Foundation, Helsinki
310
Garden terraces

311

312

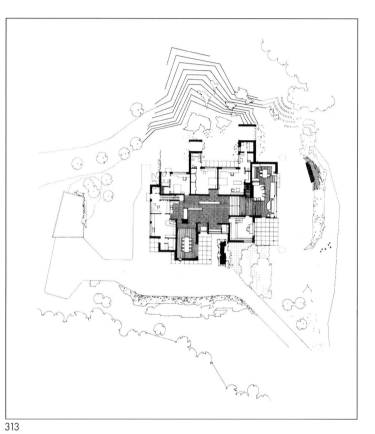

313

314

311
View from west
312
View from east
313
Site plan
314
Entrance hall

Apartment Building, Interbau Exhibition
Hansaviertel, Berlin. 1954-57

315

316

315
View from east
316
Entrance breezeway

317

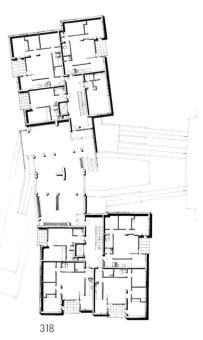

318

319

317
Upper-floor plan. Alvar
Aalto Foundation, Helsinki
318
Ground-floor plan. Alvar
Aalto Foundation, Helsinki
319
West facade
320
Typical interior (furnished
by Artek)

320

Apartment Building
Neue Vahr, Bremen, Germany. 1958–62

321
Sketchbook: plan and massing
studies. Pencil on paper,
11¹³⁄₁₆ x 8¼" (30 x 21 cm).
Collection Alvar Aalto Family
322
View from shopping arcade
323
Sketchbook: plan and massing
studies. Pencil on paper,
11¹³⁄₁₆ x 8¼" (30 x 21 cm).
Collection Alvar Aalto Family
324
Sketchbook: plan and massing
studies. Pencil on paper,
11¹³⁄₁₆ x 8¼" (30 x 21 cm).
Collection Alvar Aalto Family
325
Sketchbook: plan and massing
studies. Pencil on paper,
11¹³⁄₁₆ x 8¼" (30 x 21 cm).
Collection Alvar Aalto Family

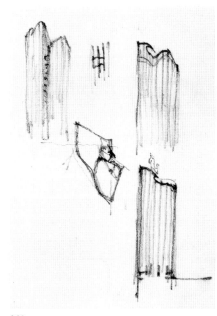

321

322

323

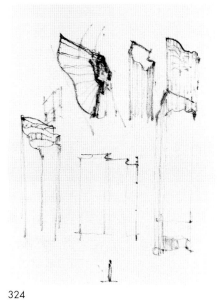

324

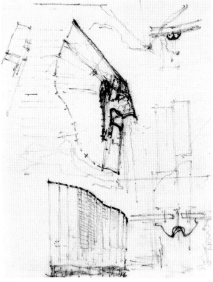

325

326

327

328

326
Typical floor plan
327
View from west
329
Exterior detail

City Hall
Kiruna, Sweden. Project, 1958

329

329
Plan and elevation sketches.
Pencil on tracing paper, sheet
11¹³⁄₁₆ x 21¼" (30 x 54 cm).
Alvar Aalto Foundation,
Helsinki
330
Plan and elevation sketches.
Pencil on tracing paper,
11⅝ x 19⁵⁄₁₆" (29.6 x 49 cm).
Alvar Aalto Foundation,
Helsinki

330

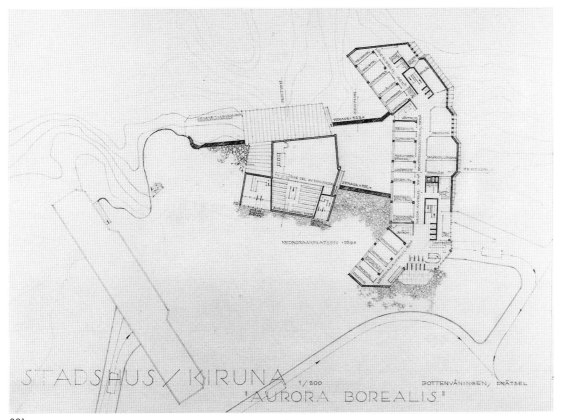

331

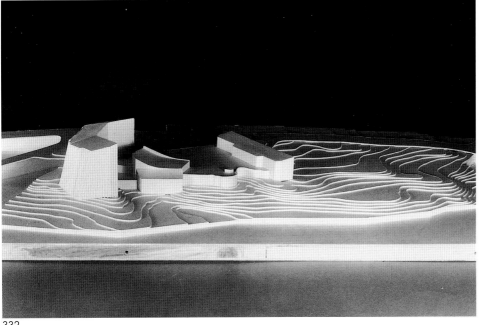

332

331
Competition drawing:
ground-floor plan. Pencil and
color pencil on paper, 23⅝ x
30½" (60 x 77.5 cm).
Swedish Museum of
Architecture, Stockholm

332
Competition model. Wood
and cardboard, 3⅞ x 27 x
17¾" (10 x 70 x 45 cm).
Swedish Museum of
Architecture, Stockholm

333
Atrium perspective sketch.
Pencil on tracing paper, sheet
11¹³⁄₁₆ x 21½" (30 x 54 cm).
Alvar Aalto Foundation,
Helsinki

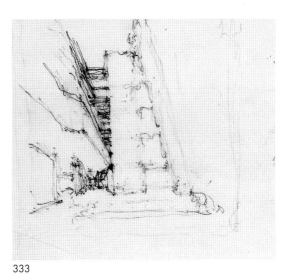

333

Elissa and Alvar Aalto and Jean-Jacques Baruël:
North Jutland Art Museum
Aalborg, Denmark. Competition, 1958; executed, 1966–72

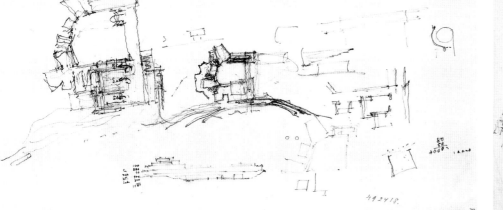

334

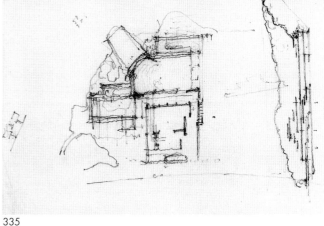

335

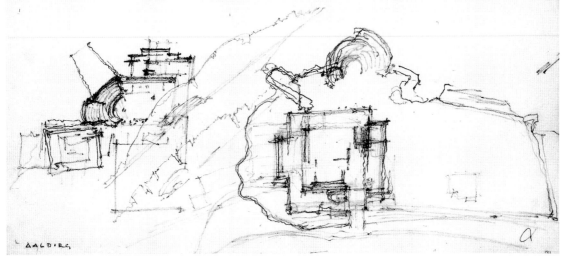

336

334
Plan and elevation sketches.
Pencil on tracing paper,
11¹³⁄₁₆ x 29⅜" (30 x 74.7 cm).
Alvar Aalto Foundation, Helsinki
335
Plan and section sketches. Pencil
on tracing paper, 11¹³⁄₁₆ x 25⅜"
(30 x 64.5 cm). Alvar Aalto
Foundation, Helsinki
336
Plan sketches. Pencil on tracing
paper, sheet 11¹³⁄₁₆ x 25¾"
(30 x 65.5 cm). Alvar Aalto
Foundation, Helsinki

337

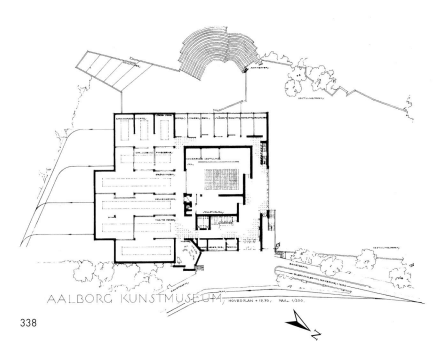

337
General view
338
Site plan with main-floor
plan

338

339

North Jutland Art Museum

339
Gallery
340
Section

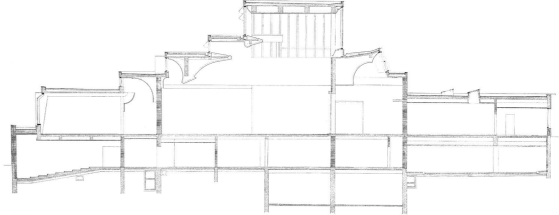

340

341

342

341
Gallery
342
Amphitheater
343
Competition model. Wood,
5¾ x 43⁵⁄₁₆ x 25⁹⁄₁₆"
(14.5 x 110 x 65 cm).
Nordjyllands Kunstmuseum,
Aalborg, Denmark

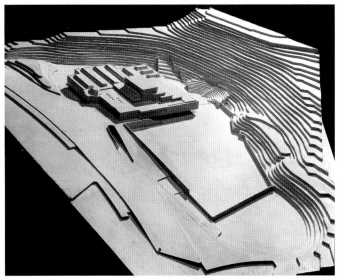

343

Cultural Center
Wolfsburg, Germany. 1958–62

344
Competition drawing: site plan. Pencil and color pencil on paper, 24 x 33¾" (61 x 85.8 cm). Institut für Museen und Stadtgeschichte, Wolfsburg

345
Competition drawing: ground-floor plan. Pencil and color pencil on paper, 24 x 33¾" (61 x 85.8 cm). Institut für Museen und Stadtgeschichte, Wolfsburg

346
Competition drawing: northeast elevation. Pencil and color pencil on paper, 24 x 33¾" (61 x 85.8 cm). Institut für Museen und Stadtgeschichte, Wolfsburg

347
Competition drawing: first-floor plan. Pencil and color pencil on paper, 24 x 33¾" (61 x 85.8 cm). Institut für Museen und Stadtgeschichte, Wolfsburg

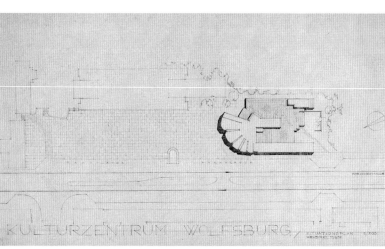

344

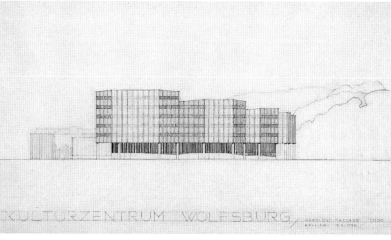

346

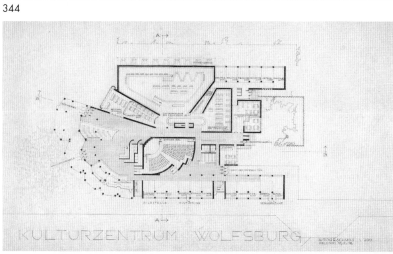

345

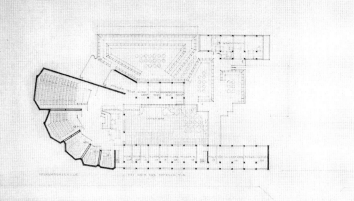

347

348

348
Northeast facade
349
Entrance lobby

349

350

Cultural Center

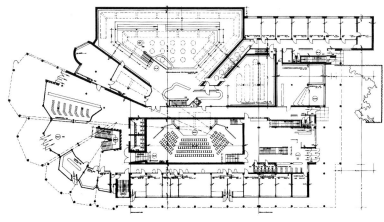

351

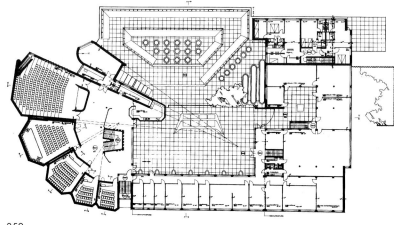

352

353

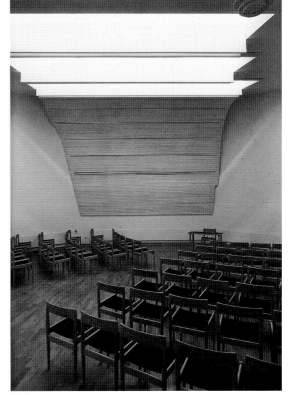

354

353
Roof terrace
354
Auditorium

355

356

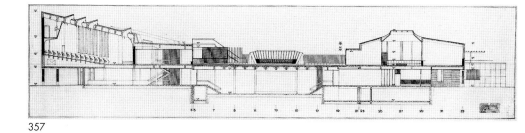

357

Cultural Center

355
Auditorium
356
Atrium with sliding skylight
357
Section. Alvar Aalto
Foundation, Helsinki
358
First-floor vestibule

358

359

360

359
Roof with skylights
360
Library

361

362

Opera House
Essen, Germany. Competition, 1959;
completed by Harald Deilmann with Elissa Aalto, 1981–88

361
Aerial view
362
Competition drawing: section
with theater and lobby
sketches. Pencil and color
pencil on vellum, 26¾ x
34¹³⁄₁₆" (68 x 88.5 cm).
Gemeinnützige Theater-
Baugesellschaft, Essen
363
Competition drawing: foyer
and parquet-level plans.
Pencil and color pencil on
vellum, 26¾ x 34¹³⁄₁₆" (68 x
88.5 cm). Gemeinnützige
Theater-Baugesellschaft,
Essen
364
Competition drawing:
ground-floor plan. Pencil and
color pencil on vellum, 26¾ x
34¹³⁄₁₆" (68 x 88.5 cm).
Gemeinnützige Theater-
Baugesellschaft, Essen

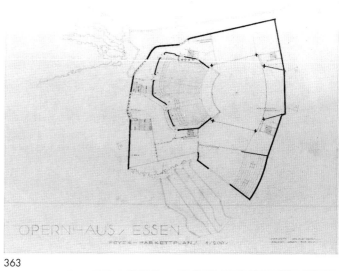

363

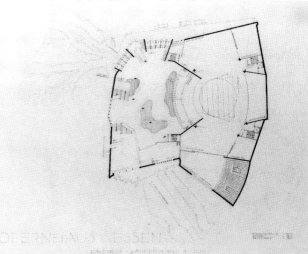

364

365

365
Theater
366
Entrance foyer and
stairway with lobby
balconies.

366

Civic Center
Seinäjoki, Finland. 1958–87

367

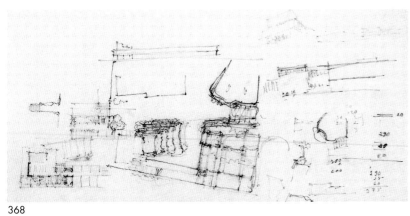

368

367
Aerial view
368
Site-plan sketch. Pencil on tracing paper, 11¹³/₁₆ x 29¹¹/₁₆" (30 x 75.5 cm). Alvar Aalto Foundation, Helsinki
369
Site-plan sketches. Pencil on tracing paper, 13 x 11¹³/₁₆" (33 x 30 cm). Alvar Aalto Foundation, Helsinki

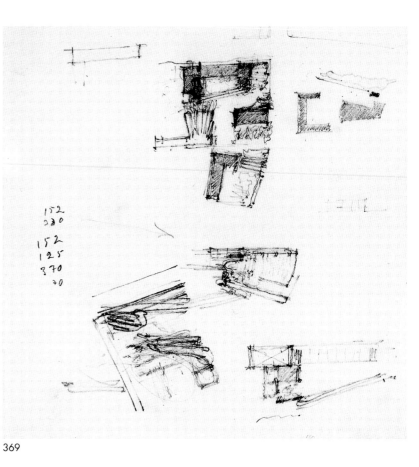

369

370

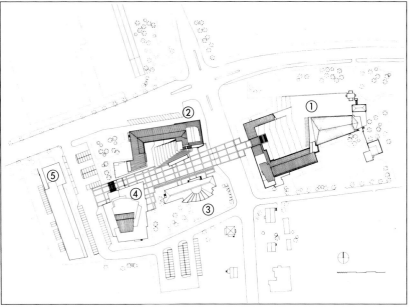

370
City hall
371
Site plan (1997; Jari
Frondelius and Peter B.
MacKeith). 1. church and
parish center 2. city hall
3. library 4. theater
5. administration center

372

Civic Center

372
View of city hall from theater café
373
View of city hall and church

373

374

375

374
View of library and city hall
from church
375
City hall

376

Mount Angel Abbey Library
St. Benedict, Oregon. 1964–70

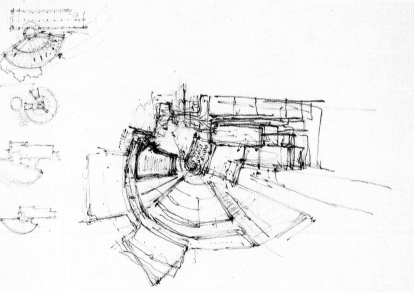

377

376
Entrance (southwest) facade
377
Plan sketches. Pencil on
tracing paper, 11 13/16 x 16 15/16"
(30 x 43 cm). Alvar Aalto
Foundation, Helsinki
378
Plan and section sketches.
Pencil on tracing paper,
11 13/16 x 28 1/8" (30 x 71.5 cm).
Alvar Aalto Foundation,
Helsinki
379
Reading room

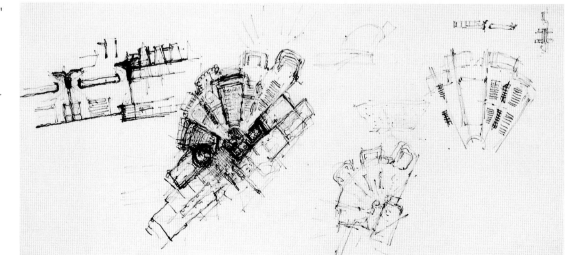

378

Mount Angel Abbey Library

380
Reading-room skylight
381
Main-floor plan. Pencil and
color pencil on tracing paper,
16½ x 27⅜" (42 x 69.5 cm).
Alvar Aalto Foundation,
Helsinki
382
Elevation and section. Pencil
on tracing paper, 16½ x
29¾" (42 x 75.5 cm). Alvar
Aalto Foundation, Helsinki

380

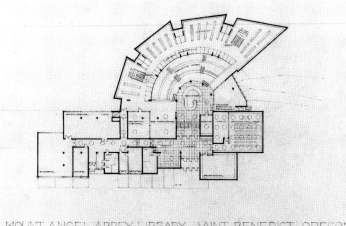

381

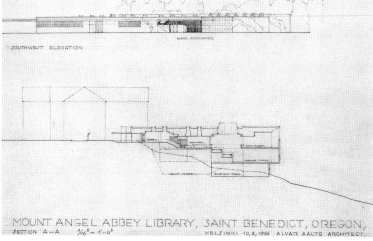

382

383
View from northwest
384
Reading room

Iran Museum of Modern Art
Shiraz, Iran. Project, 1969–70

385

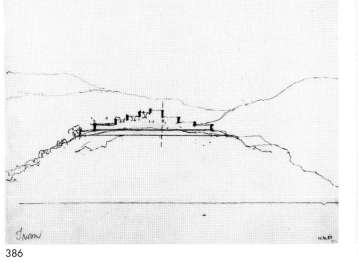

386

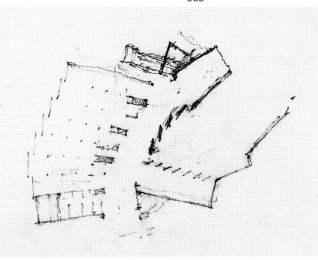

387

385
Landscape perspective
sketch. Pencil on paper, 8½ x
11" (21.5 x 28 cm). Alvar
Aalto Foundation, Helsinki

386
Section sketch. Pencil on
tracing paper, 11¾ x 16½"
(29.8 x 41.8 cm). Alvar Aalto
Foundation, Helsinki

387
Plan sketch. Pencil on tracing
paper, sheet 11¹³⁄₁₆ x 25¾"
(30 x 65.4 cm). Alvar Aalto
Foundation, Helsinki

388
Perspective sketch. Pencil on
tracing paper, 11¾ x 16½"
(29.8 x 41.8 cm). Alvar Aalto
Foundation, Helsinki

388

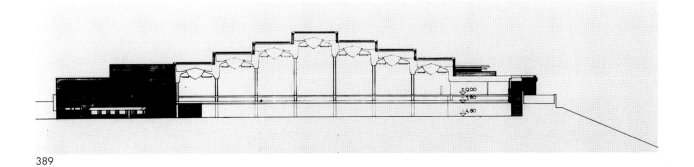

389

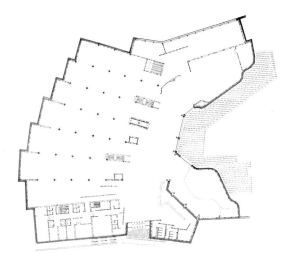

389
Section. Alvar Aalto
Foundation, Helsinki
390
Main-floor plan. Alvar Aalto
Foundation, Helsinki
391
South elevation. Alvar Aalto
Foundation, Helsinki

390

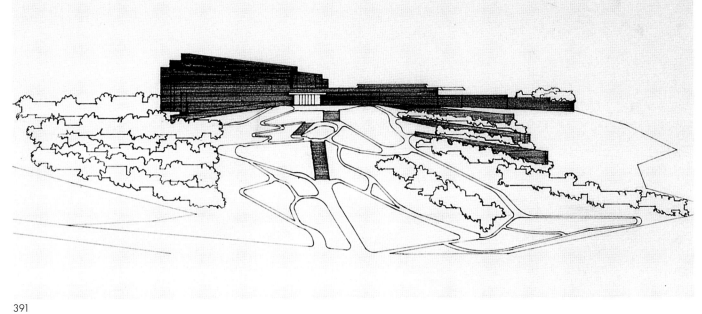

391

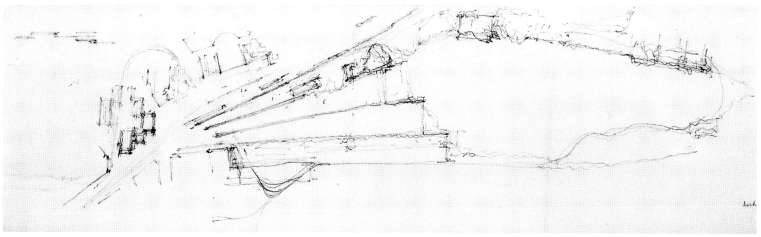

392

Helsinki Center Plan
Helsinki. Begun 1959

392
Plan sketch. Pencil on
tracing paper, 11¹³⁄₁₆ x 42½"
(30 x 108 cm). Alvar Aalto
Foundation, Helsinki
393
Model (c. 1964). Wood and
plexiglass, 4¾ x 43⅜ x 86¾"
(12 x 110.2 x 220.3 cm).
Alvar Aalto Foundation,
Helsinki

393

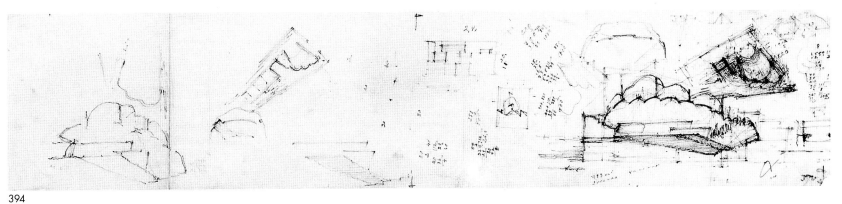

394

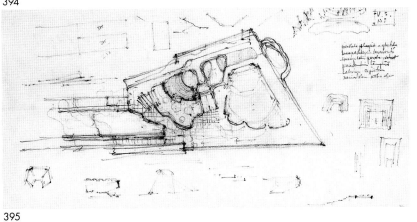

395

Finlandia Hall
Helsinki. 1962–71

394
Plan and section sketches.
Pencil on tracing paper,
11¹³⁄₁₆ x 59¼" (30 x
150.4 cm). Alvar Aalto
Foundation, Helsinki
395
Plan sketch. Pencil
on tracing paper, 11¹³⁄₁₆ x
26⅜" (30 x 67 cm). Alvar
Aalto Foundation, Helsinki
396
Aerial view

396

398

399

Finlandia Hall

397
East facade: auditorium and
stair
398
View from southwest
399
East facade
400
First-floor plan. Alvar Aalto
Foundation, Helsinki
401
Ground-floor plan. Alvar
Aalto Foundation, Helsinki

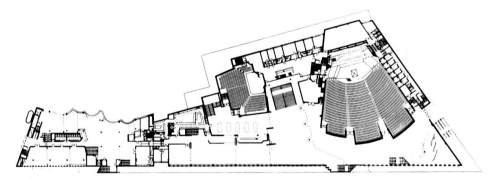

400

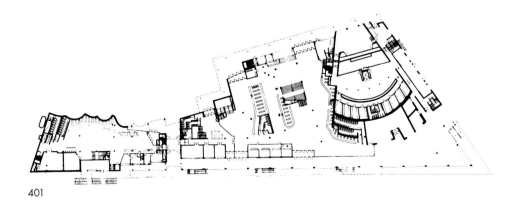

401

Finlandia Hall

402
Lobby entry
403
Small concert hall
404
Lobby and stairways to
balcony level

402

403

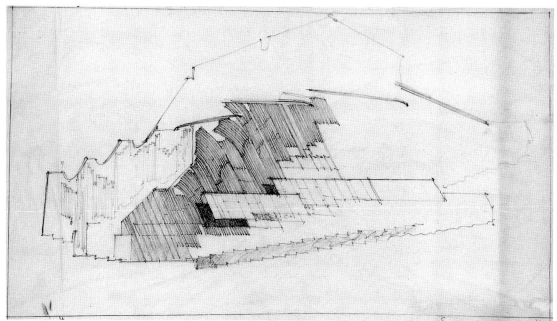

405

Finlandia Hall

405
Main concert hall:
interior elevation. Pencil
and color pencil on tracing
paper, 23¼ x 41⁷⁄₁₆" (59 x
105.2 cm). Alvar Aalto
Foundation, Helsinki
406
Main concert hall: wood
wall-relief sketches. Pencil on
tracing paper, 26¾ x 23⅝"
(68 x 60 cm). Alvar Aalto
Foundation, Helsinki

406

407

407
Main concert hall
408
View from Töölö Bay

408

A Note on Aalto as a Competitor
Vilhelm Helander

WINNING ARCHITECTURAL COMPETITIONS was one of the most important means by which Alvar Aalto received architectural commissions. The total number of competition schemes produced by Aalto hovers around one hundred, most of them for projects in Finland but also some abroad. He was awarded fifty-five prizes and commendations of which twenty-nine were first prizes (eight in international competitions).[1] Aalto's brilliant success is unparalleled in Finland,[2] and his impressive record of winning entries as well as his competitive nature remain legendary. With the exception of his extraordinary patronage from industrialists, most of his best-known works were the result of competitions. These included competitions for the Viipuri City Library of 1927–35, Paimio Tuberculosis Sanatorium of 1929–33, the Finnish pavilions for the Paris International Exhibition and New York World's Fair of 1936–37 and 1938–39, Karhula-Iittala Glass Design of 1936, Säynätsalo Town Hall of 1948–52, Helsinki University of Technology of 1949–66, and the Opera House, Essen, Germany, of 1959–88 (plates 52–72, 89–109, 130–154, 196–214, 259–276, 361–366).

For over a century, architectural competitions (whether open or invitational) have been central to the architecture culture in Finland. A large proportion of public buildings and other important commissions, from the late nineteenth century to the present day, have been assigned through architectural competitions. This noteworthy tradition is evidently responsible for the success of the modern movement in Finland and the often strikingly high level of design in Finnish architecture.[3]

The early competitions, however, were conducted without generally agreed-upon rules. This practice led to debate in the Finnish Architects' Club, the predecessor of the Finnish Association of Architects. The

Architects' Club established the first standardized competition rules in 1893,[4] and when the Finnish Association of Architects was founded in 1919, competitions were placed under its purview.[5]

The Association oversees the preparation of competition briefs, selects representatives to serve on juries, and dictates guidelines for judging. The professional members of a jury, which include architects and other building and planning professionals, are guaranteed a majority of votes.[6] The jury assiduously studies the entries, and the entire process requires at least several weeks for small invitational competitions and up to six months for major public competitions. Moreover, in addition to passing judgment, the committee produces written statements for each entry, and these are routinely published together with the projects.[7] Participating in a competition and receiving a detailed criticism is considered an important part of an architect's continuing education.

Open, "democratically" judged competitions have offered younger architects or even students an opportunity to launch their careers.[8] In this system, older architects with established careers and younger colleagues compete on equal terms (and even non-architects may enter open competitions). Aalto, for example, was still in his twenties when he won the Viipuri City Library competition. Competitions provide architects not only with the opportunity to win a commission but with personal and professional challenges as well, and many architects consider it a duty to participate in them. Moreover, the competition brief is a catalyst for developing new ideas and experimentation, and architects welcome the opportunity for periods of especially intensive creative work—a reprieve from the demanding daily routine.[9] It requires years to see a building completed, but a new architectural idea may be developed in the few weeks devoted to a competition. Preparing a competition entry thus becomes a form of focused study, and ideas and designs generated for a particular competition sometimes reemerge in later projects.

Competition rules specify guidelines concerning architectural renderings. This is intended to standardize entries for judging and to prevent their attracting attention through idiosyncratic drawing techniques and graphic styles. To counteract the brilliant wash techniques used in the earliest competitions, the rules established in the 1920s and 1930s stipulated that drawings must be presented in a more sober medium—black ink on white paper—as seen, for example, in Aalto's competition drawings for the Paimio Tuberculosis Sanatorium (plates 56–57).[10] However austere these drawings may be, they were directed at professional critics rather than at nonprofessionals. Eventually, in the 1930s, these restrictions on presentation style were criticized by the architects themselves, and consequently in the following decade the use of pencil and color pencil increased. Aalto developed his own responses to these demands: a simple and economical drawing style that took into account the limited time available to prepare a competition entry. From the late 1940s onward, Aalto used, almost exclusively, pencil on tracing paper. The main lines were emphasized in color,

often in a yellowish red, as in Aalto's entries for Säynätsalo Town Hall of 1948–52 and the Malmi Funeral Chapel of 1950 (plates 201–202, 204–205, 207, 209, 217–218).[11] From the late 1940s to the 1960s, at least, Aalto's competition entries were submitted as original hand drawings. The contemporary published versions, however, were little more than simplified line drawings void of the fine and sensitive lines in the originals. Models were only occasionally required in the 1930s, but from the late 1940s they were more commonly included among the requisite documentation for competitions. Aalto had his own model shop, with trained assistants, in his studio. This facilitated production and also provided an obvious advantage in preparing a competition entry.[12] The predilection for monochromatic models seems to have been a tradition rather than a requirement.

Competition entries have always been submitted anonymously, and Scandinavian architects have traditionally selected mottoes to identify their entries. The titles of Aalto's competition entries—Latin phrases and random sequences of numbers—are of some interest. In the early part of the century, Finnish architects often favored mottoes in Latin, Italian, or French. These references to the classical ideals of civilization and a yearning for the Mediterranean were typical of Aalto and his generation. Aalto called his project for the Finnish Parliament House of 1923–24 "Flagello" and the 1929 Vallila Church entry "Gloria" (plates 7–10, 85–87). In his postwar architecture, Aalto returned to the ideals of Nordic classicism in a new way. This is apparent in a sequence of solemn Latin mottoes: *AVE MATER ALMA, morituri te salutant* (Helsinki University of Technology), *Forum redivivum* (National Pensions Institute), *Curia* (Säynätsalo and Gothenburg Town Halls), *Sinus* (Lahti Church), *Trinitas* (Malmi Funeral Chapel), *Urbs* (Jyväskylä Pedagogical Institute), *Aurora borealis* (City Hall, Kiruna, Sweden) (plates 200–202, 204–205, 207, 209, 217–218, 259, 331–332). In other competitions Aalto favored English slogans, as an expression of modernity. Some competition briefs requested numerical mottoes, and particular numbers recur on Aalto's entries: "10791" (Central Cemetery and Funeral Chapel, Lyngby-Taarbaek, Denmark), "17991" (Opera House, Essen), and "179991" (Cultural Center, Leverkusen, Germany) (plates 220–225, 362–364). Perhaps some code is concealed. The numbers Aalto used elsewhere for Gothenburg, "48261," were at least a variation on his telephone number. On a few occasions, Aalto used telling Finnish words in reference to the main idea of the design such as *yksi taso* [one level] or *sekä että* [both and]. Perhaps his most striking motto was neither a word nor a number but rather an icon that was a key element of the design: the Paimio Tuberculosis Sanatorium window and balcony door (see plates 56–57). This motto, or symbol, called attention to modern functionalist architecture and, in particular, the ample sunlight the patients' room would receive. Clearly, Aalto's renowned sense of humor was reflected in his entry titled *Eskimoerindens Skinnbux* [Eskimo Woman's Leather Breeches] for the Karhula-Iittala Glass-Design Competition of 1936 (plates 141, 143–144).

Winning a competition did not always guarantee a commission. Many of Aalto's successful competition entries remained on paper. Among them were some of the unquestionable high points of his creative career, for example, the Malmi Funeral Chapel and Central Cemetery and Funeral Chapel in Lyngby-Taarbaek (plates 217–218, 220–225), Aalto's responses to the chapels and classical landscapes of Erik Gunnar Asplund, Sigurd Lewerentz, and Erik Bryggman; the proposal for the Kuopio Theater of 1952, an example of the combination of new building with old that was ahead of its time; and the Sports, Congress, and Concert Complex for Vienna's Vogelweidplatz of 1952–53 (plates 278–279), a building which would have opened up an entirely new perspective on Aalto as an inventor of unconventional constructions. Bad luck dogged Aalto's winning entries, in Sweden in particular. The proposal for the Town Hall in Gothenburg, Sweden, of 1955, with its slanting square and groups of buildings, is one of Aalto's finest urban designs but remained unbuilt, as did his scheme for Drottningtorget square, in the same city, of 1956, an excellent solution to a difficult traffic node and terminal group in terms of urban architecture. The unexecuted design for the Kiruna City Hall of 1958 was a fine example of Aalto's virtuosity in landscape design and plastic invention (plates 331–332). The sad fate of all these designs must be counted among Aalto's greatest misfortunes.

Competitions offer a break in the everyday routine, and the pressure of a deadline quickens creativity. Stories about how quickly a competition scheme was completed and how it had been celebrated circulate in architectural circles, and Aalto was a central figure in these legends.[13] In fact, Aalto made his competition entries with care, according to a timetable and method of working that were based on experience. He always drew preliminary sketches himself. Early in his career he sometimes drew the entire scheme himself, but generally the entire staff of the small office participated in the competition in the final busy days.[14] During the 1950s, competition proposals typically evolved in the following manner. When some interesting competition was announced, Aalto would assign an architect in the office the job of analyzing the brief. The spaces were drawn diagrammatically at a suitable scale, and at the same time the most important services were noted. Often the site was visited, but not always. Then Aalto began to sketch design ideas, which could be a long-drawn-out process. The sketches were done either in the relative quiet of his home studio at Riihitie Road (plate 129) or at the nearby Tiilimäki studio (plates 235–239). His assistant then interpreted the sketches on a larger scale, and eventually the entire office participated in the production of the finished drawings, which took a few days. Typically, the office worked throughout the night to meet a deadline. Aalto would go home to rest, returning in the morning to place the final touches on the drawings and models. Someone would rush the proposal to the post office; the others, exhausted, enjoyed some red wine.[15]

Notes

1. Aalto's prizes, however, were not easy wins. Göran Schildt observed that between the competition successes that led to the Paimio sanatorium in 1929 and the Finnish Pavilion for the Paris International Exhibition in 1936, Aalto entered twenty-two competitions without having a single one lead to a built project. Göran Schildt, *Alvar Aalto: The Decisive Years,* trans. Timothy Binham (New York: Rizzoli,1986), p. 121.

2. There is no comprehensive study of the history of architectural competitions in Finland, as such. Essays dealing with the development of the Finnish competition system and its importance to the architectural profession are found in Pekka Korvenmaa, ed., *The Work of Architects: The Finnish Association of Architects, 1892–1992,* trans. Jüri Kokkonen (Helsinki: Finnish Association of Architects, 1992). According to "unofficial" figures for the years 1892–1992, compiled by Pertti Solla, the former competitions secretary of the Finnish Association of Architects, Aalto is followed by Kaija and Heikki Sirén; among architects of the older generation, Eliel Saarinen, Erik Bryggman, and Aarne Ervi are among the top ten, accompanied by some younger architects, both individuals and groups. See Pertti Solla, "Architectural Competitions in Finland," in Korvenmaa, ibid., p. 278. The Museum of Finnish Architecture maintains a competition archive, which consists primarily of copies of competition entries but also includes jury comments and some competition briefs. Original material relating to successful and commended competition entries has generally remained in the possession of the competition organizer, while other proposals were returned to competitors after the judging and publication of the competition. The Alvar Aalto Archives in Helsinki, for example, contain primarily unsuccessful proposals that were returned to the office. The main sources for Aalto's participation in competitions are Göran Schildt, *Alvar Aalto: The Early Years,* trans. Timothy Binham (New York: Rizzoli, 1984); idem, *Decisive Years;* idem, *Alvar Aalto: The Mature Years,* trans. Timothy Binham (New York: Rizzoli, 1991); and idem, *Alvar Aalto: The Complete Catalogue of Architecture, Design and Art,* trans. Timothy Binham (New York: Rizzoli, 1994).

3. For example, see Raija-Liisa Heinonen, *Funktionalismin läpimurto Suomessa* [Breakthrough of Functionalism in Finland] (Helsinki: Museum of Finnish Architecture, 1986), which underscores the importance of competitions for the breakthrough of the new movement in architecture.

4. In addition to secrecy, they included three important principles. First, architects on the jury have the majority of votes; second, the author of a competition scheme retains copyright on his work so that if a scheme is chosen for realization, the commission must be given to the original author; and third, the architectural profession does not participate in competitions that do not meet with the approved competition rules. See Eeva Maija Viljo, "The Architectural Profession in Finland in the Latter Half of the 19th Century," in Korvenmaa, *The Work of Architects,* p. 46.

5. The rules were revised in 1929 and have subsequently been updated on a number of occasions. However, with some small modifications, the same main principles have remained in effect for more than a century. The competition rules have much in common with international practice. However, the competition principles have, perhaps, been followed more rigorously in Finland than elsewhere.

6. The most recent competition rules, of 1986, stipulate that architects or other professionals must hold the majority of votes on the competition jury. In addition to the judges appointed by the Finnish Association of Architects, generally two in number, the competition organizer may appoint other professionals, who must be approved by the competitions committee of the Finnish Association of Architects.

7. The most important source for information on architectural competitions in general is *Arkkitehti* magazine. In the earliest issues, important competitions formed the central content of the magazine. From 1958 onward, a competitions supplement appeared as part of the magazine; in 1966 this became an independent publication, *Arkkitehtikilpailuja* [Architectural Competitions]. In 1975 it was reintegrated with *Arkkitehti* magazine as a supplement. Generally only prizewinning and commended entries were published. Sometimes, however, and particularly during the years of the functionalist breakthrough, from the late 1920s onward, other proposals were included, according to competition rules, anonymously. Architects certainly often either knew or recognized the authors of these unsuccessful, but perhaps interesting, published designs.

8. Examples of this can be found from the days of the brilliance of national romanticism to very recent years. The first competition run according to established rules, which was held for the design of St. Michael's Church in Turku in 1894, was won by Lars Sonck, then a twenty-three-year-old student. The firm of Gesellius, Lindgren, and Saarinen won both first and second prizes in the competition for the Tallberg Office and Apartment Building in Helsinki in 1897, their last year as students. The tradition lives on to this day, with the success of five Helsinki architectural students in the competition for the Finnish Pavilion at the Seville World's Fair of 1992.

9. In Finland today there are approximately 2,500 architects, and it is not uncommon to find 500 entries in a major competition.

10. For a concise study of architectural graphics and presentation in Finland see Igor Herler, "Notes on Architectural Graphics for Those Concerned," pp. 2–23, in *Finnish Architectural Drawings* (Helsinki: Museum of Finnish Architecture, 1980).

11. Aalto thus created his own, undoubtedly recognizable, style of presentation. Nevertheless, it had surprisingly few imitators, and these were generally outside Finland, for example, among Aalto's former Danish assistants, in whose competition entries Aalto-like mannerisms are discernible. In general, too, it may be said that Aalto had few epigones in Finland.

12. Interview with Kaarlo Leppänen, March 4, 1997. Leppänen worked in the Aalto office from 1955 to 1975 and was the principal assistant for many projects. Leppänen stated he was Aalto's assistant for a total of eighteen competitions between 1955 and 1967, of which fourteen were international and four Finnish. The results were nine first prizes and three second prizes.

13. Schildt recounts a lively story by Aalto's Swiss assistant Lisbeth Sachs about the intensity with which the proposal for the Finnish Pavilion at the New York World's Fair was made in 1938 over three days and how the long-awaited success was celebrated in the Aalto's home and studio at a table stretching the length of the building, with the *crème de la crème* of Helsinki as guests. See Schildt, *Decisive Years,* pp. 161–164. In Aalto's career, there was particular cause for celebration in the 1950s: the entire staff of the office was taken to the Assembly Rooms in Helsinki, a restaurant designed by Aalto's teacher Armas Lindgren, in private rooms favored by Marshal Mannerheim, another Finnish national hero.

14. Schildt, *Decisive Years,* p. 44.

15. Interview with Kaarlo Leppänen, March 4, 1997.

NORWAY

ARCTIC CIRCLE

• Rovaniemi

SWEDEN

RUSSIA

• Oulu

Gulf of Bothnia

Kokkola •

FINLAND

Vaasa •
Lapua •   Kauhajärvi •   • Viitasaari
    Seinäjoki •   • Alajärvi   • Kuopio

Jyväskylä •   • Varkaus
Muurame • • Säynätsalo

Noormarkku •   Tampere •   • Jämsä
Kokemäenjoki river
Pori •   Vuoksenniska •
100 miles   Imatra •   Vuoksi river
       • Kauttua   Lahti •   • Viipuri   Lake
                                                            Ladoga
Turku •   Inkeroinen •
      • Paimio   Karhula •
Espoo • Malmi
Tapiola •   • Kotka
   Helsinki Finland

Stockholm •

Gulf of
Tallin   St. Petersburg

Chronology

Compiled by Bevin Howard

Map of Finland, showing locations of Aalto's principal architectural works, 1997 (Jari Honkonen/Decode, Inc., Helsinki; courtesy Pekka Korvenmaa)

The following chronological listing gives key events in Alvar Aalto's life, his major architectural works (all appear in the plate section), and important political events that affected the architect's life and work. Architectural works are given in *italics*.

1898
February 3: Born Hugo Alvar Henrik Aalto to Johan Henrik Aalto and Selma Hackstedt in Kuortane, Finland.

1917
Finland becomes an independent nation.

Park Café, Project.

1918
Finnish Civil War.

1921
Receives diploma in architecture from Helsinki University of Technology. Works, as a student, in architect Armas Lindgren's atelier.

Works in Arvid Bjerke's office in Gothenberg, Sweden.

1923
Meets Swedish architect Erik Gunnar Asplund at the Skandia Cinema, Stockholm.

Opens The Alvar Aalto Office for Architecture and Monumental Art in Jyväskylä, Finland.

Finnish Parliament House, Helsinki. Project (1923–24).

House and Sauna for Terho Manner, Töysä, Finland.

1924
Marries architect Aino Marsio (b. 1894). Travels to Europe on honeymoon. First trip to Italy.

Jyväskylä Workers' Club, Jyväskylä, Finland (1924–25).

Seinäjoki Defense Corps Building, Seinäjoki, Finland (1924–29).

Furnishings for Hämäläis-Osakunta Students' Club, Helsinki.

Furnishings for Seurahuone Café, Jyväskylä, Finland.

1925
August 1: Daughter, Johanna Flora Maria Annunziata, born.

Funeral Chapel, Jyväskylä, Finland. Project (1925 and 1930).

Aino and Alvar Aalto, 1947

László Moholy-Nagy and Alvar Aalto at the beach near Naantali, Finland, 1931

Atrium House for Väinö Aalto, Alajärvi, Finland. Project.

Jämsä Church, Jämsä, Finland. Project.

1926

Travels to Sweden and Denmark.

Sees Asplund's Woodland Cemetery, Stockholm, and nearly completed Stockholm Public Library.

Meets Swedish architect Sven Markelius in Stockholm.

Muurame Church, Muurame, Finland (1926–29).

League of Nations, Geneva, Switzerland. Project (1926–27).

1927

Moves office to Turku, Finland.

Töölö Church, Helsinki. Project.

Viipuri City Library, Viipuri, Finland (now Vyborg, Russia) (1927–35).

1928

January 8: Son, Johan Henrik Hamilkar Alvar, born.

Travels to France, the Netherlands, and Denmark to see modern architecture and design by Le Corbusier, André Lurcat, J. J. P. Oud, Wilhelm Dudok, Poul Henningsen, and others.

Meets Henningsen in Denmark, Lurcat and architect Alfred Roth in Paris.

Visits Johannes Duiker's Zonnestraal Tuberculosis Sanatorium in Hilversum.

Turun Sanomat Building, Turku, Finland (1928–30).

"Merry-Go-Round" Summer Cottage, Aitta maga-zine competition.

1929

Attends 2nd Congrès Internationaux d'Architecture Moderne (CIAM) in Frankfurt, whose theme is "Die Wohnung für das Existenzmini-mum" [Housing for Low-income Earners].

Elected member of the Comité International pour la Résolution des Problèmes de l'Architecture Contemporaine (CIRPAC), the inner circle of CIAM responsible for preparing agendas for meetings. Meets artist László Moholy-Nagy for the first time. Also meets architects Walter Gropius, Le Corbusier, and Karl Moser, as well as the architectural historian Sigfried Giedion.

Works on developing standard designs for projects that will be completed in the next several years: the Turun Sanomat Building (1928–30), the Paimio Tuberculosis Sanatorium (1929–33), and the exhibition, *Rationalization of the Minimum Dwelling* (1930).

Turku 700th Anniversary Exhibition and Trade Fair, Turku, Finland (with Erik Bryggman).

Paimio Tuberculosis Sanatorium, Paimio, Finland (1929–33).

Columbus Memorial Light House, Santo Domingo, Dominican Republic. Project.

Vallila Church, Helsinki. Project.

1930

Attends the Stockholm Exhibition; meets the architectural critic Philip Morton Shand.

Participates in exhibition, *Rationalization of the Minimum Dwelling,* at Helsinki Art Hall.

Travels to Brussels for the 3rd CIAM conference and a presentation of modern design from Finland.

Travels to Germany and Switzerland with his wife. Meets architects Gerrit Rietveld, Hugo Häring, Ernst May, Richard Neutra, Mart Stam, Hans Schmidt, and art patron Hélène de Mandrot, among others.

Toppila Pulp Mill, Oulu, Finland (1930–33).

1932

The Turun Sanomat Building of 1928–30 is included in The Museum of Modern Art's first architecture show, *Modern Architecture—International Exhibition,* organized by Philip Johnson and Henry-Russell Hitchcock.

1933

Moves office to Helsinki.

Attends 4th CIAM conference in Athens; meets artist Fernand Léger and architects José Luis Sert and Pierre Jeanneret. Theme of the conference is "The Functional City."

Exhibition of his furniture at the London department store, Fortnum & Mason, organized with Shand.

Shand and G.M. Boumphrey establish Finmar, a company dedicated to importing and selling Aalto-designed furniture in England. Meets architect William Lescaze in London.

1934

Founder and chairman of *Projektio*, Finland's first film society.

1935

Introduced to Maire Gullichsen, wife of industrialist Harry Gullichsen, by his associate, Nils Gustav Hahl. With Maire Gullichsen, Hahl, and his wife, Aino, establishes the Artek company to produce and distribute his furniture and glassware.

House and Studio for Aino and Alvar Aalto, Munkkiniemi, Helsinki (1935–36).

1936

Sunila Pulp Mill and Housing, Kotka, Finland (1936–38).

Karhula-Iittala Glass-Design Competition.

Finnish Pavilion, Paris International Exhibition, Paris (1936–37).

1937

Travels to Paris during the summer; meets artists Pablo Picasso, Alexander Calder, and Constantin Brancusi, and art historian Christian Zervos.

American architect William W. Wurster and landscape architect Thomas Church and his wife, Elizabeth, visit Aalto at his home in Munkkiniemi.

Standard Terrace Housing, Kauttua, Finland (1937–38).

A-House Standard Houses (begun 1937).

1938

Exhibition, *Alvar Aalto: Architecture and Furniture,* at The Museum of Modern Art, New York. The exhibition catalogue is the first book on Aalto.

First trip to the United States.

Delivers lecture, sponsored by The Museum of Modern Art, at the Dalton School in New York.

In New York meets at The Museum of Modern Art with Alfred H. Barr, Jr., director, John McAndrew, curator of architecture and industrial art, James Johnson Sweeney, future curator of painting and sculpture, Edgar Kaufmann, Jr., future curator of design, and Nelson A. Rockefeller, future president of the Museum.

Visits Finnish émigré architect, Eliel Saarinen, at the Cranbrook Academy of Art, Bloomfield, Michigan.

Villa Mairea, House for Maire and Harry Gullichsen, Noormarkku, Finland (1938–39).

Finnish Pavilion, New York World's Fair, Queens, New York (1938–39).

1939

Second trip to the United States. Supervises the building of the Finnish Pavilion at the New York World's Fair.

Lectures at Yale University, New Haven, Connecticut.

Meets architects Marcel Breuer, Wallace K. Harrison, Joseph Hudnut, and Edward D. Stone, among others.

Visits Moholy-Nagy's New Bauhaus school in Chicago, then travels to California, Arizona, and New Mexico.

Winter War, between Finland and the Soviet Union (November 1939–March 1940). Finland loses large areas of southeast Finland, including most of Karelia.

Alvar Aalto at his house, Munkkiniemi, Helsinki, 1936

Alvar Aalto in the United States, 1939

Alvar and Elissa Aalto in
their studio, Munkkiniemi,
Helsinki, early 1960s

Alvar Aalto at the
Experimental House,
Muuratsalo, Finland, 1960s

Helsinki University of Technology destroyed by bombs.

1940

Travels to the United States and delivers numerous lectures. Meets architects Buckminster Fuller and Harmon Goldstone, and historian Lewis Mumford.

Visits Edgar Kaufmann, Jr., at Fallingwater, Edgar J. Kaufmann House, Mill Run, Pennsylvania, designed by Frank Lloyd Wright.

Appointed Research Professor at Massachusetts Institute of Technology, Cambridge. This arrangement lasts briefly; he returns to Finland due to war.

1941

The Continuation War (1941–44). Finland regains and then loses to Russia its pre-1940 territories.

AA Standard Summer Cottages. Project.

1943

Elected Chairman of Finnish Association of Architects (1943–58).

Standardization Institute established in Finland.

Collaborates with Albin Stark on projects in Sweden (1942–1945).

1944

Avesta Civic Center, Avesta, Sweden. Project (with Albin Stark).

1945

Lapland War. German troops removed from Finland.

1946

Visiting Professor at Massachusetts Institute of Technology (MIT) (1946–48).

Visits Frank Lloyd Wright in Milwaukee and travels with him to his home, Taliesin, in Spring Green, Wisconsin.

Baker House, Senior Dormitory for Massachusetts

Institute of Technology, Cambridge, Massachusetts (1946–49).

1947

Imatra Master Plan, Imatra, Finland (1947–53).

1948

Travels to Rome with his wife, Aino. Visits numerous classical ruins.

National Pensions Institute, Helsinki (1948–57).

Säynätsalo Town Hall, Säynätsalo, Finland (1948–52).

1949

January 13: Aino Aalto dies after a long illness.

Gravesite at Aalto's House, Munkkiniemi, Helsinki. Project (c. 1949).

Helsinki University of Technology, Espoo (Otaniemi) (1949–66).

1950

Exhibition on Alvar and Aino's architecture, in conjunction with a comprehensive exhibition of Finnish painting and sculpture, at the École des Beaux-Arts, Paris.

Malmi Funeral Chapel, Helsinki. Project.

1951

Central Cemetery and Funeral Chapel, Lyngby-Taarbaek, Denmark. Project (1951–52) (with Jean-Jacques Baruël).

1952

Marries architect Elissa Mäkiniemi (Elsa Kaisa Mäkiniemi, 1922–1994)

Experimental House and Sauna for Elissa and Alvar Aalto, Muuratsalo, Finland (1952–53).

House of Culture, Helsinki (1952–58).

Sports, Congress, and Concert Complex, Vogelweidplatz, Vienna. Project (1952–53).

1953

Travels to Sicily and Greece.

1954

Apartment Building, Interbau Exhibition, Hansaviertel, Berlin (1954–57).

Alvar Aalto's Studio, Munkkiniemi, Helsinki (1954–56).

Master Plan for Industrial Community, Summa, Finland.

1955

Elected an Academician of the Academy of Finland (one of twelve members).

Church of the Three Crosses, Vuoksenniska, Imatra, Finland (1955–58).

1956

Maison Carré, House for Louis Carré, Bazoches-sur-Guyonne, France (1956–59).

1957

Awarded Gold Medal by the Royal Institute of British Architects (RIBA), London.

1958

Cultural Center, Wolfsburg, Germany (1958–62).

Apartment Building, Neue Vahr, Bremen, Germany (1958–62).

City Hall, Kiruna, Sweden. Project.

North Jutland Art Museum, Aalborg, Denmark (1958–72) (with Elissa Aalto and Jean-Jacques Baruël).

Civic Center, Seinäjoki, Finland (1958–87).

1959

Helsinki Center Plan, Helsinki (begun 1959).

Opera House, Essen, Germany (competition 1959, completed by Harald Deilmann with Elissa Aalto, 1981–88).

1962

Awarded Sonning Prize in Copenhagen, Denmark.

Finlandia Hall, Helsinki (1962–71).

1963

Awarded Gold Medal from the American Institute of Architecture.

Elected President of the Academy of Finland (1963–68).

1964

Mount Angel Abbey Library, St. Benedict, Oregon (1964–70).

1965

Retrospective exhibition at the Palazzo Strozzi, Florence.

1969

Elected a member of the order Pour le Mérite (the highest cultural accolade awarded in Germany).

Iran Museum of Modern Art, Shiraz, Iran. Project (1969–70).

1972

Awarded Gold Medal by the French Academy of Architecture

1976

May 11: Dies in Helsinki.

Alvar Aalto at Civic Center, Seinäjoki, Finland, 1960s

Selected Bibliography

The following listing represents a selection of books and articles on Alvar Aalto. It is divided into five sections: Writings by Alvar Aalto, Monographs, General Books, Articles, and CD-ROM. Individual listings for Aalto's writings are given only for those texts that are not reprinted in Göran Schildt, ed., *Sketches: Alvar Aalto,* trans. Stuart Wrede (Cambridge, Mass. and London: MIT Press, 1978). Special editions of periodicals devoted solely to Aalto are listed under Monographs. Additional sources are cited in the endnotes to the essays in this volume. For a detailed listing of the Aalto literature up to 1984, see William C. Miller, *Alvar Aalto: An Annotated Bibliography* (New York and London: Garland Publishing, 1984).

Writings by Alvar Aalto

Aalto, Alvar. "Architecture in the Landscape of Central Finland." *Sisä-Suomi* (June 28, 1925).

Aalto, Alvar. "Porraskiveltä arkihuoneeseen" [From Doorstep to Living Room]. *Aitta*, Special Christmas Issue (1926). Pp. 63–69.

Aalto, Alvar. "Rakenteitten ja aineitten vaikutus nykyaikaiseen rakennustaiteeseen" [The Influence of Construction and Materials on Modern Architecture]. *Arkkitehti*, no. 9 (1938). Pp. 129–131.

Aalto, Alvar. *Kokemäenjoen laakson aluesuunnitelma.* Pori: Satakunnan Kirjateollisuus, 1943.

Aalto, Alvar. "Kumo älvdal." *Arkkitehti*, nos. 1–2 (1943). Pp. 6–11.

Aalto, Alvar. "New Centre for the Town of Helsinki." *Arkkitehti,* no. 3 (1961).

Aalto, Alvar. "The Arts." In Karl Fleig, ed. *Alvar Aalto: Volume II, 1963–1970.* Zurich: Les Éditions d'Architecture Artemis, 1971. P. 12.

Schildt, Göran, ed. *Sketches: Alvar Aalto.* Translated by Stuart Wrede. Cambridge, Mass. and London: MIT Press, 1978.

Schildt, Göran, ed. *Alvar Aalto in His Own Words.* New York: Rizzoli, 1998.

Monographs

Aalto: Architecture and Furniture. New York: The Museum of Modern Art, 1938.

Alvar Aalto. London: Academy Editions; New York: St. Martin's Press, 1984.

"Alvar Aalto." *Architecture and Urbanism.* Special Edition (May 1983).

"Alvar Aalto." *Arkkitehti.* Special Issue, vol. 73, nos. 7–8 (1976).

"Alvar Aalto." *Space Design,* no. 149 (January–February 1977). Pp. 3–212.

"Alvar Aalto: Champ et Contrechamp." *L'Architecture d'aujourd'hui,* no. 191 (June 1977). Pp. 56–125.

Alvar Aalto: Das architektonische Werk. Essen: Museum Folkwang Essen, 1979.

The Architectural Drawings of Alvar Aalto, 1917–1939. Introduction and project descriptions by Göran Schildt. Garland Architectural Archives Series, 11 vols. New York and London: Garland Publishing, 1994.

Baird, George, and Yukio Futagawa. *Alvar Aalto.* Library of Contemporary Architects. New York: Simon and Schuster, 1971.

Biurrun, Javier F. *El Sanatorio de Paimio, 1929–1933: Alvar Aalto, la arquitectura entre la naturaleza y la maquina.* Barcelona: Servei de Publicaciones de la Universitat Politecnica de Catalunya, 1991.

Canty, Donald. *Lasting Aalto Masterwork: The Library at Mount Angel Abbey.* St. Benedict, Oregon: Mount Angel Abbey, 1992.

"Design and Planning: Alvar Aalto." *Progressive Architecture,* vol. 58, no. 4 (April 1977). Pp. 6, 53–77.

Ferrari, Enrico Maria, ed. *Alvar Aalto: Il Baltico e il Mediterraneo.* Venice: Marsilio Editori, 1990.

Fleig, Karl, ed. *Alvar Aalto: Volume I, 1922–1962.* Zurich: Les Éditions d'Architecture Artemis, 1963.

Fleig, Karl, ed. *Alvar Aalto: Volume II, 1963–1970.* Zurich: Les Éditions d'Architecture Artemis, 1971.

Fleig, Karl, ed. *Alvar Aalto: Volume III, Projects and Final Buildings.* Zurich: Les Éditions d'Architecture Artemis, 1978.

Hoesli, Bernhard, ed. *Alvar Aalto Synopsis: Painting, Architecture, Sculpture.* Basel and Stuttgart: Birkhäuser Verlag, 1970.

Johnson, J. Stewart. *Alvar Aalto: Furniture and Glass.* New York: The Museum of Modern Art, 1984.

Kapanen, Martti, and Satu Mattila. *Alvar Aalto ja Keski-Suomi* [Alvar Aalto and Central Finland]. Translated by Alan Robson and Tony Melville. Jyväskylä: Alvar Aalto Seura, 1985.

Keinänen, Timo, ed. *Alvar Aalto: The Finnish Pavilion at the Venice Biennale.* Milan: Electa, 1991.

Keinänen, Timo. *Alvar and Aino Aalto as Glass Designers.* Iittala: Iittala Glass Museum, 1996.

The Line: Original Drawings from the Alvar Aalto Archive. Helsinki: Museum of Finnish Architecture, 1993.

Maass, Jörg. *Alvar Aalto: Bauten für Wolfsburg.* Wolfsburg: Stadtbild- und Denkmalpflege, 1989.

Mikkola, Kirmo C., ed. *Alvar Aalto vs. the Modern Movement.* Proceedings of the 1st International Alvar Aalto Symposium. Jyväskylä, 1981.

Miller, William C. *Alvar Aalto: An Annotated Bibliography.* London: Garland Publishing, 1984.

Mosso, Leonardo. *L'Opera di Alvar Aalto.* Milan: Edizioni di Communità, 1965.

Muto, Akira, and Yukio Futagawa. *Alvar Aalto: La Maison Carré, Bazoches-sur-Guyonne, France, 1956–59.* Global Architecture, 10. Tokyo: A.D.A. Edita, 1971.

Muto, Akira, and Yukio Futagawa. *Alvar Aalto: Church in Vuoksenniska (Imatra), Finland, 1957–59; City Center in Seinäjoki, Seinäjoki, Finland, 1958–.* Global Architecture, 16. Tokyo: A.D.A. Edita, 1972.

Muto, Akira, and Yukio Futagawa. *Alvar Aalto: Town Hall in Säynätsalo, Finland, 1950–52; Public Pensions Institute (Kansaneläkelaitos) Helsinki, Finland, 1952–56.* Global Architecture, 24. Tokyo: A.D.A. Edita, 1973.

Neuenschwander, Eduard and Claudia. *Finnische Bauten: Atelier Alvar Aalto, 1950–51.* Erlenbach-Zurich: Verlag für Architektur, 1954.

Pallasmaa, Juhani, ed. *Alvar Aalto Furniture.* Cambridge, Mass.: MIT Press, 1984.

Pearson, Paul David. *Alvar Aalto and the International Style.* New York: Whitney Library of Design, 1978.

Porphyrios, Demetri. *Sources of Modern Eclecticism: Studies on Alvar Aalto.* London: Academy Editions, 1982.

Quantrill, Malcolm. *Alvar Aalto: A Critical Study.* New York: Schocken Books, 1983.

Ruusuvuori, Aarno, ed. *Alvar Aalto, 1898–1976.* Helsinki: Finnish Museum of Architecture, 1978.

Schildt, Göran. *Alvar Aalto: The Early Years.* Translated by Timothy Binham. New York: Rizzoli, 1984.

Schildt, Göran. *Aalto Interiors, 1923–1970.* Translated by Timothy Binham and Raija Mattila. Jyväskylä: Alvar Aalto Museum, 1986.

Schildt, Göran. *Alvar Aalto: The Decisive Years.* Translated by Timothy Binham. New York: Rizzoli, 1986.

Schildt, Göran, ed. *Alvar Aalto de l'oeuvre aux écrits.* Paris: Éditions du Centre Pompidou, 1988.

Schildt, Göran. *Alvar Aalto: The Mature Years.* Translated by Timothy Binham. New York: Rizzoli, 1991.

Schildt, Göran. *Alvar Aalto: The Complete Catalogue of Architecture, Design and Art.* Translated by Timothy Binham. New York: Rizzoli, 1994.

Schmidt, Dietmar N., ed. *Das Theater von Alvar Aalto in Essen.* Essen: Baedeker, 1988.

Soukka, Sirkka, ed. *Alvar Aalto Kotkassa.* Translated by Jaana Charrington and Kaija Kiviharju. Kotka: Kotkan Kaupunki, 1997.

Spens, Michael. *Viipuri Library: Alvar Aalto.* London: Academy Group, 1994.

Trencher, Michael. *The Alvar Aalto Guide.* New York: Princeton Architectural Press, 1996.

Tuukkanen-Beckers, Pirkko, ed. *En Contact avec Alvar Aalto.* Jyväskylä: Alvar Aalto Museum, 1992.

Weston, Richard. *Villa Mairea: Alvar Aalto.* London: Phaidon Press, 1992.

Weston, Richard. *Town Hall, Säynätsalo.* London: Phaidon Press, 1993.

Weston, Richard. *Alvar Aalto.* London: Phaidon Press, 1995.

General Books

Alava, Paavo. *Sunila, metäjättiën yhtiö: Sunila Oy, 1938–88.* Jyväskylä: Sunila, 1988.

Bülow, Else. *Art and Alvar Aalto.* Aalborg: Nordjyllands Kunstmuseum, 1991.

Ford, Edward R. *Details of Modern Architecture. Volume 2, 1928–1988.* Cambridge, Mass.: MIT Press, 1996.

Giedion, Sigfried. *Space, Time and Architecture: The Growth of a New Tradition.* 2nd revised edition. Cambridge, Mass.: Harvard University Press, 1949.

Kallio, Marja. *Korhonen 75.* Translated by Timo Mäkelä. Turku: Huonekalutehdas Korhonen, 1985.

Korvenmaa, Pekka, ed. *The Work of Architects: The Finnish Association of Architects, 1892–1992.* Translated by Jüri Kokkonen. Helsinki: Finnish Association of Architects, 1992.

Lehtinen, William. *Imatran yleiskaava.* Helsinki: Enso-Gutzeit, 1953.

MacKeith, Peter B., and Kerstin Smeds. *The Finland Pavilions: Finland at the Universal Expositions, 1900–1992.* Tampere: Kustannus, 1992.

Quantrill, Malcolm. *Finnish Architecture and the Modernist Tradition.* London: Spon, 1995.

St. John Wilson, Colin. *The Other Tradition of Modern Architecture: The Uncompleted Project.* London: Academy Editions, 1995.

Suhonen, Pekka. *Artek.* Helsinki: Artek, 1985.

Suomen teollisuuden arkkitehtuuria [Industrial Architecture in Finland]. Helsinki: Finnish Association of Architects, 1952.

Wallenhorst, Hans-Joachim. *Die Chronik der GEWOBA, 1924 bis 1992.* Bremen: GEWOBA, 1993.

Articles

George Baird et al. "Design and Planning: Alvar Aalto." *Progressive Architecture,* vol. 58, no. 4 (April 1977). Pp. 6, 53–77.

Baruël, Jean-Jacques. "Venne Alvar Aalto Nogle Fleve Rids." *Arkitekten,* vol. 91, no. 22 (December 12, 1989). Pp. 541–551.

Buchanan, Peter. "Aalto: Opera Essen." *Architectural Review,* vol. 185, no. 1108 (June 1989). Pp. 34–49.

Deilmann, Harald. "Vom Entwurf zur Ausführung." In Ditmar N. Schmidt, ed. *Das Theater von Alvar Aalto in Essen.* Essen: G. D. Baedeker Verlag, 1988.

Finne, Nils C. "The Workers' Club of 1924 by Alvar Aalto: The Importance of Beginnings." *Perspecta,* no. 27 (1992). Pp. 52–75.

Hewitt, Mark A. "The Imaginary Mountain: The Significance of Contour in Alvar Aalto's Sketches." *Perspecta,* no. 25 (1989). Pp. 162–177.

Korvenmaa, Pekka. "The Finnish Wooden House Transformed: American Prefabrication, War-Time Housing and Alvar Aalto." *Construction History,* vol. 6 (1991). Pp. 47–61.

Korvenmaa, Pekka. "The Crisis as Catalyst: Finnish Architecture, Alvar Aalto, and the Second World War. A Case of Strategic Decision-Making." *The Architecture of the Essential.* Proceedings of the 6th International Alvar Aalto Symposium. Helsinki, 1995.

Mikkola, Kirmo. "From the Technological to the Humane: Alvar Aalto versus Functionalism." *Abacus* (1979). Pp. 135–157.

Miller, William C. "Scandinavian architecture during the late 1930's: Asplund and Aalto vs. Functionalism." *Reflections: The Journal of the School of Architecture University of Illinois at Urbana-Champaign,* no. 7 (Spring 1990). Pp. 4–13.

Mosso, Leonardo. "Il Vogelweidplatz di Alvar Aalto." *Marmo,* no. 4 (1966). Pp. 7–51.

Poodry, Deborah, and Victoria Ozonoff. "Coffins, Pies, and Couches: Aalto at MIT." *Spazio e societa,* no. 5 (June 1982). Pp. 104–123.

Poole, Scott. "Elemental Matter in the Villa Mairea." In *The New Finnish Architecture.* New York: Rizzoli, 1992. Pp. 18–27.

Quantrill, Malcolm, and Harald Deilmann. "Opera House in Essen: Alvar Aalto, Harald Deilmann." *Architecture and Urbanism,* no. 3 (March 1989). Pp. 7–56.

Rautsi, Jussi. "Alvar Aalto's Urban Plans, 1940–1970." *Department of Architecture, Tampere University of Technology, Occasional Papers,* vol. 13 (1988). Pp. 43–69.

Schildt, Göran. "The Travels of Alvar Aalto: Notebook Sketches." *Lotus International,* no. 68 (1991). Pp. 34–47.

St. John Wilson, Colin. "'What is it like 30 years later?' An assessment of Alvar Aalto's work." *Royal Society of Arts (RSA) Journal* (London), vol. 162, no. 5463 (October 1995). Pp. 52–62.

Standertskjöld, Elina. "Alvar Aalto and Standardization." *Acanthus* (1992). Pp. 74–84.

Standertskjöld, Elina. "Alvar Aalto's Standard Drawings 1929–1932." *Acanthus* (1992). Pp. 89–111.

Viljo, Eeva Maija. "Alvar Aalto's Design for the Main Building of the College of Education [Pedagogical Institute] at Jyväskylä as an Experiment in Primitivism." In Marja Terttu Knapas and Åsa Ringbom, eds. *Icon to Cartoon: A Tribute to Sixten Ringbom.* Helsinki: The Society for Art History in Finland, 1995.

CD-ROM

The World of Alvar Aalto. Jyväskylä: Alvar Aalto Museum and Jyväskylä Science Park, in cooperation with the Alvar Aalto Foundation, 1998. Produced by mindwørks ltd.

Photograph Credits

The following credits are listed in two groups: Plates and Text Illustrations. The photographic sources are listed alphabetically by photographer, institution, private source, or secondary source. In the first group, Plates, the numbers given are plate numbers, which appear in the plate section of this volume on pages 141–301. Credits in the second group, Text Illustrations, refer to all other illustrations—in essays and chronology or section dividers—and give the numbers of the pages on which they appear. At the end of the photograph credits are captions for the images of Alvar Aalto that appear as section dividers.

Plates

Aino Aalto, courtesy Alvar Aalto Foundation, Helsinki: 111, 112.
Alvar Aalto Foundation, Helsinki: 84, 187, 212, 252, 326.
E. Ahti, courtesy Museum of Finnish Architecture: 276.
Wayne Andrews © Esto: 264.
Jean-Jacques Baruël: 337, 339, 340, 342.
Marliese Darsow: 361.
Peter Eckert/Strode Eckert Photographics: 376, 383.
Ädhäm Fethulla, courtesy Museum of Finnish Architecture, Helsinki: 399.
Kari Hakli, courtesy Museum of Finnish Architecture, Helsinki, 49; courtesy Alvar Aalto Foundation, Helsinki: 52, 397, 398, 402, 403, 404.
Heikki Havas, courtesy Museum of Finnish Architecture, Helsinki: 116, 237, 250, 251, 275; courtesy Alvar Aalto Foundation, Helsinki, 285, 315, 319, 320; courtesy The Museum of Modern Art, New York: 206.
H. Heidersberger: 348, 353, 354, 355, 356, 359.
Pertti Ingervo, courtesy Museum of Finnish Architecture, Helsinki: 127, 129, 274; courtesy The Museum of Modern Art, New York: 273.
Seth Joel, The Museum of Modern Art, New York: 63.
M. Kapanen, Alvar Aalto Museum, Jyväskylä: 21, 22, 196, 211.
Kate Keller, The Museum of Modern Art, New York: 142.
G. E. Kidder Smith, Corbis-Bettmann: 99, 106; courtesy The Museum of Modern Art, New York: 118, 208, 210, 295, 310, 311, 314, 327, 328, 350, 358, 360.

Major Kurimo, courtesy Alvar Aalto Foundation, Helsinki: 94.
Erik Landsberg, The Museum of Modern Art, New York: 59, 64.
P. Laurila, courtesy Museum of Finnish Architecture, Helsinki: 31, 36.
Eino Mäkinen, courtesy Museum of Finnish Architecture, Helsinki: 215.
Kalevi A. Mäkinen: 370, 373, 374, 375.
The MIT Museum: 181.
Leonardo Mosso, courtesy Museum of Finnish Architecture, Helsinki: 239; courtesy The Museum of Modern Art, New York: 349.
Museum of Finnish Architecture, Helsinki: 16, 101, 125, 138, 145, 236, 338.
The Museum of Modern Art, New York: 60, 66, 102, 105, 108, 132, 133, 136, 313, 322.
© 1988, Angel Otto & Friedrich Ostermann/OzOn: 365, 366.
Poul Pedersen, courtesy Nordjyllands Kunstmuseum: 341
Peter Reed: 372.
© Simo Rista: 58, 124, 203, 213, 214, 267.
Foto Roos, courtesy Museum of Finnish Architecture, Helsinki: 42, 170.
© 1997 Steve Rosenthal: 185, 188, 189, 194.
Henry Sarian-Paris, courtesy Alvar Aalto Foundation, Helsinki: 135, 137.
Ezra Stoller © Esto: 148, 153, 154, 184, 191, 192, 193, 195, 312.
Strode Eckert Photographics: 379, 380, 384.
Soichi Sunami, The Museum of Modern Art, New York: 107.
Suomen Ilmakuva Oy, Helsinki: 55, 113, 244, 262, 367, 396.
Karl and Helena Toelle, courtesy Alvar Aalto Foundation, Helsinki: 316.
Rauno Träskelin © 1997: 140, 227, 228, 229, 230, 231, 233, 234, 246, 248, 249, 253, 254, 256, 257, 258, 282, 286, 288, 297, 298, 300, 301, 302, 303, 304, 306, 407, 408; courtesy Villa Mairea Foundation, 163, 164, 165, 166, 167, 168, 169.
Marc Treib: 269.

Gustaf Welin, courtesy Alvar Aalto Foundation, Helsinki: 47, 67, 80, 100; courtesy Museum of Finnish Architecture, Helsinki: 61, 62, 70, 82, 126, 128; courtesy The Museum of Modern Art, New York: 46.

Nils-Erik Wickberg, courtesy Museum of Finnish Architecture, Helsinki: 15.

Text Illustrations

Alvar Aalto Foundation, Helsinki: 23 left and right, 24 left, 26 top right, 29, 34, 35, 51, 52 left, 56 left, 57, 58, 59 top and bottom, 60, 62 top and bottom, 86, 98, 100, 102 right, 103 left, 106, 109 left, 118, 131 bottom, 135, 310 bottom.

Aero-Lux, Frankfurt-am-Main: 110.

From *Architectural Design* (March 1965), p. 116, courtesy The Museum of Modern Art, New York: 112 bottom.

From *L'Architecture d'aujourd'hui* (December 1955–January 1956), p. 79: 125.

From Nils Aschenbeck and Hans-Joachim Wallenhorst, eds., *Modell Neue Vahr* (Bremen: GEWOBA, 1993), p. 34: 108.

Morley Baer, courtesy The Museum of Modern Art, New York: 133 left.

Arno de la Chapelle, courtesy Museum of Finnish Architecture, Helsinki: 127 bottom.

Robert Damora, courtesy The Museum of Modern Art, New York: 99.

Deutsche Fotothek, Dresden: 107 top right.

© Norman Foster, courtesy Colin St. John Wilson & Associates, London: 129 bottom.

From Kenneth Frampton, *Studies in Tectonic Culture: The Poetics of Construction in Nineteenth and Twentieth Century Architecture* (Cambridge, Mass.: MIT Press, 1995), p. 267: 128 bottom; idem et al., *Alvaro Siza: Poetic Profession* (Milan: Electa, 1986), p. 33: 132 bottom; idem, *Modern Architecture: A Critical History* (New York and Toronto: Oxford University Press, 1980), p. 227: 126.

Maire Gullichsen, courtesy Alvar Aalto Foundation, Helsinki: 311 bottom.

Kari Hakli, courtesy Museum of Finnish Architecture, Helsinki: 39, 54 left.

Heikki Havas, courtesy Alvar Aalto Foundation, Helsinki: 93, 303; courtesy Museum of Finnish Architecture, Helsinki: 38 top left, 76, 312 top; courtesy The Museum of Modern Art, New York: 2, 94.

Heinonen, courtesy Alvar Aalto Foundation, Helsinki: 19.

From *Ideias e Edifícios Atelier de Leslie Martin e Seus Associados*, p. 22: 130 left.

John Jacobus et al., *James Stirling: Buildings & Projects 1950–1974* (New York: Oxford University Press, 1975), p. 96: 131 top.

Le Corbusier, *Vers une architecture* (Paris: Éditions G. Crès, 1923), p. 152: 52 right.

F. S. Lincoln, courtesy The Museum of Modern Art, New York: 96.

Titta Lumio, courtesy Helin & Siitonen Architects, Helsinki: 128 top.

Eino Mäkinen, courtesy Alvar Aalto Foundation, Helsinki: 63, 69; courtesy Museum of Finnish Architecture, Helsinki: 45, 54 right, 55, 83, 85 bottom.

Kalevi A. Mäkinen, courtesy Alvar Aalto Foundation, Helsinki: 313.

Duccio Malagamba, Barcelona: 132 top.

Italo Marinero, courtesy Alvar Aalto Foundation, Helsinki: 312 bottom.

Herbert Matter, courtesy Alvar Aalto Foundation, Helsinki: 310 top.

Richard Meier & Partners, New York: 133 right.

Museovirasto, Helsinki: 81.

Museum of Finnish Architecture, Helsinki: 24 right, 26 left, 27 top, 33, 37, 38 top right, 46, 50, 82.

The Museum of Modern Art, New York: 25, 53, 74, 107 bottom right, 129 top right, 311 top; Mies van der Rohe Archive: 109 right, 112 top.

Eduard and Claudia Neuenschwander, *Finnish Buildings: Atelier Alvar Aalto 1950–1951* (Erlenbach-Zurich, Switzerland: Verlag für Architektur, 1954), p. 119: 127 top; p. 79: 129 left.

Theodor Nyblin, courtesy Museum of Finnish Architecture, Helsinki: 20.

Patkau Architects: 134.

Pietinen, courtesy Museum of Finnish Architecture, Helsinki: 77 left.

From Heinz and Bodo Rasch, *Wie Bauen?* (Stuttgart: Wedekind, 1928), p. 154: 107 left.

Raita, courtesy Museum of Finnish Architecture, Helsinki: 70.

Simo Rista, courtesy Museum of Finnish Architecture, Helsinki: 28, 38 bottom right.

Foto Roos, courtesy Museum of Finnish Architecture, Helsinki: 49, 75 bottom, 77 right, 79, 84 top; courtesy Alvar Aalto Foundation, Helisnki: 78 top.

Manuel Gutierrez de Rueda: 122.

Oy Sääski, courtesy Museum of Finnish Architecture, Helsinki: 72.

From Göran Schildt, *Alvar Aalto: The Mature Years* (New York: Rizzoli, 1991), p. 141: 75 left.

From Camillo Sitte, *The Art of Building Cities* (1889; New York: Rizzoli, 1986), p. 214: 61.

Mildred Schmertz, courtesy The Museum of Modern Art, New York: 130 right.

G. E. Kidder Smith, courtesy The Museum of Modern Art, New York: 117.

© Ezra Stoller Associates: 105.

Sundahl, courtesy The Museum of Modern Art, New York: 27 bottom.

Suomen Metsämuseo Ja Metsätietokeskus, Punkaharju, Finland: 85 top.

From Bruno Taut, *Alpine Architecture* (1919), p. 7: 103 right.

Marc Treib: 56 right.

From Stuart Wrede, *The Architecture of Erik Gunnar Asplund*, (Cambridge, Mass. and London: MIT Press, 1980), p. 9: 101; p. 216: 102 left.

Gustaf Welin, courtesy Alvar Aalto Foundation, Helsinki: 73; courtesy Museum of Finnish Architecture, Helsinki: 26 bottom right, 78 bottom, 80, 84 bottom.

Captions for Section Dividers

Page 19: Alvar Aalto, c. 1935.

Page 45: Alvar Aalto, c. 1938.

Page 69: Alvar Aalto at the Finnish Pavilion, New York World's Fair, Queens, New York, 1939.

Page 93: Alvar Aalto, c. 1970.

Page 117: Alvar Aalto, c. 1970.

Page 303: Aalto on his boat, *Nemo Propheta in Patria,* Lake Päijänne, Muuratsalo, Finland, c. 1960s.

Index

Trustees of The Museum of Modern Art